PENGUIN BOOKS
SUFI

Aabid Surti, born in Gujarat in 1935, is the author of over eighty books spanning across categories like fiction, poetry, theatre, reportage and comics. He is the co-creator of Bahadur, India's first comic book superhero. His environmental activism has led him to be called a 'one-man NGO', especially when it comes to water conservation. Surti lives in Mumbai.

Nachiketa Desai, the grandson of freedom fighter Mahadev Desai, is a multilingual journalist based in Ahmedabad.

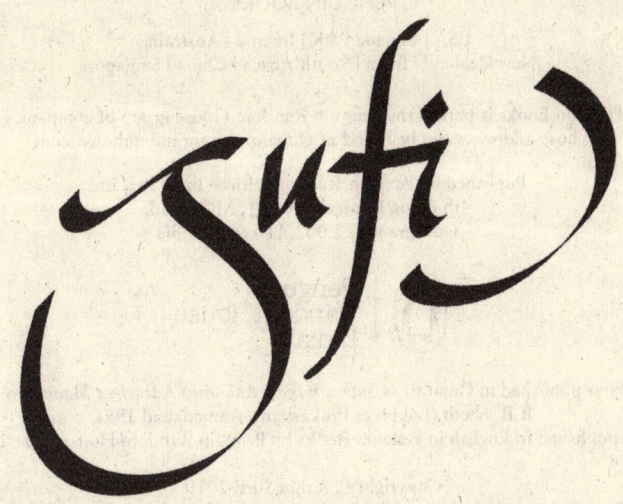

The Invisible Man
of the Underworld

AABID SURTI

Translated by
Nachiketa Desai and Aabid Surti

PENGUIN BOOKS

An imprint of Penguin Random House

PENGUIN BOOKS

USA | Canada | UK | Ireland | Australia
New Zealand | India | South Africa | China | Singapore

Penguin Books is part of the Penguin Random House group of companies
whose addresses can be found at global.penguinrandomhouse.com

Published by Penguin Random House India Pvt. Ltd
4th Floor, Capital Tower 1, MG Road,
Gurugram 122 002, Haryana, India

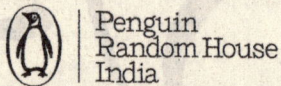

First published in Gujarati as *Sufi: Andhari Aalamno Adrashya Maanvi* by
R.R. Sheth (Lokpriya Prakashan), Ahmedabad 1991
First published in English in Penguin Books by Penguin Random House India 2019

ISBN 9780143443186

Typeset in Bembo Std by Manipal Digital Systems, Manipal

Printed at Repro India Limited

www.penguin.co.in

MIX
Paper from
responsible sources
FSC® C047271

This is a legitimate digitally printed version of the book and therefore might not
have certain extra finishing on the cover.

CONTENTS

AUTHOR'S NOTE

In the late 1980s, when I was in my fifties, I was planning to write a part of my autobiography. Coincidentally, after many years, I happened to meet Sufi (Iqbal Rupani) at a gathering in the Bandra mosque—the occasion was my cousin's nikah. As we chatted about our school days and adventures, it triggered an idea: why not write a *jugalbandi* instead of one person's life sketch?

This book is the result of a series of interviews and an investigation conducted over the course of two years (1987–88) into the golden period of gold smuggling in India. Originally written in Gujarati (1989), it appeared in Hindi (*Musalman*, 1995) and Kannada (1996). Its Marathi translation was serialized in *Mahanagar*, an evening newspaper, in 2004. Nachiketa Desai, then the associate editor, Cyber India Online Ltd, prepared the first draft of the English translation. I worked on the next three drafts. After passing through many hands and suggestions, the fifth version was edited by Shivani Tibrewala, a playwright and theatre director, and the sixth edit by a journalist friend, Rima Kashyap. The final polishing was done by my son, Aalif Surti.

When Iqbal first came to see me at my house in Bandra, we chatted for a while in the living room. The topic was theology. To be precise, it was namaz and yoga. After he left, my mother, who was resting inside and listening keenly to our conversation, came out and asked, 'Who was that Sufi?' Naturally, I was curious to know and asked her, 'How did you guess that he was a Sufi?' Her answer was, 'He sounded like an enlightened soul!'

I had got the title for my book!

1

Two boys grew up playing in the alleys of Bombay's (now called Mumbai) infamous Dongri locality. Their family backgrounds were similar. The circumstances that life threw at them were similar too. However, one was attracted to light while darkness engulfed the other. One turned out to be a celebrated painter while the other became a member of the underworld.

One of them was Aabid Surti.

The other was Iqbal Rupani 'Sufi'.

Both of them completed their education from Dongri's renowned Habib High School. Its distinguished principal, Padma Shri awardee Sheikh Hasan, considered both amongst his favourite students. Both boys had a sincere desire to study hard and succeed in life.

The similarities did not end there. As they grew into adults, neither was interested in marriage. They knew that young men struggling to make their mark in the world were not able to shoulder the responsibilities of married life. However, both were compelled by the twists of destiny into wedlock. Not only did their wives belong to the same family clan, they even had the same first names.

And yet, through all these years, growing up on the same streets, our paths barely crossed. Like ships passing each other in the dark, we passed by without realizing how similar the plans were that life held for us. Then, one day in March 1987, at my cousin's nikah in the Bandra mosque, we found ourselves face-to-face. I looked at him intently. He hadn't changed much—the same curly hair and beady eyes, now framed by wire-rimmed spectacles. He had a neatly cropped moustache and a whisper of a smile on his lips. He wore a spotless white shirt, white trousers and shoes that shone.

At first glance, he appeared to be a white-collar worker—someone who could wade into a crowd and melt into it. However, his eyes, which sparkled with intelligence, revealed something different. I expressed a desire to meet him again. He invited me home and thus began a series of rendezvous.

For two decades we had belonged to the same community, the same locality, the same school and the same mosque. Yet, beyond pleasantries, we had never spoken to each other. What would you call that? Destiny? Sitting on an easy chair on the terrace of his house, Sufi expressed the same sentiment, casting his eyes upward:

'Aabid Bhai, God has clearly said in the Holy Koran that even the leaf of a tree does not move without His will. For every living creature, He has predetermined the course of life. Someone's path is paved with petals and someone else's with thorns. No matter how hard a man may struggle to choose a different path, ultimately he will be compelled to follow the path written in his fate.'

*

Before journeying down Sufi's improbable life path further, let us familiarize ourselves with his beginnings: his home, his family and the locality where he lived. Of course, I too grew up in the same neighbourhood. Today, both of us live in Bandra, an affluent cosmopolitan suburb in Bombay. Back then, we lived near Bhendi Bazaar, in the squalid Muslim ghetto called Dongri.

The poison of smuggling and crime had entered the veins of Dongri much before Sufi's birth. Liquor dens were flourishing in the bylanes. The addiction to hashish and marijuana was shooting through the dark alleys.

This was the same locality from where the pan-Islamist Khilafat movement protesting British rule was launched just a few decades before. Maulana Mohammed Ali and Maulana Shaukat Ali, along with several other leaders of the Congress, had shepherded the campaign from here. Even today, the older generation identifies the four heritage buildings—Ibrahim Mansion, Sultan Mansion, Sharif Mansion and Kalyan Mansion—as Khilafat Manzil, home of the resistance.

Behind these four heritage buildings is Kesar Baug Hall, from where many veteran leaders, including Muhammad Ali Jinnah, Vallabhbhai Patel and Jawaharlal Nehru gave the message of unity to the nation. By 1920, even Mahatma Gandhi joined in the fray and the Indian National Congress allied with the Khilafat movement. Dongri, in those glorious days, was the centre of the freedom struggle.

As was the case with Porbandar, the birthplace of Gandhi, this once-grand place degenerated with time into a thriving hub for every vice under the sun. Racketeers big and small began to sprout like mushrooms here. Aziz Dilip—a Hindu who converted to Islam and was known by both his names—used to run a cycle shop and a transport business as a front, but in reality was the owner of three liquor dens. Ayub Lala was the don of the red-light district area of Foras Road near Bhendi Bazaar and used to operate old-style opium dens. Shankar Maratha ruled over Mazgaon and enjoyed all the debauchery he could purchase with the earnings from his liquor dens.

Before Sufi's birth, even his father, Hussain Ali, had fallen prey to the affliction of alcohol. Like a venomous snake, liquor had wound its way from the streets into nearby homes. Hussain Ali was among the first to turn into an alcoholic. Liquor became his life. His morning cup of tea would taste bitter if he hadn't had a peg or two.

Hussain Ali was basically a good-hearted man. All his life, he had been a devout Muslim who would offer namaz regularly, fast annually and read the Koran daily. He did not want to touch liquor. But, before he knew it, liquor had entered the pores of his body, flowed through his veins and emerged like fire from his eyes.

What was the cause of his tragedy? According to Sufi, 'My father used to work as a clerk under an agent at the Ghadiyal Godi docks. It was potentially lucrative work— there was the possibility of earning an extra buck on the side by under-invoicing the bags of dates imported from the Gulf. Sometimes, there would be contraband inside the crates and the importer would grease the palms of the customs officer to smuggle it in. However, for my father it was difficult to indulge in underhand transactions. Then, my mother contracted tuberculosis.'

Those days, tuberculosis meant certain death. It would evoke the same kind of fear as cancer does today. Hussain Ali could not bear it. He sought comfort in drinking. He thought he would drown all his sorrows, all his worries in alcohol. But neither did his grief decrease, nor did his problems drown.

To meet the expenses of treatment for such a deadly disease with the meagre income of an honest clerk was not possible. His meagre life savings had long been drained in settling the doctors' bills. Now, before him were two stark options: stick firm to his principles and let his wife,

Gul Banu, wither away or accept the flexible values of the changing times.

*

A similar situation had developed in my own family. My father, Ghulam Hussain, who had rolled in millions, was reduced to penury after my grandfather's shipping venture ended in bankruptcy. A man who once stood tall among billionaires like the Tatas and Birlas, who grew up like the young prince Siddhartha untouched by the shadow of sorrow, whose life was cocooned within the walls of a palatial mansion, now suddenly found himself on the footpath. One can only imagine his mental condition.

He accepted a job, but did not like it and quit. He took up another job. It was not in his nature to be a minion. He quit again. While he was struggling to support his family, he chanced upon an idea. It was not a brilliant idea, merely a desperate, ill-conceived one.

Continuing with his life story, Sufi recalled that it was a dark monsoon night. Black rain poured on the glistening corrugated tin roofs outside. In his 180-square-foot *kholi*, Hussain Ali was sitting wide awake. He could not sleep and knew that he would remain tormented until the dilemma confronting him was resolved.

Hussain Ali looked at his ailing wife. Gul Banu was observing him as well. In that moment, a flash of bone-white lightning lit up the room. In the macabre light, Hussain Ali saw two angels of death. It was as if they had come straight from the graveyard to weigh Gul Banu's good and bad deeds and release her soul.

Hussain Ali made his decision. It was like that flash of lightning had shown him the way. Just as a snake sheds its scales, he shrugged off his lifelong values and became a new man. He knew the customs officers. He knew the tricks that would get him the delivery of goods without paying the customs duty. He had never employed these ruses in the past, but now he started practising them freely.

'Does it mean,' I asked Sufi for clarification, 'that your father was also involved in smuggling?'

'Absolutely.'

'Can we call him a smuggler?'

Sufi smiled behind his moustache. This half-hidden smirk always gave an edge to whatever he said next. 'Aabid Bhai, what does the word "smuggler" mean to you?'

The images of villains from Hindi movies flashed before my eyes one after the other. The faces were ugly, menacing and scarred with stitches. Some looked like pirates, while others resembled gruesome characters from the Ramsay Brothers' horror films. Every face radiated terror and cruelty.

Distracted by this parade of hideous faces, I fumbled a reply, 'Smuggler means a person involved in smuggling.'

'And what is smuggling?'

'To bring in contraband from other countries.'

Sufi smoothly corrected my juvenile misperception. 'In the eyes of the law, smuggling means tax evasion—importing or exporting goods without paying tax.'

He continued. 'This means that anyone who evades tax can be called a smuggler. Now, you tell me, which trader or businessman in the world does not evade tax? If you concede the point then every trader is a smuggler. My father, too, had in him the genes of a trader. He, too, evaded customs duty. Whether you call him a smuggler or any other name, what difference does it make?'

Within a short span of three years, Hussain Ali earned about one lakh rupees. His swagger returned. His wife not only recovered from tuberculosis but also became pregnant. The 180-square-foot kholi turned into a haven for husband and wife. As the delivery date drew closer, Hussain Ali's devotion to God increased. So did his addiction to the bottle.

He had started with one peg—returning from the dock after a tiring day, he would drink a peg of whisky, eat heartily and sleep like a baby. One bottle would last him nearly thirteen days. Now, one bottle was not enough for even a day.

Gul Banu was tormented seeing him like that, but she did not have the courage to say anything to her husband. *What could she say? That Islam decreed that drinking liquor was immoral? That namaz and alcohol could not go together? Did he not know such fundamental precepts? Did she need to tell him?*

'What was the result?' I interjected.

'Quarrels!'

Sufi's mother was not educated. She had learnt religion from the elders of the family and the clergy. Her Islam divided the universe into haram and halal. Everything in her world was severed into black or white—moral or immoral, good deed or bad deed, truth or falsehood. Had she ever, even for a fraction of a moment, looked beyond these unforgiving partitions into her husband's inner turmoil, she would have suffered less and come closer to him.

When the oil in a lamp is nearly exhausted, the flame leaps one last time before it finally dies out. Hussain Ali's alcoholism was sparking its final blaze. The more he strengthened his resolve to quit, the more he ended up drinking. After all, actions and reactions are equal and opposite.

*

Defeated by life, my father, Ghulam Hussain, too made a last-ditch attempt. While Sufi's father had turned to smuggling because of his wife's disease, my father had turned to propitiating spirits as the last resort to end his suffering because of poverty and hunger.

In the end, he decided to embark upon an occult Islamic forty-day retreat called a 'chilla' during which he would meditate in isolation for forty nights to bring evil spirits under his control. It was said that a person who succeeded in this dangerous quest of controlling evil spirits earned magical powers. He could turn dust into gold by just blowing upon it. If he placed his hand on the forehead of a dying person, the person sprang back to life.

Like a tantric, he began chanting Islamic mantras. Every night, he prostrated himself in namaz, read selected verses from the Koran and invoked the grace of Allah upon his beleaguered family. During those days, my mother was carrying me. Only a few days remained for my birth and for my father's success in his forty-night quest to master our destiny. My mother was becoming increasingly anxious.

*

Sufi's mother, too, was no less anxious. As usual, Hussain Ali had been drinking since morning that day. He had finished a bottle by the afternoon. He had just picked up another bottle when Gul Banu's water broke.

The screw cap on the new liquor bottle was jammed. On one side was Gul Banu's increasing labour pains, on the other was Hussain Ali's increasing desperation to open the bottle. Gul Banu's pain was intensifying with every passing second. She was no longer moaning. She had started screaming.

Hussain Ali turned to look at his wife. He looked at her balloon-shaped belly, her face wheezing for breath and then he looked at the bottle in his hand. He held it by the neck and smashed it against the wall. The neck remained in his hand. The bottle was shattered. Liquor was flowing down the wall and pooling on to the floor.

On 21 November 1949, Sufi was born. On the same day, Hussain Ali kicked his drinking habit for good. He vowed never to touch liquor again and made a firm resolve to start life afresh.

*

My father was not so fortunate. The fortieth day of the chilla is critical. That night, the evil spirits are said to go on a vicious rampage and launch their final, all-out attack on the person trying to subdue them. The attack is not on the body but on the mind. A weak-hearted man cannot withstand the horrific scenario created by the blood-curdling screams of headless bodies and the wailing of toothless witches that swims before his eyes on that night. My father's heart was weaker than expected.

At the stroke of midnight, two screams were heard. One was that of my mother, who gave birth to a boy. The other was from my father, who lost his mental balance forever. Thus, fate gave me a mad father while Sufi got a loving one. Hussain Ali christened his child Iqbal.

*

After Iqbal's birth, his father not only kicked his addiction but also gave up his job under the clearing agent. Though the salary had not been substantial, it had offered scope for illicit income. Besides, one could also carry on with smuggling. The only way to keep away from such temptations was to avoid such a place—as the old adage goes, if you step into the muck, you can't avoid soiling your feet. His decision was unshakeable.

*

A similar dilemma faced Ibrahim Sheikh Kaskar, the father of Bombay's underworld don Dawood Ibrahim. Like Hussain Ali, he too had collected over one lakh rupees. His resolve to start a new life too was unshakeable.

In the 1950s, Kaskar was a head constable working with the crime branch of the Bombay Police. Those were the years when Muslim officers still enjoyed a solid reputation for crime detection. Constable Khan—famously recognized by his badge number 303—and Constable Israel too had earned quite a name.

Not just in Dongri but across Bombay the names of these three police officers sent shivers down the spines of goons. Nonetheless, one day, a gang managed to execute a daring daylight robbery in the impregnable Lloyds' Bank near Fort market.

Never in the annals of Bombay had such a well-planned and audacious heist taken place. Every newspaper carried the story with bold headlines on their front pages about the five unknown gunmen who killed a taxi driver and wounded three workers outside Lloyds' Bank before escaping with £90,000 pounds in the biggest robbery in the city's history. The entire city was abuzz.

The senior crime branch officer entrusted with this case chose Ibrahim Sheikh, Israel and Khan '303' as his deputies. Following a single clue, the trinity of the Bombay Police cracked this unprecedented case within a week.

Ibrahim Kaskar now felt there was no need for him to continue with his job. He had saved over one lakh rupees during his years of service. Besides, after the Partition, the discontent among the Muslim officers in the Bombay Police was increasingly visible.

*

Hussain Ali resigned from his job at the dock. Ibrahim Kaskar too quit the police force. Contrary to rumours, he was not suspended. He bought a shop and opened a haircutting salon. Hussain Ali also decided to start his own business.

Speculative trading in cotton was at its peak in those years. People made lakhs from thousands, and millionaires became billionaires overnight.

'What's the use of becoming a billionaire?' Gul Banu asked when she heard about her husband's plans. 'Is one lakh rupees not enough to live peacefully?'

'No,' said Hussain Ali. 'The money we have today may not be there tomorrow. I want my son to be educated. We need more money for his higher education. Will we not need to keep aside a lot more to send our son abroad to study?'

If only someone had shown him the negative side of speculative trading in cotton and told him about billionaires turning into paupers overnight by indulging in the *satta* (gambling) bazaar, he would have probably invested his savings in another business.

Ibrahim Sheikh, too, was not happy after investing his one lakh rupees in the haircutting salon. But my family's condition was the worst. We were living hand to mouth. After a prolonged illness, my father was bedridden. He would stay in bed day and night without uttering a word.

He would quietly eat whatever my mother gave him. The entire responsibility of the family fell on my mother's shoulders.

There were six members in our family. Apart from my parents and me, there were my grandmother and two uncles. The elder uncle could not be bothered with working. The younger one, Mohammed Hussain, was too young to take up a job.

My mother, who had come into the family as the daughter-in-law of a billionaire, sold off her last two gold bangles. Before this money was exhausted, it was necessary to find some work. Casting aside the dignity of her purdah, she started accepting odd jobs from neighbours.

My younger uncle, Mohammed Hussain, could not stand this. He started hunting for a job at the tender age of sixteen. Finally, he found work in the same dock that was the hub of corruption.

He soon earned the reputation of being an honest and trustworthy man. He was also involved in social work. His fame as a one-man NGO spread. However, financially, we remained where we were, in a single room in Sultan Mansion. Our prestige had increased, but not our income. We had profited in one respect—notorious underworld dons like Karim Lala, and even police officials, looked at Mohammed Hussain with respect.

One evening, Ibrahim Sheikh came to our house. 'Mohammed Bhai,' he said, 'I quit the police job and started a haircutting salon thinking that with a fixed income I could retire happily, away from all the worries of life.'

'Is it not doing well?'

'I'm finding it difficult to even pay the salaries of the staff!'

'You have a road-facing shop,' my uncle counselled him. 'Why not start some other business?'

He sat with my uncle for a long time discussing new ideas. He was confused about what he should do. And then Karim Lala cleared his confusion in a flash. He took him under his wing. Ibrahim Sheikh became the link between the don and the police. His job was to sort out Karim Lala's issues with the police. This was a piece of cake for him. He knew the price everyone in the police station commanded, from the constables to the inspectors.

*

Hussain Ali descended the staircase from his kholi on the first floor of Abbasi Manzil. To his right was Gardia School and on his left was the back of Khoja Masjid. He was always on time for namaz.

Today was Friday. He would never miss the Friday prayer. Dressed in a white shirt and white pants, he slowly crossed Munda Galli and, as he reached Pala Galli, he spotted his old employer.

'Hussain!' the man said, even before Hussain Ali could say a word. 'If you want, you can rejoin the dock. I'll be happy to take you back.'

Hussain Ali looked at him steadily. He was certain about one thing: his former boss had heard about his poverty. He did not reply. The boss too didn't need to press the matter—a word is enough for the wise.

Inside Hussain Ali's mind, a storm was brewing. The royal road to riches lay before him. He could once again become a millionaire.

With each prayer during namaz, he grappled with these disturbing thoughts. As he raised his hands seeking the blessings of the Almighty, the following words rang in his ears:

'The Merciful tests his devotees from time to time. Whether
he is a commoner or an emperor, a devotee or an imam,
only he who successfully passes the test, can proudly claim
to be a true follower.'

These words from the *pesh* imam in his address to the congregation made the agitated Hussain Ali stand still. He decided to take up a job, not in the dock but in a department store.

During the Friday namaz itself he learnt about a vacancy at a Link Bazaar store in a suburb called Bandra. He met the owner the next day and secured the job at a monthly salary of Rs 300.

*

That decade was the golden era of gold smuggling. Thanks to Union finance minister Morarji Desai's Gold (Control) Act, the value of gold had skyrocketed. The rate of gold in India was four times the international price. A gold famine raged in the country.

According to the statistics released by the Bombay Bullion Association, there were 10,000 licensed gold merchants and two and a half lakh certified jewellers in India. Together, they dealt in 100 tons of gold worth Rs 2000 crore every year. Of this, 50 per cent of the gold came from melting old jewellery, while the gold mines owned by the government accounted for just 2.5 tons issued for industrial use only.

To meet the demand, the dealers had no option but to enter into a pact with the smugglers. Haji Mastan made the most of the opportunity. Or perhaps it would be better to say that the Gujarati and Marwari traders made use of him to smuggle gold.

While the unemployed young boys from Dongri rushed to join Haji Mastan's gang, old Hussain Ali stuck to his job. His plan was working comfortably within his calculations. His salary was Rs 300. He needed Rs 100 to run the house. He would keep aside the remaining amount for his son Iqbal's future. Still, he had a feeling that somewhere something was wrong. His sixth sense told him that Allah had calculated differently. *Was Allah still testing him?* As these thoughts passed through his mind, three boys from his lane came to his door. The boy in the middle had a bloody nose.

'What happened?' Hussain Ali asked.

'Iqbal punched his nose.'

He was surprised. Ali, the boy with the broken nose and bloodstained shirt, was seven years old. Iqbal was not yet five.

'Where has that *harami* gone?'

'He ran away,' the second boy said.

Just then, a little voice piped up from behind the boys. 'Papa, I didn't run away. These three cowards came running to you to complain.'

'Come in front!'

Iqbal shoved the three boys aside and came forward. 'You had gone out to play or to fight?' An anxious Hussain Ali caught him by the wrist and slapped him. 'Speak up!'

Iqbal did not waver. He boldly replied, 'I was spinning my top alone. They wanted to play with me. While playing, my top cracked Ali's from the middle and all of them pounced on me.'

'So you broke his nose?' Hussain Ali planted a second slap across Iqbal's face. 'Come on, apologize to Ali!'

'No!' Iqbal shrieked, tenaciously holding his ground.

Hussain Ali thrashed him in front of the three boys.

*

'What you did wasn't fair,' Gul Banu chided her husband that night, giving voice to the disapproval brewing inside her.

'I know that our son was not at fault,' Hussain Ali accepted. 'But I don't want him to resort to violence to sort out his problems.'

'What will you do if three people attack you?' Gul Banu pressed on. 'Our son is not a Gandhi, and the neighbourhood we live in doesn't believe in Ahimsa. Here, might is right. Only the fearless can survive in this society and you are teaching our son cowardice?'

His wife had a point, but it was difficult for Hussain Ali to see it. His bright plans for Iqbal's future floated before his eyes. He saw him as a member of the educated and cultured elite; a doctor, he hoped. Gentlemen don't go around bloodying faces.

Hussain Ali looked at Iqbal who was sleeping on the floor. *If I do not discipline him at this tender age, he may start cracking heads when he grows up. And then maybe begin using a dagger.*

'I won't leave you,' Iqbal was murmuring in his sleep. 'I won't spare you . . .' He had decided to take revenge on the three boys who had had him punished. His subconscious mind was reverberating with thoughts of retribution.

My mind, too, was reverberating with similar thoughts at that age. However, unlike Iqbal, I had neither the strength nor the courage to seek vengeance.

2

My mother was plagued by two irrational fears. One was water and the other was exercise. She firmly believed that physical exercise caused broken bones and swimming invariably caused children to drown. 'You will go just like that,' she would say snapping her fingers. To date, I have not managed to figure out why she feared these two innocent sports. But one thing was certain: the more my mother tried to keep me away from the sea, the more it lured me.

Early one morning, when I was seven, I went to Chowpatty beach with my neighbourhood friends. We stripped naked and splashed happily into the ocean. My friends got tired after an hour and came out of the water. I stayed for a while longer. It was fun to welcome the crashing waves with open arms. At last, when I swam back to the shore, I realized that not only had my friends vanished, but they had taken my shirt and shorts with them.

My mortification knew no bounds. *How would I reach Dongri without any clothes? Even if I managed to reach home somehow, how would I face my mother?* I was about to break down when a sheet of newspaper rolled up to my feet. My eyes lit up. I lifted it and wrapped it around my waist.

At least one problem was solved—I would be able to reach home with my dignity more or less intact. Holding up the newspaper with both hands and stepping gingerly on the sand, I headed for home. However, I did not make it very far.

As I neared Opera House, a street dog came out of nowhere and started barking after me. My newspaper fig leaf slipped from my hands. I took to my heels. Chased by the dog, I dashed to Dongri in record time. My friends were waiting for me at the Char Nal crossing. Seeing me scampering stark naked, they burst into laughter. They began teasing me, dangling my clothes before me like a carrot. I could not stand their merciless teasing any more—I began wailing. *Why? Why was I being singled out!*

Finally, as if they were doing me a favour, they threw my shorts and shirt on my face and walked away. I seethed with helpless rage.

*

Iqbal was becoming more and more mischievous with each passing day. In school, he could barely sit still. He had not yet exacted his revenge on Ali and his two friends. The three hooligans studied with him at Habib High School. Iqbal was thinking up ways to strike back.

One day, during recess, he found his opportunity. Ali had snatched a pencil from one of Iqbal's classmates. Iqbal leapt into the fray and confronted the trio.

'Give the pencil back.'

'It's not yours,' Ali snapped.

Iqbal warned him. The boys playing nearby formed a circle. Now it had become a matter of prestige for the three ruffians. If they returned the pencil fearing the puny Iqbal, their formidable reputation as tough guys would take a beating. They decided to fight it out.

Iqbal attacked first and a teacher, who was passing by, witnessed this assault. Before Iqbal could teach the boys a lesson, stinging lashes from the teacher's cane rained on his back. He was stunned. He turned around. The geography teacher who resembled a globe stood before him.

Much before he returned from school in the evening, a complaint had reached home. Hussain Ali did not even look at him. He was surprised. *Why is Papa not saying anything? Why is he lying quietly on the bed?*

As he wrestled with a web of questions, Gul Banu entered the house with Dr Khimani. Iqbal backed quietly into a corner. 'There is nothing to worry about,' said the doctor after examining Hussain Ali. 'I'll take the boy with me to my clinic to get the medicine.'

After a week, Dr Khimani gravely informed Gul Banu, 'Sister, your husband was already suffering from diabetes and rheumatism. Now he has a heart problem too. You will have to be careful with his diet. No salt, chillies, condiments and oily food.' Prescribing a list of additional medicines, he warned, 'If you don't follow my instructions, his condition will deteriorate.'

Iqbal was too young to understand what 'heart problem' meant. Nevertheless, he could read the clouds of worry floating in his mother's eyes. He understood the gravity of the situation. This left a deep impression on his tender mind.

Though he was not in a position to help his father, at least he could be careful not to hurt him. It was his duty to ensure that none of his actions caused his father further anguish.

Iqbal curbed his mischief. Bedridden for a month, Hussain Ali silently observed his son's every move. The change in Iqbal's behaviour did not go unnoticed.

In the last few months, Hussain Ali had given up hope that his son would ever graduate. His hopes were now rekindled and he returned to his job the following month.

Hussain Ali lived in Dongri's Munda Galli and his workplace was in Bandra's Link Bazaar. This meant walking to Sandhurst Road station, catching a suburban train to Bandra and then walking for another ten minutes to reach the store.

The commute exhausted him, but there was no other choice. He had a dream to fulfil. He also had to keep the home fires burning. Suddenly, he saw the fire going out and his dream falling to pieces. He saw the Link Bazaar store whirling and the ground beneath his feet slipping as he swooned on the steps of the departmental store.

This was a mild heart attack—a forewarning of the bleak future ahead. Yet, he knew he could not afford to quit the job. Finally, he did not have to: Hussain Ali was asked to leave.

Iqbal was devoted to his studies and displaying remarkable progress. *If my inability to provide money were to cut short Iqbal's education, God will never forgive me.* This thought compelled Hussain Ali to hunt for another job.

After struggling for a few days, he found employment in an auto parts shop. The shop was close to home, but the salary was pathetic. The only solace was that it would keep the house running. At least his son would be able to complete high school.

This job too did not last long. The new boss was quarrelsome. He would reprimand Hussain Ali for minor lapses. At times, he would scold him for no reason. Hussain Ali could stand it no longer. He quit.

Iqbal's school fee, which had always been paid well before the due date, was now often delayed by two to three months.

One day, seeing Iqbal disturbed, Ali asked him, 'What's the matter?'

Iqbal looked at him. This was the same Ali whose nose he had bloodied. However, the incident was long forgotten and they had become friends.

'Nothing,' Iqbal lied.

'Why so down in the dumps then?'

'Eid is approaching and I don't have new clothes . . .' His voice trailed off.

'Oh, is that all?' Ali laughed and offered him a solution.

In those years, the Mazgaon docks, where foreign ships used to anchor, were the training ground for new entrants into the world of smuggling. Young men would buy imported watches, cigarette packets, a bottle of Scotch or a transistor radio from these ships and sell them to Marwari traders in Dongri.

Ali loaned Iqbal Rs 25 to start with. However, after a few days of work, Iqbal felt that there were more difficulties than income involved with this work. Besides, there was no guarantee that a ship would dock every morning. Sometimes there would be no ships the entire week.

He consulted Ali again. Ali offered a new option. 'This work is kid stuff,' he told Iqbal. 'All you have to do is to carry bottles from one place to another. You will be paid one rupee for a bottle. If you ferry five bottles, you will get five rupees, if you ferry 100 bottles, you will get hundred rupees.'

'What do the bottles contain?'

'Medicine.'

*

I was listening to Sufi's account of his childhood with rapt attention. We were sitting on the terrace of his Bandra flat. 'What kind of medicine?' I asked.

Before he could reply, his wife, Masooma, arrived with a glass of sherbet and a smile on her face. Several silent moments interrupted our conversation.

I had fixed one day of the week to meet Sufi. We met every Thursday and sat on easy chairs on the open terrace. Mostly he talked, while I listened and took notes.

I finished the sherbet and kept the glass on the table next to us. Sufi spoke again, replying to my question. 'Medicine means ethyl alcohol, which is used to make perfume, cologne water, eau de cologne, etc. However, the underworld used it differently.'

'How?'

'To make liquor, brandy in particular.'

'How old were you then?'

'I was in the sixth standard.'

I felt this incident was a turning point and so I prodded him further, 'Had Eid not come in between, the direction of your life wouldn't have changed for ever.'

'No,' Sufi hastened to correct me, 'This was just an excuse. The truth was that I had to pay my school fee to be able to continue my studies. Besides, I forgot to tell you that my mother had delivered two more children after my birth. They were younger than me and Eid was important for them too.'

There was one difficulty. Those days, a hulk named Moghul used to sell a bottle of ethyl alcohol near Moghul Masjid for six rupees. He would not accept credit, and Iqbal did not have the money to buy even one bottle.

Ali solved this problem too. He took Iqbal to a Marwari shop. Ali was three years older than Iqbal. He had been in touch with this Marwari for the last four years. His guarantee secured Iqbal a loan of Rs 60 to enable him to buy six bottles at a daily interest of 10 per cent.

From there, Ali took him through a shadowy alley behind the children's home into the dingy basement of a narrow building. Iqbal peered inside and saw a naked bulb overhead casting a pool of dim light inside.

There were more bottles than furniture in the kholi. There was only a sagging cot, a cupboard and a few clothes dangling from nails on the wall. Moghul was sitting on the cot with one leg bent at the knee, smoking a bidi.

'Chacha,' Ali said by way of introduction, 'This friend of mine is good in studies and great in fighting.'

'Is that so?'

'One day he hit me so hard that he almost broke my nose.'

Now Moghul felt it necessary to study Iqbal who was standing quietly in his khaki half-pants, a half-sleeved white shirt tucked into it. He had curly hair, beady eyes and sunken cheeks. His face was gaunt. His body was thin like a wire, 'single pasli' (scrawny) in local parlance. He wore canvas shoes.

'Have you brought the money?' Moghul finally asked after sizing Iqbal up.

Iqbal fished out six ten-rupee notes from the pocket of his shorts and laid them before him. This was the beginning of a new career. He had Ali's support. Ali had also given him the addresses of two liquor dens where he could sell the bottles. One was in Dongri, the other was in Mazgaon.

'Ali,' Iqbal said after putting the bottles into a bag, 'Why have you passed on your lucrative job to me?'

'Because you deserve it.'

'What will you do now?'

'I've been thinking of giving it up!' he said with a smug smile.

'Why?'

'I've joined Mastan's gang.'

Iqbal sold five bottles each to the two liquor dens. He earned a profit of ten rupees. He paid six rupees to the Marwari as one day's interest. He earned Rs 4, which was his net profit. In a month, he could earn Rs 120.

He returned the principal amount to the Marwari trader the following month. He spent about twenty rupees on his younger brothers, Razzak and Firoze, who did not have proper clothes or shoes.

*

I interrupted Sufi here. 'You were doing a job while you were in the sixth standard?'
'Correct.'
'What were the school timings?'
'Ten to five.'
'Then when did you find time to deliver the bottles?'
'After school hours.'

*

Iqbal would come straight home after school. He would have tea and snacks and then go out on the pretext of playing cricket with his friends. He would then make a dash from Munda Galli to Moghul's basement.

Moghul was quite pleased with him. This boy, who had started with ferrying ten bottles a day, was now ferrying forty bottles in two rounds. In the first round, he would deliver twenty bottles in a bag to Aziz Dilip's liquor den in Dongri. In the second round, he would carry another twenty bottles and walk to Mazgaon. By the time he delivered these to Shankar Maratha's den and returned home, it would be 8 p.m.

By then, Iqbal's daily income was Rs 40. But he never flaunted his money. He didn't even let his father catch a whiff of it. However, when he got new clothes for his younger brothers for Eid, Hussain Ali got suspicious.

'Where did you get so much money?' Hussain Ali asked.
'A friend of mine taught me how to sell bottles.'

'What bottles?'

'Medicine.'

'No liquor bottles?'

'Of course not.'

The talk ended there. However, when Hussain Ali came to know that his son was meeting all the other expenses of his brothers too, he was dumbfounded.

This time, he asked his wife, 'Gul Banu, is it true?'

'Yes, why?'

'Then it can't be medicine.'

'Yes, it is.'

'How do you know?'

'One day, I too had some doubts. The next day, Iqbal showed me a bottle. I opened the cork and smelt it.'

'All right, I would like to smell one too.'

'Don't you believe me?'

'Are you afraid to face the truth?'

'Yes,' she said, fuming. 'For the last six months you have been twiddling your thumbs at home. You are not earning a single paisa. My son is breaking his back to make ends meet, but you won't let him live in peace. How on earth do you want me to run the house?'

Gul Banu's last sentence carried a solid punch. It was beyond Hussain Ali's ability to counter. Discovering that the burden of the entire household was being shouldered by his schoolgoing son, he felt a wave of sadness at his plight; he was awash with guilt.

Iqbal returned home late that evening, dog-tired, and after having his dinner, he sat down in a corner to do his homework. Gul Banu had gone downstairs to fetch water. Due to lack of pressure, the water would not reach the first floor. Almost every day, people had to go down to the municipal tap with buckets to fetch water.

Hussain Ali called his son to his bedside. He put his hand on his head lovingly, found out all that he needed to and then gave him some fatherly advice. 'My dear child, there are two ways of making money: one that God approves of and the other that He doesn't approve of. When I was at the docks, I was doing the work that God does not approve of, and till today I am paying the price for it.'

'What do I do, Papa?' Iqbal lifted his head and looked straight into Hussain Ali's eyes. Behind that one sentence lurked a hundred hungry questions. *Papa, what will happen to me? What will happen to my studies? What will happen to my brothers?*

Hussain Ali did not reply. It was an answer he had yet to find himself.

*

Iqbal found the same answer that I had at his age. He used to live in a single room in Abbasi Manzil. I used to live in a similar room in Sultan Mansion. Both buildings in Dongri were in a similar condition—like hulking shipwrecks that could sink any time.

Having lost his mind, my father was bedridden. Almost all of my uncle Mohammed Hussain's salary used to go towards his treatment.

After changing several doctors, when there was no improvement in his condition, we resorted to seeking rainbows in dargahs. If someone said a particular dargah had the reputation of curing the final stages of madness, my mother would take my father there. If someone said that a particular shrine in a particular village was known for miracles, we would board a train and take my father there.

These excursions, perhaps because of the fresh air, would have some positive effect on my father's health and raise our hopes. However, such improvements would last only a few days after which he would remain confined to the same bed, the same room and the same walls. Sometimes we would see him staring at the ceiling and sometimes at the walls.

My mother took up work in more households. Her routine was the most punishing in our family. After attending to her own chores in the morning, she would get busy with work in the neighbouring homes. She would wash someone's utensils, grind someone's condiments, wash someone's clothes under the common tap of the chawl or deliver rationed milk to someone's house. After a day's rigorous labour, she would earn Rs 5.

It was not just the question of my education. There was my younger brother too. I started selling *chikki* (sweets made from nuts and jaggery), peppermint and sweet-and-sour candies. I used to sit with my cookie–candy basket on the pavement of Dongri's main road.

Iqbal would emerge from his house in Munda Galli, come to Pala Galli and sit near Khoja Masjid. His basket would contain berries, amla and other wild fruits besides candies.

*

Many decades have passed since those days. However, Sufi has not forgotten those days of struggle and his childhood friends who stood by him, particularly Kadar, who had suggested the idea of peddling by the roadside. In the last twenty years, Sufi has done business worth millions, fat bundles of bank notes have passed through his hands. Today, he lives in a penthouse terrace apartment in Bandra, while Kadar continues to sit at the pavement stall in Pala Galli.

'Whenever I go to Dongri, I think of him,' said Sufi. 'And I sit with him a while to chat.'

'If you wished, you could lift him from the pavement and put him up in a palace,' I reminded him.

'True. Sometimes, even I feel the same. God knows how many strangers I have helped without keeping a count.'

'Then why don't you?'

'He wears the shirt of a carefree person. He sits cheerfully on the road throughout the day. After earning enough to meet his requirements, he returns home in the evening. He eats a hearty dinner and sleeps contentedly. Even today, sorrow has not darkened his life. And I don't want to put the weight of money on his shoulders and take away the lightness in his steps.'

*

If we look at the life of Haji Mastan, we will find that he too went through a similar situation. He too had begun his career hawking chikki and sweet-and-sour peppermints.

In a way, Iqbal and I were fortunate. Both of us at least had a house to live in. Mastan used to live in a hut near Musafir Khana. His family had migrated from Tamil Nadu and studied in Fatimabai School near Crawford Market. Our mother tongue was Gujarati, his was Tamil.

To supplement my income, I had purchased from a second-hand bookshop some funny picture booklets by Golibar, a popular humourist from Ahmedabad, and about a dozen other children's books. I would take these to school and lend them to my classmates for a paisa per day.

To supplement his income, Mastan got a job with a roadside tea vendor. He would serve 'outdoor' customers— deliver tea in small glasses to nearby shopkeepers and offices— and daydream on a bench during his spare time.

Whenever a car passed by, his eyeballs would be transfixed. His only ambition was to sit in his own car and drive around the city. Back then, he roamed around barefoot. At the tea stall, there was more than enough work but not enough money.

He quit the tea stall, left school and landed up at the docks. Here, young children were employed to clean up the rust and paint the interiors of ship boilers. These boilers were so small that it was impossible for a man to get inside. Mastan became adept at such work.

As he grew older, his body grew too. The size of the boilers, however, remained the same. He needed to find a new job, but for that he did not have to leave the docks. He became a coolie. He was given a badge from the customs department— number 23. (Not 786, as is popularly misconstrued.)

By the time Iqbal was selling chikki, Mastan was already deep into gold smuggling. He had long fulfilled his dream of driving around Bombay in his own car.

Iqbal too tried hard to increase his income. Abbasi Manzil, where he lived on the first floor, was a three-storeyed building. Due to the low pressure of the water, the taps in the rooms on the upper floors were mostly dry.

Iqbal started fetching water during the night for the tenants who were willing to pay him. His days were now divided into three shifts: attending school in the morning, tending to his roadside shop in the evening and fetching water at night.

He would fill pots with water from the municipal tap on the ground floor, climb the stairs and fill the drums of the tenants on the second and third floors, and then climb down to the ground floor. He would carry thirty to forty pots of water and earn around Rs 3 every day.

*

'Sufi,' I wondered aloud, 'your father was a heart patient. So, one can understand why he couldn't help you. But what about your mother?'

'She was a tuberculosis patient and had outlived her prognosis. Besides, she was not keeping in good health as before.'

Seeing little Iqbal climb up and down the stairs with pots of drinking water on his head was a heart-wrenching experience for his parents. They watched him helplessly and silently. They didn't have any solution. It was particularly painful for Hussain Ali. His silence was weighed down by the question it raised. *Had he committed a mistake by asking his son to give up the path that God despised and to tread on the path that He favoured?*

Exhausted by his chores, Iqbal was sitting in his room one evening. He was yet to complete his homework and then help his younger brothers with theirs when Ali and Moghul appeared at the open door.

3

Hussain Ali glanced at Ali and focused his eyes on the hulking stranger with him—an oval face topped with bristly hair, scrubby beard and commanding eyes that drew his attention. He had a pug nose. Behind his lips, a gold tooth was conspicuous. He wore a faded green, short-sleeved Pathani shirt and a striped red lungi.

Hussain Ali was familiar with the name Moghul, but not the face. He presumed that the person accompanying Ali was his father or some other relative. 'Come in,' he said, sitting up on the bed. His wife stopped massaging his feet and got up too.

Moghul looked at Iqbal helping his two brothers with their homework, pulled up a chair and sat opposite Hussain Ali. Ali stood behind him. Gul Banu busied herself lighting a Primus stove in a corner of the same room which served as a kitchen.

'I came to see Iqbal,' Moghul began. 'I haven't met him for several days, so . . .'

'You are?'

'He's a hard-working boy,' Moghul continued without giving him a chance to speak. He was looking at Iqbal, but he addressed the father. 'He was earning about forty-fifty rupees a day when he suddenly disappeared. When I

31

inquired after him, Ali told me that he was hale and hearty. I couldn't believe it.'

An introduction was no longer necessary. Hussain Ali realized that the person sitting before him in the faded green kameez was Moghul. The filth from which he had extricated his son had, today, entered his house.

Hussain Ali suddenly found himself in an awkward situation. The unpleasant sound coming from the stove as Gul Banu tried to light it was audible in the silence of the room. She put the kettle on the stove and threw a sidelong glance at her husband. The decision was now in Hussain Ali's hands.

*

At this, Sufi fell into a deep silence and looked up at the sky.

'Sufi! What did your father decide?' I asked impatiently.

'He was not in a position to take a decision.'

'But he was the head of the family. Even your mother would not go against his final decision.'

'True. He himself was shaken up at that point, however, he did not reply either in the affirmative or . . .'

'But why?'

'A person anticipating death within twenty-four hours rises above all—sorrow and happiness.'

I simply stared at Sufi.

'How did you know that your father was going to die soon?'

'After Moghul left, he himself told us.'

'What did he say?'

'That his time was up. I didn't understand anything. After all, what was my age at that time?'

The year was 1966. Sufi was in the tenth standard. All his attention was focused on his studies.

*

Like Hussain Ali, my father, Ghulam Hussain, too announced his end beforehand. Not with an ambiguous statement like 'My time is up,' but with a calm yet explicit warning: 'No one should leave the house tomorrow, else you won't see my face ever again.'

That was a Tuesday. He had also said that if he did not die on Wednesday, he would surely leave this world on Friday.

Man has not yet understood life and its mysteries, let alone death. Who whispered into the ears of our fathers that their days were numbered? Who cautioned them to be prepared for their final exit?

We were all astonished by the way my father serenely announced his death. We did not believe him because his malaise was no ordinary sickness.

According to the doctors, not even his fingernails had any affliction. The doctors were also not willing to believe that some evil spirit had possessed him. In their view, he was the victim of neurosis. However, none of them could come to a definite conclusion about the nature of the mental disorder and its cause. We all knew that while he was trying to conquer the spirits through the forty-day chilla ritual, he had been conquered himself.

Night and day, he would lie mute on his cot. At times, one could hear him murmuring. His hands would gesticulate as if he were talking to an invisible person. Then, all of a sudden, he would fall back into his impenetrable silent world again and stare at the wall. It was because of this mental state that when he announced the precise date of his death in full consciousness, we wondered if it was another delusion and dismissed whatever he said as the ramblings of a madman.

My mother, grandmother and my uncle Mohammed Hussain huddled together to discuss the situation. They agreed on one thing: there was no harm in staying alert for the day.

The following day, before noon, my father had a seizure. No one could tell if it was a cardiac arrest or a brief fit. He was writhing in pain. My mother, who was making chapattis, rushed to his side. My uncle and grandmother too hastened across. In short order, the entire family converged around him.

Before we could comprehend anything, the storm passed. My father got up and looking at each of us said, 'Go on and get moving, nothing is going to happen to me till Friday.'

My father had had a stroke. We were now a 100 per cent sure that Friday was to be his final day. And so it happened. He left his body in the presence of all his family. I was consumed with grief but what was the use? As Omar Khayyam so poignantly said,

> The Moving Finger writes, and having writ,
> Moves on: nor all thy piety nor wit
> Shall lure It back to cancel half a Line.
> Nor all thy tears wash out a word of it.

*

Sufi firmly believed that there cannot be any deviation from what the Creator had written. One astrologer, who had seen his hand, had predicted his future.

'I'll roll in millions, yet I'll remain a pauper,' Sufi recounted the prediction. 'I'll become a billionaire and yet live like a sanyasi. I'll try to tread on the right path and yet my feet will slip towards crime. This month, I've completed the fortieth year of my life. God is a witness to how much I've struggled in these four decades to live a just and honest life.'

'For example?'

In 1980, he said, he had taken to the poultry business. When he failed, he tried his hand at the wholesale trade of prawns. In this, too, there were many complications. Recently, he took up a new occupation—buying old cars, repairing them and then selling them.

Sometimes I cannot fathom what Sufi says. For instance, he asserts that the future of all men is predestined—therefore man is feeble and helpless. He has no free will. Then, what is the use of predictions?

I asked him, 'Suppose it's predestined that I'll meet with a car accident on a particular day at a particular time. If I know this, why would I venture out of the home?'

'If a car accident is really destined for you, there will be a compelling situation that will make you leave the house.'

He gave his father's example. The date of Hussain Ali's death was fixed. He knew the exact date.

'How?'

'From his horoscope.'

'Had he got a horoscope made?'

'Oh, no! He had accidentally come across an astrologer who had prepared a rough horoscope based on the lines carved on the palm of his right hand. As per the reading, he was to get married at the age of thirty-five. That's exactly what happened. Among other such correct predictions, one was about his death.'

*

Hussain Ali was perfectly fine in the days leading up to his death. On the day before his death, he had vaguely forewarned his wife, but the following day he pointedly asked her to forgive him for whatever wrongs he had done to her, knowingly or unknowingly.

Iqbal was preparing to leave for school when he heard his father utter these words to his mother. He froze.

Gul Banu admonished her husband, 'What's wrong with you today? Why are you saying such strange things? Are you thinking of deserting us?'

'My call has come.'

The eyes of the mother and son filled with tears. Iqbal put his textbooks back in the drawer. There was no need to go to school.

'Don't be foolish,' Hussain Ali told him. 'Your presence here will not send the angel of death away. Now go, there isn't much time left for your examination.'

The father and son argued for a couple of minutes. Finally, before leaving for school with his younger brothers, Iqbal told his mother, 'Please, don't let papa go out today.'

Hussain Ali remained at home, reciting couplets from the Koran. After lunch, he told his wife, 'I'm going for a walk, just up to the street corner. I shall be back in about five minutes.'

What difference would five minutes make? Gul Banu thought. Hussain Ali left Abbasi Manzil and reached Pala Galli. For a while, he stood watching the mosque and its minaret. This was the same Khoja Masjid where he had offered namaz, sought God's blessings, listened to the sermons of the pesh imam and attended congregations. This mosque was a part of his life.

From here, he wandered up to the corner of Pala Galli and proceeded towards J.J. Hospital, almost as if he had to meet death at an appointed time and place.

The situation brings back to mind the ancient Iraqi fable. A rich sheikh was walking through the marketplace in Baghdad, when, standing across the street, he suddenly saw

Death beckoning him. The terrified man mounted his fastest horse and raced 500 miles to Samara. Later that night, there was a knock on the door. When the man answered it, there stood Death. 'Why did you beckon me in the marketplace in Baghdad today?' asked the man.

'I did not beckon you,' replied Death. 'I was merely surprised to see you, for I knew that tonight we had an appointment in Samara.'

Hussain Ali's appointment with death was near gate number 12 of J.J. Hospital. The post-mortem report revealed that he had died of cardiac failure.

'The benefit of knowing the future,' Sufi summed up, 'is to prepare man for good as well as evil omens. If the exact date of death is known, one can brace oneself to welcome it.'

Where the family had struggled to stay afloat earlier, Hussain Ali's death saw it sink completely. Hunger and sorrow besieged the family. Sorrow could still be reasoned with, but what about hunger? *What about my younger brothers? What about my studies? Who will pay the house rent, grocer's bills and the school fee?* Iqbal was devastated.

*

Hussain Ali's last wish had been to see his son graduate and live like a respectable gentleman. There was not a single straight road before Iqbal that led to this destination. So he chose the crooked one. Leaving Munda Galli, he proceeded towards Moghul Masjid.

He did not need to enter Moghul's room. Moghul was chatting with a sardar outside, at a tea stall. Iqbal stood before him. 'Uncle, can I get work?'

Moghul waved him off as if waving aside a fly.

Iqbal was about to speak again when Moghul said, 'I came to your house when I needed you. Now there is no work.'

The sardar sitting beside Moghul was listening.

'Uncle, my father is dead.'

'So, what do I do?' Moghul barked. 'Open an orphanage? Get lost. I'll call you if I need you.'

Iqbal stood there quietly for some time and left when he saw no sign of hope.

'Who was that boy?' asked the sardar who had been observing silently.

'Why?' Moghul asked, 'Do you need someone?'

'Does he have any experience in our line of work?'

Moghul nodded. 'He is also a hard-working boy.'

'Even a donkey works hard. He must also have a brain.'

'He is bright and honest too.'

'Call him back.'

Moghul turned to look for Iqbal, but he was nowhere in sight. However, he guessed that Iqbal could not have gone far. He sent a boy from the tea stall to get him.

When Iqbal faced Moghul again, his face glowed with renewed hope.

'Do you know this gentleman?' Moghul pointed to the sardar.

Glancing at him, Iqbal shook his head.

'He is Jasbir Singh.'

Iqbal looked at him again. The sardarji looked like a truck driver to him. This time, the sardarji asked, 'Will you work for me?'

Before giving him a definite reply, Iqbal asked him, 'What's the work?'

'Storing some things.'

'I don't have space.'

'Don't you have a house?'

'Yes, but it's tiny. What needs to be stored?'

'Liquor bottles.'

A shiver ran down Iqbal's spine. 'No, no, that's not possible.'

'Why?'

'If the neighbours see the bottles and inform the police, I'll be in a fix.'

Jasbir Singh laughed. His white teeth sparkled through his black beard and moustache. 'The bottles will not be visible.'

'Then?'

'They will be concealed in sacks.' Feeling the need to clarify further, he went on, 'Just like the sacks in which grain is stored.'

Finally, everything was settled. Iqbal would be paid Rs 5 per sack. Arrangements would have to be made to store about fifty to sixty sacks in the house. The entire stock would be disposed of by Jasbir Singh in two to three days and replaced with a new stock. This meant that he would get at least Rs 2000–3000 a month. However, the moot question was: where would he keep the sacks in such a small room?

On reaching home, Iqbal inspected the single-room house like a new tenant. A wooden bed occupied almost half the room. Apart from a little space in the centre, there was a cupboard, two chairs and a small writing table. In a corner was the cooking area.

When Gul Banu saw Iqbal surveying the room, she could not resist asking, 'What are you looking for?'

'A way,' Iqbal replied without looking at her.

'Have you gone crazy? A way is always outside, not inside the room,' she laughed.

Iqbal explained—he was looking for a way to store about fifty sacks so that one could earn Rs 2000 a month. Gul Banu's face lit up. She too started thinking with her son. *Can we not create space by selling the cupboard? What about disposing of the chairs? The bed can be shifted from the window to the right, near the wall.*

At last, Iqbal found a solution. The bed must be dismantled. He got to work immediately. First, he removed all the planks and stacked them on one side. Then, he loosened the joints on all four sides using a spanner. He disjoined all parts of the bed one by one and kept them near the planks. After the bed was dismantled, the small room suddenly looked like a spacious banquet hall.

How and from where were these sacks coming?

*

With Independence in 1947 came prohibition. Simultaneously, a heavy customs duty was imposed on textiles, transistor radios, cigarettes and other imported goods. As a result, the seeds of smuggling sprouted. In the 1950s, the sapling turned into a hardy plant. By the 1960s, the plant had become a lush green tree.

During these years, the shortest route to smuggling foreign liquor was from Goa to Bombay. For the poor and the working class, breweries of cheap country liquor mushroomed in residential areas in Bombay. Sion–Koliwada was the nerve centre of this flourishing trade. Ramaswamy was its don.

Just like Karim Lala and Haji Mastan ruled over Dongri, Ramaswamy held sway over Sion–Koliwada. When Varadarajan Mudaliyar challenged his supremacy, Ramaswamy's empire collapsed like a pack of cards.

Who was Varadarajan Mudaliyar, also known as Varada Bhai?

Varadarajan was born in Kalyan near Bombay on 9 October 1925. His father was a fitter in the railways. His monthly salary was Rs 12.18. Varadarajan too, like Mastan, had started his career from the docks.

Varada and Mastan led parallel lives. Mastan had left school due to poverty. Varada had left Koliwada municipal school for similar reasons. Mastan had started working in a roadside tea stall. Varada had joined a garage. Thereafter, both came to the docks. Both of them first took up work as boiler painters on a ship. Both grew up and became coolies. Then they met. Varada took advantage of this acquaintance. Mastan had already established his bootlegging network and had over fifteen boys working under him. He enjoyed the patronage of influential people.

With his blessing, Varada attacked Ramaswamy. This attack was as well-planned as a tactical army assault. Ramaswamy's liquor breweries were demolished and his gambling dens were destroyed along with the furniture and everything else inside. His men who tried to resist were thrashed within an inch of their lives. The rest surrendered at Varada's feet.

Ramaswamy was stunned. Before he could comprehend what calamity befell him, his empire was reduced to rubble. Overnight, his multi-million-rupee monthly income disappeared into thin air. His writ no more ran supreme. Within twenty-four hours, he fled to Madras with his family.

Varadarajan Mudaliyar was crowned as Sion–Koliwada's Varada Bhai. He started his own liquor breweries. He opened fifteen bars where people could drink to their heart's content twenty-four hours a day.

Liquor brewed in Varadabhai's breweries was supplied all over Bombay. This was country liquor meant for the working class. Executives and white-collared businessmen, on the other hand, demanded Scotch. The traffic between Goa and Bombay increased.

There was heavy demand in Bombay for Goa's feni (which is made from toddy palm and cashews) as well as Scotch, rum and brandy. Jasbir Singh's lorries used to ply between Goa and Bombay. His business of importing liquor illegally was thriving.

These trucks carried a large number of sacks, of which the sacks on the top contained coconuts. The remaining sacks contained liquor bottles. Post-midnight, one of the trucks would stop outside Munda Galli in Palkhi Mohalla.

This road and Pala Galli start from Dongri's Char Nal and run parallel towards Khadak. Munda Galli lies between these roads, zigzagging like an earthworm. There are three entry points to Munda Galli: one from Pala Galli, the other two from Palkhi Mohalla. It was in Munda Galli that one of Aziz Dilip's three liquor dens was situated.

*

'You said the truck would be parked at the corner of Munda Galli. Then how were the sacks unloaded and carried into the building?' I asked him.

Sufi replied with a smile, 'I was no longer alone. I too had my own gang. There were about a dozen daring Malbari lads working under me. They were prepared to risk their necks at the snap of my fingers. I would instruct them in the evening. They would stand near the lane after midnight.'

After the truck arrived, these boys would carry a sack each and enter the narrow lane. Under the cover of darkness, they would stealthily cross it, enter Abbasi Manzil, climb the stairs and dump the sacks in Iqbal's room. Iqbal would then keep these sacks in order, lay a sheet over them and sleep on top of this makeshift bed.

This continued without a hitch for some days. Iqbal repaid all his debts. The situation at home improved. The days of misery were gone. Now, Iqbal did not have to carry buckets of water. He did not have to sell chikki, candy and berries on the roadside. His studies too continued alongside without hindrance.

He was dreaming of clearing the tenth-grade examinations with a first class when an officer of the crime branch, Inspector Bharucha, got wind of his activities. This policeman was to play an important role in Iqbal's life, converting a juvenile delinquent into a hardened criminal.

I was almost the same age when Dr R.J. Chinwala entered my life. This psychiatrist-cum-author-cum-photographer would inspire me towards a very different path to progress.

4

My father's death had shaken me up. I was cold to my bones and too stunned to cry. I can't explain what the reason was because I had only received rebuffs from my father. Whatever affection I had known was only from my mother.

Painful memories of his refusal to display any affection swim before my eyes till today. I used to run towards my father's cot to sit on his lap, but he would push me away. He would then berate my mother, 'How many times have I told you not to allow the children to come near me!'

My mother would hold us close and glare at my father. She did not have the courage to say a single word in front of him. At times, when it became unbearable, she would summon a bit of courage and say, 'The world will not come to an end if you hug the children for a few minutes.' He could not tolerate such a comment and would start screaming. Then he would collapse. By this time, he was epileptic too.

This does not mean that our father did not love us. He too wanted both his sons to sit on his lap, in the cradle of his arms, to cuddle us, listen to our babble and tell us fairy tales. It was his phobia that kept him from doing so.

He had created an imaginary circle around his cot. It was his belief that if his children entered that circle, the evil spirits residing in his body would take over our tender souls.

I was too small to understand this. As a result, I did not develop any affection for my father. On the contrary, a feeling of hatred festered in a corner of my heart. *Then why did his death derail my life? Why was it that the very street urchins, loafers I should have kept away from, became my friends? What triggered my rebellion?*

With my school bag duly strapped on my back, I would leave home supposedly for school and join the gangs of my new vagabond friends to loaf around. Sometimes, we would go on a ticketless joyride in suburban trains, and at other times, we would wait outside Victoria Terminus (VT) railway station for the specially-commissioned trains carrying World War II soldiers to the docks. These narrow-gauge trains chugged slowly as they carried British soldiers to the ships waiting to take them home. We would scamper like vagrants alongside them imploring, 'Sir, give us a chocolate . . . Sir, throw us a sandwich . . . a few pennies . . .'

From the train windows, the soldiers would toss pieces of chocolate, a few coins or a packet of cigarettes. Then the smoke-belching train would lumber away into the distance. My ragged friends and I would sit on the tracks and divide the spoils. We would luxuriously smoke the imported cigarettes and eat a piece of chocolate to hide the odour.

After a month, my mother came to know about my rogue adventures. First, she thrashed me, and then she started crying. 'I toil day and night so that you can pursue your studies,' she reminded me between sobs. 'I wash dishes and clothes in the entire neighbourhood and grind chillies. It breaks my heart to see you running around town like a stray dog.'

My heart melted, and with that, my rebellion ended. I started attending school regularly from the next day. That day, I also had a time-worn Disney comic along with my textbooks. A British soldier had thrown it in the air from the train and I had caught it.

Those days, American comic books did not flood the Indian market the way they do today. Like a rare bird, a foreign comic would make an appearance once in a while. It was the first time I had seen one, albeit a tattered one.

*

A major turning point of my childhood—one that prompted me to change the course of my life—arrived most unexpectedly that day. During the snack break, I was trying to copy Mickey Mouse in different poses from the book. A classmate told me that a big artist resided near his house and that he made large paintings.

'How big?'

He spread his hands wide and said, 'Bigger than this.'

That evening, instead of going home, I accompanied my friend to see his neighbour, Dr R.J. Chinwala. His house was a haven for creative people. Photographers, painters and men of letters gathered there almost daily to discuss art and literature. Once a month, a budding poet would present poems before the august gathering.

Not only that, he had also provided accommodation in his three-bedroom apartment to an Urdu writer, who had come from Hyderabad to try his luck in the film industry, and to a painter from Gujarat who was in search of a place to start his work. The Urdu writer was Mushtaq Jalili, who would later find fame as the writer of films like Ek Phool Do Maali and Avtaar, and the painter was Yusuf Dhala.

*

I saw that Dhala had started a large canvas in the miniature style. I stood there transfixed. I did not even realize when my friend left. When I came back to my senses, Dr Chinwala was standing beside me. He asked me gently, 'Did you like the picture?'

'Yes. Can I come to see the painting tomorrow also?'

'Aabid!' He addressed me by my name. Perhaps my friend had told him about me before leaving. 'You can come every day.'

Thus began my daily visits to this house. I became a member of Dr Chinwala's extended family. Dhala was to become my guru in the field of art, while Mushtaq Jalili taught me the art and craft of storytelling. Dr Chinwala, too, was to play an important role in shaping my life. My wayward life was to take a new direction.

*

Inspector Bharucha, meanwhile, would chart out a new course for Iqbal, but there was a difference between the two courses. One was positive, while the other was negative. One led to creativity, beauty and progress while the other led to destruction, deception and ultimately ruin.

Once again, the same questions raise their heads. *Who decides these paths? Why did I come across Dr Chinwala, and Iqbal chance upon Inspector Bharucha? Was it a game of destiny or mere coincidence?*

If we look at the positive side of Sufi, he lived like a holy man. He offered namaz five times a day. He fasted for thirty days during the month of Ramadan. The big difference between Sufi and a common Muslim was that whatever Sufi did, he did it with understanding and not because a priest ordained it.

One day, his wife, Masooma, requested him, 'Iqbal, the graveyard of our community is in bad shape. The boundary walls have collapsed, the pathways inside are rough and wild shrubs have grown where there were once flower beds. If you get it repaired by spending a few thousand rupees, the entire community will bless you.'

'I'm ready,' said Sufi. 'I'm willing to spend not just a few thousands but lakhs. But on one condition—the graveyard should be Islamic.'

Masooma looked at him baffled.

He explained. 'Islam does not permit construction of concrete tombs. So, I'll first use a bulldozer to flatten all those graves constructed of marble. I'll remove the disparity between a rich man's grave and a poor man's grave. Go and get permission from the pesh imam.'

Masooma was silent.

'Aabid Bhai,' Sufi continued, 'The cemetery isn't meant for erecting mausoleums. It's meant to remind humanity that here lie mighty kings and conquerors. No one is immortal. In the end, everyone has to bid goodbye to the world. Therefore, be warned and tread on the path of righteousness.'

If you consider Sufi's negative side, his razor-sharp brain would put the biggest mafia don of the country to shame. He has done all that a don does. However, he has done it with finesse and cunning. He understands the language of the knife but does not use it. If something can be accomplished through persuasion, he does not use the gun. He believes it is wiser to grease the palms of a police officer than to challenge him.

Despite the sophistication, this aspect of his personality is a weak point to him. He resigned himself to it as his destiny. He did not want to do work that God forbid. He was compelled by circumstances. 'Because it's written,' he would say.

My own belief was different. Whether life deals you aces or not, you are free to choose the hand you play.

'If that were the case, astrology would be proved totally wrong,' he argued.

This reminds me of an event that is supposed to have occurred in the court of Emperor Aurangzeb. This emperor had total faith in Allah and the Koran, and he did not believe in astrologers or the shastras. He believed that only Allah knew the future, which is what the Koran also says. No one except Allah can claim to know the unknown. One day, his prime minister came to the court with a scholarly pandit. Aurangzeb asked him two questions. The first was: 'How long will I live?'

The pandit did some calculations and gave Aurangzeb a figure. Then Aurangzeb asked him, 'How long will you live?'

The pandit replied confidently, 'Your Highness, at present, I'm sixty years old and fated to live up to a ripe age of ninety-five.'

Aurangzeb pulled out his sword and severed his head.

To get our conversation back on track, I asked Sufi, 'Who informed Inspector Bharucha of your activities?'

He thought for a while and then continued his narration. In those years, one of Iqbal's relatives, Jafar 'Tight', was a feared goon in Dongri. Attacking him meant challenging Abdul Rehman Kaafaria, whose patronage he enjoyed. Old residents of Dongri shudder at the mention of this gangster's name even today.

The elderly people recall that Kaafaria's hand was made of steel. Just one punch was enough to split his enemy's head in two.

This was when Aziz Dilip was growing into a bloodhound, Jafar 'Tight' had become cautious. A turf war had begun between the two. Aziz Dilip had moved into the same building as Jafar 'Tight'—Velsi Lalji Building.

This building was as deceptive as Munda Galli. While Munda Galli had three entrances, this building had two: one from Pala Galli on which Khoja Masjid was located and the other from Bhimpura. The building often proved to be a portal to safety for crooks.

Many taxi drivers have also been duped here. The trick is simple. Just say, 'Sorry, I don't have enough money for the fare. I'll have to go up and get it.' While the taxi driver waits, the passenger rushes in through one entrance and walks out like a gentleman from the other one.

Aziz Dilip had started living in this centrally located building. He wanted to establish himself and lay the foundation of his network there. At the same time, he had to survive. He was not yet powerful enough to challenge Jafar 'Tight'.

Sometimes, he would return home drunk, hollering, and Jafar 'Tight' would bash him up on the staircase. 'Next time you create a row at night, I'll break your legs and stuff them up your asshole.' Aziz Dilip would silently suffer the physical and verbal assault.

It continued for a few years until Kaafaria died. This emboldened Aziz. By this time, he had laid a solid foundation for himself. He was the owner of three liquor joints.

One of his joints was in Munda Galli, another was in the playground behind New Model High School in Bhimpura and the third was in Chindhi Galli in Dongri market. He had over twenty boys, all around sixteen years of age, working under him.

Jafar 'Tight' realized that his days were numbered. It was no longer safe for him to cross Aziz Dilip's path, let alone catch him by the collar and beat him up. So, he started looking for his enemy's weaknesses to mount an attack.

He learnt that trucks carrying liquor bottles arrived after midnight, and that the stock was unloaded in Munda Galli. He assumed that the consignment belonged to Aziz Dilip. The same day, he wrote a letter and sent it to the home department.

The department forwarded it to the crime branch headquarters at VT, and it landed on the table of Inspector Bharucha. He read the complaint and deputed three men to keep vigil at the three entry points of Munda Galli that night.

It was around 10 p.m. Iqbal was mugging up history lessons, preparing for his tenth standard examinations that were to start the next day. Both his younger brothers had had dinner and gone to sleep. Iqbal's mother was awake a while longer, reading her prayer book. She too went off to sleep after about an hour.

Iqbal looked at the clock. It was 11.15 p.m. He kept one eye on his book and the other on the clock. The truck carrying the consignment was to arrive after midnight. He had already briefed his boys. They were to wait at the corner of Munda Galli at the appointed time.

A steady flow of customers had started coming to Aziz Dilip's Munda Galli joint. Echoes of raucous laughter from the den in the dead of the night died away by the time they reached Iqbal's room. The plainclothesmen of the crime branch had positioned themselves at the three entry points. They were invisible except for their piercing eyes.

On hearing a truck honk at a distance, Iqbal looked at the clock for the last time. It was 2 a.m. He closed his textbook, put it into his bag and got up. He did not need to go downstairs. His boys were trained. Sufi called these Malbari boys *taporis*.

The truck that had entered Palkhi Mohalla stopped near the entrance of Munda Galli. The plainclothesmen became alert. They saw sacks being unloaded swiftly. Young boys aged between fifteen and sixteen, slim but strongly built, were carrying a sack each and disappearing into Munda Galli. They returned, lifted a sack each and again ran into the lane.

It was difficult for the policemen to know where exactly the stock was being taken. It was risky to enter without being spotted. If they were caught, it might cost them their lives.

If Velsi Lalji Building was a blessing for crooks, Munda Galli was a haven for killers. If a killer vanished into the maze of these lanes after committing a murder, it would be impossible for the police to trace him.

*

The next day, the three policemen presented themselves before Inspector Bharucha in his cabin. 'Did the truck come?' was his first question.

The three men nodded their heads in affirmation.

'How many sacks were unloaded?'

'More than fifty,' said one of them.

'Whose consignment was it?'

'Aziz Dilip's.'

'That's not possible.' Inspector Bharucha surveyed the faces of the three men.

'Sir, that's what is stated in the complaint.'

'And you believed it?' Inspector Bharucha thundered at their ridiculous argument.

'But, sir, we saw the sacks being taken to Aziz Dilip's joint.'

Inspector Bharucha smiled. 'My dear, you saw the sacks going towards the den, not into it. Right?'

A second policeman asked, 'How come you're so sure, sir?'

'I visited that liquor den once. There isn't enough space to dump even ten sacks, let alone fifty.'

The following day, the policemen were stationed at the three entry points again. Inspector Bharucha did not want to take action before he had confirmed his suspicions. Moreover, more than seizing the liquor stock, he was interested in ambushing the culprit and catching him red-handed. This required patience and Inspector Bharucha had the patience of a monk.

5

The plainclothesmen spent two nights waiting, watching and yawning. On the third night, their vigil bore fruit. The truck carrying the consignment entered Palkhi Mohalla again. It was the same time, midnight, and the same entrance, the corner of Munda Galli, and the same routine.

Iqbal was perplexed by this unexpected consignment. The reason was that the liquor stock brought in two days earlier had not been cleared. The fifty sacks were still lying untouched. Meanwhile, another fifty had arrived. He immediately entered the dark lane. He stopped the boys carrying the sacks and went to Chandu.

Sporting the physique of a wrestler, broad-shouldered Chandu was Aziz Dilip's right-hand man. He was in charge of the liquor joint here. Chandu had met Iqbal back in the days when the young Iqbal was working for Moghul as a delivery boy.

'Yaar, Chandu!' Iqbal said, 'The new consignment has arrived. If I stock this too, we will be forced to sleep in the corridor.'

'How big is the lot?'

'Fifty sacks.'

'Of what?'

'Ten of feni . . .'

'I need feni right here. I'll keep them,' Chandu interrupted him.

'The other sacks contain bottles of Scotch, rum and vodka,' Iqbal added.

'I'll send them to the Bhimpura joint. Tell Jasbir Singh to come after two days to settle the accounts. Anything else?'

That solved the problem. Iqbal issued fresh instructions to his boys who were standing in a queue near Abbasi Manzil with sacks on their back. 'Dump the cross-marked sacks at the liquor joint. Load the remaining sacks on the handcart parked outside.'

The boys resumed work. Once again, they started unloading the sacks, and once again the cops were faced with the same dilemma: should they enter the lane or not? If they didn't do that, they would have to go back without any conclusive finding to report once again.

At last, one of them mustered the courage to enter the lane. He sneaked in like a shadow, taking cover of the darkness, and stopped at a safe distance from the joint from where he could see what was going on. At that time, ten sacks containing feni were being dumped inside. It was dangerous to stay there any longer, there was no need either. He returned.

*

Inspector Bharucha was stumped. One of the three policemen standing before him had confirmed, 'Sir, this time I saw with my own eyes. The Malbari boys were carrying the sacks and Chandu was directing them to pile the sacks up inside the joint.'

Inspector Bharucha was compelled to think seriously. After deliberating for a while, he concluded that if what he had heard was true, there must be a cellar somewhere underneath the joint. He decided to raid the place. Two days later, he left his Liberty House residence in his jeep just before 2 a.m. It takes a maximum of ten minutes from there to reach Dongri in a vehicle.

Almost at the same time, the truck stopped at the corner of Munda Galli. The boys were standing there, ready. The truck driver hopped out from his seat, went to the back and then climbed back into the truck.

Iqbal was feeling anxious. His tenth grade examinations had started. To add to his predicament, the truck that used to come twice a week had started coming every alternate day. He was concerned about balancing his studies and the growing responsibilities of a burgeoning trade.

Inspector Bharucha's jeep turned right from Metro Cinemas and reached the crime branch headquarters at VT in a minute. The three policemen, who were waiting at the main gate, boarded the jeep as soon as it stopped. One sat beside Inspector Bharucha, who was driving, while the remaining two sat at the back. The jeep roared off again into the deserted streets.

The truck was being unloaded at the entrance of Munda Galli. The driver was pulling out the sacks one by one and handing them over to the boys. The Malbari boys were disappearing into the dark lane like mice with the sacks that were being stacked inside Iqbal's room. Usually, it took two hours to empty the truck. It had been scarcely five minutes since the unloading had begun.

The jeep had crossed Crawford Market and reached Mohammed Ali Road when there was an explosion. Inspector Bharucha and the three policemen jumped out of the jeep. The rear tyre of the jeep was punctured. One of the policemen ran in search of a mechanic.

Almost an hour had elapsed. The truck was half empty by then.

The policeman returned without success. It was difficult to find a mechanic at this hour. They could not wait until morning. Finally, Inspector Bharucha decided to do the job himself. He rolled up his sleeves and took out the spare tyre.

The distance between Munda Galli and Mohammed Ali Road can be covered on foot. Instead, they had wasted two hours looking for a mechanic and changing a tyre.

*

By the time the jeep entered Palkhi Mohalla, the truck was leaving.

'Sir, the truck . . .'

Inspector Bharucha was not interested in the truck. On reaching the entrance of Munda Galli, he parked the jeep on the side and went to Aziz Dilip's joint accompanied by the three plainclothesmen. By this time, the den was almost empty.

A boy was busy cleaning the beer mugs, glasses and plates, dipping them into a tub filled with water. Chandu was tallying the night's collection, his fingers deftly counting the notes.

On seeing Inspector Bharucha, he was stupefied. One policeman positioned himself outside the entry point. The other two began searching the premises.

'Please be seated, sir!' Chandu said, recovering from the initial shock and stuffing the money into a drawer. 'What will you have? Whiskey, rum, brandy or feni? The stock arrived just today.'

'How much?'

'Enough for our requirement.'

'How much?'

'You can see for yourself,' Chandu said pointing towards the feni bottles. 'There isn't enough space to keep more than a dozen crates.'

'Where's the rest of the stock?'

'What stock, sir?' Chandu asked innocently.

Inspector Bharucha shoved the table to one side and caught him by the neck. 'Tell me, where have you dumped the stock that came in the truck minutes ago?'

Chandu understood what had happened. Someone had informed the police about Iqbal. They must have kept a watch and concluded that the stock belonged to the joint and not to Iqbal. He regained his confidence.

'Sahib, I swear we never receive more than a few crates.'

'You won't open your mouth without . . .' Inspector Bharucha raised his hand.

'Sir,' one of the policemen who was searching the premises interjected, 'there is a sword and a dagger here.'

'Listen, *dikra*!' Inspector Bharucha lowered his hand. 'Now you've compounded the crime. If you don't tell me the truth, you'll be behind bars for a whole year.'

'Sir, I've told you the truth. I don't know anything.'

All of a sudden, Inspector Bharucha gave Chandu one tight, biting slap on his ear. But this did not affect him at all. Given his Herculean physique, even a few blows felt like a tickle of feathers. After hitting him across his face several times, Inspector Bharucha realized that the giant standing before him would not squeal so easily. He would have to be taken to the lock-up for a sound thrashing.

Chandu was handcuffed. One of the policemen grabbed the boy who was washing the glasses by the hair. Before leaving the joint, a thought occurred to Inspector Bharucha. *In the maze of Munda Galli, there were only two buildings and a few sewers. One building was Gardia School and the other was Abbasi Manzil. There was no harm looking these up.*

He locked Chandu and the boy up for the time being.

*

The night was almost over. The muezzin was calling the believers for early morning namaz to Khoja Masjid. His voice sounded sweet in the soft twilight. Devout Muslims woke up rubbing their eyes. Iqbal also got up.

He had studied till late and then had the sacks unloaded in his room from two to four in the morning. He had hardly slept for an hour. This was the time he got up every day.

He cleaned his teeth with salt, gargled and went down to offer namaz. He saw two plainclothesmen and an inspector searching for something in an open sewer. He was startled. It did not take him long to guess what they were looking for.

Iqbal's first reaction was to run back. But that would mean that the time of namaz would elapse, which he did not want. From Munda Galli, he came to Pala Galli and entered the mosque. He washed his hands, face and feet and sat with the other devotees to offer namaz. He returned after ten minutes.

By this time, Inspector Bharucha and the two cops had completed their inspection of the sewers and entered Abbasi Manzil. The third cop was standing guard outside the liquor den. Every room on the ground floor was being searched. A crowd had gathered at the entrance to the chawl.

Iqbal forced his way through the crowd and reached the first floor. One thing was certain: the sacks in his room had to be disposed of as soon as possible. But where could they be dumped? If the sacks were thrown from the window, down into the gutter, there would be a loud thump. There was no time to empty the bottles into the drain. Every sack had three dozen bottles. It would take at least a few hours to empty nearly 2000 bottles.

The policemen would climb up after finishing with the houses on the ground floor. If the smuggled liquor was found in Iqbal's room, not just him but Gul Banu too would be arrested. He wanted to protect his mother.

Finally, he said, 'Ma, you leave immediately. Leave this house.'

Unaware of the police raid, she asked, 'Why?'

Iqbal explained the situation in brief and said, 'Please hurry up! By now, the search of the ground floor houses must be done. The police will be coming upstairs soon.'

Gul Banu looked at him closely. The police were searching the last two rooms on the ground floor. They were getting closer. Rudely woken from their sleep, people were cursing the police.

'Ma! There is no time to think!'

Gul Banu sat unmoving by the dismantled wooden bed. She asked him, 'Can you see these black clothes?' Gul Banu had been wearing mourning clothes since her husband's death—a long black frock and a black dupatta.

'Tomorrow is the fortieth day of your father's death.' Sensing his confusion, she added, 'I can't step out of the house till then.'

'But, Ma . . .'

Before he could say anything, Gul Banu declared, 'I won't budge from here, even if that means being handcuffed.'

Inspector Bharucha and his men arrived on the first floor and started banging at the doors of the rooms near the staircase. As soon as the doors would open, they would shove their way inside.

The third room was Iqbal's. He had locked it from inside and was sitting with his younger brothers by his side. He was barely able to breathe. He was looking at his mother sitting beside the dismantled bed, praying fervently, rosary in hand and eyes on the door. This had never happened before. Iqbal had never encountered the police. Fear was tightening every nerve on his face.

After searching the two rooms near the staircase, the police proceeded further. One of the policemen was about to knock on Iqbal's door when Inspector Bharucha stopped him.

'Why, sir?'

'Can you see this black curtain?'

The policeman glanced at the curtain over the door and then looked back at Inspector Bharucha.

'Do you know what it means?' After a brief pause, Bharucha continued, 'Someone has died in this house. The family is in mourning for forty days. We should maintain the sanctity of the bereaved family.'

Behind the door, Iqbal wiped the sweat off his forehead. He had been saved. He looked at his mother. She was still praying feverishly.

*

Before leaving Abbasi Manzil, Inspector Bharucha took the boy working in the liquor den along with Chandu. Now, he started mounting pressure on both of them, especially on the boy.

'Understand one thing clearly, dikra,' Inspector Bharucha said playing with the paperweight on his table, 'At least ten people will come forward to get Chandu released on bail, but no one will come for you. If you tell me the truth, I'll release you right now.'

The boy stared sullenly at him.

'Tell me, a truck full of sacks comes after midnight. Where do those sacks go?'

The boy was still defiantly silent. Inspector Bharucha got up, stood before him, pulled his ear and repeated the question in a menacing tone. 'Open your mouth or I will open it for you.' He pinned him back and pulled the boy's hair from behind. As the boy's face lifted, he saw two ferocious eyeballs as his nose touched another nose. He was absolutely terrified. The next moment, Iqbal's name was on his lips.

*

Inspector Bharucha was baffled. He could not believe that a high school student would be immersed in the murky business of bootlegging. He called Chandu to his cabin and started questioning him. 'Who is Iqbal?' Chandu was taken aback. The secret for which he had silently braved a thrashing in the lock-up was out. Still, he wanted to size up how much Bharucha knew. 'Iqbal? Who, sir?'

Suddenly, Inspector Bharucha picked up the paperweight and threw it at him. Chandu ducked and the paperweight hit his left shoulder. He screamed in pain. The paperweight fell down. Chandu clasped his shoulder with his right hand.

For about an hour, Inspector Bharucha threatened him and thrashed him, but he did not open his mouth. Finally, only the boy was released and, through him, Inspector Bharucha sent a message to Aziz Dilip.

When Iqbal emerged from the school gate at 5 p.m. after his geography examination, he saw Aziz Dilip waiting for him with his hands on his hips.

'Yaar!' He looked cynical but spoke with childlike sincerity. 'You will have to meet Bharucha.'

Iqbal thought for a few seconds and then said, 'My examinations are on . . .'

'If you won't go, Chandu won't be released,' he said. 'Bharucha has sent a stern warning. I sent my man twice for bail. Twice, Bharucha showed him the door.'

'He . . . he won't do anything to me?'

'No way.'

*

Next day, Iqbal had an examination in the morning. There were no classes in the afternoon. After school, Iqbal walked to VT. His heart skipped a beat on seeing the compound of the crime branch headquarters.

Steadying himself, he asked for directions and finally made it to Inspector Bharucha's cabin. He saw the nameplate on the door. He pushed the door slowly and peeked into the tiger's den.

'Who's that?' Inspector Bharucha lifted his head.

'Sir . . . It's me, Iqbal.' He stepped inside the cabin and waited shyly by the door.

6

Inspector Bharucha stared at Iqbal. Normally, he was used to seeing hardened criminals, ruthless murderers and cold-blooded mercenaries before him. But today, an innocent-looking boy dressed in a white shirt and khaki school shorts was standing before him. There were textbooks in his hand, an ink pen in his shirt and a school badge on his chest.

'Sit,' Inspector Bharucha said, closing the file on his table and pointing to a chair. Iqbal quietly sat and placed his textbooks on the table.

'Dikra, what's your full name?'

'Iqbal Hussain Rupani.'

'What do you do?'

'I study, sir.'

'Do you know my name?'

'Yes, I read it on the nameplate.'

'Have you ever read it in the news?'

'Many times, sir.'

That was partly true. Those days, newspapers published Inspector Bharucha's exploits with bold headlines. He was a celebrity.

'I'm the same Bharucha,' he said with a tinge of pride in his voice. He picked up Iqbal's progress report that was kept on top of the textbooks—as Iqbal had anticipated. He flipped through some pages and studied the results for three examinations held that year. As if his eyes had deceived him, he looked up at Iqbal again and then turned back to the report card. Iqbal had stood first in the first examination. In the next two, he had stood third and second respectively. He had secured the highest marks in mathematics and science.

Closing the progress report and putting it back on the textbooks, he muttered, as if talking to himself, 'Hmm . . . he is excellent in studies but . . .'

'But what, sir?' Iqbal could not help but ask.

Suddenly, Inspector Bharucha raised his voice, 'Dikra, my hair hasn't greyed in the sun, understand? Your cunning won't work here. If you try to act innocent, I'll skin you alive.' With this, Inspector Bharucha thumped the table with his hand. The paperweight jumped and crashed down.

Iqbal was in tears. Sobbing, he indirectly admitted his crime. 'Sir, I've lost my father. The entire responsibility of looking after my home, my two younger brothers and the school fee rests on me.'

'Does that mean you stock truckloads of contraband?'

'What else could I do?'

'Hmm . . .' Inspector Bharucha thought for a while and then asked, 'Have you ever been to Yellow Gate?'

Several docks like Ghadiyal Godi and Bhaucha Dhakka fell under the jurisdiction of Yellow Gate police station. Iqbal had started smuggling with Ali from here. Haji Mastan and the don of Sion–Koliwada, Varadarajan Mudaliyar, had also risen from here.

In response to Bharucha's question, Iqbal lied, 'No, sir.'

'All the passenger boats from Goa dock there.'

'So I've heard.'

Iqbal also knew that the boats carried, besides passengers, contraband goods.

'Buy a couple of sacks from there to meet your family's needs.' Coming to the point, Inspector Bharucha said, 'You don't have to unload an entire truck, do you understand?'

'Yes, sir. But . . .'

'But what?'

'There is a police outpost there.'

Iqbal was referring to the Yellow Gate police station. Smuggling of goods from the dock was not without risk if one did not ensure the cooperation of the police.

'Refer my name to Khanvilkar,' Bharucha said. 'He is the sub-inspector there.'

'May I leave now, sir?'

Inspector Bharucha wrote down Iqbal's address and the phone number of his neighbour and bade him farewell with a smile.

Back home, the first thing Iqbal did was to deliver all the sacks kept in the room to Jasbir Singh's customers and refit the dismantled wooden bed. Now there was no need to take risks that involved the whole family. He would be able to earn enough to make both ends meet under the guidance of Inspector Bharucha.

*

I too was to get enough to meet my needs under the guidance of Dr Chinwala. In my spare time, I began to draw cartoons. I did not have anything to guide me, except for a torn Disney comic page. I used to go to Dr Chinwala's house once a week with my cartoons. He and painter Yusuf Dhala would keenly study my work, discuss my style and encourage me.

Observing my enthusiasm for art, Dhala gave me a heavy file of past issues of 'Kumar', a Gujarati art and literature magazine. In a month, I had made ten copies of every illustration in the file. I had now gone beyond copying and had started drawing original sketches and cartoons.

Dr Chinwala was quite impressed with my work.

'Aabid!' he exclaimed, pleased with my new cartoons. 'It's difficult to sell line drawings, but it is easy to sell cartoons.' Out of a dozen cartoons, he selected two.

I expressed my doubts. 'Who will buy them?'

'Any editor will accept them gladly.'

He gave me the addresses of two publishing houses: *The Times of India*, a national daily, and a Gujarati weekly called *Chitralekha*. I had neither the guts to enter a newspaper office nor the confidence to stand before an editor. Days turned to weeks and I forgot the discussion I had with Dr Chinwala.

I had joined the Boy Scouts that year. Every year, the Scouts in Bombay celebrated 'Khari Kamayi Day': the day of hard-earned money. On that day, we would put on our uniforms and go out into the city to earn money through manual labour. One schoolboy would take with him some boot polish and a brush, and sit by the roadside to polish shoes, while another would wash cars; another boy would sell sandwiches, while someone else would sell flowers made from paper.

I thought this opportunity was a godsend. I couldn't have asked for a better pretext to sell my cartoons. If I didn't muster enough courage today and present myself before an editor, I would never be able to get rid of my shyness and fear.

I picked up the two cartoons Dr Chinwala had selected, neatly pasted them on grey poster paper, put on my uniform and left home. I knew the shortest route from my home in Dongri to the office of *Chitralekha*, which was near Fort Market. I must have taken around twenty minutes to reach there. But when I stood before the entrance, my feet felt like dead wood. The enthusiasm, with which I had come so far, had evaporated. Instead, I was sweating profusely.

Before I could turn back, a peon emerged from the door. 'Whom do you want to see?'

'Me?' I stuttered. 'I've come to meet the editor. I know he hasn't come.'

'Of course he has.'

Pointing towards the staircase, he said, 'Go upstairs.'

I entered the office like a thief breaking into a house.

I quietly climbed the stairs and reached the mezzanine floor, when my eyes fell on a young man—Harkishan Mehta—sitting on a rickety wooden chair at a wooden table. His head bent, he was busy writing an article. I guessed he was the editor.

I stood quietly.

After a while, he turned the page and looked up at me. I tried extending towards him the file in which I had brought my cartoons when he pointed a finger towards a cabin nearby. Before I could process anything, his pen got busy again. There was no escape.

As I slowly pushed the door and entered the cabin, the celebrity author and the founder editor of *Chitralekha*, Vaju Kotak, looked up at me. His face betrayed surprise when he saw a student in a Scout's uniform before him.

He might have thought that I had come to collect donations. However, there was neither a box nor a receipt book in my hands. Instead, there was a file. After contemplating me for a few moments, he signalled me to sit. I could not.

I was afraid that I might stammer if I tried to speak. Without uttering a word, I simply took out a cartoon from the file and kept it on the table. He figured that I was an upcoming artist. He picked up the cartoon, leant back and looked at it intently. I stood quietly like a student waiting for his examination result. The cartoon that Mr Kotak was looking at was a strip comprising three frames. In the first frame was a policeman patrolling a street and the words 'Help! Help! Murder! Murder!' coming out of a building nearby.

The second frame showed the policeman hurriedly climbing up the stairs. In the last frame, he is shown staring in bewilderment at a woman listening to a radio play, which is where the words had come from.

It requires not more than five seconds to take in the content of a three-panel cartoon strip. But to me, those five seconds felt like centuries. My breathing stopped and I imagined the editor dismissing me saying that my work was kindergarten stuff and that raw amateurs like me should not waste the time of such accomplished legends.

Suddenly, he burst out laughing and my eyes grew saucer-like.

'Is that all? Have you brought just one cartoon?' he asked, keeping the cartoon strip with him. I nodded. Before he could say anything more, I had left the place.

* * *

I had hit a bullseye in my first attempt. My body trembled with excitement. My self-confidence got a tremendous boost. My chest swelled with pride. It did not take me long to reach the *Times of India* office.

I was carrying two cartoons and had decided to offer the other one to *Times of India*. This was a single-frame pocket cartoon without words. In it, a pickpocket at a bus stand diverts the attention of a passenger by pointing to a signboard that says 'Beware of Pickpockets' with one hand while he picks his pocket with the other.

Once published, this cartoon became so popular that several cartoonists reworked the idea in their own style.

On entering the *Times of India* office, I walked with the triumphant swagger of Napoleon Bonaparte after he had conquered several countries. I felt as if I had won over half the world with *Chitralekha* accepting my first cartoon, but when *Times of India* accepted the second one, I felt I had conquered the other half too.

That was a memorable day for me. My first step into journalism. In a few months, I was to race ahead. I had miles to go in the worlds of art and literature.

Intoxicated by my first taste of success, instead of going home, I climbed the stairs of Dr Chinwala's building. I proudly gave him the good news. His wife, Rehmat, offered me a bowl of fruit laced with sweet cream. Dr Chinwala affectionately teased, 'We knew that you would get some good news today.' I gratefully accepted it.

Before I could start eating the fruit, Yusuf Dhala made me get up and joyfully hugged me. Mushtaq Jalili too patted me on the back. My success and joy were not just mine.

That day, like former prime minister Jawaharlal Nehru, Dr Chinwala too announced his first five-year plan. According to it, Dhala was to hold two exhibitions of his paintings. Jalili was to sell at least one story to a filmmaker, and I was to get admission to Sir J.J. School of Arts for a Fine Arts diploma course.

*

Sometimes, a thought flashes through my mind. *What would have happened if Sufi had had such an environment, if such gracious luminaries had lit up his life? Would the brilliant class topper have followed in their footsteps? Would that have changed the course of his life?*

I recollect an article I had read in a magazine in which scientists proved that if a child was taken from a slum and transplanted to a cultured family, raised in a healthy, secure environment, then the child could grow up into an adult fit to compete in any field.

Sufi says it is a game of destiny. If his stars were brighter, his grandfather would not have been a gambler—his grandfather speculated in cotton—and his father would not have been a smuggler. And he would not have been born in Munda Galli.

*

Joy and sorrow do not ruffle Sufi's placid demeanour. When he is happy he does not seek the company of beautiful women, nor does he turn to liquor when he is depressed. When he rolls in millions, the expression on his face does not change. Nor does his face fall when he falls upon bad days. He is like Kipling's 'Man' who can 'meet with Triumph and Disaster and treat those two imposters just the same'. He knows how to live content with whatever he has.

Iqbal has learnt to live this way from hard experience. Experience which spans the extremes of life: from the pits to the peaks, the unimaginable highs and the unbelievable lows, the dark path of crime and a godly way of life.

*

Inspector Bharucha, instead of scaring him away from crime, had made the path easier for him. Now, Iqbal did not have any fear. Nobody could touch him. Inspector Bharucha had given instructions to Sub-inspector Khanvilkar of Yellow Gate police station on the phone to take good care of Iqbal.

'How did you know that?' I asked Sufi.

'I'd met Mr Khanvilkar before embarking upon the new venture. He not only surprised me by calling me by my name but also offered me a seat.'

'Still, I'm unable to understand one thing,' I questioned him. 'Why should Inspector Bharucha act like your shield? Why should he turn a little cub into a dangerous wolf?'

'So that he could use me to his advantage in the future.'

'How?'

He laughed, asking me a counter question, 'You want to know everything in one sitting?'

I kept quiet. He continued his narrative.

*

When Iqbal was in the eleventh standard, passenger boats used to ply between Bombay and Goa. These boats were quite useful for those who did not want to travel by train. Comparatively, the journey also cost much less. The *Konkan Sevak* was one such boat.

These boats used to come twice a week and anchor at Ghadiyal Godi. Besides passengers, these boats also carried liquor, especially feni. This had become a cottage industry. Besides feni, the brandy, whisky and rum made by the then-famous Kodak Distillery were also in demand in Bombay.

As advised by Inspector Bharucha, Iqbal used to buy just two or three sacks. Every sack contained two dozen bottles of cashew feni and three dozen bottles of liquor made by the Kodak Distillery.

Each bottle of feni cost Iqbal Rs 11. Its selling price was Rs 14. Thus, he made Rs 3 per bottle. On the liquor made by Kodak, he made Rs 5 per bottle. For three sacks—two of feni and one of Kodak liquor—he would earn Rs 300. Thus, he made a neat profit of around Rs 600 a week.

Though Iqbal was happy, there was a slight hitch. On the days when the boat anchored, he could not attend school. He had to wait at the dock from morning. He had to lift the stock, put it in a taxi and supply the bottles to different joints. Sometimes, he had to spend the entire day doing this. However, it did not worry him too much. He would borrow notes from one of his classmates the next day and copy the lessons that he had missed.

This routine continued for some months. Soon, his relatives came to know about his adventure. They were shocked. Could it be true? Hussain Ali's son, a bootlegger? A racketeer? At such a tender age?

The following day, Iqbal went for Friday prayers. The elders, who used to smile warmly at him, turned away as if he was a leper, while those who glanced at him had no affection on their faces. Was he being ostracized?

After the prayers were over, the elders surrounded him in the courtyard of the mosque. Some of the devotees, instead of going home, stayed back to watch the spectacle. One of the elders started reprimanding him. 'Aren't you ashamed? Your booze business is a blot on the name of our clan.'

Iqbal listened silently. It was a hot, humid day in May. He could feel droplets of sweat forming on his back and under his chin. 'We are humiliated . . .' another elder proclaimed. 'People are spitting on our faces,' he said.

A third one threatened, 'If you dare go to the docks tomorrow, I'll come to your house and thrash you in front of your mother.'

'I won't go,' Iqbal declared sincerely. 'But how do we survive?'

'Beg!' The first elder growled.

The second one took a wiser route, 'Is crime the only solution to poverty? There are hundreds of poor Khoja brethren in our community. Do all of them survive on bootlegging?'

This homily had the desired effect. Once again, Iqbal quit the path of the devil and started following the path that God had ordained. The struggle began afresh. It was his final year of high school. He wanted to secure a first class and join college. He had to fulfil his father's last wish.

*

I did not have to pass the matriculation examinations. For me, the certificate was not important. Neither was a certificate needed to join Sir J.J. School of Art. I discussed the matter with Dr Chinwala. He had taken my father's place. He was firm that it would not be proper to join art school after leaving my studies midway. 'How many months are left for the final examinations?' he reminded me, 'Only five.'

Iqbal was preparing for the final examinations in earnest. I was preparing for the finals with zero interest and under compulsion. I felt like a Sherpa who carries the load of the mountaineers and climbs towards the peak. Moreover, there was no facility at home to study, neither in the day nor at night. I started studying under the dim light of our chawl passage every night.

My family's financial condition had improved slightly. Because of his honesty, my uncle Mohammed Hussain had received a salary raise at the docks. However, in order to make both ends meet, my mother still washed dishes in other houses. To contribute, I used to meet my expenses by drawing cartoons. The same year, Sri Shani, the editor of Gujarati weekly *Chet Machandar*, started my cartoon strip titled 'Batukbhai'. Today, this strip is more popularly known as 'Dhabbuji'.

*

Iqbal's financial condition was deteriorating day by day. The funds collected through bootlegging were dwindling. By the time his matriculation examinations were to begin, the family was down to its last pennies. His class teacher issued a warning: 'Those who don't pay the examination fee by tomorrow won't be allowed to sit for the examinations.'

The examination fee was just Rs 16. The following day was the last to submit the form. Iqbal had Rs 12. What was he to do for the remaining amount? He thought fast. He was prepared to do anything to meet the shortfall except beg—it was not in his nature to spread his hands before anyone for alms.

He came to Pala Galli after school. There was a flower shop opposite Khoja Masjid. He saw a boy placing an order for a bouquet. The florist did some calculation, asked for some money as advance and returned a Rs 5 note to the boy.

The boy put the receipt and the note in his pocket and turned to leave. Iqbal accosted him, slapped him hard and pulled out the money from his pocket. The boy was stunned. Before he could realize what had happened, Iqbal had disappeared into Munda Galli.

7

The declaration of the matriculation examination results was more of a relief than anything else. I had managed to scrape through all subjects. However, I had topped the class in drawing. Iqbal, on the other hand, had scored well in practically every subject.

He got a first class. He had secured 91 per cent marks in mathematics and 75 per cent in science. In physics and chemistry, he scored 71 per cent. We know the circumstances under which he had given the examinations. His financial problems had not been solved yet. In fact, they were getting worse. He wanted to join college. *But how? Should he sell candy on the street? Or lift pots of water?* It would break his back and he would still barely be able to make ends meet, let alone go to college. This time, he thought of a new venture. He decided to start his own brewery.

*

Glancing at the notes I was taking, he interrupted, 'Aabid Bhai, this wasn't exactly a brewery. It was an industrial unit that manufactured alcohol from tincture iodine.'

'That amounts to manufacturing liquor.'

'Yes.'

'Where did you learn it?'

'Moghul used to do the same.'

Tincture iodine is nothing but ethyl alcohol mixed with iodine. Its original colour is brown. Iqbal used to store tincture iodine in a drum. A vessel was kept inside this drum, which floated four inches below the top with the help of a steel pipe that pierced through its sides. This pipe was three inches longer at one end and bore through the drum where a rubber tube was attached to it. Before covering the drum, one pound of hypo solution was added to fifty pounds of tincture iodine. Then the stove under the drum was lit.

'This hypo solution is the same which is used by photographers in the darkroom?'

'Yes,' he said. 'Adding hypo has two benefits: it converts the brown tincture iodine into a colourless liquid and it also helps speed up the distillation process.'

When the tincture iodine comes to a boil, the steam rises and touches the lid, dropping into the vessel in liquid form. The liquid comes out of the drum through the steel pipe and is collected in a container. This pure alcohol is then bottled and sold to liquor joints.

Iqbal used to make 100 bottles of liquor in a day on an average. The cost of producing one bottle came to Rs 4.5–5 and was sold for Rs 7. However, the sales were not very high. He earned around Rs 80 by selling thirty-five to forty bottles a day.

Iqbal's newfound prosperity bothered Moghul. Originally, this racket belonged to him. Now, Iqbal had started supplying liquor to his customers. It was natural for Moghul to be furious. He sent two warnings to Iqbal. Iqbal ignored the threats and continued expanding his business.

Moghul was to Iqbal what an elephant is to a mosquito. Moghul was strong enough to reduce Iqbal to pulp in a few seconds. However, a duel requires not just brute force but self-confidence too, which Iqbal had aplenty. Armed with courage and cleverness, a David can slay a Goliath.

*

Iqbal was returning alone late one evening after supplying liquor to Shankar Maratha's Mazgaon joint. He found himself out of breath by the time he reached Noor Baug marriage hall. He stopped for a while. Perhaps he was tired. However, words like tired, exhausted and drained had never been part of his vocabulary. He was accustomed to criss-crossing the city daily on foot. He had never felt this way.

Lost in thought, Iqbal rested against an electric pole. There was a wedding taking place in Noor Baug hall. He could hear the brass band playing and see a tree decked up with lights inside the gate. It was dark all around. In the midst of this darkness, the dazzling festivities were in full swing.

After he caught his breath, Iqbal started walking again. Just then, Moghul surfaced like a shadow from the corner of a shop and stood before him. Iqbal felt like a great wall had suddenly appeared in front of him. He stopped.

The two of them were a few steps apart now, facing each other. Words were unnecessary. It was a matter of survival for both.

Moghul had assumed that the mosquito would look for an escape route; perhaps he would try to dart into a nearby building. Instead, Iqbal stared unblinkingly at him, working out a strategy to attack the elephant.

Moghul took a step forward. Iqbal was ready. He had spotted a bamboo stick nearby. If only he could get his hands on it, he could easily teach Moghul a lesson. Moghul took two more steps forward. Now only three steps remained between the two. Moghul was ready to attack. And attack he did. He charged at Iqbal with lightning speed.

Instantly, Iqbal jumped aside, picked up the bamboo stick and hit Moghul on his back with all his strength. Moghul did not even flinch. Iqbal raised the stick again, but Moghul caught his hand and snatched it from him.

Now the stick was in Moghul's hand. He started thrashing Iqbal who had covered his face and head with both hands. At every opportunity that he got, Iqbal rained punches on Moghul's face. He was determined to fight till the end.

One of his punches hit the ogre square on the nose. But neither did his cartilage rupture nor did his nose bleed. On the other hand, Iqbal continued receiving a barrage of bone-crushing blows.

Inside the Noor Baug wedding banquet, the gay tune of the brass band was reaching a crescendo and outside its gate, the number of beggars was growing steadily. They had collected to watch the pomp and spectacle of the rich under dazzling lights. However, here on the dark pavement, there was just a dog, tail wagging, watching Iqbal from a distance.

Iqbal found that he was wheezing again. *Why? Why were his punches getting weaker?*

Abdul Rehman Kaafaria's punch could split open the head of his opponent like a coconut. Iqbal's punch could at least break a nose!

He had received several crackling blows from the bamboo stick. He did not have the strength to take it any more. Just when Iqbal was about to collapse, Moghul saw a jeep coming from the Dongri police station side. As if nothing had happened, Moghul threw the stick and walked away.

Iqbal entered a building nearby and hid in the passage. The police jeep, which was on routine patrol duty, went past. While leaving the building, Iqbal lurched forward and collapsed. It was only then that he realized how badly he had been beaten up. His back was swollen and he could feel an excruciating pain shooting though his head.

He leant against the wall, gathered whatever strength he had left and stood up. Dongri was just a few minutes' walk away but he took half an hour to reach there.

Instead of going home, he entered Palkhi Mohalla. Dr Khimani's clinic stood at the entrance of Palkhi Mohalla. Its closing time depended on the number of patients. Iqbal entered the clinic and sat down on a bench. He was drawing slow, ragged breaths. His entire body was afire with pain.

He realized that there was no other patient waiting in the clinic. He stood up again and entered the cabin.

The doctor took one look at him and knew that somebody had beaten him up. This was nothing new for him. He examined the nose, flashed a torch on his eyes and tongue, inspected the throat and placed the stethoscope to check if the vitals were intact.

'Aren't you Hussain Ali's son?' The doctor asked, administering a painkiller.

Iqbal nodded in the affirmative.

'What work do you do?'

Iqbal was forced to think as he swallowed the tablet.

'Look, beta,' the doctor said affectionately, 'you suffer more if you keep secrets from a doctor. It's obvious that you have been badly beaten up. But I can't figure out how you contracted asthma.'

Iqbal now understood why he was having difficulty breathing, why his punches carried no strength. He could guess the cause, but he did not consider it appropriate to reveal it to the doctor. The polite doctor too did not press him further.

That night, once the painkiller took effect he fell asleep. But it was a fitful sleep. His subconscious mind kept admonishing him that God had sent asthma as a warning because He did not want him to distil liquor. God wanted him to follow the path of righteousness. *Was it necessary to earn money through crime?* Moreover, his chest had become hollow with asthma and it would be impossible to survive in the underworld with this condition. It was necessary to find some honest way of making a living.

When Iqbal got admission to Bhavan's College, the condition of his family was like that of a race car that had gone into a tailspin. Iqbal was to play this game of snakes and ladders, as far as finances were concerned, throughout his career. One moment, he would be on the pinnacle of success, and the next moment he would fall into a deep, dark chasm.

*

My joy knew no bounds when I got admission into Sir J.J. School of Art. However, my mother was downhearted. She wanted me to be a doctor or a lawyer. At least, I would be getting a job with a minimum salary of Rs 1000.

'What work will you get after spending five years in J.J.?' She asked me with a tinge of hope in her voice. I did not have an answer to her question. I had only enthusiasm, euphoria and dreams that meant nothing to my mother.

To console her, I said that I would become an art director with an advertising agency and earn more than she could imagine. However, I don't know why she did not believe it. In my heart there was no conviction—perhaps my face betrayed that. She simply gazed at me. I would not be surprised if she was seeing in my face the ominous future that awaited me after college. My life's real struggle was to begin after I completed five years in college. I too was to get lost somewhere in destiny's game of snakes and ladders.

When my uncle, Mohammed Hussain, came to know that I had got into Sir J.J. School of Art, his warm brown eyes sparkled. He surveyed me from top to bottom, pulled out three Rs 100 notes and offered them to me.

I was surprised because I had never seen so much money at once. By this time, Iqbal was playing in thousands. I, however, did not know what to do with the Rs 300 I had got.

'Will you go to college in tattered clothes?' my uncle asked. 'Go get yourself a decent set of clothes for college. And yes, monsoon has set in, so don't forget to buy a raincoat and gumboots.'

Thinking that I might run short of cash, he gave me one more Rs 100 note. 'For the first time, a boy from the Surti family will go to college. It's not a joke—you must look your best.'

Do not for a second entertain the notion that my uncle had hit a jackpot. His monthly salary was Rs 1200. Nevertheless, he lived like the large-hearted Hatim Tai, the legendary Prince of Arabia. This was why many a time his salary would shrink to half by the time he reached home from his workplace in Ghadiyal Godi. Yet, we were happy.

Now, there was no need for my mother to work. Our family was back on track. Whatever the shortcomings might have been, we could at least eat two meals a day. Iqbal was not that fortunate.

*

In the game of snakes and ladders, you roll the dice and climb up if you come across a ladder. The last time Iqbal had thrown the dice, he had climbed a small ladder. He had enjoyed the bliss for a few days. But then he was trapped by a snake waiting with its jaws wide open. He had fallen back to where he had started from.

Of course, he was no more a child. He had left his school uniform of khaki half-pants and white shirt behind. Now, he was a young man who dressed in sparkling white attire that made other boys pale in comparison. His favourite outfit was an immaculate, white, long-sleeved shirt and a pair of white trousers.

Though he was not muscular, he had the guts to challenge a giant. His body was slim but fit and hot blood flowed through his veins.

His asthma was history by now. Had he not given up distilling liquor, the disease would have stayed with him forever. The days of selling candy and berries were in the past too. The only thing that remained by his side was hunger.

His college, Bhavan's College of Arts and Science, was near Chowpatty beach. In the first month of college, he did not even have the bus fare to go to Chowpatty from Dongri, a distance of three kilometres. He walked to college and back home every day.

*

'One day, I returned home hungry and thirsty,' Sufi said. 'I realized that the kitchen stove had not been lit. Both my younger brothers, who were still in school, had gone off to sleep without food. Mother was up and staring at me blankly.'

Iqbal was not shocked. He knew that the home front would collapse, but he did not imagine that it would happen so soon.

Putting his books down, he filled his belly with water from the earthen pot. Then he went to the mosque to offer prayers. He preferred to offer namaz at Khoja Masjid because it was close to his house. Besides, there was serenity in the sacred atmosphere of the mosque. Incidentally, whenever Hussain

Ali felt confused, he too used to go there for peace of mind. In this regard, Iqbal was following his father's footsteps.

After offering namaz, he sat in the mosque's courtyard for a long time. His stomach growling with hunger, he kept on thinking about the future. It was 10 p.m. He had spent almost two hours there. God had not offered as much as a hint as yet. He glanced at the inky sky as if he hoped to read God's word there. But there was nothing. Finally, he got up and came out. To discover that God had heard his prayer after all. Rashid Parkar, who was standing at the florist, approached him.

'*Kya, saale*! Planning to be a mullah?' he joked looking at Iqbal. 'I went to your house and your mother told me that you would be in the mosque. When I looked inside, you were praying. Since then, I've been waiting here for you.'

(In similar circumstances, Hussain Ali had met an acquaintance who had informed him about a vacancy in Link Bazaar and he got the job the next day.)

Iqbal knew Rashid Parkar. He was the eldest of five brothers. All of them stayed in Ranmal Building in Pala Galli and were much ahead of Iqbal when it came to illicit activities.

Iqbal asked Rashid, 'What's the work?'

'Fetching water.'

In underworld parlance, liquor bottles were called 'water'. Rashid needed an additional reliable man to smuggle in a large quantity of liquor bottles. The work was that of a helper (in other words, that of a coolie). There was little need for intelligence. Iqbal had a long reputation in Dongri as an honest and daring boy, that's why Rashid had come to him personally.

'How much will I get?'

'Rs 200 per trip.'

Iqbal thought of his family. He thought of his mother sitting hungry and his two brothers sleeping without food. He said, 'I'll take half the money as advance.'

If you hire a coolie who demands an advance, you will be surprised or perhaps take it as a joke and burst out laughing. Rashid burst out laughing.

'Good joke, *saala*!' he thumped Iqbal on the back. 'Listen, come in the night tomorrow.'

'If you don't give me an advance I won't come.'

'Yaar, you know how it works in our business. No one gives . . .'

'Okay. If not hundred, give me seventy-five.'

Finally, it was settled at Rs 50. Rashid gave him five notes of Rs 10 each and went his way. Iqbal went to a restaurant nearby, got four plates of biryani packed and came home. He saw that his mother also had gone to sleep without eating.

He emptied the four packets into a large vessel, woke everyone up and sat down with them to eat. The rice and mutton dish he had bought was like a banquet for them. They ate ravenously. In no time, the vessel had been licked clean.

He washed his hands, wiped them clean and stuffed the remaining Rs 30 into his mother's purse. 'This is for tomorrow,' he said.

His mother wanted to ask: *Where did you get it from?* But by now, she had accepted the reality. Families living in the filth of Munda Galli had no right to complain about the foul smell. Instead she said, 'I have never tasted such delicious biryani in my life.'

*

The following day, Iqbal left his house late in the evening and went to the corner of Pala Galli. There, two Ambassador cars stood waiting. In the first car, there were six people, including the driver. In the second, there were five. Rashid was sitting next to the driver. He opened the door and Iqbal sat beside him on the front seat.

Both the cars headed towards Ghadiyal Godi. Since traffic was thin at that hour, it took them just seven minutes to reach the dock. Except for the drivers, all the other men—ten in all—got out. Both the empty cars were to return later.

This was a new experience for Iqbal. He was to learn how an organized network functioned. He was to take one more step into the world of smuggling. He was already knee-deep into it. Now he was to sink up to his waist in its murky waters.

At the dock, fishing boats and steam launches were anchored at the jetty. The sea was calm. The reflections of the lanterns on the boats were dancing upon the water. The sky was dark. It was the beginning of the monsoon. Dark clouds, sleepily turning and twisting in the sky, were floating overhead.

Rashid walked ahead and the gang, which included his four brothers, followed. After a few steps, they reached the pier. Below them was the sea, the boats and the mild ripples caused by the waves.

From one of the steam launches extended a wooden plank. Rashid stood on one side. One after the other, every member of the gang stepped on to the plank and boarded the boat. The last one to come was Rashid, after which the plank was removed. The launch started with a whirring sound and headed out into the sea.

The moon made a brief appearance from behind a dark cluster of clouds and disappeared again. A mild breeze was gathering momentum. The launch was heading forward, cutting through the water.

The lighthouse came closer. The silhouette of a ship started taking shape. Iqbal was looking at it wide-eyed.

He had comprehended a little so far: they were heading towards the *barpani* (a place off the coast where ships that are unable to dock at the pier anchor) to take the delivery of 'water'.

After an hour's journey, the steam launch came close to the ship, which was from Hong Kong. Its Chinese captain was waiting on the deck. The time for the meeting had been fixed.

Who had fixed it? Where had it been fixed? Iqbal's questions remained unanswered. He still had a lot to learn. He was to graduate with flying colours, not from college, but from the underworld.

A rope ladder was thrown down from the ship. Rashid gave one half of a Rs 10 note to Iqbal and said, 'Give this to the captain and tell him to keep the stock ready. We will return at 1 a.m. to take delivery.'

Iqbal put the note in his pocket and held the rope ladder tightly. Carefully, he climbed up nearly thirty-five feet. The captain extended his hand. Taking it, Iqbal placed his foot on the railing of the ship and jumped on board.

It was huge even for a cargo ship. He could see three ghost-like sailors standing at a distance on the deck. All of them looked Chinese, like the captain.

Iqbal pulled out the bank note. The captain opened his wallet, extracted the other half carefully and compared the two pieces until he was convinced that both fragments were of the same note.

He smiled. Iqbal delivered Rashid's message, 'We will be back by 1 a.m. Okay by you?'

He nodded in agreement.

Iqbal again steadied his foot on the railing of the ship. Several questions flashed through his mind as he climbed down the rope ladder. *Who had torn the Indian currency note in two and given one piece to the captain? Where and when was it passed on to him? From where did Rashid get the second piece?*

On reaching the last rung of the ladder, he stepped on to the roof of the steam launch. From there, he jumped down to the deck.

'Everything went off well?' Rashid asked.

'Yes.'

The launch sputtered to life again. They were to return after idling for three hours in the dark. The launch, instead of heading towards the shore, was going in a different direction. Iqbal observed quietly. Piercing through the water as well as the darkness, the launch powered ahead with an audible whir of the engine. When the eerie roar of the ocean merged with it, the atmosphere reverberated into a nightmarish dimension.

Now the water was not as calm as before. Waves were slapping the launch on either side. The sky had grown darker. There were signs of an approaching storm.

8

The lantern, which cast a faint light inside the launch, started rocking. There were eight men apart from Iqbal and Rashid Parkar. Along with the light from the lantern, their shadows were also dancing. From the lights twinkling in the distance, Iqbal could tell that they had travelled from Bhaucha Dhakka (Ghadiyal Godi) to the barpani and were now heading towards Uran island. They had spent another hour at sea.

Soon, the coastline of Uran became visible. There were six to seven steam launches anchored at the pier. Finding a vacant place, Rashid anchored for an hour. The lantern had died a while ago. A shroud of darkness engulfed the ten men.

After some time, the light from the distant lamp posts started percolating through the boat. The ten passengers emerged like shadows.

Rashid owned the launch. The boatmen were his employees. They were used to the darkness. As soon as the launch stopped, they all got busy. They were responsible not just for the upkeep of the boat but for cooking and serving meals too.

Within half an hour, a piping hot meal of fish and rice was ready. Because of the chilly sea breeze, everyone was famished. They wolfed down the food silently and were ready to move again. Another hour had elapsed.

In the third hour, the launch returned and steadied itself by the ship's side. Compared to this giant vessel, the launch looked like a minnow swimming by the side of a whale.

Iqbal raised his wrist and glanced at the tiny watch. Suddenly, there was a flash of lightning. The ship and the launch were lit up for a moment and then plunged into darkness again. It was exactly 1 a.m.

The captain was ready on the deck. In three hours, he had taken out 175 crates of liquor from the storeroom and stacked them up on the deck. Each crate contained twelve bottles of foreign liquor of a common brand.

*

Today, instead of the terrace, we were sitting in his bedroom. He was relaxing on the double bed. A pillow supported his back. I had pulled a chair from the dining room.

'Let me get some points clarified before we proceed,' I interrupted.

He nodded.

'I want to know whether the ship from Hong Kong was really a cargo ship.'

'Absolutely. These ships leave Hong Kong with legal cargo. But they also carry contraband goods.'

'If it was a cargo ship, why did it not anchor at the dock?'

'Because it didn't have cargo bound for Bombay.'

'So if it had cargo for Bombay, it would have come ashore.'

'Certainly.'

'Then what about the captain's manifest?'

The manifest is a list that the captain has to present to the customs official upon entering a port. This list contains details of all the goods on the ship. Naturally, the list does not include contraband items. I guessed that the customs officials

were bound to confiscate illicit items if they cross-checked the
goods on the ship with the list.

Sufi proved my guess wrong. 'The Chinese captain of
the Hong Kong ship had cleverly noted in the list even the
prohibited goods, including the 175 crates of liquor. He had
listed these crates in the column meant for the consumption of
the seamen. No customs official can object to that.'

'You mean no one will suspect anything even after seeing
heaps of crates?'

'There is no scope for doubt because the ship, after
stopping at different ports, returned to its country of origin
after four to six months. The crates of liquor were sufficient
to meet the needs of these seamen during such a long voyage.'

Convinced with Sufi's explanation, I asked him to clarify
another point. 'The seamen were not ignorant of the fact
that their captain was involved in trafficking. If one of them
informed the police, would the captain not lose his job?'

Denying such a possibility, Sufi revealed a shocking truth.
'Just as Rashid Parkar and his gang were part of this smuggling
business on land, the captain and his gang were doing the same
at sea. They were part of a racket. After keeping 50 per cent
of the profits, he would distribute the rest among the crew
members. Moreover, the business did not require investment
of capital.'

Whenever a trustworthy captain was about to leave
Hong Kong on a voyage, the local wholesale traders would
happily offer him liquor on credit. Even today, the business
of smuggling runs on verbal commitment. There is neither
a written agreement nor any guarantee. If someone becomes
greedy and betrays trust, he won't find a place to hide. He will
be hounded and killed.

The Chinese captain of the Hong Kong ship too had
carried 175 crates of liquor to Bombay with only a verbal

assurance to the suppliers. Here, he would trade the liquor bottles for silver bricks. He would then sell these at a hefty profit in Dubai and from there buy Japanese fabrics.

The ship would then proceed to either Mombasa or Dar es Salaam. There, he would sell the fabrics and pick up clove. His profit would multiply again. On his return, he would make another stop at Bombay to unload the clove and take opium in return.

Opium is in great demand in Hong Kong. One gets an idea of how profitable this zero-investment business is from the fact that during a two-month trip, the captain could earn as much as he would have in two years. On an average, a captain's monthly salary in those days was about Rs 25,000. This single stint helped him earn around Rs 6,00,000 in one voyage.

'One last question,' I asked. 'You had mentioned that the foreign liquor on the Hong Kong ship was of a common brand. What did you mean by that?'

'A consignment that comprises liquor of the same grade and same price,' explained Sufi. 'In the case of this particular transaction, there were bottles of Red Label, Johnny Walker, White Horse, Black & White and Vat 69.'

After satisfying all my queries, Sufi continued with his story. Under the supervision of the captain, the crew members started lowering a dozen crates held together in a net.

Iqbal was standing on the roof of the launch along with Rashid. The rest of the men were positioned on the deck below. Everything had to be done swiftly and efficiently.

As soon as the net would come close, Iqbal and Rashid would pull it towards the roof and begin handing one crate after the other to the men standing below them. They, in turn, handed over the crate to two others. The crates passed through different hands before reaching the last two men standing near the cellar who stacked them neatly on the floor.

After the first lot was emptied, Rashid placed in the net a different crate. This contained silver bricks. Iqbal tugged the rope to signal. Soon, it was pulled up. Before the next lot could come down, there was another crack of lightning and it started raining.

There is a vast difference between rain in a city and rain in the open sea. In the city, because of tall buildings and other structures that act as buffers, the force of the rain is halved. Here, in mid-sea, there is nothing to block the whip of the wind and the stinging rain. Though the ship shielded them on one side, the wind was ferocious on the other side.

The launch started to sway. The boatmen tried their best to keep the launch steady. Standing on the roof of the cabin, Iqbal and Rashid were dripping and trying hard to keep their balance when the second lot came swinging down. Again, the routine of pulling the crates and passing them along began. However, this time the task was not that easy.

At great risk of being swept away like upturned umbrellas into the sea by the stormy gale that accompanied the rain, both men were forced to proceed with caution.

By the time the fifth lot came in, Rashid was sneezing. He went down on his knees and opened a crate. He pulled out the first bottle he could lay his hand on and opened it. After he gulped down a quarter, his body was instantly invigorated.

'You . . .' he said offering the bottle to Iqbal, 'take a shot.'

Iqbal did not take it. The wild rain was streaming down his hair and face.

Rashid growled, 'Saala! I'm telling you. You must drink. Drink or you will die here.'

Iqbal swept aside the wet hair from his face. 'Liquor is forbidden by Islam.'

'Then take it as medicine, yaar!'

Iqbal did not budge. For him, even the finest liquor in the world was repulsive. Rashid did not insist. He took two more swigs and presented the open crate to his mates below. They were overjoyed.

In order to withstand the rain and the storm, one bottle each was enough for the men. They had to last another two to three hours. The work that had begun at 1 a.m. was to continue until dawn. It was just 2 a.m.

Iqbal and Rashid were busy on the roof despite the wind slapping them and the sea pounding their boat. Rashid was now working less and guzzling more. His sneezing had stopped a while ago. Iqbal, meanwhile, had started shivering.

He had been getting drenched for over an hour now, but he was diligently carrying out the work assigned to him.

Seeing the net empty, he placed another crate of silver bricks and shook the rope. The net was pulled up. He lifted his head to look up when a drunk Rashid lost his balance and toppled on him. Iqbal fell flat on the roof of the cabin. Rashid lay over him, still clutching the bottle in one hand.

He tilted the bottle into Iqbal's mouth. 'When I say you drink, you have to drink.' He had become delirious in his inebriated state.

Iqbal pushed away the bottle with his right hand. For a moment, Rashid was surprised. 'What the fuck . . .' The next moment he felt embarrassed. Slowly, both of them stood up.

It was no longer possible for Rashid to stand on the rocking boat. His words slurring, he admitted, 'Yaar, I'm totally high.'

The net came down with a new lot. Iqbal caught it quickly and pulled at it. His earnestness left the others touched. In the meantime, Rashid had climbed down.

For the next two hours, Iqbal battled the storm alone, shivering in the rain, water dripping from his clothes. The consignment continued to be loaded. When he received the last lot, it was 4 a.m. The work done, he slithered down from the roof and collapsed.

By this time, Rashid had had a glass of lime juice and had come back to his senses. Thereafter, he had slept for two hours. Now, he was looking down at the unconscious Iqbal. The other men were standing in a semicircle. The steam launch was racing towards Bombay.

Rashid felt a twinge of concern. *Is he dead?* He held his fingers below Iqbal's nostrils. He could feel Iqbal's warm breath, but he still had some doubt. He held Iqbal's wrist and was shocked. 'He is running a high fever!' Before the launch could reach the Ghadiyal Godi jetty, both of Rashid's Ambassador cars were waiting on the dock with a truck. Soon, all the men got working again.

The boatmen lifted the crates from the steam launch and handed them over to men who passed them on to others standing in a row. The crates were loaded on to the truck. Lastly, an unconscious Iqbal was also hauled out in the same way as the crates.

There was no space in the car for him to lie down. So, Rashid placed him on top of the crates in the truck. As a precaution, two men sat beside him.

By the time the caravan of the three vehicles left the dock and headed towards Dongri, it was dawn. The rain had stopped but the sun was still not visible. Fat raindrops were still dripping from the buildings and trees and flowing as rivulets into the sewers.

As the vehicles turned towards Dongri from Wadi Bunder, Iqbal's eyelids fluttered. He could see an overcast sky above and a speeding truck below him. His body seemed to be on fire, shivering and shuddering. Rashid's men, who were accompanying him, covered his body with a tarpaulin sheet.

That did not seem to make any difference. Along with Iqbal's body, the tarpaulin too started shaking.

After reaching Dongri Char Nal, the cavalcade took another turn. The truck was leading, followed by the two cars. On entering Pala Galli, the vehicles stopped. They were at Rashid's house, which doubled up as a godown.

Stepping out of the car, Rashid rushed to the truck and asked, 'Has Iqbal regained consciousness?'

One of the men nodded, adding, 'But his condition is serious.'

Instructing his men to unload the goods, he ran in search of a doctor. After about half an hour, he succeeded in waking one up. By this time, the truck had been emptied. The 175 crates of foreign liquor had reached the godown. Iqbal had been carried by the men and made to lie down in Rashid's house.

After inspecting Iqbal, the doctor declared, 'He has pneumonia.'

*

Interestingly, I was to develop typhoid at the same time.

It is a pleasure to leave the claustrophobic confines of school and step into the carefree college campus, but not every student has this privilege. While there are several reasons for that, the main one in places like Dongri is poverty.

In those days, most students of Habib High School belonged to the lower middle class and below. Our headmaster, Sheikh Hasan, had devoted his life to motivating such students. Within the Muslim community he had fought for education and against hunger, but he could not combat poverty.

A look at the alumni of Habib High School will reveal top engineers, doctors, lawyers and artists, as well as successful gangsters, smugglers and criminals. One cannot come across such a stark contrast among students of any other school.

Stepping into college is like taking a leap into adulthood. On joining Sir J.J. School of Art, I felt as if my childhood had been left far behind. What lay before me was the golden freeway of teenage life, bedecked with flowers. A new world, new friends and new experiences awaited me.

As far as looks go, I didn't look like a Bollywood chocolate hero, nor was I a strapping Mr Universe. Like Iqbal, I was an ordinary student. Short crew cut hair, pointed nose, thick-framed glasses in front of my eyes, high cheekbones, long neck and a skinny body. Yet, I was popular. More than boys, girls were attracted to me. *Why was it? Was this also karma?*

In my very first year at J.J., I performed well both academically and in sports. I won the table tennis championship every year. I was awarded a scholarship for securing a first division every year. In fact, I received scholarships all five years at college. Moreover, I also won the best actor award in the inter-college Hindi drama competition.

The same year, an Iranian girl decided to organize a three-day excursion to a *chikoo* orchard and farmhouse owned by her family in Dahanu. She asked me if I thought it was a good idea. Who could say no to a weekend in nature?

We sat together and prepared a list of students: six boys and six girls. We decided to leave Bombay on Thursday. We were to spend Friday and Saturday in Dahanu and return on Sunday evening.

The day before we were to leave, a shooting pain pierced my forehead. I could not imagine the reason. I swallowed two pills. The ache stopped.

I was packing when my head started pounding again. For some time, I was confused. *Should I go for the trip or not?* It was my first year at J.J. and my first trip. In my excitement, I did not bother about the headache, took two more painkillers and left.

My friends were waiting for me at Dadar station. One friend had put on a straw hat. The girls were in jumpsuits, jeans, skirts and tees. I was dressed in a pink handloom shirt and dark pants. Everyone was cheerful; my headache too was gone thanks to the pills.

We dashed into the compartment as soon as the train arrived at the platform. The hitherto sedate train compartment turned into a boisterous party. We reached Dahanu in two hours, singing and dancing throughout the journey.

The orchard was not very far from the station. The weather was perfect. The sky was cloudy. The road was wet in patches. Perhaps it had rained the previous night. When we reached the farmhouse, it was 10 a.m. The sea was roaring in the distance.

We opened the windows and a soft fragrance wafted into our rooms. Outside, there were century-old mango trees. I couldn't help but think that the rustle of the leaves we were enjoying was the same sound the former British owners of this estate must have enjoyed on lazy weekends.

But I had not come here just for escape. I had brought my sketchbook and paints along. I had planned to spend half the time sketching diligently and the rest with my friends.

But I could neither enjoy time with my friends nor sketch. No sooner had we settled down than the headache started again. This time, it was accompanied by a fever. Outside, my friends were preparing for a game of musical chairs, chattering loudly. And here I was all alone, sitting beside a window, watching them silently.

Suddenly, the Iranian girl asked, 'Where is Aabid?'

I moved away from the window. I did not want to be a spoilsport by telling them about my sickness. She came to my room looking for me. I was running a high temperature. It was no ordinary fever: it was typhoid.

I spent the rest of our days in Dahanu taking pills and shots from a local doctor. In Bombay, I consulted our family doctor, Dr Dastoor, who asked me to get admitted to a hospital.

I spent a month and ten days in Habib Hospital. I had become so weak that I did not even have the strength to swipe at the flies squatting on my face.

*

Iqbal suffered from pneumonia for about ten days and recovered dramatically. Nevertheless, his lungs were not as strong as before. His eyes, too, had sunk into their sockets. A day's work as a helper had proved to be expensive for him.

The only consolation was that Rashid Parkar was so impressed by his dedication and honesty that he gave him Rs 300 as bonus over and above the Rs 200 he had promised. All that money was drained in meeting the household expenditure and medical bills.

After recovering, Iqbal went to meet Rashid. He spotted him near the Dongri taxi stand.

'Can I get some work?'

'Didn't I tell you?' he shot back, still remembering the harrowing experience of that night. 'If you had taken a peg or two, you wouldn't have been in such a sorry state.'

'But . . .'

'Then you started preaching: liquor is taboo in Islam. Now, just tell me if liquor is fucking taboo, why did God make it?'

Iqbal was not interested in any philosophical debate. 'Rashid, I've come for work.'

'Listen, buddy. You won't be able to work for a few more days. The fact is that you still need some rest. Secondly, the tapori in whose place I had taken you for a day has come back.'

Iqbal was disheartened. He went to Haji Ali and sat on the parapet by the seaside, his back to the dargah. The sun was about to set. He cast a long shadow across the road. The vehicles, which were leaving the city after work and heading home towards the suburbs, were trying to crush his shadow. Even then, after every vehicle passed, his shadow emerged on top. Whenever a car would cross him, the shadow would jump over it and then spread across the road in its wake again. He seemed to be playing yet another game of snakes and ladders when he saw Inspector Bharucha's jeep speeding in the opposite direction, towards the city.

His eyes sparkled. He stood up and tried to run on the pavement, parallel to the jeep that was on the other side of the road. Traffic sped dangerously between them.

9

Iqbal ran till he reached a petrol pump and stopped abruptly. He laughed at his foolishness. It was not possible to outrace a jeep. Besides, what was the use of overtaking it? What did he expect from Inspector Bharucha?

When he pondered over it, he realized that the sight of the jeep had given him hope. Perhaps, Inspector Bharucha would have shown him some way out of his misery.

He watched the jeep speed away when suddenly, to his surprise, it stopped near Cadbury House and made a U-turn. It came towards him. He felt hopeful again. His eyes gleamed. The jeep stopped where he was standing, at the petrol pump. Inspector Bharucha got down and headed straight for the manager's glass-paned cabin.

Why didn't Inspector Bharucha notice him? He should have smiled at him at least. He had simply turned his face away as if Iqbal did not exist. From the pavement, Iqbal could see two other men inside the cabin. The young man sitting in the owner's chair was probably the manager. The other was a Sikh. He was sitting on the opposite chair. He looked sly, like a guy with ulterior motives, someone who would act for self-gain at the expense of others. Iqbal could not guess who he was.

Hesitantly, he approached the cabin and stood there with a blank face. Inspector Bharucha was talking to the Sikh. Iqbal assumed the Sikh was Inspector Bharucha's friend. The two of them were discussing something animatedly. Iqbal could see everything but hear nothing.

After some time, Inspector Bharucha spotted Iqbal from the corner of his eye. For a moment, he was unsure, but then his face softened. He came out.

'Dikra!' He inspected Iqbal from top to bottom and added, 'The last time I saw you, you were like a pony, and today? You look like a horse—but not a racing stallion, a buggy horse. You look as deadbeat as those horses that pull the Victoria carriages. Are you all right?'

Iqbal nodded.

'Then straighten your back,' Inspector Bharucha said firmly, slapping Iqbal's back. 'Lift your head high. Now tell me, how is work going?'

'Bad.'

'Why? Did all the boats sink?'

Inspector Bharucha was still under the impression that he smuggled liquor from Ghadiyal Godi.

'No, sir.'

'Then?'

'I need to earn some more, sir.'

'Has the greed bug bitten you too?' Inspector Bharucha joked. 'Do you know that old saying: greed destroys goodness first?'

'True, sir.'

'Then?'

'I'm able to manage the household expenses, but not my college fee.'

Inspector Bharucha stared at him for a few moments. He was pleasantly surprised to know that Iqbal had finished school and joined college.

'What percentage did you get in the matriculation examinations?'

'I got a first class, sir.'

'Well done.'

Inspector Bharucha thought for a while before asking him, 'Which college do you go to?'

'Bhavans.'

'What are your plans for the future?'

'I'll try to get into a medical college and become a doctor.'

'That'll be quite expensive.'

'That's why I've come to you.'

'Hmm . . .' Inspector Bharucha was silent for a while. Then he abruptly asked Iqbal if he knew how to drive.

'Yes.'

'I don't mean the Victoria.'

'Yes, sir.'

'I'm talking about car, a motor car.' He repeated the question with some emphasis, 'Do you know how to drive a car?'

'Of course, I know how to drive a car . . . and also how to drive over someone with a car.'

Inspector Bharucha got the message and smiled. 'Stay at home tomorrow. I'll contact you.'

Iqbal was about to say something when he remembered that the first time he had gone to see Inspector Bharucha at the crime branch headquarters, he had noted Iqbal's address and the phone number of his neighbour as well.

*

I stopped Sufi here. 'When did you learn how to drive?'

'We had to take out the smuggled goods from Ghadiyal Godi in a taxi. One cannot do that unless the taxi driver is your man. Whenever we took the contraband goods out of the dock, I used to sit beside him and watch him closely. Gradually, I started driving the taxi under his guidance. Of course, I drove as a hobby then.'

*

The next day, Iqbal stayed at home all day, waiting for the call. It was a holiday. There was no work and he was getting bored. He glanced at his watch again. Of course, he had checked a hundred times since morning.

It was 5 p.m. He could not resist the temptation of going out for a stroll. He got up and was about to step out when he saw his neighbour approaching. Stopping midway in the passage, he informed Iqbal, 'There is a phone call for you.'

He went to his neighbour's house.

'What are you doing, dikra?' Inspector Bharucha's voice was loud and clear.

'Nothing.'

'An idle mind is a devil's workshop. You should be studying.'

'College just opened, sir. Lectures haven't started yet.'

'You must top the class in college too.'

'Yes, sir.'

'Be at the petrol pump at 6 p.m.'

Instead of going out for a walk, Iqbal changed two buses— there was no direct bus from Dongri to Haji Ali—to get to the petrol pump. Inspector Bharucha was already in the cabin. He got up when he saw Iqbal coming close.

'Sit here, dikra,' he said, pointing to the chair he was sitting on. He himself moved towards the entrance of the cabin. Before leaving, he added, 'I'll phone you again.'

Iqbal saw his jeep speeding away into the distance before turning around. The manager sitting opposite him was engrossed in the ledger, perhaps adjusting some invoices.

Iqbal turned his head again. He saw the Sikh guy on his left. It was the same man he had seen the previous day. *Perhaps he was Inspector Bharucha's man. But he did not look like a cop.* Since he had not been introduced, Iqbal turned his eyes away. The burly Sikh unconsciously slid his hands into his pant pockets and jingled some keys and coins.

Outside the cabin, it was work as usual at the petrol pump. Cars and taxis were arriving, stopping there for some minutes and leaving after getting their petrol tanks filled. Iqbal watched all this through the transparent glass panes. There was nothing else to do.

Around 9 p.m., the Sikh brought two large club sandwiches. He gave one to Iqbal and ate the other one himself.

'Can I get some water?' Iqbal asked after finishing his sandwich.

The Sikh got up, went up to the water filter outside and brought him a glass.

Iqbal drank the water and got up with the empty glass. The Sikh, too, got up and took the glass from Iqbal. He wasn't letting Iqbal move out of sight. *Had Inspector Bharucha instructed him not to let Iqbal leave?* He did not even know why he was being made to wait.

He ran out of patience by 10 p.m. 'How much more time will it take?' he asked the man, looking at him. He simply shrugged.

At 11 p.m., Iqbal got up. 'I must go now. I think Inspector Bharucha might have got busy somewhere.'

The Sikh told him to sit down. 'If that were the case, he would have informed us over the phone.'

'Are you sure?'

'Yes.'

'What's your name, sir?'

'Bali.'

Iqbal did some quick thinking. *Bali knows where Inspector Bharucha is. That means Bali must be from the underworld or an informer, or both.*

Exactly at 1.30 a.m., the phone started ringing. Iqbal grabbed the receiver. Inspector Bharucha's voice echoed from the other end, 'Are you awake?'

'I'm wide awake, sir. Your man, however, is fast asleep.'

'Really?'

Iqbal placed the receiver near Bali's open mouth. Bali had fallen asleep on the chair with his head rolled back. He was snoring loudly.

'Convinced?' Iqbal asked Inspector Bharucha.

'Wake up that bastard and ask him to bring you.'

'Where to, sir?'

'He knows where.'

Iqbal replaced the receiver on the cradle and shook Bali. He got up with a start. Iqbal gave him Inspector Bharucha's message.

From Haji Ali, Bali took him to Worli's Lotus Theatre in a taxi. The roads were empty. The crowd from the last show had dispersed. The place was deserted. The gaslight poles, which were some distance away, illuminated a limited area.

Inspector Bharucha's jeep was parked a short distance away from the theatre. He was leaning on a Fiat car parked nearby. He addressed Iqbal, 'Do you like this car?'

Iqbal moved his hand over its body. Though it was covered in a thin sheet of dust, the navy blue car looked new. 'It's nice,' Iqbal said. *Did he make me wait for hours just to appreciate this car? Or is it a stolen one?*

'Get inside.'

Iqbal opened the door. As he entered, he spotted two jackets on the seat. He felt the lining of one of the jackets and realized that there were gold biscuits inside it. He knew from experience that, generally, one jacket carried 100 pieces.

He looked out of the car window. Inspector Bharucha suppressed a smile. Iqbal smiled back. 'What do I do with the jackets?'

Inspector Bharucha handed him a small chit. 'There is a chemist's shop near Pydhonie police station. Be there by 11.30 a.m. tomorrow. A jeweller will be waiting for you there. Hand over both the jackets to him.'

Now Iqbal's brain started piecing the puzzle together. He had finally unravelled the mystery behind the seven-and-a-half-hour wait at the petrol pump.

After leaving him at the petrol pump, Inspector Bharucha must have gone to raid some smuggler's den and seized a consignment of jackets there. Then, he must have removed two jackets from the lot and made a note of the rest in his official register.

'How do I find the jeweller?'

'He will find you.'

'How do I confirm that he is the right person?'

'He will offer you a Rs 1 note. Check the number on that bank note. It should match the number on the chit I've given you.'

Iqbal took out the chit from his pocket and glanced at it. There was a long number on it.

'Anything else?'

'This car . . .'

'Enjoy it for a few days. I'll ask for it when I need it,' said Inspector Bharucha.

Iqbal slid into the driver's seat and sped away.

On reading the newspaper the next day, Iqbal patted his own back. His guess was right. The story of Inspector Bharucha's heroic raid was all over the front page.

Inspector Bharucha had intercepted a taxi near Juhu beach. Bali was his informer in that area. According to the report, thirteen jackets (which meant there were fifteen) and other contraband goods had been found in the taxi. These included Japanese wristwatches and transistor radios.

Iqbal put down the newspaper and looked at the clock. He had to deliver the jackets at 11:30 a.m. It was only 7 a.m. He had an omelette and bread for breakfast and while having a cup of tea realized that he had missed fifteen days of college. He would have to borrow notes and devote all his attention to his studies now. If not, his hopes of becoming a doctor would remain a pipe dream.

By 8 a.m., his younger brothers Razzak and Firoze had woken up. Both of them were rubbing their eyes when Iqbal told them to get dressed quickly. They looked at him blankly. There were still two hours to go before school.

By the time they completed their daily chores and strapped on their schoolbags, it was 9 a.m. Gul Banu could not understand what was happening.

'Iqbal! What's the hurry?'

'I'm taking them out for some fresh air,' he replied, looking at Razzak and Firoze standing near the door.

'Now?'

'Now . . . In the car.'

'Car?'

'I'll take a round of Chowpatty and drop them to school before the bell.'

'But where did you get a car?'

'It belongs to a friend, Ma. I have to return it next week.'

The Fiat car was parked in Palkhi Mohalla outside Munda Galli. Iqbal opened the door, signalled both of them to get in and sat in the driver's seat. Both his brothers were still standing outside, looking at the car with amazement. Razzak was caressing the car's body as if it were a puppy.

Iqbal turned the key and started the car. Hearing the whirr of the engine, Razzak and Firoze jumped in and sat beside him. Crossing Palkhi Mohalla, they turned left. Since there was less traffic at that hour, the car moved fast, crossing Bhendi Bazaar, Nal Bazaar, Gol Deval and Prarthana Samaj to reach Chowpatty in a few minutes.

With the ebb of the tide, the sea had withdrawn. On the beach, there were only as many people as one could count on one's fingers. Some of them were strolling, while the others were basking in the mellow morning sun. Iqbal did not stop the car but turned towards the Hanging Gardens on Malabar Hill. At the top of the hill, he parked the car. Here, standing near the railing, one could see all of Bombay city.

Both the brothers held the railing and stared, amazement writ on their faces. The fog over the city had almost dispersed and the sun was still soft. From here, tall buildings looked like toys. One could see dense smoke belched out by the mill chimneys forming clouds overhead.

Iqbal went to the hawker selling ice candy nearby, bought two and gave one each to his brothers. Their faces lit up. Iqbal's mind wandered back to his own childhood.

He had grown up almost like an orphan. Nobody had taken him for an outing or a picnic, nobody had ever offered him a sweet. Both his parents had spent their life struggling to survive.

Around 9.30 a.m., Iqbal got his brothers back into the car. He chose a different route to go back and drove from Mount Pleasant Road towards Nepean Sea Road.

At 9.40 a.m., he stopped near the main gate of Habib High School. Razzak and Firoze got down, waved back at him proudly and ran inside. Iqbal then drove towards Pydhonie.

*

He was there before the appointed time. Parking the car near the chemist's shop adjacent to Pydhonie police station, he crossed the road. From the other side of the road, he could closely observe the jeweller who was supposed to take the jackets. He wanted to spot the jeweller before the latter identified him.

It was almost 11 a.m. The streets start getting crowded in this area well before 9 a.m. By now, from the way people were bustling about, it appeared as if a bomb was about to be dropped on the city. Everyone was scurrying about. There was quite a crowd at the chemist's shop with people hollering above each other. Not far off, pigeons feasted on grains strewn across the pavement, while others roosted on the heritage buildings.

Iqbal was surveying the view when he realized that a man wearing a dhoti and shirt had stopped near the chemist's shop. He had a Gandhi cap on his head and wore glasses with a wire frame. Like Iqbal, he too was quietly scanning faces.

Iqbal was convinced. He crossed the road and tapped the man lightly from behind. Startled, he turned around and stared at Iqbal blankly. Iqbal did not need to say anything. He proceeded towards the car. The man followed. Both of them sat inside the car. Iqbal turned on the ignition and began driving.

The man was still wondering how Iqbal had recognized him. At last, to satisfy his curiosity, he asked him. Iqbal ignored the question and inquired, 'Where is the note?'

The man immediately took out a Rs 1 note from his pocket and placed it before him. By this time, the car had crossed Mohammed Ali Road and reached Flora Fountain. From here, it turned towards Gateway of India and stopped. Iqbal compared the number on the currency note with the number written on the chit Inspector Bharucha had given him. The numbers matched. Iqbal kept the note as proof of delivery, took out the jackets wrapped in brown paper from under the seat and gave them to him. 'Where can I drop you?'

Iqbal dropped the man near Princess Street before 1 p.m. and came to Haji Ali. Inspector Bharucha was waiting for him in the cabin at the petrol pump. Iqbal parked the car and entered.

'Everything went off well, dikra?'

Iqbal handed him the chit and the currency note. Inspector Bharucha glanced at the two numbers for a moment and smiled. He pulled out ten Rs 100 notes from his pocket and placed the Rs 1 note on top. 'This is your share.'

Putting the notes into his pocket, Iqbal got up.

'Are you in a hurry?'

'Yes. I have to attend college in the afternoon.'

'Hmm . . .' Inspector Bharucha got up too and patted Iqbal on the back. 'I'm sure you will make a name for yourself one day.'

Sitting in the car, Iqbal wondered whether Inspector Bharucha had congratulated him for his dedication to his studies or for having delivered the two jackets. One thing was for sure: Inspector Bharucha had taken notice of him for being an honest young man. He was to smuggle gold worth millions under Inspector Bharucha's patronage.

*

'Aabid Bhai!' Sufi interrupted his narrative to ask the same old question, 'What is smuggling?'

I knew the answer this time. 'Duty not paid on export or import of goods that are surreptitiously brought into or sent out from the country.'

'Now tell me, who will you call a smuggler? The man who legally sends gold from Dubai to India? The boatman who brings the gold in his boat to India? The gang that takes the delivery of the gold from the boatman in the cover of the night? The invisible mafia that receives the payment from the jeweller? And don't forget, this invisible man has never played an active part in trafficking. Just tell me who will you point an accusing finger at and brand him a smuggler?'

10

When I returned home after spending over a month in Habib Hospital, I felt as if I had left my body behind. What returned home was just a skeleton. It was difficult for me to stand, let alone move, without support.

Iqbal had been lucky. He had recovered from pneumonia in just two weeks. I spent another fifteen days at home. All these days, I fondly remembered the hospital. There, from the window facing the west, I used to see the open sky, my eyes filling up with the crimson colour of the setting sun. Sometimes a flock of birds would fly past in formation. Reclining on the pillow, I also observed with interest the compound of the juvenile remand home across the street from the hospital. Time flew by.

Back home on the first floor of Sultan Mansion, my dimly lit room had only one window. The iron bars on the window resembled a prison cell. Moreover, the window overlooked an open sewer. At times, when it overflowed, a head-splitting stench filled the room. Like the worms that lived in the gutter, we too had become accustomed to the foul smell. But after spending a month in the hospital, I had lost my immunity to it. Worse, I had become accustomed to certain luxuries.

I had developed a fondness for the sunlight that percolated through the window there. It would slowly spread all over my bed. I loved it. We used to play together. I would interlock my fingers and place them against the sunlight. This would cast a shadow over the white bedsheet. In a few days, I learnt how to create shadow images of around twenty animals. But in my gloomy room there was no scope for the sun to even peep in. I did not have the strength to go outside for a glimpse. There was no way out. Moreover, it was not my nature to sit idle.

Watching the little rascals in the children's remand home, I started thinking about subjects for children's stories. I was thinking about them from the point of view of comics. The three impish characters—Sonu, Bhagu and Lakhudi—who became a craze after being published in the children's Gujarati monthly magazine *Ramakadu* were born during this period.

Prior to this, I had never done any creative writing nor had I thought about it. Of course, I used to look out for ideas for pocket cartoons and comic strips. But the visualization of a complete story to make a four-page comic book was a different ball game altogether.

I wrote about half a dozen stories. One evening, after I had recovered, I went to Dr Chinwala's house. He was not at home, but Mushtaq Jalili was sitting there reading an Urdu classic by Ibrahim Jalis. To be honest, I had gone there hoping to meet him.

Seeking his opinion, I narrated to him my ideas for children's stories in Hindustani. He looked at me for a while and then asked, 'Aabid, would you like to work with me?'

'What?'

'I write for films and I need an assistant.'

'But I've never written anything.'

He laughed. 'Who wrote these stories?'

'I did . . .'

There must have been some freshness in my concepts, or else this writer would not have asked me to join him.

Besides, by working with him on his stories, I would be able to learn his technique. Every writer has his or her own way of thinking and his or her own style. Jalili had developed his unique method of developing powerful characters. I could not resist the temptation of learning this secret and so I accepted his proposal gladly.

Dr Chinwala's house had proved to be a double boon for me. Here, I got two teachers in one go. I had Yusuf Dhala for painting and Mushtaq Jalili for writing. Jalili, in fact, once told Dhala, 'Aabid writes weird but wonderful tales with magical elements.'

*

One can also say that, in a way, Inspector Bharucha's patronage had proved beneficial for Iqbal. He had successfully completed the task of delivering the two jackets. In turn, he had received Rs 1000—Rs 500 per jacket. He was also presented an additional Rs 1 for good luck.

Half this amount was spent on settling the grocer's and other bills. Before the remainder was exhausted, Inspector Bharucha assigned Iqbal the task of delivering one more jacket for which he got Rs 500. After that, he did not get a phone call from Inspector Bharucha for two months.

The financial situation of Iqbal's house was precariously hanging by a thread once again. Tension fluttered its owl-like wings once again. He realized that it would be difficult to survive as Inspector Bharucha's carrier because the uncertainty of the work had started affecting his studies.

The first-year examinations were approaching. Iqbal's worry was not whether he would pass or not. He knew he would be able to clear every subject easily by going through the notes a week before the examinations. But he did not intend to just get through; he wanted to secure a first class with distinction.

He was trying hard to concentrate on his studies when his neighbour knocked at the door. 'Iqbal! There is a call for you.' Iqbal placed the book upside down and got up immediately. At the neighbour's house, he picked up the receiver and said, 'Hello!'

It was Inspector Bharucha on the line. He told him to come to the garage in the lane adjoining Bhavan's College the next day between 1 and 2 p.m.

Iqbal left college during the recess and reached the garage at seven minutes past one. Inspector Bharucha was already there. There were some problems with his jeep, which is why he had come there to get it repaired.

On seeing Iqbal, he smiled warmly. When he did not get any reaction, he asked, 'Dikra, you are looking like a dead duck. Is anything wrong?'

'My examinations are approaching.'

'If a bright student like you starts worrying about the exams, what will become of the others?'

Iqbal put his concerns on the table. 'The Rs 500 you gave me last time is finished. If I don't get regular work, how will I concentrate on studies?'

'Hmm . . . that is true.' After a moment's thought, Inspector Bharucha said, 'Okay, I'll make some arrangements. Are you busy this evening?'

Iqbal shook his head.

'Come to the petrol pump at 6 p.m.'

He understood. It was the same routine again. Inspector Bharucha would give him one or two jackets. As the carrier, Iqbal would deliver them to some jeweller and again earn anywhere between Rs 1000 and Rs 500. He would have to survive like this.

By the time the examinations ended, Inspector Bharucha had given him two more assignments. On both occasions, he was given one jacket for delivery.

Then one day, Inspector Bharucha explained, 'Understand, dikra. I know your problem. But I'm not in a position to give you regular work. Whatever I'm doing isn't my business. Beyond earning some extra money on the side, I've no interest in it. But you don't worry, I won't let you down. You are honest, you have the right to live and progress in life.'

Both of them were sipping lime juice standing by the Haji Ali parapet, facing the sea. The tide had covered the narrow serpentine pathway that led to the mosque.

'Have you seen Gaylord Restaurant?' Inspector Bharucha spoke at last.

Iqbal nodded.

'Go there and ask for Singh at the counter. He will be sitting inside somewhere.'

'What do I tell him?'

'Just take my name. He will know.'

'What is the best time to see him?'

'Between 5 and 7 p.m.'

Iqbal looked at his wristwatch. It was already 4 p.m. He looked up at his godfather for permission.

'Go with God, dikra.'

*

'What's your opinion about Inspector Bharucha today?' I interrupted Sufi.

'In what context are you asking?'

'Whenever you faced a crisis, he stood by you. Of course, his method of helping you was not ideal. Still, he was your godfather. He wasn't interested in just his own well-being but yours too.'

'If he was really concerned, he should have slapped me hard on our very first meeting.'

'Then how would you have survived?'

Sufi looked up at the sky, as if he had not heard me. We were sitting on the terrace of his house. 'I was a juvenile delinquent. Bharucha picked me up from a pothole and tossed me into a well. Then he pulled me out from the well and threw me into a lake. I came out of it only to dive into the ocean of crime.'

Taking a deep breath, he added, 'It's all God's will. Had He wanted, an angel would have dropped into my life too. Like your mentor Dr Chinwala, he too could have become my shepherd. Forget it. Destiny had already carved out my path. There is no point blaming anyone.'

He pulled out his glasses and began cleaning them with one end of his long kurta. After an interminable pause, he continued with his narrative.

*

Iqbal crossed the road and boarded a bus for Churchgate. Gaylord Restaurant was close by. During the bus journey, he couldn't help but think that the person he was going to meet must be a Sikh. He was taking a guess based on the surname 'Singh'.

Who was he? What was he? How did he fit into the world of crime? He did not yet have answers to any of these questions. Still, he was confident that Inspector Bharucha's contact would not be an ordinary person.

Alighting at Churchgate, he glanced at his wristwatch again. He had arrived ten minutes before time. He spent some time at Eros Theatre gazing at the posters of the film *Chase a Crooked Shadow*.

Around 4.15 p.m., he crossed the road and asked the man sitting at the counter of Gaylord Restaurant for 'Mr Singh'. The man pointed to a table. Iqbal turned to see a broad-shouldered man wearing a light brown safari suit sitting there, immersed in thought. He was not wearing a turban as Iqbal had expected, but had well-combed hair.

Iqbal walked up to him.

'Mr Singh?'

The man lifted his head and took in the young man standing before him in an immaculate white shirt and pants with ice-blue eyes.

'Inspector Bharucha asked me to see you,' Iqbal said, pulling a chair and sitting down. There was a table between them with a half-finished cup of coffee on it. In the ashtray were a couple of cigarette stubs. One cigarette was dangling between Singh's fingers.

Generally, he had observed that Sikhs do not smoke. Iqbal's brain started working. This man was smoking, and he did not have a beard and moustache like most sardars. On the contrary, he had a clean-shaven square face with prominent eyebrows.

'What will you have?' Singh asked Iqbal.

'I don't drink.'

Taking a drag, Singh decided to pull his leg. 'I was asking about tea.'

'That's what I meant.'

He seemed to be surprised. 'Don't you drink tea in the morning?'

'Two cups.'

'Then what's the harm in having one now?'

Silence descended for a while. Finally, Iqbal took the lead and said, 'I hope Inspector Bharucha briefed you about me.'

'He has. But I believe in first-hand experience.'

'Try me.'

'From what he said, there cannot be any doubt about your honesty.' This time, Singh took a sip of coffee and stubbed the cigarette. 'He also said that you are a daredevil driver who knows how to drive a car and also drive over someone with it.'

Iqbal's probing eyes were focused on Singh's face. This is what he had told Inspector Bharucha.

'Now tell me, till date, how many people have you run over?'

'None.'

'Then, should I assume it was a bluff?'

Singh was surprised when he heard a firm 'no' from Iqbal.

'Of course. Inspector Bharucha has complete faith in me, and I don't give my word lightly. Still, if you don't believe me, as I said earlier, try me. Whom do you want me to bump off?'

'Not a human being,' said Singh, picking up the cigarette packet and pulling one out. 'Two jackets need to be disposed of.'

'Can you clarify?'

'There are two jackets lying in an apartment on the third floor of a building. They have to be picked up from there and thrown into the backyard.'

Iqbal instantly did the math in his head. One jacket has 100 gold biscuits in its lining. One biscuit weighs 116 grams. Hence, 100 biscuits would weigh 11 kg and 600 grams. In 1966–67, the price of gold was Rs 180 per *tola* (11.5 grams). Accordingly, one jacket was worth Rs 1,80,000. *What circumstances had compelled him to discard these jackets? If it was just about throwing these away, even a child could do the job.*

'No,' said Singh, reading his thoughts. 'The cops have encircled the building since the last three days.' He flicked the lighter and lit another cigarette, gazing steadily at Iqbal.

Now Iqbal figured out what was happening. The apartment that Singh was referring to belonged to his men. It was being used to store contraband. In the last trip, over twenty-five jackets had arrived. Meanwhile, somebody had informed the police. Before they could take action, almost all the jackets had been delivered. Except for two.

On inquiring with the neighbours, the police learned that no tenant lived in that apartment. Sometimes, one or two persons would come there with a suitcase and leave in an hour or so. The police got more suspicious, but they did not know how much contraband was stored inside. They were hoping for a major catch—it would be front-page news.

The question was whether to break open the door or not. It was easy for them to barge in, but doing so would only yield smuggled goods, not the smugglers. Hence they decided to stake out the building.

'How many cops are on duty there?'

'Six.'

'They must be in plainclothes!'

'Right. One of the six is hiding somewhere on the third floor, two of them are keeping watch in the lobby and interrogating any suspicious-looking person who enters, and the remaining three are posted around the building.'

Iqbal could not help but whistle in admiration. The building was under observation on all sides. Moreover, one of the policemen was somewhere outside the closed apartment, keeping a watch on the door. If any fool dared to open it, he would be caught red-handed.

'Now tell me, can you do it?' Singh exhaled a ring of smoke.

'I want to know the geography of the apartment.'

'Two bedrooms, a hall, kitchen and two bathrooms.'

'Sketch out a rough layout for me.'

He immediately took out a pen, folded the tablecloth partly and started drawing on the glass top. 'You will get off the lift on the third floor here. From this point, you will go through the passageway, cross two doors and come to the third one.'

While drawing up the plan, he was explaining it too. 'When you open the door and enter, there is a large drawing room. From here, you have to go into this narrow passage. Here, on the left, is the door to the bedroom. It's in this bedroom under the mattress that the two jackets are concealed. You have to take them out and throw them down from the bathroom.'

'Is there a window in the bathroom?'

'No, but there is a ventilator. There are glass plates fitted into it at an angle.'

'That means I'll have to remove the glass plates before throwing the jackets down.'

'What's the need to remove them? Just break them.'

'I can't do such a foolish thing.'

'Why?'

'Because the broken glass that falls on the ground will make a crashing sound.'

'Won't the jackets make a sound when they fall?'

'No. The jackets are made of cloth. There is a possibility that because of the gold biscuits inside there may be a muted thud. But that will not attract attention. Secondly, I don't want to throw away such precious jackets.'

'Then?'

'I plan to carry them out and personally gift them to you.'

Singh's eyes opened like flashbulbs. His eyebrows shot up. 'Listen, Iqbal! There is not just the risk of going to prison but also the risk of losing your life. And you're still young . . .'

Iqbal remained silent.

'If you are undertaking this job and putting your life on the line just to prove a point, know this: you have come to me on Inspector Bharucha's recommendation. To tell you the truth, I have full faith in his words. Till date he has never been proven wrong.'

Iqbal patiently heard him out then reminded him, 'You haven't given me the name of the building and the address yet.'

Singh concluded that the novice sitting across the table was pig-headed. *He is knowingly jumping into the fire. If someone wants to commit suicide, even God cannot help him.*

Handing over the keys to the apartment, Singh gave him the address. The name of the five-storeyed building was Sagar Darshan in the posh Warden Road locality.

'One last question. What are the names of the people who live on either side of this apartment?'

'To the right lives a foreign couple. Their names are Suzy and John Langdon. On the left lives a Parsee gentleman whose name I don't know, but his surname is Irani.'

And then, as if he still doubted Iqbal's words, Singh asked, 'When will you go?'

'Tomorrow.'

'At night?'

'Only thieves operate at night. I'm a gentleman,' Iqbal quipped, getting up. 'I'll see you tomorrow at this time.'

'Just a minute. If by chance the jackets are with you, don't drop in here. I have a room at Natraj Hotel on Marine Drive. Meet me there. And if the police catch you, remember, we never met.'

Iqbal put the key ring on his finger and, playing with it, went out.

Coming out of Gaylord Restaurant, Iqbal was reminded of how late it was. The sun had set ages ago. For a while, he stood thinking. A concrete plan had taken shape in his mind while discussing the matter with Singh. Now, the only thing that remained to be decided was the time that he would enter the building. Instead of heading home, he decided to visit Taj Mahal Hotel. For that, he had to go to Kala Ghoda after crossing Oval Ground. It was a ten-minute walk from there.

Stepping on to the soft grass of the playground, he decided to go to Sagar Darshan between 1.30 and 2 p.m. That being the lunch hour, there might be slight slackness in the watch.

After entering the hotel, he went straight to the florist's counter, took out a Rs 100 note and placed an order for a bouquet.

'Where do you want it delivered?' the florist, a Parsee gentleman, asked opening the receipt book.

'I'll collect it myself tomorrow morning.'

'Would you like to place a card?'

'Yes, a birthday card.'

'In whose name?'

'Suzy Langdon.'

'From?'

'John Langdon.'

'Wonderful! I'm filled with joy whenever a husband remembers his wife's birthday and sends flowers to her. You can collect the bouquet any time after 11 a.m.'

Iqbal thanked him and left.

11

The taxi was hurtling through the streets of south Bombay. Iqbal had collected the bouquet from Taj at 1.05 p.m. He had taken the taxi from there and was going to Warden Road. He had placed the bouquet carefully beside him on the seat.

He cast a cursory look at the bouquet and felt that it was good value for money. Along with thirty roses were four stems of the rare tiger lily from Singapore. The bouquet was placed in a ceramic pot bound by thin silver wires.

The taxi crossed Marine Drive. The October sun was bright enough to make you forget the heat of May. The parapet on Marine Drive was empty, the footpath was desolate and there was hardly any traffic.

The main thing that worried Iqbal was the prospect of the woman Suzy not being in Bombay and thus drawing the suspicion of the policemen. *Maybe she is in Bombay. What if he bumps into Mr and Mrs Langdon at the entrance?* The bouquet he had ordered had John Langdon's name as the sender.

The taxi crossed Chowpatty, reached Kemp's Corner and turned left. After some time, taking one more turn towards Breach Candy, it stopped near the footpath across Sagar Darshan.

Iqbal did not want to get down here and cross the road. Like a lord, he wanted to take the taxi into the courtyard and get down at the lobby in front of the policemen. 'Driver! Take a U-turn and enter that building.'

The driver grimaced but took a U-turn. The taxi entered the courtyard and stopped near the entrance. Iqbal settled the bill, gave a generous tip and got down with the bouquet. Two policemen in plainclothes stood before him.

Iqbal observed that one of them was stubby and pot-bellied while the other was athletic, well-built and sported blue sunglasses.

Before they could ask him anything, Iqbal forwarded the card of the florist and requested, 'Will you please guide me to this lady?' He had asked so innocently that both the cops looked at each other and then at Iqbal. The shorter policeman took the card and glanced at it. The man with the blue sunglasses too craned his neck over his shoulder.

The name 'Suzy Langdon' was written clearly on the card. Beneath it was a birthday greeting in English: Many Happy Returns of the Day. At the end was the name of the sender in cursive letters and the Taj florist's monogram printed along with the words: With Best Compliments.

There was no room for suspicion. Everything was in order, yet the towering policeman with the sunglasses asked, 'What's your name?'

'Michael.'

'I think I've seen you somewhere.'

Iqbal too was thinking the same. He had seen this smart-ass somewhere but could not place where. And then Iqbal remembered. His legs began shivering.

This was the same policeman who was part of the raid on Aziz Dilip's joint in Munda Galli three years ago with Inspector Bharucha. It was dawn. Iqbal had left home to offer namaz when the two had come face-to-face. Those days, Iqbal was in school and wore half pants and half-sleeved shirts. Today, he was dressed in a full-sleeved white shirt, white trousers and white shoes.

'Sir,' Iqbal said promptly, 'My job is to go from place to place delivering bouquets. Perhaps I dropped into your building too sometime.'

Before the policeman could think any further, a girl who looked like a domestic help came out of the building with a shopping bag. Seeing the bouquet, she asked, 'To whom is it to be delivered?'

The rotund policeman looked at the card once again and said, 'Suzy Langdon.'

'She is our memsahib,' the maid said instantly. 'Give—I'll take it to her.'

Iqbal's heart skipped two beats, but on the third, he came up with a bright idea. 'Very sorry,' he interjected, before the smiling maid could grab the bouquet. 'After delivery, I need to take madam's signature on the receipt.'

Disheartened, she said, 'Okay. Go up to the third floor. It's the last door to the left of the lift.' Thanking her, Iqbal took the card from the policeman and was heading for the lift when suddenly the maid, with new-found concern, said, 'Wait, I'll come with you.'

Iqbal was in a fix.

*

She marched ahead. Iqbal followed her. After a few steps, they stopped at the lift. The maid pressed the button to call for the lift.

'Why take the trouble . . .' Iqbal tried desperately to shake her off.

'What trouble? This is for our memsahib. I'd have helped you even if it was for some other tenant.' She then asked Iqbal the question he was dreading, 'Who sent it?'

The lift arrived and, opening the door with one hand, Iqbal entered. The maid followed him and closed the door. 'It's neither madam's birthday nor Christmas today.' Pressing the third floor button, she asked again, 'Who has sent it?'

'Mr Langdon.'

'Really?'

'What's there to be so surprised?

'But . . .'

'If a husband loves his wife, can't he send her flowers?'

'That's true,' said the maid looking at him closely, 'But Mr Langdon isn't here, he is in America since the last one month.'

The lift was slowly moving up. By the time it crossed the first floor, Iqbal came up with a convincing reply. 'The order for this bouquet has come from America.'

'How?'

'Like there is an arrangement to send a telegram from one country to another, florists too have their own arrangements.' As if he were explaining this to a child, he said, 'If your madam wants to send flowers to her husband in America, she can place an order with our shop in Taj Hotel. We will deliver the flowers in America on the day and time she wants us to.'

This was not a lie but a fact, and it had the desired impact on the girl. She was glad. Her boss was a doting husband. Why wouldn't he remember his wife and order flowers for her from America?

As the lift crossed the second floor, drops of sweat appeared on Iqbal's forehead. He had successfully duped the two policemen downstairs, but what about the third one? Iqbal did not have any idea where he could be hiding on the third floor. Would he be keeping guard outside the closed apartment? Iqbal did not have a clue. Moreover, the maid was sticking to him like a leech.

Besides, he had not brought the bouquet of flowers to deliver. He had taken it with him only as a pretext to get into the building. On reaching the third floor, he had planned to throw it into a garbage can.

The presence of the housemaid had ruined his plan. By this time, he was realizing that things had come to such a pass that perhaps he would have to return like a fool without accomplishing anything.

As he and the maid stepped out of the lift on the third floor, the third policeman with closely cropped hair appeared before him like the djinn from Alladin's lamp. Although he was muscular, he looked like a half-baked man. 'He has come with me,' said the maid before Iqbal could say anything. 'Our sahib has especially ordered these flowers to be delivered from America.'

The policeman glanced at Iqbal for a second and went back to where he had come from. He had chosen this place after much deliberation. Sitting on the stairs that led to the fourth floor, he could see anyone trying to climb up while no one could spot him. Besides, he could also keep an eye on the lift.

Again, the girl moved ahead. Cursing his stars, Iqbal followed her. A few steps later, she stopped and pointed from afar. 'There. The fourth and the last door, can you see it?'

'Of course.'

'That's our sahib's flat. Got it? Can I leave now?'

Iqbal thanked the maid from the bottom of his heart. She entered the lift and went down. Iqbal walked up to the third apartment and glanced back at the lift. Neither could the policeman sitting on the stairs see him, nor could Iqbal see the cop.

Immediately, he set the bouquet down, took out the key from his pocket and inserted it into the keyhole of the door. A soft clicking sound travelled through the silent corridor.

The sound caught the policeman's ears. Half his attention was on opening his lunch box containing puri-bhaji and the other half was on the sound. He presumed that Suzy Langdon must have opened the door.

Iqbal entered the apartment quickly, closed the apartment door from inside and fastened it with a latch. Now, he had to do his job in the shortest possible time. Every second mattered.

He was leaning on the door of the large drawing room. He took in everything at a glance. Though nobody lived there, the room lacked nothing. He saw the sofa set, centre table, sideboard, the chandelier dangling from the ceiling, the wall-to-wall carpet, a TV and VCR, a well-stocked liquor bar, luxurious printed curtains shielding the window and the oil paintings on the walls. He looked to his right.

There was a narrow passage, as Singh had explained. Taking a few steps, he came to the door to the first bedroom. He turned the doorknob slowly. The same care had been taken to furnish this room as well.

A round double bed, a bedside table lamp, a dressing table and indoor plants were all colour-coordinated. A painting, a nude in vibrant colours by Modigliani, was placed over the double bed.

He lifted the mattress and saw two jackets under it. He took off his shirt, placed it on the side table and lifted one jacket. It was heavier than a suit of armour. Iqbal had already calculated exactly how much it weighed: 11 kilos and 750 gms.

*

While eating his lunch from a tiny plastic lunch box, a thought bothered the policeman. He had heard the click of the opening of the door but nothing after that. *How could that be possible?* Someone should have said something? At least Suzy Langdon should have spoken. He gulped down his lunch, set it down on one side and got up. He peered down the corridor.

The last apartment belonged to the Langdons. The door was closed. He became suspicious. *The maid had left, but what about the young man?* He strode down the passage purposefully.

*

Iqbal wore one jacket on his chest and the other one on his back. When he tried to put on his shirt, he realized his foolishness. He had calculated everything, except that after putting on the shirt, his chest would swell like that of a bodybuilder.

He stood before the dressing table and looked at himself. He was stunned. One would not be as surprised to see an old lady enter a salon and leave a young woman, as one would be if an ant entered an apartment and came out looking like an elephant!

*

When Suzy Langdon, dressed in a sleeveless purple T-shirt and shorts covering only half her thighs, opened the door, the policeman was standing before her.

'Yes?'

'A young man had come to deliver a bouquet to you.'

'Where is he?'

'I also want to know the same.'

'What?'

'Where has he gone?'

'He is not here.'

'Sure?'

'Then, have I hidden him in my cupboard?' Suzy Langdon laughed, displaying her ample cleavage.

A rush of thoughts passed through the policeman's head. *This foreigner is a seductress whose globetrotting husband is always out. The young man may be her lover. It won't be surprising if she has hidden him inside the house for a quick one.* But how could he confirm? He did not have a warrant to intrude into the privacy of a tenant. And until he could confirm whether the young man was inside this woman's house, he could not ascertain whether he had sneaked into the adjoining apartment.

He was standing there perplexed when Suzy Langdon smiled and said, 'I don't mind if you want to search my house.'

Now the policeman was alarmed. Immediately, he bolted to the lift and rang the call bell thrice at an interval of three seconds. This was an emergency signal to his colleagues keeping watch downstairs.

The short policemen standing in the lobby rushed towards the lift while the tall one with the blue sunglasses ran to call his three colleagues who were keeping vigil around the building.

*

Iqbal slumped on the sofa in the drawing room. His computer-like brain had ditched him today. He had realized there were loopholes in all his getaway plans.

It would be easy for him to throw the jackets out of the window and come out of the main door like a gentleman. The law would not be able to do much without any evidence. But what about the bravado he had shown before Singh?

At last, he had a brainwave. Though this too was not his brightest idea, he decided to implement it nevertheless. The policeman guarding the third floor was sitting on the stairs by the wall, he thought. He could stealthily go down the steps. On reaching the ground floor, he would not rush out but wait for a group of tenants to step out, mingle with them and thus slip out of the building. This was possible because the policemen were keeping strict watch only over the people entering the building.

He got up from the sofa, reached the door and was about to open it when the doorbell rang. His hands froze. A barrage of questions swarmed his mind. *Who could have rung the bell? Some neighbour? But why should the neighbours do that? He did not know any of them. No one knew that he was inside!*

The doorbell rang again. He became cautious. Surely, the policemen had guessed. He was now certain that if he opened the door he would land straight into the police's trap and be handcuffed. The bell kept ringing. Iqbal ran back to the bedroom. This time, he locked the bedroom door from inside and hauled up the round double bed to block the entrance.

*

Hammers were now being used to open the main door. It would take the policemen at least a few minutes to break it open. After that, they would need a couple of minutes to break open the bedroom door too. Iqbal needed more time. He went into the bathroom and locked it from the inside too. The sound coming from the hammers hitting the main door was so loud that it could be heard in the bathroom.

Iqbal was not worried. He was thinking fast. The bathroom was made of white marble and was as big as Iqbal's house. Everything was sparkling white. The jacuzzi had been carved out of Makrana marble. Dressed in spotless white, Iqbal stood in it like a marble statue. His eyes were fixed on the ventilator.

The main door lock gave way. Two policemen rushed inside with revolvers. Four others followed behind, providing cover.

Outside in the corridor, the neighbours had gathered. These included Suzy Langdon, Mrs Irani and a dozen others. 'You see,' Suzy Langdon said to no one in particular. 'The bouquet lying on the centre table was brought for me by that young man.'

Iqbal was pulling out the glass panes from the ventilator and placing them on the commode. He was hoping to escape from the ventilator and slide down the drainpipe. One of his fears was the policemen downstairs. He did not know that all of them were upstairs. The other fear was that some tenant from the buildings nearby may raise an alarm on seeing him come down the drainpipe. However, there was less likelihood of that happening. He did not expect people to be standing at the window at this time of the day. Moreover, the distance between this building and the next was more than fifty feet. A seven-foot-tall compound wall separated the two buildings. Besides, he could see a tall tree with thick foliage beyond the ventilator. Surely, it would cover him.

The lock on the door of the bedroom cracked with a snap but the door did not budge an inch. The policemen knew that there must be some obstacle behind it. Four men applied pressure on the door. Two others stood behind them, prepared for any sudden attack. Inch by inch, the door started giving way.

Iqbal had succeeded in getting out of the ventilator with much difficulty. His body was dripping in sweat. His chest had bulked up on account of the two jackets and the ventilator was very narrow. Besides, the jackets weighed almost twelve kilos each. Getting through the ventilator carrying so much weight was like pulling a camel through the eye of a needle.

He was standing on the ledge outside the ventilator. First he looked down and saw no one. Then he looked across and what he saw made him freeze.

He blinked and again looked at the opposite building. He saw a young girl standing in the balcony of the fourth floor. The girl was also staring at him. His legs shook. He felt giddy and was afraid that he might fall down. No one survives a fall from the third floor.

Who was that girl? Why wasn't she screaming?

Before climbing down the pipe, he thought of a new strategy: he put his hand through the ventilator window, picked up the glass panes stacked on the commode and placed them one by one into the grooves of the ventilator, beginning with the top slot.

The policemen, meanwhile, had succeeded in opening the bedroom door. The double bed had budged to the left. They rushed inside.

There was no one in the room. The door to the bathroom too was closed. They cursed their luck. Until now, no big-time racketeer had outwitted them as smoothly as this kid.

Immediately, they mounted an all-out assault on the bathroom door. They were like tigers in rage. If they caught Iqbal alive, they would first beat the shit out of him—*the law be damned*—to vent their anger.

Iqbal slid down the pipe slowly. Once he reached the first floor, he jumped on to a strong branch of the tree. His task was now easy. The compound wall separating the two buildings was close by. Making his way through the foliage, he reached the wall and jumped into the compound of the adjoining building.

Meanwhile, the bathroom lock too broke open. The doors of the house had not been easy to break because the house had been designed by racketeers. But one thing the policemen were sure of was that this was the last door. They had finally trapped him like a cornered rat.

The short policeman, with a revolver in hand, shoved open the door with his shoulder and stepped inside. Two others followed him, while the remaining three watched from the entrance to the bathroom. The marble walls were bare. The marble tub too was empty. There was a lid on the commode. All the glass panes on the ventilator were intact. Where the hell had the boy gone? *Had he turned into a fly and flown away?*

The policemen looked at each other with their mouths open.

*

Before leaving the compound of the adjoining building, Iqbal thought of the girl again. He looked up. She was still standing on the balcony and staring at him.

Iqbal was certain that the girl was from his college and his class. Both of them had appeared for the first-year examinations together. *What was her name?*

He strode out confidently now, taking long, firm steps. Now, he was safe. On coming out of the compound, he spotted a parked taxi, as if it was waiting for him. *What luck!* As he strode towards the taxi, the door opened, and from inside, a familiar voice said, 'Come in, dikra.'

He was stunned.

12

Seeing Iqbal standing confused outside the taxi, Inspector Bharucha got suspicious: what if the disciple gave the guru the slip!

Their relationship was like that of a master and disciple. Whatever progress Iqbal had made was because of Inspector Bharucha. It was because of him that Iqbal had left behind small-time crooks like Moghul and Ali, and joined Singh's international gang.

Inspector Bharucha stretched his hand out of the taxi, caught Iqbal's wrist and pulled him inside. The taxi sped away.

Both of them were seated side by side on the back seat. Both of them were silent. It was not safe to say anything in the presence of the taxi driver. They were immersed in their own thoughts. Iqbal was wondering who had informed Inspector Bharucha. *How did he know that I would emerge from Singh's flat with two jackets at that particular time? Not only this, he knew the exact place—outside the gate of the neighbouring building—and had been waiting patiently in the taxi.*

The fog of confusion lifted after a while. Iqbal remembered that when he had tried to enter the building with the bouquet, the policeman with the blue sunglasses had said that he had seen him somewhere. That man was Inspector Bharucha's deputy. That meant this too was Inspector Bharucha's operation!

His guess was correct.

Inspector Bharucha had been alerted by his informer Bali: twenty-five jackets had arrived at Sagar Darshan building on Warden Road. He did not know which gang owned the apartment. It would not have mattered even if he had known that the apartment belonged to Singh. Once an FIR was lodged, friendship was the first victim.

Before Inspector Bharucha could act, most of the jackets had been delivered, only two remained. This was when Inspector Bharucha's men had surrounded the building.

Iqbal also got answers to his other questions. Before the main lock was broken into, Inspector Bharucha must have been given the description of the young man with the bouquet. He must have surmised that this could be no one but Iqbal. He must have rushed in a taxi and kept a watch on the building. It is possible that he might have seen Iqbal climbing down the drainpipe and understood the plan.

As the taxi crossed Kemps Corner and turned towards Babulnath, the other mystery also was solved: the name of the girl he had seen in the balcony of the opposite building. Longing to connect the face in his memories, his lips quivered and the name burst forth.

'What did you say?'

Hearing Inspector Bharucha, Iqbal said, 'I didn't say anything.'

'Who's Kusum?'

Iqbal was alarmed. That was the name of the girl. The name had slipped out of his mouth unwittingly. 'She is a student at my college.'

'Really?'

'Of course.'

'When did you seduce her?'

'I don't even know her.'

The taxi driver looked into the rear-view mirror and smiled. He presumed that the two were father and son.

'If you lie, I'll skin you alive.'

'I've told you the truth only.'

'Then how come her name was on your lips?'

'Sir, sometimes I think aloud.'

The taxi turned into the lane behind Bhavan's College and stopped near the garage. Inspector Bharucha's jeep was being repaired there. He paid the taxi driver and got down. Iqbal followed him.

The manager was standing near the entrance. 'Jeep is ready.'

'I'm not,' Inspector Bharucha scoffed. 'Is there someone at the back?'

'A mechanic is resting.'

'Throw him out.'

The manager marched ahead. Both of them followed him like soldiers. Iqbal observed that the garage, which looked compact from outside, extended like a telescope inside. The noise inside was unbearable.

A mechanic was scraping the paint off a car, creating that incessant screech that can get on your nerves, while another was hammering a dent on the body of another car. The engine of a third car was being taken out, while another vehicle was waiting for a new coat of paint. There were pools of oil in some places and balls of thread and dirty rags lying around the grease-stained floors.

Winding their way through all this and crossing a wooden plank laid over an open gutter, they reached the back of the garage. A makeshift room had been created there using tin sheets. The manager went in and came out with the boy who was sleeping inside.

'Welcome dikra,' said Inspector Bharucha, sounding more than polite.

Iqbal knew it was time to face the music. He would be lucky to be allowed to leave in one piece for he had unwittingly interfered with the guru's case. His escape from Singh's flat with the two jackets would surely dent his guru's reputation.

Inspector Bharucha entered after him. There was a bench and a few tyres piled up. There were four empty drums in a corner. On the tin wall hung the mechanic's clothes.

Inspector Bharucha pointed towards the pile of tyres for Iqbal to sit on. He sat quietly. Before saying anything, Inspector Bharucha paced up and down the room twice. 'Do you know just how foolish you have been?'

He resumed pacing up and down the garage. 'Can you imagine what will come of this?'

'What, sir?'

Unexpectedly, Inspector Bharucha slapped him hard. 'You bastard! Trying to act smart!' All his pent-up anger came out through his eyes, face and clenched fists. 'My image will be tarnished in tomorrow's newspapers. My superiors will question me. Did I send six men from the department to keep vigil or enjoy a picnic?'

Cursing, he stood behind Iqbal, hit him on the back with full force and then screamed in pain. He had forgotten that under his shirt Iqbal was still wearing the jackets containing the gold biscuits.

Iqbal sat quietly. He knew that if he opened his mouth before his raging guru now, he would be in for it. Inspector Bharucha continued with the tongue lashing for some more time, intermittently kicking and punching him. Finally, he stood squarely before Iqbal, caught him by the hair and said, 'Tell me, do I throw you behind bars or cut your balls off right here?'

'Sir, that you should have done when I met you for the first time at your headquarters.'

Inspector Bharucha was not prepared for this answer. His grip on Iqbal's hair loosened. He looked at him steadily for a few seconds. 'Was it a mistake to have taken pity on you? Was it my fault that I stood by you in your starving days? Who gave you the opportunity to join college? Was that my crime?'

Challenging Iqbal with a barrage of questions, he thundered again, 'Tell me, you scoundrel!'

'I can't say for sure that you helped me out of pity. But I can say confidently that you have made a big mistake by teaching me honesty.'

'What do you mean?'

Iqbal stood up and looked straight into his eyes. 'You introduced me to Singh. He gave me the first assignment to dispose of two jackets. I carried out the job with total honesty. Why? Because you had vouched for me, that I was an honest person. What did I get in return for my integrity? Three slaps, ten kicks and seven blows. Moreover, you pulled my hair, twisted my ears, throttled my neck . . .'

'Enough, enough! Wasn't it your duty to inform me before poking your Pinocchio nose into my affairs?'

'Had I known, I'd have certainly consulted you.'

Iqbal's truthfulness seemed to have convinced him. 'Hmm . . .' Inspector Bharucha became thoughtful, took a few steps and sat on the bench nearby. 'I understand. You have spoilt my case unwittingly, but the law doesn't recognize ignorance.'

Iqbal did not fully comprehend the last statement. Inspector Bharucha explained, 'Suppose a man catches a stray chicken, cooks and eats it. The next day he is charged with theft. In that case, he cannot escape punishment saying, "I thought there was no owner." The law does not recognize ignorance.'

'What has that got to do with me?'

'You will have to atone for your ignorance,' Inspector Bharucha ordered from the bench. 'Dikra, take off both the jackets!'

*

In the evening, when Iqbal reached Hotel Natraj, Singh had already opened a bottle of White Horse. This was his daily routine. After sunset, he would come to his room and start drinking. He would finish off at least one bottle by midnight. Sometimes, there would be friends with him and sometimes he would invite those with whom he wished to curry favour. This last category of people included politicians, bureaucrats, police officers, etc.

Today, there was a call girl with him. It was she who had opened the door. Reclining on a pillow, Singh was sitting on the double bed, his legs outstretched. He had a glass in his hand. A plate of shami kebabs was on the white bed sheet.

After Iqbal entered, the girl closed the door and stood near the window with her back to them. Across the road at Marine Drive, the sea was beating hard against the tetrapods shielding the shore. The girl's miniskirt barely concealed the outlines of a graceful, perfect body. Iqbal guessed this beautiful teenager was new to the profession.

He turned and looked at Singh who was keenly observing him. Gradually his cold blue eyes focussed on Iqbal's chest and stopped there. He had not believed that the kid standing before him would triumph. Even if he was lucky and succeeded in his mission, it would be impossible to come out with the jackets. From the bulkiness of Iqbal's chest, it was evident that he had one on him. *Where was the other one?*

Before Singh could say anything, Iqbal went to the bathroom, removed the jacket and returned. 'Sorry, Singh,' he said, folding the jacket and placing it on the double bed, 'I couldn't live up to my words.'

Singh was intrigued. *The boy was different. He was expressing regret at not being able to get both the jackets.*

Even if he had not brought this one, who could have questioned him? Who would have known? After all, he had clearly instructed Iqbal to throw the jackets down from the bathroom and return.

Singh also knew that one jacket was valued at Rs 1,80,000. One would rather lose both jackets but not get into trouble with the police. Besides, for global traffickers dealing in millions, this was loose change.

Singh gestured to him to sit. 'What happened to the other jacket?'

'I had to gift it to my guru.' Sitting on the sofa facing Singh, he narrated the entire incident. At the end he added, 'Inspector Bharucha wanted to confiscate both the jackets. After much haggling, I settled for one.'

Iqbal rose in Singh's esteem. 'Kiran!' he addressed the call girl. 'We need one more glass to celebrate.'

Before she could move, Iqbal reminded him, 'I don't drink.'

'Hope you aren't feeling shy?'

Iqbal laughed. 'This bottle of White Horse is one of the most expensive whiskies in the world. No one declines it out of politeness.'

'Please understand, Iqbal. I'm pleased with you. Whatever you ask for,' he looked at Kiran proprietarily and then back at Iqbal with a smile, 'you will get it.'

The hint was obvious. He could demand the sixteen-year-old beauty who charged Rs 2500 for an evening, which in the mid-1960s was more than the monthly income of most families in Dongri. On the other hand, he could have kept the jacket worth Rs 1,80,000 and become a prince from a pauper.

'Ask, man, whatever you desire.'

Iqbal took out from his pocket the bill of the florist from Taj Hotel and placed it before Singh. 'What's this?' Singh looked at Iqbal confused.

'Rs 100 for the flowers, plus Rs 18.50 for the taxi fare.'

Singh burst out laughing like a firecracker. Till then, Kiran had been looking at both of them by turns, like a spectator at a tennis match. She now focused her gaze on Iqbal and realized that her seductive body, which made all men weak, was a fistful of dust for this young man. He had not accepted her, even for free. Singh doubled up laughing.

*

My cartoons may not have made readers laugh, but they did tickle them. I had started with *Chitralekha*. My cartoons had also been carried by the *Times of India*. In *Chet Machhandar*, I had discontinued my cartoon strip, which was called 'Batukbhai', and introduced a one-page cartoon feature called 'Prof. Chhelbatau' instead. It met with instant success. In *Ramakadu*, my trio of mischievous cartoon characters, Sonu, Bhagu and Lakhudi were a rage among the Gujarati readers, especially children.

The first two years at art school are for general grounding, to find our voice. Quite early, I discovered that I had a talent for line drawing. It paid off. On standing second in the first year, my tuition fee was waived and I also got a scholarship. Yet art material was so expensive that I needed a part-time job. I confided in Mohan Barodia, a friend of Mushtaq Jalili.

Those days, Mohan, who had also become my close friend, was an assistant with famous film director Shakti Samanta. After pondering over my problem for quite some time, he finally said, 'Aabid! I've only one solution to your problem and that's the film industry. I can get you a job there. But you will have to do donkey work.'

I asked for a night to decide. After giving it serious thought, I felt that this was the only field where I could express my feelings, because filmmaking involves several forms of art. Also, I was not in a position to accept a ten-to-five job anyway. In the film industry, I would be required only when a film was being shot.

*

I joined Samanta's team. The film was called *Singapore*. Mohan was the chief assistant director there. He had two juniors working under him. I was given the fourth position. Like in government offices, where a peon is sarcastically referred to as a 'third-grade officer', I was the fourth assistant director—my work was even lowlier than that of a government peon.

After a shot was ready, I was required to sweep the floor and mop it with a damp cloth. Sometimes, I had to run to the property room carrying the sandals of the lead actress or to the make-up room with a cup of tea for the actor. Amid such menial work, one day I was given an important task and that was to give the 'clap' with the clapperboard—my first step towards direction.

I was ecstatic. Here was an ocean of knowledge for me to dive into. It used to take two to three hours between shots to change the lighting. I started reading during these breaks. I began with Saratchandra Chattopadhyay's classic *Devdas*, sitting in one corner of the set. Saratbabu was Jalili's favourite writer and he insisted that I read all his books.

The shooting took one and a half years to complete, by which time I had read all of Saratbabu's works. A new world had opened before me. Powerful Bengali characters floated before my eyes. For the first time, I was inspired.

If Saratbabu can write a book, why can't I?

I would provoke myself in this way from time to time in order to push myself in every area of creative life. In the field of cartoons, my aim had been to achieve what Walt Disney accomplished, while in the field of painting, Van Gogh challenged me. Now in literature, Saratbabu became my goal.

*

Iqbal's target was Singh. As he came closer to Singh, his resolve grew firmer. Singh also liked him. Who would not like an honest young man who offered namaz five times a day, did not have any vices and was educated, daring and sharp?

Like Mohan Barodia had started my new life from the lowest rung, Singh did the same for Iqbal. He was assigned the job of a 'carrier'—like a college graduate being made a school fresher again. Iqbal was not interested in the work, but he kept quiet. It was not yet time to fly.

The vacations were over and college had reopened. From the first year, Iqbal was promoted to 'inter'. He could join a medical college if he did well this year. For that, he needed to study hard. He decided to join Bhola Coaching Classes.

While stepping back on the college campus, he remembered Kusum—the girl with a sharp nose, a determined chin and a clean, intelligent gaze. He stopped for a while. *Who was she?* She was like any other student in his class. Whenever they came across each other, they would smile formally and go their own ways.

He also knew that Kusum was in love with another boy. He had seen her getting into that young man's car more than once. Yet, he felt disturbed. *What did Kusum think seeing him climb down the drainpipe? Had his image as a gentleman been wiped off her mind? Why was he bothered by such questions?* But the very next moment, he got the answer and his feet headed towards the lift. *How did it matter if his image had received a battering? It had been about two months since that incident. Perhaps she had forgotten about it over the vacations.*

*

The first hour was free. He took the lift to the fourth floor and sat in the library. The book *Baburnama* lay in front of him. He was not interested in literature, but he loved books from which he could learn something new about religions. He was particularly interested in studying Islam.

He wanted to know why, like men, religions too grew old? Why, like the soul leaves the body, virtue leaves religion, making it defunct? Why did blind followers proudly hug the corpse of religion?

He got up after about an hour to return the book. Kusum, who was turning the pages of a magazine, got up too. His attention was drawn towards her. Their eyes met. For the first time, he observed that she had an impressive face, handsome, rather than beautiful. Cinnamon eyes, ebony hair and a wide, white smile. She gave the impression of a sound mind in a sound body.

She smiled.

Both of them came out of the library together.

'You forgot to return my smile today,' she reminded him.

'I'd have definitely returned it had that been a regular one.'

'Oh! Was it a special one?'

'Wasn't it?'

'You are a strange fellow.'

'Thanks for the compliment.'

'To be frank, I've been flooded with questions since I saw you in the first year.'

Iqbal just listened while walking with her.

'I've never seen you carrying comics or cheap paperbacks. Even today, you were reading a translation of *Baburnama*, a heavy historical volume.'

Iqbal was excited. Forgetting everything, he blurted out, 'Do you know who imposed a ban on cow slaughter first?'

'Babur?'

'True. Our library is a treasure trove of knowledge. We can see the world through its windows.'

'You're right!' she agreed, stopping near the lift. 'But I prefer to look at the world from my balcony.'

This simple statement hit Iqbal like a bolt of lightning. He squirmed as questions swam before his eyes. *What was her motive? Was she amused with what she had seen from the balcony or was she disturbed? Why had she punched him with an iron fist within her velvet glove?* He retreated into a chilly silence, pretending to be unfazed. He pondered over her words. One thing was certain: she meant well for Iqbal, else she would not have kept him in mind—that is if her statement 'I've been flooded with questions ever since I saw you first' was to be believed. Truth be told, she had been observing him since the first year of college.

As the lift arrived, both of them entered quietly. The two young hearts, chatting like intimate friends a few moments ago, had become strangers. Kusum, obliquely observing the changing colours on Iqbal's face, sensed that she had touched a sore spot.

'Sorry, did I say something wrong?'

Faced with a direct question, he reflexively blurted out, 'Oh, no.'

'Then why are you silent?'

'I was asking myself how different is the view of the world when seen from the window and from the balcony.'

The lift stopped and Kusum opened the door. 'Did you get your answer?'

'In the first case, we get a limited view because we are constricted by the limits of the window frame. In the second, we get an unlimited view because there is no obstruction. But if a person sees, hears and speaks within the limits of his or her needs, they will never be sorry.'

With this sharp comeback, he stepped out of the lift and, without turning back, went towards the classroom.

*

In the evening, he registered with Bhola Coaching Classes and reached Natraj Hotel. Kusum was still in his thoughts. *Was it necessary to get even?* The answer was negative. However, he was compelled to do so because it had become part of his nature. In the world of crime, in which he lived, it was customary to reply to a brick with a rock.

On seeing Singh, he closed Kusum's chapter and opened a new one. He had made up his mind to put an end to his role as a carrier. 'Please understand, Singh,' he sat on the sofa facing him, trying to persuade Singh as he relaxed on the double bed, 'No one employs a graduate as a peon. My condition is exactly like that. The work of delivering jackets from one place to another belongs to untrained rookies. You must have realized by now that I'm not that.'

Singh listened to him attentively, took a sip from the crystal glass and asked, 'What do you want?'

'Crossing.'

Crossing, in underworld parlance, meant unloading contraband goods from one ship to another at mid-sea. He had accompanied Rashid Parkar once—though only as a porter. But Iqbal was born to give orders, not to receive them.

'Have some patience,' Singh said, 'You'll be promoted at the appropriate time.'

'I want to know when that time will come.'

'Very soon, the boss is pleased with you.'

'Boss?'

'There is someone above me too.'

For the first time, Iqbal felt that he had made the wrong choice. Singh was merely one step of a long ladder.

13

Shakti Samanta's film ended and with it went my job. Before I could experience the pangs of unemployment, Mushtaq Jalili succeeded in selling his story 'Begana' to producer–director Sadashiv Rao Kavi.

After a series of failures, another of Jalili's stories was to be made into a film. He introduced me to the new producer as an assistant director. I got a new job.

In those days, actor Dharmendra had just arrived in Bombay to try his luck. He had signed a few B- and C-grade films like *Dil Bhi Tera Hum Bhi Tere*. *Begana* was Dharmendra's first social message drama—his first family film. This was an excellent opportunity for him to work with a successful director, Sadashiv Rao Kavi. Kavi had already made a name for himself with *Bhabhi Ki Chudiyan* that starred Balraj Sahni and Meena Kumari.

There was only one assistant director, Prem Kumar, in the unit. He alone handled the work of three assistants. After I joined him as junior assistant, he transferred a bulk of his workload to me. That also gave me more opportunities to learn. I gained experience in new fields like song-recording, editing and dubbing.

During the shooting of my previous film, *Singapore*, my work was confined to Bombay. I did not go with the unit

when it went abroad to shoot. Being the second-in-command
in the direction team here, I received my first opportunity to
go out of Bombay for a location shoot. The place was Agra. A
song was to be shot in the lawns of the Taj Mahal.

If my memory serves me right, the five-star hotel,
Clarks Shiraz, had opened in Agra the same month. We had
reservations there. Dharmendra was staying in the room next
to mine. He was a friendly and happy-go-lucky person, and I
had an amiable temperament too, so we got along well.

Dharmendra had that special quality of easily mixing
with anyone, just like sugar mixes with milk. He could put
his arm around the shoulder of the spot boy in the unit and
chat like they were childhood friends. Perhaps this was the
key to his success.

I was interested in his life, in what he said. Mostly, he
would talk and I would listen. We would return to the hotel
every evening after the shoot wrapped for the day. He would
open a bottle and start talking. The more he drank the more
cheerful the atmosphere would become.

'Aabid, would you like to succeed in life?' He would ask
me invariably after polishing off half the bottle.

I would give him the same reply, 'Who doesn't want to
succeed?'

'Then you have to drink.' He would place the bottle
before me. 'Start today. Be great tomorrow!'

I would take the bottle from him and change the topic.
This continued for a few days. Then one day, he grew wise
to my tactic. That day, instead of handing me the bottle, he
prepared a peg.

'Take it.'

I had never tasted liquor. Alcohol never held any charm
for me. Though I had smoked a few cigarettes as a child, I was
never addicted. Liquor had not been a part of my upbringing.

Since early childhood, I remembered being told that Islam forbade liquor.

'TAKE IT!' Dharmendra yelled.

I tasted liquor for the first time. I liked it. It dispelled the fatigue of the day-long shoot. That night I slept soundly and woke up fresh and cheerful.

I had one peg with Dharmendra every night for as long as we stayed in Agra. That was my limit. I did not want to get drunk and lose my senses. I just wanted to keep my mind and body well-oiled.

I have come to accept certain truisms with regard to liquor. Never touch it when you are in trouble or feeling depressed. If someone drinks in sorrow, the urge to drink more will take him over. This was the tragedy of Devdas. First, he consumed liquor, then, liquor consumed him. It is true that liquor is like a poisonous snake. But even snake venom can be an elixir for one who knows how to control it. In the hands of the wise, liquor awakens the ruddy glow of life in a dull face.

*

Iqbal, meanwhile, had lost the radiance on his face. He was facing several problems all at once. After joining Singh's gang, he had got stuck on the first rung. He had no interest in doing the work of a delivery boy: he wanted to rise to the top, and fast.

The other problem cropped up in college. Kusum's boyfriend, Sharad, got suspicious. It became obvious that Kusum was giving special attention to Iqbal. Sharad presumed that he was trying to woo her.

Iqbal's third problem was unexpected. His two younger brothers, Razzak and Firoze, were still in school. Firoze, like him, was devoted to his studies, but Razzak had lost interest. His grades were plummeting. In the last examinations, he had failed three subjects. As for the other subjects, the less said the better.

Iqbal was not unaware of it. One day, some boys from the lane turned up at his door. Iqbal was about to leave for college when they blocked his way. He saw blood dripping from the face of the boy standing in the middle.

In a flash, Iqbal's past came back to taunt him. He recalled the day when he had broken Ali's nose. Then too the boys from the street had come to complain to his father. Hussain Ali had beaten him black and blue.

Today, he had taken his father's place. History was repeating itself. He had no solution. Knowing Razzak, he was certain his brother would not improve even if he walloped him. Perhaps, he thought, persuasion would have a better impact.

He pacified the boys and went to college where he saw Sharad leaning on his car, accompanied by a gang of five others, waiting for him. Pretending to be unaware of their presence, Iqbal continued walking. The moment he came close, Sharad raised his hand and blocked his way. 'What's the hurry?'

Iqbal looked straight into his eyes. 'I come here to study, not to fritter away my father's money.'

Sharad caught him by the collar and pulled his face towards him. 'I thought as much, that you come here only to study and not to romance girls. So remember, if you ever try to make a pass at Kusum, you won't go home in one piece.'

Iqbal did not consider it worthwhile to react. He knew that Sharad took great pride in his strength. Besides, he had his cronies for backup. Iqbal did not want to play hero and challenge them. At least in the college, he wanted to maintain his image as a well-behaved and serious student.

Sharad shoved him before releasing him. Iqbal smoothed his crumpled shirt and entered the college.

*

It was the day of the biology practicals. For the first time, the students were to dissect a frog and study the external and internal structures of its anatomy. One preserved specimen was kept on its back on each table in the lab amidst seven students.

The table allotted to Iqbal included Kusum. Sharad saw this from a distance and his eyes turned bloodshot, but he was helpless. He also knew that Iqbal had nothing to do with it. The dissection tables were allotted in alphabetical order. Both Iqbal and Kusum's last names began with the letter 'R' which is why they were standing side by side.

Iqbal noticed Sharad from the corner of his eye and felt uneasy as well, but he too was equally helpless. Had he been given the option to switch tables, he would have. He neither wanted to hurt anyone's feelings nor invite trouble unnecessarily. Finally, accepting the situation, he requested the lecturer, 'Sir, with your permission, can I begin dissecting the frog?'

The lecturer was surprised. Today was the first day of biology practicals. He was to demonstrate to the students how to dissect a frog. But he did not know that Iqbal had come prepared. At Bhola Coaching Classes he had seen the dissection of frogs. He had tried it at home too. It was child's play for him now.

Kusum shuddered. There was a great difference between Kusum and Iqbal's upbringing. He was a non-vegetarian while Kusum grew up as a strict vegetarian in a Jain family. She could hardly bear to watch the dissection of a frog, let alone perform it. She began feeling queasy.

She wanted to escape from the class, but that was not possible. She too wanted to join medical college and become a doctor. If she could not watch, how would she dissect? If she could not dissect a frog, how would she operate on a human body?

She suppressed her feelings and looked at the frog nervously. Iqbal had a scalpel in his hand. Like a surgeon, he held it on the frog's neck and slowly sliced through the muscles and breast bone. The rest of the students watched in awe as the frog's belly opened up.

Kusum's eyes widened. Her mouth was agape. She felt nauseous. She put her hand over her mouth. This did not help. Darkness engulfed her. Swooning with dizziness, she fell on Iqbal. Throwing the scalpel on the table, Iqbal held her in his hands. She was unconscious.

The lecturer rushed from the front of the class, while Sharad leapt from the left. The lecturer gave Sharad a piercing look that made him return to his table. Iqbal was still standing in his place, holding Kusum. He was caught in a bind.

The lecturer motioned to him. Iqbal followed, carrying Kusum. They crossed the passage and came to the staff room. Iqbal laid Kusum down on a long table. The lecturer switched on the fan.

As the blades moved with a whirring sound, Kusum came back to her senses. She stared at the moving fan for a while. Suddenly, she remembered everything and sat up.

'I'm sorry, sir,' she said softly to the lecturer. Then she glanced at Iqbal and looked down embarrassed.

'Sir, my experiment is incomplete. Can I go back to the lab?' asked Iqbal.

'Sure . . .'

Kusum stepped down from the table. 'Iqbal! I'm coming with you.'

Iqbal stopped near the door of the staffroom. He was as surprised as the lecturer.

'It is not compulsory,' the lecturer said.

'Sir, if I don't get rid of this revulsion, how will I be able to progress?'

She proceeded towards the class.

'What happened?' she asked Iqbal.

'Don't you know?'

'I only know that suddenly there was this darkness before my eyes and I passed out.'

'You passed out and fell into my arms,' Iqbal chuckled. 'I carried you here in my arms.'

'Really!'

'What's there to be surprised about?'

'Did you not find me a bit heavy?'

Iqbal stopped and looked at her. This time, Kusum did not lower her gaze. They looked deep into each other's eyes. In those few tender moments, Iqbal realized that Kusum loved him sincerely.

*

When Iqbal arrived at Singh's hotel room in the evening, Singh was not there. But Kiran was. It was she who answered the door and welcomed him in. He wondered where Singh, who always came before 7 p.m., had disappeared.

Before entering the room, he asked Kiran, 'When is he expected?'

'I don't know.'

He was about to turn away when Kiran said, 'He has asked you to wait.'

Iqbal entered and Kiran shut the door firmly behind him. He became alert, though there was no reason to be.

Nobody keeps the door open. And if the room belongs to a smuggler, the question of leaving the door open does not arise at all.

He crossed the bed, sat on a sofa and looked at Kiran. She was at the window. 'Are you afraid of me?' she asked impishly, focusing her kohl-lined eyes upon him.

Iqbal had not expected such a question. Truth be told, he was nervous. His heartbeat had increased because he was sitting alone in a closed room with a girl—and Kiran was not just any ordinary college girl. Kiran sensed his uneasiness.

In response to her question, he compressed his lips and mutely gestured a 'no'.

'Then why are you sitting on the edge?' she said, chuckling. 'Rest your back. Be comfortable . . .'

It was true that he was sitting upright on the edge of the sofa as if someone was about to attack him. Kiran moved across from the window, stopped in front of him, put her hands on his shoulder and gently pushed him so that his back rested on the sofa. She then sat on the bed opposite him.

Until now, Iqbal had not really looked at her properly. Now he had no other option but to face her. If he did not look at her, he ran the risk of betraying his shyness to her.

'Am I not beautiful?'

'You are.'

'Am I not young?'

'But of course.'

'What would be my age?'

'Seventeen?'

'Right. Yet you are ignoring me?'

Iqbal wondered where she was heading with this line of inquiry.

'I'm not accustomed to staring at the opposite sex.'

'If one doesn't look at a beautiful girl, it can be construed as an insult to her beauty.'

'My religion doesn't say so.'

'What does it say?'

'One should lower one's eyes before women.'

'I'm not a woman. I'm a girl.'

'What do you want?'

'I want to talk to you for a few minutes like a friend.'

Iqbal could not believe her.

'Why? What did you have in mind?' Kiran smiled mischievously.

He realized this girl was not as naive as he had thought after their first meeting. On the contrary, she was as sharp as a razor. For the first time, he felt she was worthy of cultivating as a friend.

'What do you think I had in mind?' he asked her instead to wriggle out of the trap.

Kiran laughed. Her white teeth sparkled from behind the sherbet-coloured lips. 'Iqbal! What do you want to hear? The truth or a lie?'

'Whichever suits you.'

'You thought the same as every other man thinks about me—that I was trying to seduce you, right?'

Iqbal accepted the charge.

'But you forgot one thing. It costs Rs 2500 to spend a night with me.'

'Why?'

'Why what?'

'Why did you pick this profession?'

'What if I ask you the same question?'

Iqbal was stunned.

Kiran was selling her body because of some compulsions. Iqbal was involved in trafficking. *What was his compulsion? He had already saved about Rs 5,00,000. What was his excuse now?* He was a delivery boy. He wanted to be in the shoes of his boss. *Why?* Because the profession of smuggling, the dream of that elusive land of milk and honey, had become his blood and was coursing through his veins. It had become contagious and spread all through his body.

He got up. Kiran realized that her words had pierced Iqbal's heart. This pricked at her conscience but she did not stop him.

When he opened the door to step out, Singh stood in front of him like a wall.

Singh put his arm around Iqbal and brought him back into the room. Kiran got up from the bed and returned with a new bottle of whisky from the cupboard.

Singh sat on the bed, reclining on a pillow. He was silent. His clean, square face looked serious. He was tense about something and it was visible in his cold eyes.

Iqbal sat on the sofa to his left. Coming between them, Kiran dialled room service and placed an order for ice cubes and snacks. As she walked up to the window and looked out, the sea waves were breaking on the tetrapods.

Soon, a waiter brought ice cubes, glasses of water and a bowl of pistachios in a tray. First, Singh prepared a peg and downed it in one straight gulp. As if it instilled life into his body, he looked at Iqbal and smiled.

'Now, tell me,' he said, preparing the second peg, 'What do you want to hear first? The good news or the bad news?'

Iqbal's mind was still in turmoil. Kiran's words were reverberating in his ears. His father, Hussain Ali, had given up smuggling after making about Rs 3,00,000. At that moment, he too was thinking along those lines.

If he wanted, he could earn enough interest from the Rs 5,00,000 he had to take care of the household expenses and meet the cost of his college education too without any hassle. What was the need to go deeper into the quicksand now?

'Iqbal! What happened?'

'Nothing.'

'Did that slut say anything?'

On hearing herself being referred to in such an uncomplimentary way, Kiran turned. Singh looked at her questioningly. She just shrugged and turned again to look out of the window.

Taking the first sip from the second peg, Singh spoke to Iqbal. 'Okay. Let me give you the good news first. Your spirits will lift and touch the sky.'

Iqbal stared at him.

'Starting next month, you'll be going for the crossing.'

14

Iqbal's desire to progress in the field of bootlegging had borne fruit. Finally, he was to enter the world of crossing—to leave the first rung and climb on to the next. Now, the sea would be his territory.

He thought for a while and asked Singh, 'How did the boss suddenly become so benevolent?'

'Because your stars are bright. Else, there are so many kids like you who just waste away as delivery boys.'

Iqbal still could not understand. His sixth sense told him that something was amiss.

'Now the bad news,' Singh continued, finishing his second peg. 'Last week, one of our launches was seized by customs.'

'What was the value of the consignment?'

'Rs 2,00,00,000.'

Iqbal's brain started working. The launch had left the shore and gone past the lighthouse into the sea, up to 40 *bams* [one bam equals six feet] for crossing. There, it picked up the consignment mid-sea from a Dubai ship and, while returning, was intercepted by the customs' motorboat.

'How many of our boys got caught?'

'There were eight. Seven jumped into the sea and escaped. Only one held his ground.'

'Why?'

'Because the captain goes down with his ship!' Singh said lightly and then added, 'Hamid Bhadak was the captain. He had been going with the team for crossing for years.'

Now, the scenario became clear. Hamid's place had fallen vacant. Iqbal had all the attributes to replace him.

'Don't we have customs officials on our payroll?'

'Absolutely right.'

'Then?'

'This operation was carried out by the marine guards.'

Naval ships keep a constant watch over the country's sea frontiers. Normally, whenever the captain of such a ship spots smugglers at sea, he alerts the Coast Guard. Once the Navy is involved, it becomes imperative for the Coast Guard and customs to look into the matter seriously. In rare cases, Navy officers arrest the pirates and hand them over to the customs. This was the worst possible situation. And that is what had happened with Singh's launch.

After a while, Iqbal asked, 'What will happen to Hamid?'

'He will be hanged.'

'I can't believe it. Leave aside a sentence, I haven't heard or read about a person involved in trafficking ever being hanged.'

'You aren't wrong. Hamid stabbed a customs official who died on the spot.'

'But why?'

'There was an altercation. As it is, Hamid is short-tempered. He could not control himself.'

Normally, if a member of the gang is arrested, one of the best lawyers is engaged to free him. Had not Hamid committed this stupid act, he too would have come out on bail within twenty-four hours and resumed work.

Iqbal was thinking fast. His thoughts were getting mixed up again. There was a forked road ahead of him: one path was full of adventure, the other was dull and drab. One promised thrill and romance while the other led to a mundane life. There was a challenge at every step on the crooked path while the straight road was flat.

Willingly, Iqbal opted for the adventurous path. Knowingly or unknowingly, in that moment, he ignored the ancient way of the prophets and adopted the road that Allah did not approve of.

Hussain Ali too had considered the same truth but decided to follow the path of divinity, the path that Allah liked. Of course, at that time Hussain Ali was over forty-five years old. He had learnt a lot in life. Iqbal was still to gain that experience. He had just crossed the age of twenty. He had youth, enthusiasm and vigour. His heart was craving to do something daring, something unimaginable. He could not give up the opportunity of crossing, could not resist the alluring call of the sea. He had experienced the thrill once already. He thought about it calmly and estimated the risk involved: crossing meant not just the occasional possibility of being robbed at sea, but putting one's life in jeopardy every night that he went out into the darkness.

Those were the initial days of gold smuggling, and they were really difficult. The Arab launches carrying jackets with gold biscuits from Dubai were robbed not just by the pirates but also by the Coast Guard. Instead of seizing the goods, the officials would loot them and sink the launch. Still, the 1960s can be described as the golden period of gold smuggling. This was because a whopping Rs 300–400 crore of black money was transacted during this decade.

*

I stopped him at this point. 'Sufi, I still haven't understood the exact meaning of smuggling.'

'We have discussed this in detail.'

'If smuggling means not paying duty on the import or export of goods, which section of the law is a case of smuggling tried under? If, for example, a trafficker is caught with gold, can he not be freed after paying the customs duty?'

'Aabid Bhai. If this could be settled so easily, how would lawyers buy imported cars and magistrates live in luxury?'

He explained in detail: several court judgments use the word 'smuggling' but till date they have failed to define it. If the government catches a smuggler even today, he is charged under sections 165 (1-A) and 165 (1-B) of the Customs Act, which prohibit the possession of contraband goods and not paying customs duty on the import and export of goods.

If there is more than one person involved, they are charged under section 120 (B) of the Indian Penal Code instead of the above Act. This section now accuses two or more persons of indulging in criminal conspiracy.

The judgement which most clearly defines 'criminal conspiracy' dates back to the case of Mirza Akbar during the British era: on page 259 of the Privy Council's judgments, the judge noted that 'the conspiracy comes to an end after the goods are confiscated'.

The same judgment was cited in 1979 in the case of the disappearance of the cans of the film *Kissa Kursi Ka*, in which Sanjay Gandhi was charged with criminal conspiracy. Following the recovery of the cans from a godown, Gandhi was absolved of the charges.

In short, the law on criminal conspiracy is as weak as the law on smuggling. Hence, it is not surprising that the law is unable to cause any harm to the traffickers.

*

When Iqbal returned home after meeting Singh, he felt pride at seeing his younger brother sitting in a corner completing his homework. Firoze had the same zeal for studies that he had. The confidence of getting admission to college on his own merit was visible on his face. *But what about Razzak?* The youngest one had still not returned home. Iqbal looked at the clock. It was 9 p.m. He looked at his mother. Gul Banu was busy preparing dinner.

'Where's Razzak?' Iqbal asked.

'Must be loafing around with his friends.'

'You should make him study!'

'If only he listened to me!'

Iqbal changed into a vest and pyjamas and sat cross-legged on the floor to have his dinner. With each morsel, he thought of his youngest brother.

He had cajoled and threatened Razzak but this had had no effect on him. On the contrary, he had gone from bad to worse. Sometimes, Razzak would come home after thrashing someone and at other times with a black eye himself.

'Did he come home after school?'

Before Gul Banu could answer, Firoze stuffed his books into his bag and replied, 'After tea, he slipped away to play.'

A little later, he added, '*Bhaijaan*, neither is he interested in studies nor in school. I told him to do his homework with me, but he refused.'

'What did he say?'

'He didn't want to be a barrister.'

'What does he want to become?'

'The don of Dongri.'

'Did he say that?'

'No, but he says such things while playing in the street.'

Iqbal realized that the situation was out of control: words no longer had any effect on Razzak. After finishing dinner,

Iqbal washed his hands and brought out a cane from behind the cupboard.

Gul Banu looked at him from the corner of her eyes. 'Are you going to punish him?' Appalled at the thought, she put away the used utensils in a corner of the kitchen area.

'I'll thrash him till he realizes his errors.'

'Did you realize yours?'

'What?'

'Your father used to thrash you. Did that stop you?'

Iqbal was forced to think again. His father used to cane him mercilessly whenever he came home after beating somebody. The next day, he would hunt down the boy who had complained and take revenge. *Could Razzak's life end up just like his?*

He threw away the cane. Gul Banu picked it up and hid it behind the cupboard. Iqbal realized that it was only natural that his mother should pamper her youngest the most.

Razzak appeared exactly at 10.30 p.m.

Both his hands were behind his back and his shifty eyes were looking for a way out; he had not expected Iqbal to be waiting for him.

Slowly, he started backing out. He was about to escape when Iqbal leapt and caught him by the neck. 'What are you hiding?' Iqbal asked, dragging him inside. Firoze quietly looked at him from near the window. Gul Banu also thought it wise to remain quiet.

'Show me! What are you holding in your hands?'

'I won't.'

Unwillingly, Iqbal slapped Razzak so hard that it left an imprint on his face. Razzak hit the wall swirling and collapsed. The three plates of bone china that he held tightly also fell down and broke into pieces.

Iqbal looked at him wide-eyed. It did not take him much time to understand that these were stolen plates. He lifted

Razzak by his wrist and slapped him again, twice. 'From where did you steal these plates?'

In an equally loud voice, Razzak replied, 'I've not stolen them.'

'From where did you get them?'

'There was a goods truck parked in the lane. All the boys were removing plates from it, so I too pulled out three.'

'Didn't you feel ashamed?' He raised his hand again, but Gul Banu stepped forward and held him back.

'Enough! That's enough! You want to kill my boy?'

'Maa . . .' Iqbal turned towards his mother, 'If you don't teach him a lesson now, you will be digging your own grave.'

*

That night, Iqbal could not sleep peacefully. He kept writhing in pain. He did not want his brothers to take up the path he had chosen. On the contrary, his innermost desire was that both his younger brothers pursue their studies, join college and progress in life. If they wanted to go abroad for higher studies, the road was clear. They should secure good jobs, get married and lead a happy life.

Hussain Ali had had similar dreams for Sufi.

Iqbal was lying on the bed. He had taken his father's place. Both the brothers had made their beds on the floor and were sleeping by their mother's side. He gazed at Razzak steadily till sleep overcame him.

When he got up in the morning, both the brothers were getting ready for school. It was 9.30 a.m. He was surprised. He had never slept till so late. Normally, he used to get up before the muezzin's call for morning prayers. After brushing his teeth, he used to offer namaz at the mosque. Today, there had been a break in the routine.

He smiled at Razzak and beckoned him to come close. He wanted to affectionately hug him and apologize. He wanted to talk to him warmly for a few minutes to forget last night's episode.

Razzak shifted the school bag from his shoulder on to his back and moved towards him. But suddenly, he turned and left. Firoze was waiting for him on the stairs. Both brothers climbed down together.

Iqbal was not offended. The young one was naive, still angry. Everything would be forgotten in a day or two and Razzak would be his usual self again. He would become a worthy student once again. But despite reassuring himself repeatedly, why was he feeling uneasy? *Why wasn't he able to believe his own words? Was he deceiving himself?*

*

Puzzling with these questions, he reached college and, from a distance, noticed Sharad. He was waiting for Iqbal with his gang by his car. Iqbal became cautious but did not hesitate. Stopping would have meant displaying weakness. Turning his back would have meant admitting cowardice. He was not a coward. Kusum collapsing on him was not his fault. Lifting Kusum and taking her to the staffroom as per the lecturer's instruction was not a crime. Then why should he be afraid?

He came straight towards the blockade and nonchalantly held Sharad by the neck. 'If you think I'll be frightened by your five puppies, then you are mistaken.'

Sharad was stunned. He could barely utter a few words. 'But . . . but, we hang around here . . . . just like that.'

'I'll tell you once again,' Iqbal said releasing his neck, 'I'm neither interested in your girl nor in any other. If you ever try to poke me again, I'll break your bones along with your car. Get it?'

'Buddy, you are getting upset for no reason.'

'Were you not waiting to catch me off guard?'

'Not at all!' Sharad had gauged the situation. 'On the contrary, we wanted to invite you to my birthday party.'

Iqbal knew that he was lying. His offensive had turned the tables. Sharad was extending a hand of friendship. Iqbal accepted the invitation.

The lecture had already started. Iqbal sat quietly in his place. Kusum's seat was next to his. She glanced at him. Iqbal's entire attention was on the lecturer. This year was important for him. If he got good marks, he would get admission into medical college. It was not just important for him to get through the examinations but also to score a distinction. This was also the reason he attended Bhola Coaching Classes in the evenings.

*

After having lunch in the canteen, Kusum came to the backstage area of the theatre adjoining Bhavan's college looking for Iqbal. He was offering namaz at the time. She watched him quietly. The theatre was empty. There was one dim bulb lighting up the wing. Under the pale light, Iqbal's figure resembled that of a shadow puppet. At times, he stood up straight with both hands extended to seek blessings and at times placed his hands on his knees and bent forward.

After the namaz, he sat for his closing prayers. Kusum advanced slowly and came beside him. He gestured to her to keep silent, finished his prayers and stood up.

'Do you come here often?' Kusum asked.

'It's very peaceful here at this hour. Besides, no one disturbs me.'

'Does my presence here disturb you?'

'Not me, but your boyfriend is already disturbed.'

'Who told you that he is my boyfriend?'

Iqbal thought for a while before replying. 'How else would you describe a boy who considers you his personal property?'

'Madness. Craziness. One-sided love.'

'If this is true, then I think you should clarify it.'

'I tried once.'

'What did he say?'

'He asked me who was in my life if not him.'

'What did you tell him?'

'I've yet to reply.'

'You aren't bound to. Yet, if there is someone you love, you should tell him.'

Placing both her hands around his neck, she became emotional, 'Iqbal, I love you. Look into my eyes. You live in every pore of my body.'

Slowly disentangling her hands from his neck, he said, 'That's called madness, craziness, one-sided love.'

Kusum was shocked. She felt as if someone had crushed her dreams just like someone crushes a cigarette stub.

'Kusum, I know you are disturbed by my frankness, but it's true. Neither do I love any other girl nor do I have time for love. Don't you know me?'

The sight of Iqbal climbing down a pipe from Sagar Darshan building flashed through Kusum's mind. Into that image merged the ringing of a bell, making her realize that recess was over. There was no scope for arguing now.

*

Iqbal brutally uprooted the sapling of first love before it could bloom. The same year, love sprouted its tiny leaves for the first time in my life. I had time to nurture this fragrant plant. There was peace in my life.

I had two sources of income: journalism and the film industry. My cartoons were being published in different magazines. After introducing four pages in colour in the monthly *Ramakadu*, a two-page cartoon comic 'Doctor Chinchu Ke Chamatkar' was launched in the Hindi magazine *Parag*. There was additional income coming in from the film industry. Moreover, I was getting a scholarship from art school.

We were drawing still life that day. There was a wooden block in the middle of the room covered by a violet sheet. On it was placed a transparent jar containing a sunflower. Behind it was a white china plate.

All the students were sitting in a semicircle around it and drawing the arrangement on a sheet of paper with a charcoal stick. My right hand was busy drawing and the left was groping for an eraser. Not finding it, I looked away from the drawing and started looking under bench. To the left. To the right. Suddenly, my eyes were transfixed. Suraiyya was sitting by my side.

This was our second year in college. We must have crossed each other on several occasions, on the stairs and in the classroom, but had never cared to look at each other. Today, as we locked eyes, it was like we were meeting for the first time. An electric current seemed to have passed through us in those few moments.

Suraiyya was neither as beautiful as a fairy nor as petite as a poet would imagine nor as buxom as a photographer's model. Her skin was wheatish, her nature was quiet and her eyes were mesmerizing.

I had not fallen in love, but I jumped willingly into it. I was to conquer the peaks of success one after another. My first novel, *Tutela Farishta* (Broken Angels), was to be born after the tragic end of this unforgettable affair.

*

Iqbal too had made progress in the underworld. He had climbed one more rung. The boss, whom he had never met, was pleased with him. He had given Iqbal an opportunity, through Singh, to experiment.

Iqbal was standing at the entrance of the hotel room. Singh was drinking alone sitting on the double bed. Iqbal's eyes scanned the room for Kiran and settled on Singh's square face.

'Relax!' Singh made him sit comfortably near him and handed him one portion of a half-torn Rs 5 note. Before he could ask, Singh said, 'You will be going for crossing on Saturday night.'

The window was open and a salty wind was blowing in from the sea, making the curtains wave. Had Kiran been there, her hair too would have danced like waves.

'How much are the goods worth?'

'Five crores, but our stuff is just Rs 1.5 crore. The rest belongs to the syndicate,' Singh explained.

'Syndicate' meant a group of four to five small traffickers. Sometimes they got their goods loaded with a big player's consignment from Dubai on a commission basis. In a way it was a joint venture.

Iqbal's eyes again drifted to the window. The room was the same, the walls were the same, the sofa was the same, the curtains were the same and yet something seemed amiss.

'Kiran hasn't come today,' Singh remarked, reading Iqbal's mind.

He stared at Singh and wondered: *was he really missing Kiran?*

15

I am yet to unravel one of nature's mysteries: why were there always more girls in my life than boys? Even today, my friends tend to be women. Society tries to label such relationships: is the woman my sister? My cousin? My girlfriend? There has to be some socially defined role. Whenever society's questions find their way to someone's lips, I am compelled to reply: 'If two men can be best buddies, and two women can be best friends for life, why can't a man and a woman simply be best friends?'

My answer did not satisfy anyone then and, even today, my friends are suspicious. I do not care because I know that society is used to seeing everything in black and white. Anything without a label becomes cause for worry and fear.

It was an altogether different matter with Suraiyya. Despite being in her second year at the J.J. School of Arts, no boy had ever entered her life. It was love at first sight.

We were drawn to each other like the opposite poles of a magnet. Yet, I did not have the courage to invite her to watch a film or a play with me. I did not even have the nerve to take her to the family room of an Irani restaurant for a cup of tea.

After thinking about it till late in the night, I made up my mind. Two months had passed since we had grown close. If I didn't take the initiative now, my youth would pass.

'Suraiyya!' I spoke to her the next day, 'Can you come this Saturday?'

She lowered her eyes and then looked up smiling. 'Where to?'

I wanted to say 'picnic', but the word did not find its way to my lips.

'To the zoo!' I was a perfect candidate for the loony bin.

'To the zoo?'

'I want to draw some sketches of birds and animals.'

She did not refuse.

There was a flutter of warmth and excitement in the pit of my stomach. My joy knew no bounds.

*

I started hectic preparations. There were still three days to go before our date. I bought a stylish new shirt and a tin of shoe polish and a brush as my shoes had not been polished for months. I ironed the best pair of trousers I had and put them under the mattress on my cot.

*

On Saturday morning, under the mild January sun, I reached the Victoria Gardens zoo half an hour early. We had fixed our rendezvous for 9 a.m. Just to while away time, I opened my drawing pad and started sketching passers-by.

My sketchbook and I were inseparable. My charcoal pencil produced a running commentary on life. I sketched on buses, in trains, waiting at the dentist's, while eating at Udipi restaurants—indoors or outdoors, it was all the same to me.

I did not have to wait long for Suraiyya. She came fifteen minutes before the appointed time. I couldn't take my eyes off

her. She looked like a fairy in a baby pink churidar. A ribbon
held her hair together in a ponytail. She had a sketchbook in
one hand and a basket in the other. I could not imagine what
the basket contained as it was neatly covered with a white
napkin.

I asked her.

'I've brought some sandwiches and fruit.' I was thrilled.
We were to spend the whole day here, but the idea of lunch
had not occurred to me. Suraiyya had taken charge from our
very first date.

We entered the zoo and, after crossing the vast green
lawn, reached the monkeys' cage. Here, there were both
monkeys and hefty langurs. We started drawing quick sketches
in different poses.

I had collected some information about Suraiyya in the last
two months. She stayed in the girls' hostel on Marine Drive.
That meant her family was not from Bombay. She had come
here for her studies. 'Suraiyya! What does your father do?'

'He died in a plane crash when I was a child.' She had a
faraway look as she spoke. I expressed my regret.

'My mother lives with her two elder brothers and
their families,' she added. 'We have a departmental store in
Mombasa.'

It was evident that she had come from abroad. It was also
obvious that she belonged to a rich family.

'What about your father?' she asked.

'My father too died when I was a kid,' I said and thought
it prudent to give her some more information so that she
didn't remain under any impression that I too belonged to an
affluent family like hers. 'My uncle works in the dock. Our
family survives on his salary,' I added.

We left the monkey cage and walked towards the birds.
'You disappear for a few days every month.' She placed the

basket near her feet and started drawing the birds. 'Where do you go during those days?'

I realized that though I had started taking an interest in her only in the last couple of months, she had probably set her eyes on me much before that.

'I assist during film shoots. That's my secondary source of income.'

'What is the primary source?'

'Journalism.'

She lifted her face from the sketchbook and looked at me. There was a gleam of respect for me in her eyes.

In the afternoon, we ate sandwiches and apples sitting on the grass in Victoria Gardens and had tea in the canteen sitting on wooden benches. It was winter. We did not realize when the sun set.

When I returned home after dropping Suraiyya at her hostel, every cell in my body was tingling with joy. My drawing pad too was full of ecstatic sketches; I had secretly sneaked some sketches of Suraiyya too.

I looked at those sketches till midnight. I heard the clock strike twelve. Finally, I fell asleep at 12.30 a.m.

*

Iqbal was awake. That Saturday night was important for him. It was his first crossing as the leader of a gang. The caravan of two Ambassador cars stopped at Bhaucha Dhakka. It was a dark night. One could see from the jetty the outline of naval ship *Vikrant* which patrolled the sea. It was anchored at a distance. Because its lights were dimmed, it appeared like a shadow.

The lanterns from half a dozen motorboats anchored at the dock were swaying with the gentle waves. Their reflections were swinging too. One of the steam launches, *Al Kabir*, belonged to the gang.

During the day, as a cover, *Al Kabir* ferried passengers between Bombay and the nearby Uran Island. At night, it continued its real job: carrying traffickers for crossings.

Iqbal got down from the car with his men and took his place in the launch. The boatman turned off the lantern and moved the vessel slowly in the direction of the lighthouse. Iqbal stood on the deck. He was wearing a sky-blue sweater over a full-sleeved white shirt. He had a belt around his waist and a pair of white trousers and white shoes.

He had to take extra care to keep them white, but that was not his concern as of now. His eyes were trying to pierce the darkness. The only thing visible to him, besides the lighthouse and the naval ship, was the dark sky on which some stars were twinkling.

He moved from the deck and sat on a bench with his gang. He noticed they were all sitting glumly, shivering in the cold. The only thing interrupting the silence was the whirring sound of the engine and the slapping of the waves against the launch.

*

The thought of Hamid struck Iqbal while glancing at the seven-member crew. It was Hamid who had led these men for a crossing last time. 'Since how many years had Hamid been doing the crossing?' he asked Dagdu who was sitting next to him.

Dagdu was a Maharashtrian with an awful, grating, croaking voice like that of an old crow. But he was a friendly person. He had begun his career as a corrupt coolie at Victoria Terminus railway station. From there he had progressed and joined the gang.

'I've worked with him for nearly six years,' he told Iqbal.

'It must have been at least eight years,' said another man.

'Hamid was lion-hearted, but the bastard had a weakness: his anger. No one could predict when he would explode,' said a third.

Michael, sitting across him, vouched, 'That's why we had secretly nicknamed Hamid 'bhadak' [hot-headed]. The best part was when he came to know about his nickname, he laughed heartily.'

'Not only that,' Dagdu interjected enthusiastically, 'he proudly told his wife also.'

'Is he married?'

'He has seven children. The eldest is in college.'

'How old is Hamid then?'

'Must be over forty, has a slender build but he is not skinny,' croaked Dagdu. 'But, boss, why are you asking us all these questions?'

Iqbal liked being addressed as 'boss'. For the first time, somebody had looked at him with respect.

'Perhaps I can be of help to him.'

'Forget it, man,' said Altaf, a weirdo with a drooping moustache who was sitting next to Michael and had remained silent till now. 'He is beyond help.'

*

As they inched closer to the lighthouse, Iqbal got up. He stood atop the launch. His beady eyes stared into the darkness as if trying to sense danger. After a while, when the siren of 'all clear' sounded in his mind, he took a deep breath of salty air. *Al Kabir* crossed the lighthouse and stopped at a distance. The rendezvous location must have been nearby since the depth of the sea at this point was not more than 40 bams.

This was the place chosen for the crossing. It was somewhere here that the launch from Dubai carrying gold worth Rs 5 crore was to appear. Nothing was visible because of the darkness.

Iqbal fished out a matchbox from the boatman standing behind him, lit a matchstick and held it in his hand. It burnt out shortly. After waiting for a minute, he lit another matchstick. There was no wind, but it was bitterly cold. His hands were shaking.

A few days before, New Year's Eve had been celebrated here. Light bulbs had decorated *Vikrant*, *Shivaji* and other boats, and laser lights had beamed into the skies, turning this same opaque midnight into day.

Iqbal lit the third and last matchstick. When that too burned out, he continued to stare into the darkness. He had performed his duty. He had informed the launch from Dubai about his presence and the location of *Al Kabir* with the lighting of the three matchsticks. Now, it was the turn of the invisible foreign vessel to do so.

After a five-minute wait, the first matchstick was lit. From that distance it looked like a twinkling star. Iqbal's eyes were fixed in that direction. The boatman standing behind him took two steps forward. They watched silently.

Just like Iqbal had lit each matchstick after a minute's interval, three matchsticks burnt out from the launch across. Iqbal threw a glance at the boatman who started *Al Kabir's* engine and ferried them close to the launch from Dubai. After the engine stopped, he extended a boathook towards the opposite launch, fixed it firmly and brought both the launches side by side. His assistant fixed another boathook from under the launch.

Iqbal observed that there were not more than five men on the other launch. Of these, two appeared to be either Indians or Pakistanis. The other three were Arabs. One of them was the leader.

Iqbal took out the torn Rs 5 note kept carefully in his trouser pocket and, extending his hand, gave it to the Arab. He immediately took it and with the help of a small torch, compared it with the other half of the note that he had.

The transfer of gold biscuits worth Rs 5 crore was about to begin at 2 a.m., in pitch darkness under the open sky. There was tension on both sides. No one knew what might happen, but everyone knew that on successful completion of the operation, each of them would get Rs 25,000. Iqbal was to get double the amount.

After confirming that both the portions belonged to the same currency note, the Arab lifted the torch and looked at his face carefully. He had never seen Iqbal before. It was natural for him to want to be fully reassured before handing over the goods, so he threw a question to Iqbal.

'What's the value of the goods?'

'Five crores.'

'To whom does it belong?'

'One and a half crore of goods belongs to us and the rest to the syndicate.'

The Arab was satisfied. He signalled to his men. On this side, all of Iqbal's men took position to accept delivery of the 300 jackets. One took position on the upper deck and another on the lower deck—their work was to keep vigil. In case of a sudden attack, everyone could escape by jumping into the sea. Two entered the cellar. The remaining three placed themselves at intervals between the cellar and Iqbal.

At first, a rope was cast from the opposite launch. Iqbal caught one end and handed it over to Dagdu, who was standing behind him. He in turn gave it to Altaf who was waiting at some distance. Iqbal kept on pulling the rope until one end reached the cellar. The process was similar to pulling the string of a kite after it is cut. But it did not end there.

Like shirts on a clothesline, the jackets started sliding down the rope. There were 100 gold biscuits sewn into the lining of each jacket, and Iqbal kept count as he pulled at the rope. The chain of jackets was passed from one launch to the other and from one hand to another until it reached the cellar.

Michael, one of the two standing inside the cellar, was pulling the jackets along with the rope, while the other disengaged the jackets and stuffed them into jute sacks. Already, five sacks were full.

This was just the beginning. Work was going on at a feverish pitch. There was no question of taking a break until all the jackets arrived safely. As Iqbal's count crossed the figure of 150, a beam of light swept across the sea. Both the launches were illuminated for a second before darkness descended again. Iqbal sat down and held his breath. The Arab, who was passing the jackets from the opposite launch, froze. The beam had come from *Vikrant* that was anchored at a distance.

Had they become suspicious? Had they seen both the launches doing the crossing? The questions were many but the answers were none. Yet, it was necessary to exercise caution. Iqbal's career would end on debut if anything went wrong with his first assignment.

He shot an order to the Arab, 'Make it quick.'

Again, the rope was pulled and the dangling jackets were transferred from one launch to the other. The speed accelerated. When the figure reached 265, another beam of incandescent light from the naval ship pierced through the darkness. This time the searchlight stayed locked on the two launches. They lit up like little floating lamps.

*

A momentary shiver ran down Iqbal's spine. He was certain that he had inherited Hamid's jinx. There was no doubt any more that the naval ship had spotted them. The captain would now immediately inform the customs collector. Shortly after, the Coast Guard would rush in to raid them. An identical catastrophe had befallen Hamid last time.

The beam of light remained steady for a few seconds and then moved away. Silence replaced the light. Every man felt a knot in his stomach. Everyone was unusually quiet.

'Boss!' Dagdu could stay silent no more. 'We should jump into the sea if we want to avoid arrest.'

Michael, Altaf and the rest of the men had stopped working.

Iqbal tried to reassure them, 'Only thirty-five jackets are left.'

'The temptation of these jackets will get us trapped,' Michael argued.

Altaf too concurred, 'It's better we leave the goods and flee.'

'Don't forget, the consignment is worth Rs 5 crore,' said Iqbal and turned towards the Arab. 'Let the rope come.'

As the rope slackened from the other end, Iqbal started pulling it. The jackets started landing near his feet. His colleagues were confused. Taking advantage of their dilemma, Iqbal tried to persuade them. 'This is not just our consignment, the syndicate has also pitched in. It is our duty to save it even at the cost of our lives.'

'But, boss!' said Dagdu, 'If all of us are arrested then the gang's work will come to a standstill.'

'That's my responsibility.'

'What do you mean?'

'I'll take you back to the shore safely.' Pulling the last jacket, he ordered the boatman, 'Start the launch!'

The two boatmen, who were keeping the launches steady side by side, loosened the bamboo and unhooked the vessels. They pressed their boathooks against the outer wall of the other launch to push away.

Meanwhile, Altaf and Dagdu, trepidation etched on their faces, had reached the top deck. According to their calculations, the raid would occur on their way back. They did not want to risk returning in the launch.

Iqbal's problem was that if both of them jumped into the sea, the others would also lose courage and follow suit.

He rushed towards them, caught them by their necks and pulled them back violently. Dagdu roared as he tumbled down on the wooden floor. Altaf was annoyed. He stood up and delivered an unexpected punch. Iqbal felt a pain in his jaw. With his tongue, he explored his mouth and tasted blood.

The blood got his right arm into motion like a spring from which came a punch, a punch as terrible as the pain he felt. Altaf tried to attack again. Stopping his blow with one hand, Iqbal dealt another blow to his nose. He fell down. His nose started bleeding on to his drooping moustache and then on to his shirt. He was not going to forget this incident.

'Who else wants to jump?' Iqbal challenged the other six, readying his fists like a boxer. No one had the guts to look into his bloodshot eyes.

*

Al Kabir started again. Iqbal turned towards the boatman, wiping the blood from his lips with the back of his hand and said, 'There is no need to take the launch back to Bhaucha Dhakka.' The boatman was intelligent. He turned towards Uran Island. Iqbal leaned over to Altaf and offered a friendly hand, 'Come, get up.'

Rubbing his nose with one hand, he took Iqbal's hand with the other and got up. The furrows on their brows eased up. They smiled at each other.

'You were panicking needlessly.' Putting his hand around Altaf's neck magnanimously, Iqbal brought him to the bench. 'Sit! A peg will clear your nose and your head.'

From the boatman, he got a bottle of country liquor, gifted it to him and went to stand atop the launch. From here, he was able to see the faraway lights of Uran Island. As the coast came closer, the lights became brighter and sharper.

He started wondering: *if the captain of the naval ship had informed the customs collector over the phone, why had the Coast Guard not appeared?*

From the roof, he stepped down on to the lower part of the launch and searched far into the darkness to see if he could hear anything. He could neither see the light of any customs boat nor hear any engine.

He presumed that they must have been late. Perhaps they were waiting for *Al Kabir* at its original destination of Bhaucha Dhakka. Anchoring safely at Uran Island, Iqbal was relieved of all tension, but little did he know that the enemy had devised a unique plan of action.

16

There were fifteen sacks in all. Twenty jackets were stuffed into each bag. Each jacket contained a hundred gold biscuits. The consignment worth Rs 5 crore had landed on Uran Island.

There was no other way to ferry the consignment from here to Bombay but by road. The sea route would take just one hour, but the road would take over two. The journey would also be more tiresome.

'Dagdu!' Iqbal beckoned him, 'We need to arrange for a tempo.'

Dagdu was an old member of the gang. 'Boss, I know a transporter here. But . . .' he said doubtfully, 'I'm not very sure if he would be ready to come at this early hour.'

'Call me if he needs convincing.'

Dagdu faded away into the cold fog of dawn.

Iqbal saw that the rest of his men had made seats out of the sacks and were sitting shivering on them. Some were trying to keep warm by smoking a bidi or a cigarette. Altaf was still holding on to the bottle of country liquor and relishing the last few drops.

Iqbal lifted his eyes. The metallic grey sky was changing its colour gradually. The rim of the clouds had begun to turn silver.

On the horizon, across the sea, a roseate glow of light was emerging as Dagdu arrived with a tempo.

Iqbal saw that there were two taxis behind it. He was happy to see Dagdu's wisdom. He had proved his proficiency by arranging for transport at this odd hour on a desolate island.

'Boss,' he said, jumping out of the tempo, 'today is really our lucky day. Some chaps from the tourism department arrived in these taxis last night.'

'How much did the tempo guy want?'

'Thousand bucks.'

'So much?'

A thousand is insignificant in a business of crores. Perhaps if Iqbal hadn't seen poverty and hunger up close, he wouldn't have felt this momentary pinch.

Dagdu added with a chuckle, 'We need to make the payment in advance.'

'All right,' he said, reluctantly handing over ten Rs 100 notes to Dagdu.

'Where is the consignment to be delivered?'

'To our Mazgaon godown.'

The formalities were completed. The consignment was loaded on to the tempo. Before the tempo was ready to move, Iqbal and his men had piled into the taxis. As the caravan started from Uran, the first rays of the morning sun greeted the earth once again.

*

The tempo had a bumpy ride over the uneven rural roads. The two taxis followed it at a cautious distance. The gang had stayed up throughout the night. As the journey began, most of the men dozed off; some started snoring like foghorns.

Iqbal sat wide awake. It was not possible for him to sleep in the taxi. Till the consignment was delivered, he had to stay alert. His prime responsibility was to keep a watch on the tempo, but not because the tempo driver would try to pull a fast one; that didn't worry him. Suppose the tempo caught the attention of some traffic policemen and they stopped the vehicle for random checking, they would all literally be caught napping.

*

The procession of three vehicles crossed the bridge to enter Panvel and turned towards Bombay—past a tea stall where a waiting customs official in mufti noted down the registration numbers of all three vehicles and, barely able to conceal his smile, headed for the nearest phone booth.

*

There was still one and a half hour's journey remaining. Iqbal was sitting next to the driver of the first taxi. The smugglers' modus operandi was time-worn; the risk therefore was extremely high. If only one could reduce the risk, the work could be accomplished more speedily and easily. Take the case of delivery of goods during the crossing. The long-standing practice was that a man from the Dubai launch would hand over the jackets one after another to the man on the boat that had come to receive the consignment. Instead of this, Iqbal had once given Singh the idea that all the jackets could be kept ready for delivery, tied along a rope.

Singh was thick-headed. The idea went in from his right ear and escaped through the left. There was a reason for this too. Whose idea it was? Iqbal's. And who was he? A novice in the field of smuggling. What was his experience in crossing? Zero.

Moreover, though the jackets could be transferred from one boat to another faster this way, there was also the increased possibility of a slip up in counting the jackets because of the speed involved, or worse, even deliberate fraud.

'Singh,' Iqbal had argued, 'till today has it ever happened to you that there were less biscuits in a jacket than you paid for? Mutual trust is the foundation of our business. The day the trust dies, the business of smuggling will die too.'

Singh began to ponder. Iqbal's claim was not an exaggeration. In today's corrupt world, smuggling was the only profession in which one still could find 99 per cent honesty, if not hundred. Businessmen, meanwhile, had buried their souls six feet under.

Now the genius of Iqbal's idea hit home; he decided to carry out the experiment at least once. To Iqbal's surprise, on his very first crossing, all the jackets had come tied to the rope.

*

As the convoy entered Chembur, another customs official, who had been smoking cigarettes since morning, cross-checked the numbers of the three vehicles against the information from Panvel: the tempo and two taxis, which had passed him a few seconds ago, bore the same number plates.

*

Iqbal was immersed in deep thought. After crossing the eastern suburbs of Bombay, as the taxi speeded west, he felt more and more convinced that there was a need to introduce big changes into their business; in fact, the entire system from ground up needed to be radically overhauled. And he was the only one who could do it.

He was educated—in his second year of college—he could devise fresh solutions for the age-old problems that confronted smugglers at every step. Otherwise, most of the people involved were illiterate. Even the few who were educated clung to the traditional ways of bootlegging like a female monkey sometimes clings to her dead infant thinking it is alive.

After giving it serious thought, Iqbal concluded that the first and most important need was to bring about sweeping changes in the system of crossing itself because that's where the risk was highest.

When two ships meet mid-sea and, like two lovers, remained glued to each other for hours, it is bound to invite suspicion. The fact that the entire operation was carried out under the cover of darkness did not reduce its risk. Like walls have ears, the darkness has eyes.

Was it not possible to find a way to transfer the consignment from the Dubai ship to the boat coming to take the delivery without them actually meeting?

Even as he put this question, he heard a critical voice echoing within his sleep-deprived brain. *My dear Iqbal, this would be possible if you were a magician: you could just say abracadabra and, lo and behold, the consignment would fly into the air from the Dubai ship and land in your delivery launch! You are a talented college student, how come you don't get such simple logic? Of course it is necessary for both boats to be side by side for the transfer of any goods.*

'No!' his lips quivered. This is already possible if the smuggling is carried out through the land route. For example, a vehicle carries the goods up to the Bombay city limits and returns after stashing them at a specified place. A while later another vehicle picks up the goods from the same secret location.

Why can't the same technique be applied at sea? Something clicked in his brain. Gradually, the idea began to crystallize— an idea which was to revolutionize the technique of crossing.

*

As the caravan entered Bombay's western suburb of Andheri, Iqbal asked the taxi driver to stop. The taxi driver signalled the tempo ahead whose driver saw it in his side-view mirror. All three vehicles stopped near an Udipi restaurant.

The men dozing in the taxi woke up. At first, they thought that they had arrived at the godown, but then they cast their eyes across the suburban street. They looked at each other. Everybody had the same question in their eyes: *What was the need to stop here? The Mazgaon godown was just a forty-minute drive from here.*

'Dagdu!' Iqbal said, settling the taxi fare. 'We need to arrange for another tempo.'

For the first time, Dagdu lost his temper at Iqbal. They had already entered Bombay, were about to reach the godown and Iqbal wanted to change the tempo.

'Boss . . .' Before he could protest Iqbal had reached the second taxi. He checked the meter and settled accounts with the driver.

'Michael!' Iqbal called out to Michael who squeezed out of the taxi yawning with Altaf. 'You keep a watch here till Dagdu arranges for a new tempo. I'm taking the others for breakfast.'

'Is it necessary to change the tempo?' Michael asked.

Iqbal nodded and entered the Udipi restaurant with the five men.

*

'Sufi!' I stopped him to seek a clarification. 'How did you get this sudden idea of changing the vehicle?'

'Divine inspiration! Or call it a flash of intuition, if you will.'

'So you knew all along that the customs officials were keeping a watch on your vehicles!'

'Had I known, I wouldn't have committed the blunder of entering the city. Instead I would have gone to Vapi or Surat.' Pausing for a while, he added, 'In spite of having been exposed mid-sea, we had not been raided till Andheri. This fact was bugging me constantly. Maybe that's why my subconscious mind jolted me!'

*

After twenty-five minutes, the caravan proceeded again. Iqbal had brought two packets of grilled sandwiches for Michael and Dagdu. They were eating their breakfast in the taxi. The new tempo was racing ahead.

It was a Sunday. It was almost eight in the morning. The crowd of passengers in the suburban trains heading into the city was gradually thickening. The sparse traffic too had increased but today being Sunday, at least the city's vehicles would not be forced to a snail's pace.

After crossing Ghodbunder Road and reaching Bombay's posh Bandra suburb, even this fantasy was shattered. Everyone sucked in their breath: ahead of them, as far as the eye could see, snaked an unending jam of vehicles heading into the city.

Iqbal understood. The customs and police officials had jointly set up a barricade near Mahim. They had placed empty drums in a serpentine arrangement in the middle of the road so that all vehicles would have to slow down.

Long-distance taxis and goods carriers were subjected to special inspection.

This action had been ordered immediately after the caravan of three vehicles had vanished beyond Ghatkopar. The fifth customs official had informed the police over the telephone that a tempo and two taxis had crossed him, but they bore different number plates. Moreover, in this uncertainty, he could note down the number of the tempo but missed the taxi plates.

*

Dagdu, who was sitting at the back, was alternately looking at the long queue of vehicles and then at Iqbal—the boss he had abused just a few minutes ago. His new-found respect for Iqbal bordered on reverence.

Had they not changed vehicles at Andheri, the police, on checking the numbers of the vehicles, would have separated the tempo and the taxis from the queue and inspected them. The result: they would have been caught red-handed with gold worth Rs 5 crore, and all of them would have been thrown behind bars.

Signalling the driver, Iqbal brought his taxi from behind the tempo to the first lane. Watching it from the second taxi, Michael too changed lanes. The caravan quietly dispersed into the crowd of furiously-honking vehicles.

First, the tempo entered the serpentine blockade and one of the customs officials, Khan, directed its driver to park aside. There were a few cars behind the tempo. After that was Iqbal's taxi.

Seeing their tempo being flagged aside, Iqbal felt dizzy. Everyone's blood ran cold. Their labour had gone down the drain and, with it, their share of Rs 25,000 each.

Now it was the turn of Iqbal's taxi to enter the serpentine obstacle course. There were two cars ahead. Slowly, the taxi entered after them. A second customs official, accompanied by the police, was standing guard.

Iqbal poked his head out of the window and asked innocently, 'Sir, anything wrong?' The official glared at him. Iqbal drew his neck back in, apologizing. Turning towards the driver, he bluffed, 'You see, the public don't even have the right to ask!'.

His taxi passed through the barricade. Now Iqbal wiped the perspiration off his brow. His other colleagues started breathing smoothly. Michael's taxi, which had gone ahead of them, had stopped near Mahim church. He was watching intently. Customs official Khan was inspecting the tempo driver's licence. As Iqbal's taxi slowed down near him, Michael asked, 'Now what do we do?'

'There is no point waiting here. Whatever is written will happen. Let's be optimistic. We will wait for the tempo at Mazgaon.' Iqbal then turned towards Dagdu at the back and asked, 'I hope you have given the correct address to the driver.'

Dagdu nodded and then warned, 'But, boss, if the tempo gets caught, then there will be a raid at the godown.'

There was no doubt about that.

Both the taxis drove off again. In half an hour, they crossed Byculla, turned for Mazgaon and stopped near the godown. Iqbal paid the fare to both the drivers and entered the nearby Irani restaurant with the others. While placing the order for eight cups of tea, he thought it was necessary to give Singh a report of today's failure.

*

Singh had woken up a while ago. Nervously scanning the headlines of the *Times of India*, he was thinking hard.

Iqbal had taken two Ambassador cars for the crossing. Both the cars were to return before dawn. He was alarmed to find that the cars had returned at 3 a.m. On questioning the drivers, he had been told about the catastrophe—the launch being spotted by *Vikrant*. Despite this, both drivers had waited at Bhaucha Dhakka for almost an hour. According to their guess, the gang's launch, *Al Kabir*, had headed for Uran Island.

At least there was some consolation for Singh, the launch had not been raided mid-sea. He slept for four hours more.

Now, as he sat and read the newspaper, the wrinkles on his forehead became even more pronounced. His thick eyebrows knotted. There was no news from Iqbal. *What had happened to the consignment? Had they been arrested?*

He was distressed and his wife, who was preparing to send the children to the park, noticed. Singh had three children, one son and two daughters. The son was still in kindergarten. The daughters were in the third and fifth standards respectively.

The three children came to him, sports equipment in hand. For a few minutes, a smile lit up his face. In turns, the children kissed him on the cheek and left with the nanny. His face turned grim again.

His wife picked up the empty cup from the table before him and replaced it with a hot cup. Singh folded the newspaper and looked at her. 'How many more cups will you make me drink?' He had had four cups already.

'I'll serve you till your frayed nerves calm down.'

He knew that his wife wanted to know the cause of his worry. However, he did not want her to know about his connection with the underworld.

He was still thinking of an answer when the telephone rang. He grabbed the receiver. 'Bad news, Singh.' It was Iqbal. 'We crossed the ocean but sank on the coast.'

Singh did not get the hint. Scratching his head, his eyes followed his wife who was heading into the kitchen. He liked the way she walked—there was still some charm in her.

*

After giving a detailed account over the phone, Iqbal said, 'The tempo got caught before Mahim but we have all reached Mazgaon safely.'

'Are you sure the tempo has been caught?' Singh confirmed.

'Had the police released the driver after questioning, he would have reached with the consignment by now.'

Iqbal was speaking to Singh from the public booth at the entrance of the Irani restaurant. While on the call, he was also keeping a watch on the godown across the road. Suddenly, he heard the tempo's engine. He turned his neck and saw it heading towards the godown.

'Good news, Singh! The tempo has arrived.'

He was about to put the receiver down when Singh yelled, 'Iqbal!'

'Yes?'

'Can you see a police van behind the tempo?'

'No.'

'Be careful, the customs might have laid a trap.'

Singh's suspicion proved correct.

The customs officials had separated the tempo from the queue and interrogated the driver. He had told them everything that he knew. The consignment had come from Uran Island. The tempo had been changed at Andheri and the consignment had been transferred.

'How many people were there?'

'I don't know exactly, but they followed me in two taxis.'

'Where are those taxis?'

The tempo driver paused to think.

'Disappeared in the traffic.'

While two officials interrogated the driver, another opened the tempo and started inspecting it. His eyes popped out on finding jackets containing gold worth Rs 5 crore. He called his two assistants and started counting.

'Where was the consignment to be delivered?'

'Mazgaon.'

'Are you familiar with the place?'

'No, sahib, I've never been there before.'

After the gold had been counted, the consignment was officially confiscated in the presence of five witnesses and sent to the headquarters in a police van.

*

Two customs officials, Khan and Rustomji, got into the empty tempo. The third gave instructions to the driver. 'As soon as you park the tempo near the godown, the men from the gang will come running towards you. If they ask, just tell them that you were released after questioning. The moment they open the door, we will pounce on them.'

Before leaving he also warned the tempo driver, 'Just remember, if you try to act smart, you will rot in jail for at least ten years. And if you cooperate, I promise, we won't involve you in this case.'

The tempo driver was innocent. He simply nodded.

*

After replacing the receiver on the cradle, Iqbal returned to the restaurant and joined his gang. The second round of tea had been ordered. Since Altaf was drunk, he was still hungry. He ordered a bun maska.

Meanwhile, the tempo driver had inquired about the exact address from the shops nearby and parked the tempo near the godown. He got down from the driver's seat and was leaning against the bonnet. He could not see Iqbal and his colleagues, but Iqbal could see him clearly from the restaurant.

Watching him closely, Iqbal divined that there was something fishy going on.

'Dagdu!' he said, casting his eye on the gang. 'After drinking tea, all of you leave.'

'What about you, boss!'

'I want to know how this cat-and-mouse game ends. I'll sit here till it is over.'

At five-minute intervals, all his gang members left the restaurant one after the other.

Iqbal sat alone. His face was calm but his mind was racing. *Could he still retrieve the situation? No, he couldn't salvage anything more than what he got, or what he didn't get.* After a few frustrating moments, a strange idea came to him.

The customs officials had foiled his very first crossing. He would avenge this. For the rest of his days, he would become their worst nightmare.

17

Time seemed to have sprouted wings. The days were flying past like a flock of birds soaring across wide open skies. Everything appeared to be a dream. Those were the days of youth, joy, ecstasy and love. I could not believe my luck—a poor fisherman had cast his net and caught a mermaid. For me, Suraiyya was no less precious than a mermaid.

'You look radiant!' she remarked one day, gazing into my eyes. The radiance was both physical and emotional, as if sunlight, and not blood, coursed through my veins: it was the look of love.

The shooting of the film *Begana* was over and so was my contract. Now, there was no need for me to work as an assistant director. The income from the cartoon strips was enough to support my studies and my love.

Besides, I had lost interest in the film industry. During shoots, I could not attend college for days together and it was getting impossible for me to stay away from Suraiyya for even a day.

Whether it was a working day or a holiday, we used to spend the entire day together—sometimes strolling barefoot along Juhu beach, arms around each other's waists, in the cool of the evening, or standing on the cliffs at Bandstand, watching the water rush, break and mill around the rocks below us. Before it got dark, I would go to her hostel to drop her off. Like me, many Romeos would hang around the main gate exchanging sweet nothings with their beloveds until the last minute before the hostel gates closed. Across the street, the Arabian Sea murmured indulgently, sending wave after wave of salty breeze to caress us.

As twilight fell, and the moment of separation approached, the tempo of our talks increased. The scene resembled that of a railway platform, our restlessness similar to the one among passengers and their relatives at the time of the train's departure. As if we were going to be separated not for just one night but for years together, we would remind each other of every trivial thing that came to mind.

Then, the sadistic bell would pronounce the closure of the main gate of the girls' hostel. Suraiyya would enter the gate after giving me one last, long, deep kiss. I would then return home.

Today, neither Suraiyya nor I was in a hurry to go. At my request, she had managed a late pass, enabling us to spend an hour more together. We were sitting head to head and hand in hand in the garden of the aquarium next to the hostel, solemn, listening to the whistling of the westerly wind. Suraiyya had been looking pensive since the morning. After spending half a day in college together, I invited her to the Eros theatre to watch a hilarious comedy called *Southern Yankee*. I laughed loudly throughout the film, while she sat grim-faced as if she was watching a Shakespearean tragedy.

'How did you like the film?' I asked her later, pretending to be unaware of her mood.

'It was good.'

'Then, *jaanu*, why didn't you laugh even once?'

'I did laugh, but I don't hee-haw like you, displaying all my teeth.'

Her answer was correct but not convincing. I knew that something was bothering her. I had an inkling that something must have happened the previous night. However, she was not willing to tell me.

Perhaps she did not want to burden me. It was possible that she was hesitating because we were having a good time and she did not want to spoil the day.

I lost patience in the garden. 'Suraiyya! Don't you forget, we haven't chosen each other to share only happiness. I've as much right over your sorrows. Tell me, what's the matter?'

She looked straight at me and tears welled up in her eyes. She put her head in her hands and cried as if she would never stop. I felt a curdling pain in my stomach; I had never seen Suraiyya weeping before. I gathered her in my arms and drew her close. She put her head on my shoulder. I caressed her back to console her. After a while, her sobs ceased and she said, 'My roommate committed suicide.'

I lifted her face. Suraiyya revealed more details: her roommate, a girl named Anusuya, had jumped from the terrace the previous night. The hostel was a five-storeyed building. Falling on the stone-paved ground, her skull had cracked.

'But she was a fountain of laughter!' I said, wiping her face with a handkerchief. 'She always had a smile on her face. What provoked her to . . .'

'Her boyfriend ditched her,' Suraiyya said, looking me in the eye. 'Aabid, you won't abandon me, will you?'

Forgetting the gravity of the situation, I burst out laughing. 'You dodo! Why would I abandon you?'

'Even now, girls flock around you in the college.'

'They're my friends, you're my life. If at all anyone has a reason to fear being jilted, it's me, not you.'

'You think I'll betray you?' She was taken aback.

'No, but a situation may arise in the future that would leave you helpless.'

'Like what?'

'There is a barbed fencing of wealth separating us. I'm poor and you are rich. One cannot ignore reality.'

'You know that I don't believe in that nonsense.'

'Let's hope the elders in your family don't believe in it either.'

'It won't make any difference even if they do.' She sat up like a queen full of confidence. 'If they try to pressurize me, I'll walk out of the house and come to you wearing just the clothes I have on.'

I pulled her close and held her in my arms once again: these words, and her self-assurance, were enough for me.

It was almost 9 p.m. The October moon was smiling above us and the sea breeze was playing with the leaves on the ground. Walking back slowly from the garden, we arrived at the hostel. The Gorkha watchman opened the gate for her. That night, I watched every step Suraiyya took until she disappeared into the hostel.

*

Iqbal too watched with full concentration. He was sitting alone in the Irani restaurant. His eyes were focused on the tempo and its driver near the godown across the road. Two hours had passed.

His imagination was running wild. He was asking himself question after question, but he could find no answers. There were gold biscuits worth Rs 5 crore in the tempo. But the driver was waiting outside for two hours. This could only mean one thing: customs officials were somewhere in the area.

But if this guess was right, then the driver should have made eye contact with them at least once. But that had not happened. Had the driver been released after interrogation?

Half an hour more went by. The tempo driver had started his duty early in the morning. He had neither had tea nor breakfast. Besides, he was getting bored standing alone.

He headed into the Irani restaurant for a cup of tea. Iqbal immediately turned away, although he knew that the driver had not seen his face clearly earlier either. When the consignment had been offloaded from the tempo from Uran and loaded on to this tempo by Michael and Dagdu, Iqbal was having breakfast in an Udipi restaurant nearby.

Still, Iqbal did not want to take the chance of the tempo driver spotting a familiar face so close to the godown. The driver sat in an empty chair near the entrance. A cup of tea was placed before him.

Iqbal got up slowly, settled the bill and walked out. He had decided that before the driver finished his tea, he had a chance to peep into the tempo like a casual passer-by. He was certain that the customs officials were not hiding anywhere outside the van. *Were they hiding inside?* The thought made him stop in his tracks.

Behind him, the driver was having tea. The tempo stood in front of him. Iqbal only needed to take two steps and open the door. But the deadly question that had occurred to him left him frozen.

He thought quickly. If the customs officials were hiding inside, they would have suffocated by now because of the lack of ventilation.

While he was thinking, the rear doors of the tempo opened with a bang. Iqbal was stunned for a few seconds. Fortunately, the doors opened outward. He had the advantage of cover from the door. He walked away in the opposite direction.

Their faces flushed with frustration, Khan and Rustomji, after emerging from the tempo, first stretched their legs and then looked at the driver's seat. Hurriedly finishing his tea, the driver rushed back cursing his luck.

'Sahib!' he began pleading. 'I hadn't even had a single cup of tea since morning. I just went to the restaurant and you came out.'

Both officials now looked at the closed doors of the godown. No one had come to take the delivery. The godown was locked. That meant the gang had caught wind of their plan.

'Who's the owner of this godown?' Khan asked the tempo driver.

'I told you, sahib. I don't know anything. In fact, I've never come to this area before to deliver goods.'

They did not doubt the driver's sincerity, so they let him go after noting down his name and address. Now, they began exploring the neighbouring shops.

From a grocer's shop, they got the name of the owner of the godown—Abdul Sattar. He dealt in antiques like haveli doors, carved grills and wooden statues. On further inquiry, they also got the address. The owner's house was not very far. Engaging a taxi, they left in the direction of Bhendi Bazaar, hoping to find some leads.

*

Being a holiday, there was lethargy in the air. When Iqbal arrived at the hotel room to meet Singh, he was once again sitting alone, glass in one hand, legs outstretched on the bed. A thought struck Iqbal. *Had he sacked Kiran?* Then he smiled at his own naïveté. Kiran was a call girl; Singh was a womanizer. It was more likely that he had lost interest in her.

Immersed in his thoughts, Iqbal lowered himself on to the sofa opposite the bed when a new girl emerged from the bathroom. On seeing a stranger she paused for a second and then turned towards the window and stood there with her back to them.

'Like her?' Singh taunted, taking a sip.

Iqbal gave the girl a cursory glance and didn't say anything.

'Don't like her?'

'Singh! Five crore rupees went down the gutter and you are trying to pull my leg!'

'If crying over what's lost could bring it back, then I am prepared to sit with you and beat my chest.'

'Don't you think it's necessary to discuss this matter?'

'To discuss what exactly?'

'Hamid is behind bars. And . . .'

'You don't have to worry about that. DK has engaged the best lawyer for him. He will be out on bail in a day or two.'

'DK?'

'Our boss.'

This was the first time Iqbal had heard about DK.

'That doesn't change the situation. This week, we've lost consignments worth Rs 6.5 crore.'

'Will discussing help get them back?'

'No. But if we apply our minds, we can avoid such disasters in the future.'

Singh's blue eyes twinkled with interest. He forgot his drink for a few minutes. 'How?'

'By giving up crossing.'

'Are you in your senses?'

'You are drinking, not me.'

'If we stop crossing, how will the transactions take place?'

'That's what I'm going to drill into your head.'

A concrete plan had taken shape in Iqbal's mind while coming to Bombay from Uran. He explained this plan to Singh in detail.

'On a fixed date, the ship from Dubai will come to the appointed distance of 40 bams, stuff all the jackets in a gunny bag and dump it into the sea.'

'What? What did you say?'

Iqbal repeated himself.

'Forty bams means 240-foot deep waters, right?'

Iqbal nodded.

'Dump the bag with the whole consignment into it?'

'True.'

'And then send deep-sea divers to fetch it?' Singh taunted, 'That's your bright idea?'

'No.'

'Then?'

'The bag will be tied to a sturdy 250-foot-long nylon rope.' At the upper end of the rope, a piece of thermocol will be tied. The bag will sink while the thermocol, being light in weight, will float. The next day, it won't take much time for our launch to locate the floating thermocol near the light house.'

Singh now brought his forgotten glass to his lips and drained it in one gulp. He stared at Iqbal with newfound respect and awe.

'Are you with me so far?' Iqbal asked him after a while.

He nodded like a puppet.

Iqbal continued to explain the second phase of the operation, but only after ensuring that he had succeeded in driving the point home. 'We need not lift the consignment from the same spot because that might draw someone's attention.'

'Then?'

'We only have to look for the thermocol, tie that end of the rope to our boat and tow it to a safe place.'

'Are you sure the boat will be able to tow the heavy gunny bag?'

'Of course.'

'How?'

'The weight of solid matter reduces in water.'

Singh realized that if Iqbal's plan worked, the risk involved in crossing would drop from 99 per cent to just 1 per cent. The launch could be brought from the lighthouse either to Versova or Madh Island, both of which were on the western coast of Bombay.

However, there was some risk in Iqbal's idea. In the current modus operandi, before carrying out the transaction, two halves of one currency note were matched by the parties—this satisfied both parties. Second, in a direct transaction, there was little possibility of cheating. Iqbal was playing blind.

But upon thinking further, he remembered Iqbal's words: *our business runs on trust. The day this trust dies, the business of smuggling will die too.*

Singh had been involved in trafficking for many years. It was true that he had never been cheated of a single paisa, otherwise any thug hell-bent on duping him could have found several loopholes even in the traditional system. One could easily place copper biscuits in place of gold in the jackets. Who would notice the difference under the tension of crossing?

Moreover, until today, no one had torn open the jackets during transfer to check, simply because until today there had been no double-crossing.

'My dear Iqbal! Let's celebrate with a drink, just today—then don't drink ever.'

Iqbal stood up.

'*Arrey*! Sit down at least. Relax, I won't force you.'

'I haven't been home for the last twenty-four hours.' With that, Iqbal walked out.

For the last twenty-four hours Iqbal hadn't slept either. On reaching home, he did not even change his clothes. Removing only his sky-blue sweater and shoes, he had barely stretched his legs on the wooden bed when sleep overtook him.

*

When his eyes opened on Monday morning, a clerk from the customs department was standing at the door with a summons. He signed, accepted and read it at the door itself. He had been asked to present himself at the Directorate of Revenue Intelligence (DRI) office at 11 a.m. sharp. His hands started shivering. Summons from the Crime Investigation Division (CID) of the customs sent shivers down the spines of even seasoned criminals.

It was 9 a.m. Both his younger brothers were still sleeping. Gul Banu was standing by the stove preparing breakfast. Iqbal thought fast. *Should he present himself at the DRI office or not? Would they arrest him if he went there? Lock him up? Thrash the daylights out of him?*

Before he could think any further, his neighbour appeared, 'Iqbal, there is a call for you.'

Iqbal was not the only one who received the DRI summons. Singh had received one too. He was calling Iqbal.

'Singh! I was thinking of calling you up when . . .'

'I suspected that you too might have received the same.'

'How did it happen?'

'They arrested the owner of the godown. He must have disclosed our names. But you need not worry. Legally, the customs officials can't touch us.'

Iqbal wanted to ask several questions, but here at his neighbour's house, he could not speak out openly. Of course, he could listen to Singh's advice without fear.

'Now listen!' Singh was whispering into the receiver. 'They will threaten you, frighten you and use all kinds of lies, but don't admit to anything.'

'Okay.'

'Point number two: you'll have to smarten up a bit too. Do you have a suit?'

'No, why?'

'At least buy an expensive tie. Remember, we are respectable businessmen, not crooks, and we need to leave that impression.'

Iqbal put the phone down. When he returned to his room, Firoze was awake. The youngest brother, Razzak, was still fast asleep on the mattress beside the bed. From the edge of the bed where he sat, he gazed at Razzak's face that looked perfectly at peace with the world.

Iqbal was worried for him. Razzak never did his homework. For that, he received a caning at school almost every day. But there is a limit to how much you can punish a student. His teachers were fed up of beating him. Now, they simply threw him out from the class. This is exactly what Razzak wanted. Instead of going out of the class, he would go out of the school. Every time Razzak went rogue,

Iqbal brought him back on track. But all of Iqbal's efforts to reform his young brother had failed, leaving him helpless. He had only one option left.

Razzak was in the sixth grade. He had failed the last two years. There was no indication to suggest that he would succeed this year. Iqbal decided to get him a job where he could learn some skill so that someday he could start his own business.

Iqbal's other worry was his own examinations. If he hoped to join medical college, he had to somehow secure at least 80 per cent this year. Only then would he be able to fulfil his father's dream of becoming a doctor.

However, the question begged to be asked: did he still want to become a doctor? The answer was not a straight no. He still harboured the passion—the outline of which had been etched into his mind since childhood. Hussain Ali's words 'my son will become a doctor when he grows up' still reverberated in his ears ever so often.

He decided to sincerely pursue his studies. There were still two months to go for the final examinations and that was enough time to prepare.

He fixed his eyes on the calendar on the wall opposite him. Today was Monday. On Friday was the birthday party for Sharad, Kusum's so-called boyfriend. To allay the growing bitterness between Sharad and him, Iqbal had accepted his invitation. He decided upon Saturday as the day that he would begin preparing earnestly for the finals.

*

At 10.30 a.m. sharp, dressed in a white shirt, pants and shoes, he climbed down a flight of stairs and after crossing Munda Galli arrived at Palkhi Mohalla. He engaged a taxi for the

DRI office. As the taxi picked up speed, his palpitations increased. *How would this day end?*

On the way, he stopped near Handloom House. He remembered that Singh had insisted that he wear a tie.

Iqbal went to the tie section. While selecting one, a thought crossed his mind: *no one in his family had ever worn a tie*. It was but natural that he did not know how to knot it. He selected a lemon-yellow one that looked bright on the white shirt. Pretending to knot it, he asked the salesman behind the glass-topped counter, 'Is there a mirror?' The salesman pointed to the changing room in a corner. Iqbal looked in that direction. Fortunately, it was locked as a customer was inside.

He requested the salesman, 'Can you please help me? I'm in a hurry.'

The salesman came up from behind the counter and knotted his tie. He settled the bill and came out. Sitting in the taxi, he felt that he was not wearing a tie but a noose that the DRI had prepared for him.

18

Iqbal's taxi crossed Electric House and entered Colaba. The DRI office was located above Waldorf Hotel. The CID of the customs department occupied the entire top floor.

Iqbal stood before a clerk at 11 a.m. sharp with the summons paper. The clerk pointed to a cabin. It belonged to Deputy Collector Khan. He was forty-five and athletically built. Clad in a safari suit, he had an impressive-looking face. He had greyed before his time but the salt and pepper hair only added to the aura of dignity.

Khan took the summons from him, glanced at it cursorily and then smiled. 'Sit,' he said pointing to a chair. Then he spent some time going over the file that lay before him on the table.

Iqbal sat quietly. He was feeling awkward because of the tie. His hand nervously fidgeted with the knot from time to time.

Khan jotted something down on the last page of the file and got up. Iqbal too had to stand up with him. Khan came around the table and put his arm around Iqbal's shoulder. Walking with him, Khan began with some small talk.

'What do you do?'

'I'm a second-year student.'

'Since when have college students started wearing ties?'

Iqbal realized that Khan had noticed his uneasiness. He confessed, 'I've worn it for the first time.'

Khan stopped to slightly loosen the knot. 'Nice colour. It looks very smart on your white shirt. Where did you get it from?'

'Handloom House.'

They started walking again. There was an empty room ahead. Khan took Iqbal inside and locked the door. Iqbal observed the stark white walls in the dimly lit room that stared at him.

For furniture, in the centre of the room, there was a long table and a chair without armrests. There was a bulb dangling above the chair. There were two windows in front that looked out on the road, but they were covered by curtains.

He made Iqbal sit on the chair, pulled the table away from the centre of the room and parted the curtains. Sunlight washed across the room. Taking a few steps, he stood before Iqbal.

'You must be aware of why we have summoned you here,' Khan began in a friendly tone, having worked on building up a rapport. 'And . . .'

'Sir . . .' Iqbal interrupted. Khan tried again.

'My name is Rahim Khan Pathan. How old are you?'

'I'm twenty-two running.'

'Then I'm like your father, yet you may call me Khan.'

'Mr Khan!' Iqbal said, defiantly continuing his incomplete sentence. 'I've still not been able to figure out why I'm here!'

Khan sized him up and then stared straight into his calm eyes. He realized that sitting before him was not a soft kernel but a hard nut.

'You said you are a student, right?'

'Yes, sir.'

'Which college?'

'Bhavan's.'

'What are the timings?'

'Normal. From 9 a.m. to 4 p.m.'

'What's your attendance?

'I go almost daily. Only today . . .'

'Forget about today.'

'I attend regularly.'

'Last year, you were absent for forty-five days.'

Iqbal felt a knot in his stomach. If this was correct, it meant that the customs officials had been investigating him for months. Otherwise, how did they arrive at the exact figure which even Iqbal did not know?

'Sir, it seems that there has been some mistake.' Iqbal spoke coolly but his brain was desperately trying to look for a way out of this corner.

'Mistake!' Khan's face now began betraying the hardness of a seasoned cop. 'Is your college attendance register wrong?'

'I didn't say that, sir,' Iqbal said without flinching.

'Then tell me, where were you on those days? Otherwise I will read out each day's detailed account of your misdeeds from my file.'

Iqbal's legs started shivering. This was the first time he was being interrogated. He had not expected to be attacked with statistics and evidence. Still, he did not lose his nerve. One of Singh's bits of advice was etched in his mind. Singh had warned him on the phone: 'They will threaten you, scare you and use all kinds of lies, but don't you confess anything.'

'Please read them out, sir!'

'What?'

'Each day's account. Let me also know what I did during forty-five days of absence!'

Khan's intense brown eyes softened, betraying defeat: the rat who had been sniffing the cheese a moment ago was now running away from the trap. In truth, Khan was unaware of Iqbal's activities. He only got two names, Iqbal's and Singh's, from the owner of the godown.

That was enough for him. He was capable of extricating other details. This was just his first move. He had speculated that if Iqbal was involved in trafficking then surely there would be a shortfall in his college attendance—to trap him, he had bowled a bouncer, but Iqbal had cheekily hit a six. Thanks to Iqbal's defiant stand, he had ended up in a trap himself.

'Iqbal!' said Khan, his voice dipped in honey. 'I'm not your enemy, but your friend, a well-wisher. If you tell the truth, rest assured you will receive our full cooperation.'

Iqbal was now certain that Khan had been bluffing. If he really had evidence, he would not have softened like butter.

'Sir, I'm telling you nothing but the truth.'

'What?'

'I was indeed absent for a few days.'

'Be precise. How many days?'

'I did not keep count.'

'What did you do?'

'Rest.'

'Rest?'

'Bed rest on doctor's advice.'

'For what?'

'I'm an asthma patient, sir.'

Iqbal had asthma a few years earlier and he had been using it as an excuse till date. Even at college, he still used this medical condition to explain his absence. 'Whenever I get an attack, I'm forced to take complete rest.'

'Hmm . . .' Khan started pacing the room. 'Tell me, how many members are there in your family?'

'Four, including me, sir.'

'Who are the other three?'

'My mother and two brothers.'

'Brothers are older or younger?'

'Younger.'

'They must be studying, right?'

This time Iqbal guessed Khan's plan even before he could make his next move. Anticipating the next question, he said, 'One is in high school while the other is working.'

Again, Khan was knocked back: had Iqbal said that both his brothers were in school, he would have definitely asked where the money to run the house came from.

His frustration at being outplayed was now clearly visible on his face, but he was standing behind Iqbal.

'Where does he work?'

'In a footwear store.'

It was that very morning that Iqbal had decided to terminate Razzak's education and get him a job at a footwear store. His neighbour, on whose telephone he received calls, was the owner of a shoe shop.

'Where's the shop?'

'It's near Pydhonie in Jambli Mohalla.'

'What's his salary?'

'Rs 800, sir.'

'So, the younger brother slogs and the elder brother has fun in college! Which Hindi film did you pluck this idea from?'

'I don't watch films, sir.'

'Then where did you get this story from?'

'This is not a story. It's my life, my misfortune, my tragedy.'

'Really?'

'Many a time I feel like quitting college and taking up a job, but then I won't be able to fulfil my father's dream.' Iqbal's lips quivered dramatically. 'Sir, before he died, my father held my hand and made me promise that I would become a doctor. Now you tell me, how can I quit college?'

'Of course not,' Khan said coming in front of Iqbal, 'but you may quit telling lies.'

'Lies?'

'We both know that whatever you are saying is far from the truth. There is still time. Tell me the truth.'

'Sir, will you please tell me why you don't believe me?'

'Because your mouth smells foul.'

'Not possible, sir! I use Binaca toothpaste.'

'Shut up!' Khan screamed.

Iqbal fell silent.

Both of them stared at each other. Iqbal had the wide-eyed gaze of a child while Khan's eyes were bloodshot. He was not a fool. He could clearly see through Iqbal's mask, but he was unable to break through it.

Nonetheless, he was confident that sooner or later he would be successful in his endeavour. He looked at his wristwatch and, without uttering a word, opened the door and walked out. Iqbal remained seated. As he was wondering where Khan had disappeared, a peon brought in some sandwiches and a cup of coffee.

It was only then that he realized it was lunch time. The duel would start again after lunch. The game of cat and mouse would pick up again. He was unable to guess how many more hours it would take. The only satisfaction he had was that he was enjoying the game.

He sipped the coffee and took a bite of the sandwich, his thoughts turning to Singh. *Where was he? Both of them had received summons from the DRI. Both had been asked to present themselves at 11 a.m. Was Singh too being interrogated in one of the adjoining rooms?*

*

Khan entered the room at 2.30 p.m. and started with an ingratiating smile again. 'Did you enjoy the sandwich?'

'Of course.'

'For once you spoke the truth.'

To Khan's attempt at bonding with humour, Iqbal fired back. 'Sir, to tell you the truth, this was the only lie I've spoken so far.'

'What?'

'The sandwiches were stale, like toilet paper. See for yourself. I've not eaten more than two bites.'

Khan was shocked. He had not expected that in the second innings, this kid would take his wicket in the very first ball. He came straight to the point: 'The tempo driver says that you had loaded the consignment on to his vehicle from Andheri.'

'Which tempo driver, sir?'

By now, Khan was so annoyed that he felt like breaking all of Iqbal's teeth. But he had been trained to not break the law. Suppressing his rage, he patiently clarified, 'The same driver who brought the consignment from Andheri to the Mazgaon godown.'

'But how does that concern me?'

'He says it concerns you.'

'That isn't possible. I've not been to Andheri in the last six months and you are saying that I loaded the consignment on to the tempo! When, sir?'

'Yesterday morning.'

'Yesterday was Sunday. I spent all day at home. And if I was at home, how could I be in Andheri?'

Khan began pacing around Iqbal once again. 'So you'll not give up your game!'

'Sir! I have replied truthfully to all your questions. I don't understand why you are connecting me with a place I didn't visit and with a tempo driver whom I've never met.'

'How did he know your name?'

'There are countless Iqbals in this city.'

'But you are the only Iqbal Rupani.'

'That doesn't prove that I loaded some consignment on to some tempo!'

'And if I prove it?'

'I'm ready to be hanged.' Iqbal loosened his tie a little more as he defied Khan for the second time.

He was confident. No one could harm him without proof. Charges can also be hurled against the prime minister, but what was the meaning of such charges unless they were substantiated with evidence? While the police put anyone behind bars by cooking up charges, customs officials were helpless in such cases. And here, a customs officer was standing before Iqbal, not a police officer.

'Who's Singh?'

The sudden question shook Iqbal up slightly. His rebellious defiance gave way to gentle innocence again. 'Which Singh are you referring to, sir?'

'How many Singhs do you know?'

'Two.'

'What do they do?'

'They study with me in college.'

'I'm not talking about students.'

'I don't know any other Singh.'

'But he knows you well.'

'Maybe.'

'Maybe?'

'He may know me.'

'And you don't know him?'

'That's right.'

'Do you think it's that simple to make a fool out of me?'

'Sir . . .'

'He knows you but you don't know him?'

'Millions of people know Dilip Kumar. That doesn't mean that he knows all of them.'

'You aren't Dilip Kumar.'

'I've nothing to do with your Singh.'

'Are you sure?'

'A hundred per cent sure.'

'Think again.'

'There is nothing to think about.'

'Don't you carry out smuggling jobs under him?'

'How can I work under somebody I don't even know?'

'Is it a lie that he had sent you on Saturday night for crossing?'

'A blatant lie.'

'Is it also a lie that you got the consignment landed on Uran Island?'

'I think you are looking for some other Iqbal.'

'You loaded the consignment on to the tempo, came to Andheri and . . .'

'Sir! Please leave me alone. I'm really fed up.'

'Is that so?' Khan looked at his watch and chuckled.

Iqbal was perplexed. His brain was working at full speed. This much was certain that he was standing before the jaws of an unknown trap. *But what was the trap?* His computer brain seemed to have failed him in this time of crisis.

'Why so quiet now?'

'To be frank, my brain is getting all scrambled.'

'If you had brains, you would have cooperated, Iqbal. Anyway, that's your hard luck. What can anyone do if a ten-year sentence is written in your destiny?' Khan walked up to the window and resumed talking.

'I gave you all the opportunities. But you turned them down by telling one lie after the other. I really feel bad for you.

Believe me, I'm not happy sending an intelligent young man like you to prison. I will regret it. Your youth will turn to dust and your father's last wish will be buried under it. Don't tell me then that I didn't warn you.'

He walked towards the door and paused after a few steps. 'Do you feel like confessing even now? Or should I bring the report about your relationship with Singh with photographs?'

Before Iqbal could reply, the door opened. Khan's colleague Rustomji was standing at the threshold. Iqbal was familiar with his face. Both these officers had been on duty at the serpentine barricade set up at Mahim. They had also come to the godown hiding in the tempo.

'Singh has confessed,' Rustomji said casually, as if discussing the weather.

'Really!' Khan turned to Iqbal with a triumphant smile. For the first time, Khan saw sweat on Iqbal's forehead.

'Here is the confessional statement,' Rustomji said giving four typed sheets to his colleague, 'with his signature.'

Khan scanned through the typed pages. 'Seems like the ringleader's name is missing.'

'Singh fears for the safety of his family if he reveals the name.'

'How many members are there in his family?'

'A wife and three children. If we can assure him of their security, he is prepared to divulge that too.'

'What did you tell him?'

'What could I say? Providing security cover means posting security guards at his residence. Moreover, the kids are small. They go to school. We would have to take responsibility of their security as well.'

'Tell me,' Khan asked Rustomji, glancing once again at Iqbal who was intently listening to the conversation, 'how did you get Singh to spill the beans?'

'I had him under surveillance for the last two years. I knew his weakness: he wants to maintain a "Mr Clean" image before his wife. So I threatened him that if he didn't cooperate, I would hand over the file to his wife and expose him completely.'

'As it is, every man stands exposed before his wife,' Khan joked.

'Seems like your interrogation is still incomplete. Should I send in Singh?'

'Is he still here?'

'I've kept him waiting.'

'Just a minute.' Khan went up to Iqbal and said, 'Now tell me, are you signing your confession too or should I call your boss to refresh your memory?'

'Call him, sir,' Iqbal said, gathering his last ounce of courage.

Rustomji left to call Singh.

*

Iqbal was like a defeated gambler, and a defeated gambler always plays the last game with gusto. He had nothing more to lose. *If Singh had really admitted to everything, then he was bound to be locked up with him. But what if he had not confessed?* This last hope was as thin as the strand of a cobweb. He was still not prepared to accept defeat; it was not in his nature to surrender.

As soon as Rustomji entered the room with Singh, Khan said, 'Here is your boss. Now, do you have to say anything?'

Iqbal glanced at Rustomji and Singh. Singh wore a deadpan expression. Iqbal turned to Khan and declared, 'I don't know him.'

'Rustomji!' Khan said, 'Read out Singh's statement.'

'My statement?' Singh was surprised.

'Shut up!' Rustomji shouted.

'But how can you have my statement when I've not confessed to anything?'

The game was over. Both the officers accepted failure. There was no reason for them to keep the suspects under custody.

A while later, they saw Iqbal and Singh emerge from the building, arms draped over each other's shoulders, engage a taxi and zip off to Natraj Hotel to celebrate their victory.

'Rustomji!' Khan said bitterly, 'Until I put these two goons behind bars, my soul won't rest in peace.'

19

Before Sharad's birthday party on Friday evening, Iqbal met Singh at Gaylord restaurant. Singh would usually be there every day between 4 p.m. and 6 p.m.

'Iqbal! I spoke to DK about your fancy ideas on crossing.'

'What did he say?' Iqbal sat across Singh. Over Singh's shoulder, his gaze wandered to a heavyset Gujarati businessman dressed in a white kurta-pyjama, sitting a few tables away.

'He agreed to try the idea out before implementing it.'

'A trial run!'

'We will put stones equalling the weight of 100 jackets in a bag tied to a nylon rope and dump it in forty bam-deep waters. Then, you will pull it with a steam launch up to the Versova coast.'

'There is no need to experiment,' Iqbal said flatly.

Singh scowled. Iqbal's eyes rested on the Gujarati businessman again. He recalled seeing him the last time he had come to meet Singh. Who could this elegant *baniya* be?

'I have full confidence in my idea,' Iqbal added, looking back at Singh. 'Besides, I'll be going on two months' leave from tomorrow.'

'For what?'

'To prepare for my final examinations.'

The reply made Singh ponder.

'It's a matter of just an evening,' he implored. 'Can't you spare it?'

'No.'

'But . . .'

'I don't have time to waste. If you don't trust me, you can take Dagdu and Michael along and try it out.'

Singh reluctantly accepted this suggestion.

The stocky Gujarati got up and walked over to Singh, asking for a matchbox. Singh flicked the lighter. The Gujarati lit his cigarette and went back to his seat. Iqbal figured that, like Singh, he must be a regular here.

*

It was after 7 p.m. that Iqbal reached Sharad's bungalow on Carmichael Road. Entering the stately gate, he saw that the front door was at the far end of a lush green courtyard—a tiled pathway led up to it. Crossing the pathway, he drew close to the entrance when his foot touched something soft: a cat was hiccupping and writhing in pain. It perplexed him.

A moment later, the door opened and he forgot about the cat: he was dazzled by the spectacle before his eyes. The posh, high-ceilinged hall was exploding with colourful balloons and crepe ribbons. Rock and roll was blasting from a record player. Under a shiny glitter ball, boys and girls were dancing like they were possessed. Magical shards of lights kaleidoscopically floated across the walls. It looked like a dream world.

Treading lightly, Iqbal sat on a sofa set against the wall. In the darkness, he could see the play of lights dancing across ecstatic faces, but it was not possible to discern the dancing faces clearly.

In any case, he had little interest in them. He had come here just as a formality. In fact, he felt like an alien. He had planned to sit for a while and leave after greeting Sharad.

As the song ended, the disco lights went off too; the house lights came on. All the faces were visible now. He knew most of them because they were from his college. The others were perhaps from St Xavier's or some other college. But every one of them, he guessed, was blowing up daddy's hard-earned money.

After the dance, all the couples dispersed and sat down on the chairs and sofas arranged against the wall. Kusum was sitting across him in a chair placed against the opposite wall. She was chatting animatedly with a boy.

She had not yet noticed Iqbal, who began looking around for Sharad. *Where was he? Had he not been part of the last dance? The guests were partying while the host was absent!* Iqbal stood up to check in the next room when his friends spotted him. 'Hello, Iqbal!' someone called. 'Hi, Iqbal,' another shouted. Kusum now looked up and observed him silently.

Exchanging smiles with friends, he made his way up to Kusum.

'Where is Sharad?'

'Maybe in the kitchen! You are late.'

'It took me some time to locate the address. The cake must have been cut, I suppose!'

'Cut, eaten and digested.'

They were talking like friends, yet Iqbal did not miss the note of melancholy in Kusum's voice. 'I've not yet wished Sharad,' he said.

'Come, I'll take you.' Kusum stood up.

Before they could move, the house lights went off. The colourful dance lights returned along with the ear-splitting music. The young boys and girls, who had taken a break, started dancing jerkily to 'Rock around the Clock'. It became difficult for Iqbal and Kusum to weave their way through the sweaty crowd.

'Kusum, I'm feeling suffocated in this strange, westernized world.'

'To tell you the truth, I was planning to slip away after wishing Sharad.'

'Is it necessary to greet him?'

'Won't he feel offended?'

'Everyone has taken note of your presence here. If you want to slip away, this is a great chance. Go. Go away.'

Iqbal continued to stand. He was caught in a dilemma. The raucous music was reverberating in his ears. Strange lights were swinging across his face.

'Believe me, Iqbal. The darkness is to your advantage, no one will notice you.' Kusum held his wrist and began to guide him towards the main entrance.

'But . . .'

'The dance will last for at least fifteen minutes. And Sharad won't let you go before dinner. So unless you intend to sacrifice two hours of your life . . .'

Bumping and weaving through the crowd, they stopped at the main entrance. Or rather, it was Iqbal who stopped her.

Iqbal's conscience pricked him. To leave without saying hello would be an insult to the host. *Why was Kusum pressing him? Why was she desperate that Iqbal should leave as soon as possible? Did Kusum fear that there would be renewed tension between Sharad and him because of her?*

Little did he know that he would get the answers to all these questions the following day.

*

The lights came back on again in a while, and with them surfaced Sharad's face, smiling at both of them. He had probably come from some adjoining room and joined the dance halfway.

'Hi, Iqbal! Planning to escape?'

'Not at all,' he quickly replied, with a touch of guilt. 'How can I leave without meeting you?'

'You can't leave without dinner either. The party has just begun. It will gain momentum after midnight. If you wish, you can stay back for the night. We will have breakfast together in the morning.' Then turning to Kusum he asked, 'What do you say? Should he be allowed to leave early?'

'Not before midnight.'

Kusum's reply surprised Iqbal. Just a couple of minutes ago, she was pushing him out. *Why?* Once again, the question faded away unanswered.

Iqbal shifted his attention from Kusum to Sharad. 'I'm accustomed to going to bed by 9 p.m. It is really painful to stay up late. I'm sure you won't make anyone suffer on such an auspicious day.'

Sharad pretended to think before replying. 'Hmm . . . you got me there. I won't force you, but I can only humbly request you not to leave on an empty stomach.'

'This is not a humble request,' Iqbal laughed. 'This is called an order. I know the food isn't going to be served before midnight.'

'At least you can taste my birthday cake right away.'

Iqbal could not refuse.

Pleased, Sharad put his arm around his neck and told Kusum, 'You come along too. In your presence, Iqbal will eat a piece or two more.'

Suddenly, rock music started playing and Kusum found an excuse to stay back. Sharad went ahead with Iqbal.

'How many bedrooms are there in this bungalow?' Iqbal asked, making small talk.

'Six. My mother and father use one bedroom, while another is for my sister and this . . .' he said, pushing a door nearby, 'is my own bedroom.'

Iqbal glanced through the door. Sharad's bedroom was air-conditioned. *Every room in this mansion probably had an AC!* The wall across was covered with a large Beatles poster. His eyes spotted a model of the Taj Mahal enclosed in a glass case, a radio, a cuckoo clock and an aquarium with piranhas. As for furniture, there was a walk-in closet and a cupboard fitted into the wall. Silk curtains were draped over the windows, below which there was an exquisite bedstead. Imported crystal statues sparkled on the sideboard.

'So what do you think?' Sharad asked proudly.

'It's like a dream.'

Crossing the passage, they entered the kitchen. The kitchen was as spacious as a bedroom. The designer tiles on the walls glowed in the soft light.

'This cake is known as the king of all cakes.' Sharad made Iqbal sit on a bar stool and passed him the cake from a table.

Iqbal saw that only three slices had been eaten from the round six-inch cake. Taking a piece, he asked, 'Is this your birthday cake?'

'No, that has been polished off.'

'What about this one?'

'A friend of dad's sent it to me with his best wishes. You'll have to finish it.'

'So much!'

'Listen, buddy! I've already accepted your request to leave before dinner. To compensate, you will have to lick the plate clean.'

'It's really delicious.'

'Why shouldn't it be? After all it has come from the Taj Hotel.'

As he savoured the slice, Iqbal had a doubt. 'What did you say its name was?'

'I haven't told you. I thought you'd know the name of the king of all cakes.'

'I hope this isn't the one called the black forest cake?'

'The very same.'

'Sorry, I can't eat this.'

'But, you have already relished one piece.'

'Had I known, I wouldn't have touched it.'

'Why?'

'Because it contains liquor.'

Sharad burst out laughing. 'What a joke! It contains only as much alcohol as is used in certain medicines. Have you never taken a tonic?'

'I don't remember having taken one knowingly.' Iqbal wiped his hands with a towel.

'Sorry, my friend. Had I known earlier . . .'

'Forget it.'

The two walked out of the kitchen.

'I never had the slightest idea that you were such a fanatic when it comes to alcohol.'

'You said it—a fanatic. At this moment I am feeling like a Brahmin who has mistakenly tasted beef!'

Sharad stared at him wide-eyed. It was 10.30 p.m. Half an hour later, Iqbal engaged a taxi to return home.

*

To reach Dongri from Carmichael Road at that hour takes not more than ten minutes. But once the convulsions started, time seemed to stretch endlessly. A series of convulsions, starting suddenly from his legs, violently shook Iqbal's body and reached up to his head, which was bursting with pain. His body temperature started rising. Eating the cake containing alcohol had shaken him up mentally. He felt as if he would die before reaching home.

'Driver!' he hissed, gritting his chattering teeth. 'Faster!'

The driver was surprised. 'I want you to reach home, not the graveyard.' He was driving at full speed.

Iqbal did not have the strength to reply. He lay down on the back seat.

*

When the taxi stopped at the corner of Munda Galli, the driver turned back and realized the gravity of the situation. He opened the back door and helped Iqbal out. The boys working in Aziz Dilip's liquor den were surprised. They wondered how Iqbal, who never ever touched alcohol, had come home drunk.

The taxi driver managed to haul the staggering Iqbal up to the first floor of Abbasi Manzil. At home, everyone was asleep. The driver knocked on the door twice. Gul Banu opened the door. For a few moments, she simply stared blankly. The first thought she had was that her son had been beaten up in a gang war.

'Ma!' Iqbal let go of the taxi driver and tried to enter the room. On the very first step, he buckled at his mother's feet like a broken puppet.

Before Gul Banu could understand the situation, the taxi driver told her, 'The boy is suffering from high fever. Please call a doctor immediately.' Without claiming his fare, he went down the stairs.

At once on her knees, Gul Banu held her son's wrist and immediately pulled her hand back as if she had been stung by a scorpion. Iqbal's body was indeed scorching with fever. His head was rolling from side to side. There was no time to think.

She woke up Firoze. *Where would they get a doctor at this hour of the night? All the clinics in Dongri closed at 11 p.m.*

'What happened to bhaijaan, Mummy?" Firoze asked, rubbing his eyes.

'He has a fever. Take a large vessel, fill water and mix two spoonfuls of salt in it. We need to put a wet cloth on his forehead.'

By the time Firoze came back with the water, Gul Banu had managed to get Iqbal on the bed. She placed a stool close by. Firoze placed the container on it. Gul Banu sat on the edge of the bed, folded a handkerchief, dipped it in the water, rinsed it slightly and spread it across Iqbal's forehead. Firoze stood there staring. He had never seen his elder brother in such bad shape. He wanted to ask his mother if his big brother would be all right when Iqbal muttered, 'Ma, my stomach is on fire . . . entire body is burning . . . if the agony doesn't stop, I'll . . .' His head stopped rolling.

He had fainted.

Firoze, who had suppressed his emotions all this while, started crying. Gul Banu's body was racked by sobs as intense as hiccups and tears were streaming down his cheeks. She thought Iqbal was dead.

Dazed, she leapt up. As she ran out of the house, somewhere in the distant nocturnal quiet, a clock struck two. Once again, she remembered that no doctor was at hand this late. She reluctantly returned and saw that Iqbal had started coughing—a sign of life. She was relieved. Iqbal's eyes were still closed. Intermittently, convulsions of dry cough would compel his body to jump off the mattress.

Ignoring Firoze's sniffling sobs, Gul Banu stoically dipped the handkerchief in water, and this time placed it on Iqbal's belly. His body was so hot that the water in the handkerchief evaporated in a few seconds. She again dipped the parched handkerchief in salt water.

After repeating the process every few minutes, Iqbal's body temperature dropped slightly but his coughing continued. This raised doubts in Gul Banu's mind. *What type of fever is this? No one coughs so severely in fever.*

The voice of the muezzin wafted in from the nearby Khoja masjid. Dawn was about to break: the night was almost over. Firoze had fallen asleep weeping. The ringing call of 'Allahu Akbar' (Allah is great) raised Gul Banu's hopes.

*

After a while, the neighbour's door opened. Adjusting his skullcap, he crossed Iqbal's doorway and froze on spotting the scene inside.

'Sister, what happened?'

Gul Banu explained the situation in brief: 'The coughing has ceased but his temperature has started shooting up once again.'

He stepped inside and holding Iqbal's wrist exclaimed, 'I guess the temperature is around 104 degrees! If it rises further, it could affect his brain.'

Rushing out, he assured Gul Banu, 'I will return with a doctor soon.'

Iqbal's neighbour Noor Mohammed was fifty-five years old. He was a kind-hearted, God-fearing soul always ready to help. Only last month, Iqbal had withdrawn his brother Razzak from school and got him a job at Noor Mohammed's footwear shop.

He returned in half an hour with the family doctor, Khimani, who had been woken up from a deep slumber.

The doctor entered, followed by Noor Mohammed who was carrying his bag.

Dr Khimani examined Iqbal's tongue and eyes, while listening to all the details from Gul Banu. He was shocked. All the symptoms she described were that of poisoning. 'What did he have for dinner last night?' he asked, taking out a thermometer from his bag and inserting it in Iqbal's armpit.

'He wasn't home. He had gone out for a birthday party.'

The doctor pronounced that it was food poisoning. He might have eaten something rotten, because of which poison had spread throughout his body. If the diagnosis was correct, he presumed the same food must have affected other guests at the party.

The doctor was unable to say anything more because no one else could corroborate what Iqbal had eaten last.

Iqbal was still unconscious. The doctor gave him a shot and turned to Gul Banu. 'When he opens his eyes, give him these two tablets. He will vomit. If he doesn't, rush him to Habib Hospital.'

He got up. Noor Mohammed, who was quietly standing behind his chair, picked up the doctor's bag and left with him.

When the shot took effect, Iqbal opened his eyes and was dazed by what he saw. There were no faces before him, only foggy forms; he couldn't recognize anyone.

He focused on Gul Banu. The woman looked familiar— he had a feeling that he had seen her somewhere. On trying harder, the hazy face came into focus. 'Ma! Has Razzak left for school?'

'No, son.'

'Why?'

'He has a job now. It was you who had pulled him out from school and put him there.'

Suddenly, the haze descended again. Puzzled, Iqbal asked, 'Ma, when will Razzak return from school?'

Gul Banu felt like crying. The poison was affecting his brain. In his delirium, Iqbal was repeating himself over and over again.

*

After some time, Noor Mohammed returned from the clinic and got busy. He placed his hand behind Iqbal's back and raised him. 'Iqbal! Take these two pills.'

Where are the pills? Who is asking me? The voice had drowned in a haze. Gul Banu brought her hand near his lips and put the two pills inside his mouth. Then she gave him a glass of water. He washed down both the pills one after the other.

Noor Mohammed eased him back on to the bed. Gul Banu was deeply touched by this gem of a man, a perfect model of humanity, who ungrudgingly tended to her son as his own. 'Brother! You have been on your feet since morning. I'm sorry you missed your morning prayers.'

'I've only done my duty. As for the prayers, if for a day I offer namaz a little late, my Allah won't be annoyed.'

'But you will be late for work too.'

'It's only 8 a.m. I can wait for at least one more hour. You please pray that Iqbal vomits soon.'

Getting up from the edge of the bed, Gul Banu picked up the *tasbih* and sat on the mattress on which the two children were sleeping. Noor Mohammed too started praying fervently.

*

After ten minutes, Iqbal felt nauseous. Gul Banu put down the tasbih, picked up a bowl and sat on the bed. After five more minutes, Iqbal sat up with a start. His mouth was bent over the bowl. His vomit was black. Gul Banu and Noor Mohammed were bewildered.

Had the doctor not told them before, Gul Banu would have thought that the black vomit was a result of some black magic or voodoo.

She got up and started washing the bowl in the kitchen. Noor Mohammed's face relaxed. He was not needed here now. Taking Gul Banu's leave, he left.

After about an hour, Iqbal recovered slightly. He could hear his mother fumbling around the small kitchen. He could think clearly. In his semi-conscious haze, his brain processed a word he had heard the doctor say: 'poison'.

Did the doctor guess right? Had he been a victim of food poisoning? Or had someone tried to poison him?

20

I qbal lay in bed thinking. The events of the previous evening flashed before his eyes.

He had gone to Sharad's bungalow on Carmichael Road to attend his birthday party. There, in the kitchen, he had eaten just one slice of cake. *Was that cake so rotten that it had caused food poisoning?*

He had read about several such instances in the newspaper where all the guests at a dinner party took ill after eating sweets made from milk and had to be hospitalized. However, this could not have happened at Sharad's house. The piece that he had given Iqbal to eat was from a special cake. It was not the same cake that the rest of the guests were served. This was the black forest cake from Taj Hotel. When Iqbal had taken a piece, there were already about three pieces missing.

Who could have eaten those pieces?

He thought of the sick cat outside Sharad's bungalow. When he had entered, the cat had been writhing in pain. By the time he left, the cat was dead. *Had it had a piece of that special cake?*

Gradually, a seed of suspicion started sprouting in his mind. He thought of Kusum. He had found her behaviour strange: as if she wanted to shove Iqbal out of the bungalow before he could touch anything. Iqbal had been unable to understand her then. Now, the mystery had begun unravelling.

Sharad had laced the cake with poison. The cat had pounced on it first. Maybe the cat smelt the egg in it. Kusum must have somehow known about the cake being spiked. Despite this, he felt certain that she was not a part of the poisoning conspiracy. Had she known it could prove fatal, she would have warned him clearly.

Kusum still had a soft corner for him. Sharad's attitude was different. He was not only a coward but vicious and vengeful too. Pretending to extend a hand of friendship, he had tried to stab him in the back.

*

'Sufi!' I interrupted his narrative. 'What exactly do you mean by poison?'

'What was mixed in the cake is called arsenic.'

'How did you know?'

'The symptoms of my illness were the same as those caused by arsenic. For example, fever accompanied by cold, dry cough, dilation of the pupils, loss of memory and black vomit are clear indications of arsenic poisoning.'

I recalled having read in a history book that Napoleon too was killed using arsenic and that he too suffered the same symptoms.

*

This incident had shaken Iqbal. Though the poison was ejected from his body through the vomit, its after-effects persisted: he could not see clearly. Whenever he tried to focus on an object,

a fog would start rolling in his eyes. This did not affect his daily
chores because they did not require concentration. *But what
about his studies?*

He had planned to start preparing for his examinations
from Saturday. Unfortunately, he was bedridden for a week
due to the weakness caused by high fever.

He picked up a book lying on the bed. As soon as he tried
to read, the black letters would blur into clouds and float away.
He felt his heart sink.

*

The next week, he went to Dr Khimani's clinic. 'Doctor, how
can I appear for examinations if I can't read? And if I don't
appear for the examinations, I'll lose one full academic year.'

'There is no need to panic. Your eyesight will be normal
in about a month.'

'One month!' he cried. 'For me, each day is precious.
Doctor, I want to study medicine. And for that just passing
marks won't do.'

'You don't start digging a well after your house catches
fire, do you?' the doctor chided him. 'What did you do
throughout the year?'

Iqbal did not reply. As was his nature, he had left everything
to fate. Whatever had happened in his life had always been
beyond his control. *Was he in control of whatever was happening
now?* Every morning, as soon as he woke up, he would open
a book and see the black letters turning into storm clouds and
his face would darken too.

*

Suraiyya and I were floating on bright, happy clouds. For
us, the question of preparing for examinations did not exist.

Wherever we went, we had our sketchbook and colour pencils ready.

At times, we would board a train from Bombay and reach Khandala. When we were tired of capturing the landscape on paper, we would rest in the lap of nature. The sky smiled at us, the trees serenaded us. It was an unforgettable experience, lying silently on the green earth and looking at the turquoise sky— 'gazing at God's window' as the Czech proverb says. This was our world, with its rarefied air and perfect rolling hills, solitary but always holding the promise of adventure in its hush.

Suraiyya could not remain quiet for long.

'Life is so soft and gentle,' she would muse to herself, 'like a rabbit's fur.'

I would point out, 'In Japan, more than a million innocent people were killed. An entire city was wiped out.'

'Sometimes I feel I'm living out a dream!'

'Israelis bombarded the Palestinian settlement and massacred more than 300 people.'

She would wonder aloud, 'Who colours the rainbows of our dreams?'

I would reply, 'The death toll in communal riots in Bhiwandi has crossed 500.'

This time, as if she heard me for the first time, Suraiyya sat upright. 'Aabid, you're a pessimist.'

'I just stated the truth about life.'

'Please explain, how are we concerned with that truth?'

'If our feelings are numbed, then we aren't.'

'You mean to say that I'm insensitive?' She didn't wait for a reply. 'Here there is greenery, there are flowers, butterflies, a flowing spring, the sweet aroma of the air, you and me. And there, far away a man is killed—one we have never seen, with whom we have no relation. You think it's a sign of your sensitivity to grieve over his death and trample over these fragrant moments. I don't feel that way.'

I sat up and accepted her argument. 'Now, even I don't feel it is right.'

'Read this letter!'

She took out an envelope from her purse and handed it to me. I observed postage stamps of Kenya across the envelope: it was obvious that the letter was from her home.

I took out the letter and read it. The expression on my face changed. Of course, the problem was not that serious. Suraiyya's mother had called her to spend the vacation with the family.

'Did you go there last year?'

'Nope.'

'And this year?'

'I'll go if you permit.'

I felt torn. She had every right to visit her mother once a year. I could not stop her just because of my selfishness.

'Suraiyya, only you can take that decision. I won't be a hurdle.'

'Then can I go after the exams?'

'You have all the right.'

'You are willingly giving me permission, no?'

'To tell you the truth, it is with a heavy heart.'

'Then I won't go.'

'Look, the vacation is one and a half months away. Do you feel it is right to sour these romantic moments by worrying about it now?'

She laughed. We walked back silently, hand in hand, autumn leaves under our feet. There was no need for words, nor was there any desire to break the sublime silence.

*

After the affliction in his eyes was rectified, Iqbal studied hard for a month, day and night, and secured 67 per cent marks, just over the 65 per cent required for getting admission into medical college.

*

Suraiyya and I were in the first five on the merit list. To double our joy, Suraiyya decided to postpone her visit to Mombasa that year too. I decided to give her an expensive gift. My budget was limited to Rs 100. The problem was what to buy with that budget.

A sari?

She had a number of saris: banarasis, silks, kanjeevarams. In college, she dressed simply. However, while accompanying me to a movie or going to a restaurant, she wore exquisite clothes.

Sandals?

With the question came the reply: In love, an offering of shoes is not advisable.

Perfume?

I bought a bottle of the legendary Chanel No. 5 and went to the hostel to present it to her.

She accepted it gleefully and put a proposal before me: a girl from her hostel was going to Nainital—Suraiyya wanted both of us to join her.

'But will you get permission?' I asked.

'No one, including our hostel superintendent, will object to my escorting a dear friend.'

'But what about me?'

'Only my friend and I know this secret,' she said, and then added with a mischievous smile. 'Even you don't know it.'

Now I understood.

I spent two days preparing. Before leaving, I needed to wind up several assignments. I had to submit comic strips to *Ramakadu* and *Parag* for the coming months. My comic strip 'Batukbhai' in *Chetmachandar* had failed to find favour and was discontinued. However, the one-page comic story, 'Prof. Chelbatau', had become quite popular. In the meantime, the editor of *Chetmachandar*, Shani, started misusing his pen—and brush—to indulge in yellow journalism. This, however, had not impacted me yet.

There were times when I would detest Shani, and there were moments when I would pity him. The creator of an immortal character like Nathubhai, who had the potential of becoming the Walt Disney of not just Gujarat but the entire country, was slipping into the sewer because of his misdeeds. To top it all, he had also started drinking recklessly.

His decline had begun. Court case after court case was being filed against him. The people he tried to blackmail through his weekly were no ordinary people. He had not spared even the powerful local politician Dhebarbhai.

As a result, physical assaults began. The legal cases were only a pretext to harass him, to compel him to leave Bombay in order to stand trial in the courts of Junagadh or Rajkot. As soon as he stepped into enemy territory, he was beaten black and blue. He would return to Bombay sometimes with bandages and sometimes on a stretcher.

I was thinking of discontinuing 'Prof. Chelbatau' when Shani started abusing the leaders of my Khoja community in Bombay. I finally had a valid reason for leaving *Chetmachandar*.

During those days, Dr Dharmavir Bharati joined *Dharmayug*, a *Times of India* publication, as its editor. He created a special space on the magazine's last page for a comic strip where he wanted to feature an Indian cartoonist. He tried initially with some established cartoonists of the time. Some comic strips lasted a few weeks, while others became stale after a few months. There was no option but to offer the opening to an upcoming cartoonist. I received an invitation.

In the excitement of going to Nainital, I hadn't had the time to create a new character. However, I also did not want to lose the opportunity of gaining a foothold in the exalted Times group. In the rush before departing for Nainital, I picked up the originals of my old cartoon strip 'Batukbhai', which the Gujarati readers had rejected, and submitted them to the *Dharmayug* editor with a new name: 'Dhabooji'.

*

Our train went only as far as Pathankot. From there, we were to take a bus till Nainital. The journey took two days, but I was told it was not at all boring.

When we boarded the train from Bombay, Suraiyya's cheeky friend, Lubayna, had already settled in with her baggage under the seat. We too parked our luggage and while sitting across her, looking at her chestnut-brown hair—which was so long that she could sit on it—the first thought that struck me was that Lubayna knew that Suraiyya and I were in love and it was but natural that we would prefer to spend most of our time with each other. *Would she not feel lonely?*

'Are you from Nainital?' I asked her as soon as the train started.

'Lubayna is from Pune,' Suraiyya answered.

Till then, I had been under the impression that she had a family home in Nainital, which is why she had invited us along. My mind rebelled—I should not have joined the trip. I would be required not only to look after Suraiyya but, despite my unwillingness, keep Lubayna in good spirits as well. The presence of a third wheel between two lovers is not a pleasant experience.

After about ten minutes, the train stopped at Dadar. To
Suraiyya and my surprise, a jovial, athletic youth entered
our compartment and offered his hand. His clasp was warm
and surprisingly gentle for such a big-built man. He was
Anil, Lubayna's boyfriend. He was affluent and rather sweet,
but completely under her thumb. I marvelled at her: now I
understood her game.

She wanted to spend her vacation with her boyfriend
outside Bombay. But how would she get permission from the
hostel superintendent? Therefore, she persuaded Suraiyya.
Unwittingly, we too had fallen prey to this conspiracy of
love.

Anil's arrival rid me of a major headache. Now, we could
fully enjoy our trip. Each day flew past. As Suraiyya often said,
we were dream-dwellers.

*

If we were floating on the clouds, Iqbal was trying to plant his
feet firmly on the ground. He had grim realities to face. The
time for a crossing was coming up.

'Iqbal!' Singh perked up on seeing him after a long time.
'Your new idea is fantastic.'

'Did you try it?'

Happily, Singh opened a bottle of Scotch. 'Yes, under my
own supervision.'

Singh had taken two of Iqbal's colleagues, Dagdu and
Michael, on the steam launch and dumped a bag stuffed with
stones into the sea. The bag was tied to a nylon rope. The
other end of the string was tied to the lower hull of the steam
launch. The bag was then dragged from Indira dock to Uran
Island. Once Singh pulled out the bag from the water safely,
he was convinced it worked.

'Still, we can't call it an absolutely secure method.' With this, Singh smiled into his glass, swirled it, drank up with a flourish and commented, 'Of course, the risk at sea has been reduced, not on land.'

That was true. The consignment could be dragged under the sea to Madh or Versova, but it could attract attention when being loaded into vehicles. Moreover, if an informer gave a tip-off to the customs, there would be no way to avoid danger.

'We can also find a way out for that. How many customs officials are on our payroll?' Iqbal asked.

'Five.'

'Are they loyal?'

'More than dogs.'

'Okay.'

Iqbal was quiet after that.

'What do you mean by "okay"?'

'We will have to assign a task to one of them.'

'Where?'

'At the place of landing.'

'Where do you plan to land the next consignment?'

'At Versova.'

'What will that officer do there?'

'We will have to inform the officer in advance.'

'About what?'

'About the details of the consignment so that he can keep all the papers ready with him.'

'Papers?'

'A record of seizures—a *panchnama*.'

'Without carrying out a raid?'

'Singh!' Iqbal couldn't resist a snort of laughter. 'It seems that you have left your brains at home today. Listen, that will be a bogus record, so that if honest officers like Khan and

Rustomji carry out a surprise raid, our officer can tell them that it is his case.'

Now, the blueprint sparkled before Singh like a Christmas tree. If this happened then the officers honestly carrying out the real raid would not be able to interfere in their colleague's affairs. They would be compelled to return empty-handed. The officer on the gang's payroll could then prepare a weak case and present one or two dummy accused before the magistrate so that these fellows too would be released.

'But what about the consignment?'

'The consignment will remain with us.'

'What about the consignment list recorded in the panchnama?'

'There are several ways to deal with that. The record can be destroyed and replaced with a new one, or it can be disclosed that the accused fled with the entire consignment.'

Singh was speechless. Such a well-choreographed waltz between the police and criminals could revolutionize the field of smuggling. But that was not the reason behind Singh's astonishment. He was amazed by the lightning speed with which Iqbal's brain computed solutions. For Singh, it was no less than one of the wonders of the world.

That day, Iqbal had not even required time to think; no sooner had Singh presented a new problem, than Iqbal had shot back a brilliant solution. *The time was ripe to arrange his meeting with the boss.*

Iqbal had been hinting at it for the last few months, and he had been avoiding it saying that it wasn't time yet. This had heightened Iqbal's curiosity. After all, who was DK, under whose invisible umbrella they were working? Who was this mighty man whose reach was far beyond the long arm of the law? Who knows how many police and customs officers were in his hand? He held judges of the lower and higher courts in his pocket like trump cards.

His desire to meet the boss had not been fulfilled till date. Today, he felt that he had to make some special move to compel DK to request him for a meeting. But for that, first it was necessary to snare Singh.

Singh was keenly observing Iqbal's face. He got an inkling of what Iqbal was trying: the baby sparrow was testing its wings.

He cancelled the meeting with DK that he had mentally fixed. Pleased with himself, Singh's face lit up: he realized he was yet to praise Iqbal's brilliant idea. He effusively said, 'Yaar, that stuff inside your skull . . . is it a brain or a computer?'

As if Iqbal too was waiting for such a move, he proclaimed, 'You'll know it after I get Hamid released from the hangman's noose.'

Singh was caught off guard.

DK had engaged Bombay's best barrister to get Hamid acquitted of the charge of stabbing a customs officer to death during crossing. He had been able to help Hamid come out on bail but had thrown up his hands about the final verdict.

'I don't believe it,' said Singh.

'Because you are Singh, not DK.'

'At least try to convince me!'

'That won't help.'

'Then?'

'DK pays the barrister Rs 50,000 for every court appearance to fight the murder case. If he wants Hamid scot-free in just Rs 500, tell him to contact me.'

A stunned Singh stared shell-shocked at him.

21

After Iqbal left, Singh fell into deep thought. *Could Iqbal's claim be trusted? Would he be able to rescue Hamid from certain death? Was he more intelligent than the seasoned barrister fighting the case?*

The answer he got to all these questions was the same: NO. The barrister's fee for appearing in court was Rs 50,000 a day. Over Rs 36,00,000 had already been spent on Hamid's case. What had been the result?

Zero. Nothing.

To be fair, before accepting the case, the barrister had apprised them that the odds were fifty-fifty. However, as the case had stumbled towards the final hearing, the 50 per cent chance of winning had come down to just 5 per cent, while here Iqbal was claiming that in just Rs 500 he could legally . . .

Singh's train of thought came to an abrupt halt: Iqbal had not told him whether he would save Hamid legally or illegally. He could be planning to smuggle Hamid across the border into Pakistan. But that would be risky.

If the plan failed, Hamid would undoubtedly be in a fix. The entire case would be ruined. The 5 per cent chance of success would become a minus 5 per cent because there would be no option of filing an appeal. Even the President would reject a mercy petition. DK would never approve of this.

DK had a big heart. He reciprocated with equal measure the loyalty of his gang members. He would stand by his men like a rock in times of crisis. Why else would he waste lakhs of rupees on a tapori like Hamid?

Singh returned to his thoughts once again. Iqbal had demanded only Rs 500 to secure Hamid's freedom. This amount would not be enough to get across the border. One would have to bribe security officers on both sides of the fence. This would cost a minimum of Rs 2000–5000.

Iqbal must have planned a master stroke. He could not fathom what it was and Iqbal would never disclose it. *Would it be wise to discuss the matter with DK? What if he mentioned it and DK dismissed the possibility with a laugh?* He would sink into the earth out of shame. Even if DK didn't laugh him off the face of the earth, there was another possibility, more terrifying than the previous one: what if Iqbal's genius scheme turned out to be full of loopholes? DK would shoot a frozen look at Singh. And DK's icy glare was as deadly as an icicle dagger.

No, he couldn't take the risk of blindly pitching Iqbal before DK. Yet, he made up his mind to mention the subject casually to DK when the opportunity arose in the next few days. He would see which way the wind was blowing before deciding on a course of action.

But if Iqbal's plan proved workable, Singh's stock would rise in DK's eyes; he would be applauded for grooming a promising young cub like Iqbal.

Finally, he removed a diary from his pocket. A consignment of gold was scheduled to arrive from Dubai on Thursday night. Iqbal was to sail out to take the delivery early on Friday morning. Singh was to meet the boss the same evening to report on the crossing. He would get a chance that very evening to present Iqbal's idea—at least he would be able to work it into the conversation somehow. He marked an asterisk in his diary for Friday; a habit he had inculcated for remembering important things.

*

On Friday morning, Iqbal, after offering the early morning prayers, left from Bhaucha Dhakka along with his gang. The stars were fading in the sky and the wind was picking up speed. He was standing on the deck of *Al Kabir*. The new method of crossing he had introduced was to be put to test today. But he was not nervous—he had confidence in his judgment and the trial run had proven him right.

As *Al Kabir* crossed the halfway mark to the drop location, dawn broke over the horizon. After crossing the lighthouse, the launch slowed into a neutral gear.

Iqbal and his colleagues bent over the handrail in search of the floating piece of thermocol. They did not have to look too hard.

With the first rays of the sun falling on to the surface of the sea, they spotted the thermocol at a distance, gleaming like a diamond. Everyone saw it at the same time. The boatman turned the launch in that direction.

Soon, the thermocol, along with the nylon rope, was pulled into the launch with the help of a boathook. One end of the rope was fastened to the stern; the other end was tied to a bag that lay 240 feet under the sea.

Al Kabir was on the east side of Bombay. Its engine whirred to life and began chugging towards the west, towing along gold worth Rs 2.5 crore.

Iqbal was chuckling. His new method had not only reduced the risk factor but had also solved several other problems. Earlier everyone had to stay awake throughout the night during the crossing. Hours were wasted transferring the jackets from one boat to another. It was, overall, a nerve-racking and back-breaking job.

In contrast, this felt as if they were headed to Elephanta Island for a picnic—Iqbal and his seven colleagues looked fresh and buoyant.

After about an hour, the boat completed the semi-circular route and arrived at Versova beach. Here, customs officer Bhonsle, who was on the gang's payroll, was waiting for them in his jeep and two Ambassador cars.

Bhonsle received Rs 1000 every month from the gang to turn a blind eye to their activities. But that day it was different—he was asked to be present to provide security cover to them. In case of a genuine, unexpected raid, he would announce that he had already seized the goods. Also, given the special security needed for the operation, his jeep was to pilot the convoy of the two Ambassador cars carrying the gold to ensure that nothing untoward happened on the way.

The bag was hauled ashore before *Al Kabir* dropped anchor. Ten minutes later, Iqbal and his colleagues were seated in the Ambassador cars. The bag was stuffed into the boot of one of the cars. It was 8 a.m. Iqbal signalled to Bhonsle from the front seat of the first Ambassador. He started the jeep. Both the cars followed.

The gang had never known such security till date. Everyone applauded Iqbal's intelligence. Until then, only Dagdu had called him 'boss'. Now, all of them did.

'Boss!' Michael spoke from the back seat, 'now I too will have to get admission into your college.'

'For what?' asked Iqbal, his eyes fixed on Bhonsle's jeep ahead.

'To learn all these new tricks! Inside this skull is only sawdust. Such brilliant ideas don't come to me!'

*

Bhonsle looked back on reaching Andheri. Iqbal received the signal he had been waiting for: had DRI officers been waiting, they would have been ambushed by now.

He signalled Bhonsle whose duty ended here. Besides, he lived in Andheri. After having tea and breakfast at home, he had to report for state duty. Near the railway crossing, Bhonsle's jeep turned and headed towards Andheri (East). Both the Ambassador cars went towards Parle. Iqbal, instead of taking Ghodbunder Road, chose the Juhu-Parle bypass.

There were two reasons for this. First, the population was thin there. There were just a few scattered bungalows and dwellings. Work was on in full swing to reclaim the rest of the land. Second, on the main road, there was the likelihood of attracting the attention of the traffic police or other hawk-eyed officials, especially if they found themselves crawling in a traffic jam.

His judgement was spot on, but his luck was dented. A little further, Iqbal's Ambassador jolted to a stop and pitched to one side. The car following it also had to brake. Dagdu jumped out and dashed up to Iqbal.

Both realized that what the driver had thought to be a puddle was in fact a foot-deep ditch—the front tyre was stuck inside it.

Immediately, the rest of the gang gathered around too and, with much difficulty, heaved the car out. At the same time, in the distance, they spotted a police jeep coming towards them. Everyone froze for a few seconds.

Iqbal made a snap decision and asked Dagdu and his other cronies from the second car to sit in his car—the car which carried the precious Rs 2.5 crore cargo.

*

The police jeep raced towards them and stopped in front of the first car. 'Dikra!' said the man who stepped out of the jeep and smiled at Iqbal. 'We're meeting after quite some time, isn't it?'

Iqbal stared at Inspector Bharucha. *Was Bharucha there at this early hour by accident or by design? Had someone tipped him off?* The next moment, Iqbal remembered Bali, who was Inspector Bharucha's informer for the Juhu-Parle beat.

Iqbal's guess was almost correct. Only, he did not know that Bali's seafront apartment faced Versova beach. A fitness fanatic, he went jogging early every morning to keep fit. Today, as usual, he had woken up at the crack of dawn. Standing in his balcony brushing his teeth, his eyes fell on the two Ambassador cars; Bhonsle's jeep had not arrived then.

He understood: just like the once-revered Gandhi cap had become a symbol of corruption, the Ambassador car had become a symbol of smuggling.

He immediately dialled Inspector Bharucha, waking him up.

'Sir, I'm seeing signs of a massive haul.'

'Where?'

'There are two Ambassador cars parked close to the fishermen's settlement near my apartment. The consignment is likely to arrive here.'

Within minutes, Inspector Bharucha got ready and sped away in his jeep. As it was still very early, the roads were deserted. Even the gaslights on the footpaths had not yet been turned off. A distance which, during rush hours, usually took more than an hour now took him just thirty-five minutes. After crossing Mahim, he came upon the arterial Ghodbunder Road that linked the city with the suburbs.

Had Inspector Bharucha decided to continue down that road to Versova, he would have missed Iqbal. But, to save time, he left the main road, and after crossing Lido Cinema entered Juhu.

On reaching Juhu-Vile Parle Development Scheme, his eyes caught sight of the two cars standing in the middle of the road. He did not know that the person he was going to confront was none other than his disciple.

*

Recovering from the initial shock, Iqbal replied, 'It's true, sir. We are meeting after a long time.'

'Where did we meet last? Do you remember?' Inspector Bharucha peeped into one of the cars.

Iqbal walked behind him, his attention unwaveringly on Bharucha. 'Anyway, let me remind you,' the officer continued, 'that last time we met at Warden Road near Sagar Darshan building.'

He stood behind the first Ambassador car and opened its boot. It was empty. He shut it and, without looking back, walked towards the second car. 'But I'm sure that you won't forget today's meeting for years.'

Iqbal quietly followed him. When Inspector Bharucha stopped near the second car, he too stopped. The officer looked at Iqbal's men sitting inside. 'Are these your boys?'

Iqbal nodded.

'My, my! You have made quite some progress. Will you please ask these gentlemen to step out?'

Iqbal signalled to them. His men, along with the driver, came out. Inspector Bharucha looked inside and then went towards the boot.

'Dikra, can I ask you a question?'

'Sure.'

'Will you tell me the truth?'

'I don't lie.'

Inspector Bharucha let out a snort of laughter.

'I've never heard a bigger lie. Nevertheless, I'll ask. Where did you do the crossing?'

'You won't believe it.'

'What?'

'I don't do crossing.'

'Then did this manna [holy offering] drop from heaven?'

Saying this, Inspector Bharucha dramatically opened the boot with a jerk. Inside, in the bag, were jackets containing gold biscuits.

'I already told you that you won't believe it.' Iqbal gently closed the boot.

Annoyed, Inspector Bharucha opened it again. 'How much is it worth?'

'Rs 2.5 crore.'

'Tell your taporis to put it in my jeep.'

'I'll take out two jackets for you.'

'Didn't you follow what I said?'

'But, sir . . .'

'Pull out the bag and keep it in my jeep.'

'It's worth Rs 2.5 crore. You won't be able to digest it alone.'

'You aren't wrong. My appetite may be limited, but you know very well that our government's hunger is insatiable.'

'What will you gain by seizing the consignment?'

'I'm on duty here.'

'That's why you are entitled to two jackets. Two jackets mean 200 gold biscuits, you also know that.'

'What do you think I am!' Inspector Bharucha gave Iqbal a tight, biting slap. 'You think everyone is a racketeer like you?'

Iqbal was stunned. It had been a stinging slap. His face had turned red. His ears reverberated. His eyes had turned bloodshot. His gang members, who were standing at a distance, watched bewildered.

'Put the bag in my jeep!' Inspector Bharucha barked forcefully this time.

'Sir,' Iqbal said nursing his cheek, 'even I know how to use force.'

A lightning-sharp blow exploded below Iqbal's ear. The brute force spun him on to the car's bonnet. His jaw jarred with the impact: never before had he been hit so hard.

'You bloody bastard!' Iqbal heard Inspector Bharucha snarling. 'You're threatening me! I can skin you alive right here and make shoes out of your hide.'

Slowly, Iqbal steadied himself and turned towards Inspector Bharucha. His head was splitting with pain. Darkness swirled around his eyes. He was seeing this side of his guru for the first time. *How did this happen? Where was the good old Inspector Bharucha that he knew?*

He turned his eyes and looked into the barrel of a revolver. Inspector Bharucha stood pointing it at him. He glanced across at his team. All eyes were on him.

'Sir!' he said, making a last-ditch attempt to broker a deal, as a line of blood stained his impeccable white shirt. 'I don't believe in violence. If two jackets aren't enough, please take one more.'

'If you utter one more word, I'll blow your brains out,' Inspector Bharucha warned. 'Take out the bag!'

Wiping the hot blood away from his lips, Iqbal looked at Dagdu who was standing a little behind and to Inspector Bharucha's right. In a flash, he leapt like a panther. Before the inspector could realize what was happening, his neck was in Dagdu's iron grip and he felt a cold knife on his throat. One signal from Iqbal and Dagdu would slit it.

In the blink of an eye, the tables had turned.

Inspector Bharucha was stunned. Iqbal first took two steps forward and snatched the revolver. Then he turned towards his gang members.

'Close the boot.'

Michael ran across and slammed it shut.

'I won't spare you!' Inspector Bharucha yelled. 'I won't leave any of you alive. I'll wipe out your entire family from the face of this earth!'

Ignoring him, Iqbal shot another order. Michael and half of his gang sat in the second car. The driver started the engine, backed away a little and drove away.

'Dagdu!' Iqbal said, holding the revolver to Inspector Bharucha's chest. 'Hurry up! All of you leave. . .'

'What about you, boss?'

'That's Bharucha's concern, not yours,' Iqbal said, smiling confidentially. 'It's not fair that he should return empty-handed. I'm going with him to the police station.' Dagdu could not comprehend anything. For a few moments, he stared blankly at him. It was his duty to obey orders. He slowly pulled the knife away from Inspector Bharucha's neck.

The second Ambassador left, stirring a cloud of dust in its wake. Now, only two persons stood on the deserted road. One was the guru, the other was the disciple. But it was difficult to discern who was who.

*

After both the cars were no longer visible, Iqbal removed his finger from the trigger and offered the gun to Inspector Bharucha. 'Sir, your revolver!'

Snatching it, Inspector Bharucha put it back in the holster. Before he could explode, Iqbal said, 'You can arrest me and take me to the police station.'

'Did you think that I would let you go scot-free?' Inspector
Bharucha said, grabbing his hair and dragging him to the jeep.
'You rabid dog! You pointed my own revolver at me.' Kicking
Iqbal in the back, he made him climb into the jeep. 'Now you'll
see how I break your bones and ribs in the lock-up.' Inspector
Bharucha stomped his way to the steering wheel.

The jeep roared to life and sped to the nearest police
station. Iqbal sat quietly. He knew that Inspector Bharucha
was seething with rage. And when a person's blood pressure
shoots up, he loses the ability to think rationally.

Reality would dawn on Inspector Bharucha once his
temper cooled. Iqbal was prepared to stoically suffer a couple of
slaps and blows to satisfy the inspector's ego; he was hardened
far beyond his years.

*

When the jeep stopped in the police station compound,
Inspector Bharucha once again tried to grab his hair. 'Sir!'
Iqbal said, stopping him this time. 'Please. Be courteous, at
least as long as my guilt isn't proved.'

'You get down first!'

'Sir, I volunteered to come,' Iqbal reminded him, jumping
blithely off the jeep.

Inspector Bharucha dragged him by the wrist and presented
him before Duty Officer Ratnakar who looked shocked.
Ratnakar did not know Inspector Bharucha personally because
they belonged to different zones. Still, the rugged face looked
vaguely familiar.

Inspector Bharucha introduced himself. Ratnakar now
remembered: he had read about his exploits in the newspapers
in connection with gold smuggling. The report had effusively
praised this much-decorated crime branch officer.

'Sir!' Ratnakar jumped up saluting and gestured towards a chair. 'What can I do for you?'

A livid Inspector Bharucha refused to sit. 'Lodge an FIR and put this swine behind bars.'

'Go ahead, sir.' Ratnakar instantly sat down and picked up a ballpoint pen.

'Name, Iqbal Rupani. First offence, trafficking gold worth Rs 2.5 crore into Bombay.'

Taking a seat, Iqbal interrupted, 'Proof?'

'Shut up!' Inspector Bharucha screamed at him. 'The second offence, obstructing an officer from performing his duty by placing a knife at his throat.'

'Who put the knife, sir? Me or someone else?'

Ratnakar forgot about the FIR and gazed at them steadily.

'The third offence. He snatched my revolver and pointed it at me.'

Iqbal kept quiet.

'The fourth offence, he tried to bribe me.' Noticing Ratnakar's hand still and head up, he asked, 'Have you noted this down?'

Ratnakar had written just the name, nothing else. 'I'm listening, sir.' He pushed a chair with his leg for Inspector Bharucha to sit on—a diligent action that went unnoticed.

Now, Iqbal spoke evenly to the duty officer. 'Sir, all these charges are baseless. I'm totally innocent. Ask Mr Bharucha that if I smuggled gold worth Rs 2.5 crore into Bombay, where is it? If I had placed a knife on his neck, where is that knife? If I had his revolver, would he have been able to arrest me? Despite this, if you don't believe me, you are free to lock me up. But before that, as a citizen of this country I'm entitled to exercise my rights.' After a theatrical pause, Iqbal concluded with a victorious flourish, 'I want to talk to my advocate.'

Ratnakar turned to Inspector Bharucha askance. 'Do you have anything to say, sir?'

Inspector Bharucha stared in black melancholy. His empty eyes were fixed on an unseen wall in front of him—the hard, unforgiving, unbreakable wall of reality.

'Mr Bharucha! You are my senior and much more experienced than me. You must know that the words of a policeman alone don't carry any weight in a police case. Sorry, sir, but without any evidence, I can neither lodge an FIR nor put this young man behind bars.'

By now, Inspector Bharucha had realized his foolishness. He had misjudged Iqbal. Just like a son is always a kid in the eyes of his father, Iqbal was still a child according to Inspector Bharucha. He had first met Iqbal when he was in school and had turned up at Inspector Bharucha's office dressed in a half-sleeved school shirt tucked into baggy khaki shorts.

That image of a baby-cheeked Iqbal with the boyish smile faded today. A new boundary had been drawn between the guru and disciple. It seemed as if the disciple had toppled the guru and taken the high seat.

Realizing this bitter truth, Inspector Bharucha's taut back slackened and his shoulders fell. Once again, he looked at Ratnakar. Then he looked at Iqbal and slowly shuffled out of the police station.

As Iqbal got up to leave, Ratnakar indicated to him to be seated. 'You have a message.'

'A message! For me?' Iqbal asked, astonished. 'That's not possible. Nobody knows that I'm here.'

'Not even your men?'

'What men?' he said, feigning innocence. 'Sir, I'm an ordinary college student.'

Ratnakar continued with a chuckle, 'They must have guessed that since Inspector Bharucha had arrested you from my section, he would bring you here.'

Iqbal realized that Ratnakar knew much more about him than he had let on.

'What is the message?' he asked warily.

'DK has asked you to call him up.'

Iqbal stared at him in disbelief.

22

Iqbal's first meeting with DK happened in his apartment. Singh accompanied him. The three of them were seated on the sofas in the drawing room like the three ends of a triangle. Iqbal was sitting opposite DK. Between them was a luxurious glass centre table.

Iqbal was trying hard to suppress his desire to laugh out loud. His tragedy in that moment was similar to what mine had been when, one day, Iqbal had asked me, 'Who is a smuggler?' and the twisted, gory faces of Bollywood villains had swum before my eyes. Iqbal had had a somewhat similar illusion about DK. The man played in crores. His name—initials only—was whispered with awe and fear by everyone right from the chief minister to members of the municipal corporation. High court judges and inspector generals of police felt a shiver of significance when they were invited to his private parties. He was not just a hidden grandmaster of the political game, he was the puppeteer who pulled the strings of the state government.

What did he look like?

Sitting across Iqbal was an ordinary-looking Gujarati dressed in kurta-pyjama. He had an oval face, broad nose and a short neck. He was stocky and about five feet six inches tall.

Moreover, Iqbal was familiar with this face even though there was nothing special about it; if he dressed in kurta-pyjamas and mingled in a crowd, no one would cast a second glance at him.

Perhaps Iqbal's attention too would not have been drawn towards him had he not seen him more than once at Gaylord Restaurant, sitting by himself with a cup of cold tea and a cigarette. The last time he had gone to meet Singh there, he had seen him waiting for someone. It was during that meeting that DK had come across to ask Singh for a light.

Iqbal had not paid much attention then. In a public place, if a stranger asks a person sitting nearby for a light, it does not establish a relationship between the two. Singh had flicked the lighter and DK had thanked him and returned to his seat. It was as if he had nothing to do with Singh.

Now, Iqbal understood the reason for this behaviour. Not to speak more than required in a public place is the first rule of the underworld. The second rule is to not make an introduction only out of formality. That's why, though DK had been sitting right there, Singh had not introduced Iqbal to him.

*

Sufi follows this rule even today. If I am with him and any of his former acquaintances visits him, Sufi dispenses with the formality of introductions. Just the other day, an Indian prisoner who had escaped from a Dutch jail came to meet Sufi in Bombay. He was six feet tall, taut-shouldered and smooth-skinned. Dressed in a sharp shirt and trousers, he looked like a young tycoon to me. Sufi and I were sitting on his terrace discussing his first meeting with DK. Sufi did not feel it necessary to introduce us. However, after the man left, Iqbal explained, 'The guy was caught in Holland running drugs. Legally, our police can't arrest him now. But they can harass him to skim some money. That's what he fears.'

*

Though this was their first formal introduction, DK knew everything about Iqbal. Singh would brief him regularly about every minute detail. He knew that Iqbal was a man of redoubtable abilities and had joined the gang on Inspector Bharucha's recommendation. He had first proved his mettle by escaping from Sagar Darshan building with two jackets. Back then, he had felt obliged to make an offering of one jacket to appease Bharucha but in this latest exploit he had made his guru eat dust. In between these two defining episodes, Iqbal's innovations in the archaic methods of smuggling had not escaped his attention.

Today, for the first time, they were sitting face-to-face. In the spacious hall of this luxurious fourth-floor apartment facing Marine Drive, they had just completed the formal introductions. Across the gently heaving sea, the sun was about to set. A kaleidoscope of gold and purple and orange filled the ever-changing sweep of the sky.

DK's plump wife, who had a tired, resigned face, ambled in with a coffee tray, placed it on the transparent centre table and went away. Iqbal was not given to drinking excessive tea or coffee, but since DK himself offered him a cup, he thanked him and accepted it. Singh took the other cup.

Taking the first sip, DK turned towards Singh. 'Have you brought the keys to our Colaba apartment?'

Singh put down the cup, took out the key from his pocket and offered it to Iqbal. He did not accept it because he did not understand what was happening. He looked to the boss.

'From today, that apartment is yours.'

Singh placed the key on the coffee table and slid it across to him. Iqbal was bewildered. He looked at the key and then at DK.

'You live in Dongri, right?'

He nodded.

'In a single room?'

'Yes.'

'The Colaba house has two bedrooms and is fully furnished. You can move in right away.'

Iqbal remembered the luxurious apartment in Sagar Darshan building. There were more than a dozen such properties under DK's possession but under different names. They were used for meetings and storing contraband.

Iqbal felt an urge to return the key. He could not stay with his mother and two brothers in a place that may be used for illicit business. However, returning the key would have meant insulting DK and he did not want to offend the boss in the very first meeting. After a couple of days, he would cook up some excuse to return the key.

He put the empty cup down and picked up the key. Now another question popped up in his head. *Why was he being gifted such a royal apartment? He had just made a beginning in the gang. He had just moved from being a carrier to crossing. He was yet to take the plunge into the big league of gold smuggling. Who sends the smuggled gold to India? At what rate? Who is the gold merchant who takes it off their hands in India? How is foreign exchange transacted? Who are the local industrialists who buy it? How many of them are active? Where are they located?*

Iqbal had started his career in smuggling by selling one or two jackets given to him by Inspector Bharucha. Here, gold worth crores of rupees landed every month. *Where did it disappear?*

In the vast ocean of smuggling, Iqbal was a small fish. When someone gifts a small fish a vast blue lake, questions are bound to arise.

After some deliberation, Iqbal realized that by offering him an apartment, DK had not done him any favour. Through him, the gang had earned profits worth lakhs of rupees. For example, at Sagar Darshan, though he had been told to throw away two jackets, he had managed to retrieve at least one and hand it over to Singh: one jacket meant 100 gold biscuits worth Rs 1,80,000. In the 1960s, that was a colossal amount. And now again, he had outwitted Inspector Bharucha and managed to deliver gold worth Rs 2.5 crore.

A fully-furnished flat in Colaba was not worth over Rs 10 lakh. In a business that had a turnover of crores, this amount was insignificant. DK had appraised him shrewdly before bestowing the gift on him.

He also noted another point after meeting the big boss. Till now, he had been under the impression that Muslims dominated smuggling. This impression had been false.

*

'Sufi!' I grabbed the opportunity to ask him a few questions that had been bothering me too. 'There is a general impression in the minds of the common people that smuggling and Muslims are synonymous. Why?'

'Because of the media. Propaganda. The newspapers have only focused on the pygmies involved in the business and not touched the giants.'

'Why?'

'There is more than one reason. One could be that the real godfathers don't want the publicity.'

'But can't the journalists expose them?'

'How? The masterminds work from behind the curtains and enjoy prestigious positions in society. And when such a VVIP gives out exclusive information to a journalist that Mastan is a smuggler, he happily dashes to the press with the story.'

'Was Mastan not a smuggler?'

'He was, but a small fry. His bosses were Marwari industrialists. Does the name of the Chamadia family ring a bell? Their names were splashed in the newspapers for the first time around 1961.'

'I recall three Chamadia brothers who were convicted for gold smuggling.'

There were seven brothers in the Marwari family: Poonamchand, Laxmipat, Bhuramal, Balchand, Gyanchand, Kundanwal and Girdhari. As a cover for smuggling, they had set up three international offices: one was in Lagos, another in London and the third in Hong Kong.

Besides gold smuggling, they were also involved in the foreign exchange racket. For that, they used their travel agency in Lagos. They had siphoned off large amounts of foreign currency from Nigeria by issuing bogus airline tickets from that office.

Had they not offended the religious sentiments of the people, including parliamentarians, by stealing antique statues from Indian temples, they would never have been exposed. Those who operate in the shadows should not crave the limelight. This was the second blunder they committed.

'Haji Mastan worked under one of the brothers, Girdharilal. Gold came from Dubai, Mastan's gang did the crossing and delivered it to Girdharilal.'

Yet, if we ask a reader even today how many 'smugglers' he or she can recall, they would mention the names of at least two Muslims.

Deputy Customs Collector Daya Shankar's views in his interview to Gita Manek of *Sandesh* reflected Sufi's thoughts on this issue: 'The impression that a smuggler is always a Muslim is baseless.'

The fact is that members of all communities are engaged in underworld activities in India. For example, in Dongri, where Muslims are a majority, the Muslims naturally dominated the underworld. Similarly, south Indians dominated Sion–Koliwada. It is not surprising that Varadabhai ruled like a king there. Marathas dominated the Lalbaug–Parel area where no Muslim or south Indian dons staked a claim. In the underworld, religious fundamentalism is almost absent. It won't be far from the truth to say that they believe in coexistence.

If we examine the composition of DK's gang itself as an example, he was a Gujarati Hindu businessman, but his fast-rising right-hand man was Iqbal, a Muslim. Iqbal worked closely with Singh, a Sikh. Those working under them included Dagdu, a Maratha; Michael, a Christian; and Altaf, a Muslim.

Gang members are chosen based not on their religious affiliations but their strength and usefulness. Whether the gang belongs to DK or Dawood, it makes little difference: one would find the same communal harmony. This does not mean that they do not indulge in gang wars. At times, these wars assume a communal colour, but primarily these are fought for survival or for expanding territories of influence. On both sides, members from various communities join the fray.

For further proof, let us take a quick look at India's history. Shivaji fought till the end against Aurangzeb. Was it a holy war? If that was the case, none of the Muslim chieftains in his army would have participated. Tipu Sultan invaded neighbouring Hindu states—this much is a fact. But was it a holy war? If that was the case, Tipu Sultan's ten Hindu chieftains would never have supported it.

Coming back to the subject at hand, another important issue comes to mind. In 1978, it was widely publicized that many yesteryear smugglers had taken a public oath before Jayaprakash Narayan to renounce crime and turn into builders. How many of these so-called smugglers who had pledged to give up illicit businesses were the real godfathers who operated from behind the scene? None. Those who attended the function were only the ones who had already been exposed by the media. Where are the rest who continue to leer in the darkness? Who are they?

Only a handful of people know these secrets because they are the links between the godfathers and the gangs. People like Singh, for example, who is the single point of contact between DK and the rest of the gang. A player like Iqbal would perhaps have spent his whole life without knowing who DK was had he not played the trump card—Hamid.

Beside this point person, if there is anyone else who knows this secret, it is our government. The home department of every country has a watch list of most-wanted criminals, and our government is no exception. A reader may ask: if the government knows everything, why doesn't it act?

The answer lies in the fact that every politician needs these godfathers from time to time, particularly during election time when they desperately need donations for campaign financing. Besides, to the political parties that are likely to emerge victorious, these godfathers also lend the muscle of their armies of goondas. Not just these big dons, it is common knowledge that politicians knock on the doors of petty criminals and small-time racketeers too during election time.

The nexus between the government and the mafia is unbreakable. The don of Sion–Koliwada, Varadabhai, had publicly named a former chief minister who had approached him for help during elections. He further claimed that a former finance minister owed him his seat. But provoking the government publicly proved to be a costly mistake. (The big bosses never make such silly mistakes, which is why they remain godfathers for many decades.) Varadabhai was at the peak of his influence at that time. He enjoyed full support from Mastan—after all, both of them had worked their way up from the docks together. No one had the guts to walk tall in Varadabhai's area. But soon after this incident, to his misfortune, an honest officer entered his territory. This was Deputy Commissioner (DC) V.C. Pawar.

With a view to undermine the unimpeachable DC Pawar, Varadabhai started exposing other corrupt policemen in his department—with concrete evidence. This did not go down well with the police. Ultimately, Varadabhai had to flee Bombay and settle down in Madras where, after a few years, he breathed his last.

When one Varada dies, another Varada replaces him. When one Mastan retires, another Mastan fills the vacuum. When one government falls, another comes to power. Both these power centres exist with each other's blessings; they cannot survive without each other's support.

These godfathers come before us in the garb of industrialists or social reformers. Sometimes, they win elections and assume the seat of power, at other times they sit amidst us wearing kurta-pyjamas. If we take out a protest march against corruption, they humbly bear all expenses. When Bombay was under prohibition, the bootleggers' bosses used to organize the largest rally against the evils of drinking—that too on the day of Mahatma Gandhi's birth anniversary.

*

Finishing his coffee, Singh put down his cup and looked at the other two sitting silently. Iqbal's eyes were surveying the flat. If one ignored the antique furniture, the flat looked quite modern. It blended old-fashioned beauty with the latest in modern convenience.

Finally, DK turned to Singh and broke the silence. 'Do you have Rs 500?'

He immediately took out five hundred-rupee notes and handed them over to DK, who offered them to Iqbal.

'For what?'

'To save Hamid from the noose.'

Iqbal slipped the folded notes into his pocket. Dazzled, Iqbal had completely forgotten about his proposal to save Hamid using just Rs 500.

'Don't hesitate to ask for more if you need it,' DK gibed.

Iqbal did the math on his fingers and declared, 'No, I won't need extra. In fact, taking into account all the petty expenses, I'll be left with some balance.'

DK's expression changed swiftly from sarcasm to surprise. His intellect could not grasp what miracle this young man could pull off in court, which a barrister charging Rs 50,000 for a day's appearance was unable to manifest. Yet, he had the confidence—the young man sitting across him had already proved that he was not among those who made empty boasts. Moreover, Iqbal was laconic and DK respected those who talked less. After all, another rookie in Iqbal's place, upon getting the rare chance to meet the boss, could have tried to establish his indispensability by bragging about his achievements.

'DK,' Iqbal said, addressing him directly for the first time, 'don't you want to know how I will save Hamid with five hundred rupees?'

Since the past few days, Singh had been desperate to know Iqbal's mysterious plan. DK, however, knew how to hold his curiosity. Iqbal too was just gauging him: had DK replied in the affirmative, Iqbal would have smiled.

'Hamid is out on a bail bond worth Rs 10 lakh,' Singh blurted out. 'If you are planning to send him to Dubai, forget it. DK won't approve of that.'

Iqbal continued to look at DK as if Singh didn't exist. DK said nothing, leaving it to Iqbal to decide whether or not to disclose the answer. But a smile briefly flickered inside his eyes.

Iqbal caught this. That is when he realized that while DK was as shrewd as he had imagined him to be, he also had far more depth than he had anticipated.

'Iqbal!' DK said to him before he left with Singh, 'If you succeed in giving Hamid a fresh lease of life, I'll make you a partner in our business.'

Iqbal was surprised, but Singh's eyes almost popped out of his head.

23

With my first step on to the soil of Nainital, I looked up at the stunning sky with the intensity of a landscape painter trying to imprint a vision upon his mind. I had never seen such a crystal clear, azure blue sky before. Catching its reflection, Naini Lake rippled with the same crisp shade of blue.

We were a cheery gang of four: Lubayna and Anil, and Suraiyya and me. We had on us only as much baggage as hippies would carry. Our hands were free, all our essentials hanging off our backs in bulky, crammed rucksacks. Anil had carried a guitar too.

It was the summer holiday season so Nainital was overrun with tourists. Instead of staying in the hill station, we took the state transport (ST) bus to a nearby village, Bhavali, and set up camp in a dharamshala.

Every morning, we used to take the ST bus into Nainital, spend the entire day there and return to our camp by the last bus. Despite the exertion of our day-long wanderings, every night, Anil would always play at least one song before going to bed; all the boys working in the dhaba below the inn would come up to listen to him.

The following day, we would head out to Nainital again. There, Suraiyya and I would try to capture the colours of nature with our watercolours, while Lubayna and Anil would explore restaurants and cafés.

*

'Aabid!' Suraiyya said one day. 'Nainital looks more dazzling by night than during the day.' I could see what she meant. The rippling reflection of the jewelled lights in the Naini Lake looked astounding. In fact, I too was itching to capture this nocturnal beauty. However, there was a problem of time. Our camp was quite far if we chose to walk, and the last bus was at 11 p.m. If we missed that bus, we would have to spend the night in a hotel in Nainital, which our pockets would not permit. Moreover, it being the peak tourist season, all the hotels were full. There was not even standing room in the local dharamshala.

Suraiyya had already figured out a solution.

'If we start drawing by 7 p.m. we can comfortably finish by ten.'

We had just found the perfect spot on the hill when another problem cropped up. The spot, while ideal in the sense that one could get a full panorama of Naini Lake from there, was rapidly getting dark. That meant we could not paint at the same time.

I suggested, 'You paint first while I hold the torch over your paper.'

'Oh no!'

'What difference will it make if I paint tomorrow?'

'You paint today, tomorrow will be my turn.'

'No, Suraiyya, basically it was your idea.'

'I merely echoed your thoughts. Tell me the truth! Didn't you want to capture this scene with your brush?'

Conceding, I pulled out my handmade paper pad, watercolours and the box of wax crayons, and was soon immersed in drawing. Suraiyya stood behind me, holding the torch over my shoulders and observing me.

First, I drew a rough sketch with a pencil, then deepened some of the lines with black waterproof ink and filled in some colours with the wax crayons. Lastly, I prepared a wash of blue and, using a thick brush, spread it all over the paper meticulously. The wax in the crayons resisted the watercolour wash. This made the daubs of crayon colours look like the sparkling reflections of the lights in the blue lake: a splendid effect!

(This painting, however, was fated to meet with tragedy. On reaching Bombay, I exhibited it in a group show. The first art connoisseur who entered the gallery booked the painting. My chest swelled with pride. The show was on for a week. During those seven days, nine other art lovers liked the same painting and I had to disappoint them all since it had been spoken for. The tragedy was that the gentleman who booked it never turned up to take the delivery nor make the payment on the final day.)

I became aware of the time only after completing the painting. It was already 10.30 p.m. There was just half an hour left for the last bus. Anil and Lubayna were to meet us there. This was our routine.

Hurriedly, we packed up, clambered down the hill and dashed for the bus depot. Both of us were aware of the fact that we did not have much time, but it was necessary to make a determined attempt.

'Why didn't you warn me? Didn't I tell you to stop me before 10 p.m.?' I chided Suraiyya.

'Don't shout at me. The painting was coming out so well that I didn't have the nerve to disturb you.'

*

By the time we reached the depot, the last bus had left. For a while, we stood looking at each other. *Now what?* There was sky above, earth below and the dark night closing in around us.

If I were alone, I would have slept on the verandah of a shop or under a tree. *But what about Suraiyya?* She guessed my predicament and asked, 'How much time will it take to reach Bhavali on foot?'

'At this time of the night?'

'It's just 11 p.m. now. We can reach in a couple of hours, chatting as we go along.' To lighten the air, she added, 'We've walked together so often on moonlit nights. Let's enjoy a moonless night.'

It was not a terrible suggestion. Besides, what option did we have? We held hands and started walking. In my free hand, I held the torch whose circle of light walked ahead of us.

There were shadowy silhouettes of hills, bushes and trees looming on both sides of the path. Wherever the torchlight fell, everything sprang to life. Sometimes, when the gnarled branches of a dry tree lit up, it looked eerie. At other times, the shadows on rocks assumed ghastly shapes. The steady chirping of the crickets was suddenly pierced by the roar of a wild animal, sending shivers down our spines.

As if this torment of nature wasn't enough, to complicate things further our torch betrayed us. Truth be told, its battery cells did appear to be weak when we started from the bus depot. However, we didn't expect it to ditch us in the middle of nowhere. We were plunged in complete darkness. Now the full terror of the night descended on us. We could not even see our hands. Though Suraiyya was right next to me, I could not tell if she was there.

I pulled her closer, slipping my hand around her waist. We could neither go ahead nor go back. There were neither ridges before us, nor trees beside us; neither a mountain looming above us nor a road below us. We were standing somewhere alone in the midst of an ocean of darkness, our hearts thumping with fear.

'Suraiyya!' my voice quivered in the silence, 'I think we will have to spend the night here.'

'What do you mean here?'

Her question was valid. How could we spend the night at a place where nothing was visible? We could not sleep where we were standing—in the middle of the road. If a truck happened to pass, we would perish here unsung, even though no vehicle had crossed the stretch so far.

I thought for a while and said, 'I remember seeing a tree to your left. At least we can sit all night under it, if not sleep there.'

Before we could come to a decision, in the distance we saw a torch. It raised some hope. Some unfortunate soul like us must be going on foot! The next moment, I was suspicious. *What if it was a bandit?*

I did not even have any weapon to defend us. Nothing more intimidating than the painting materials in my rucksack. In the pitch dark, we could see no road on which to run and no place where to hide. Even a blind dash for cover was not possible: the darkness had robbed us of all sense of direction.

We stood there for a while, clinging on to each other, when suddenly we were lit up by the torchlight. Our hearts pounded in unison. We couldn't see the face of the stranger. As he drew closer, we started breathing normally again.

From his features, he appeared to be a tribal. He held a torch in one hand and a spear in the other. He was wearing a rough-hewn jacket and had a loincloth wrapped around his waist. He had a blanket on his shoulder too. We looked at each other in wonderment.

Composing myself, I explained. 'Our torch has failed and we want to reach Bhavali.'

'You won't get anywhere without a torch in these parts. If you wish, you can walk with me to the town.'

I looked at Suraiyya. She was looking back questioningly at me. *What would we do in the middle of the night in the town? Where would we spend the night?* We were considering these questions when the tribal handed me his torch, placed the spear by his side and lit up a bidi.

An idea struck me. 'Bhai,' I said while returning the torch. 'Can you give us your matchbox?'

After a momentary hesitation, he handed it over. We thanked him and were about to proceed on our way when he asked, 'Do you have any weapon?'

'No, why?'

'What if a cobra appears? There are also wild animals.'

'But this is a pukka road?'

'The road may be pukka, but it passes through a dense forest.'

'Has any wild animal ever attacked a traveller?'

'Once or twice a year, particularly when the traveller is unarmed.'

I had Suraiyya beside me and my youthful vigour and courage with me—I decided we would walk towards Bhavali. Before parting, the tribal made an announcement that made us freeze. 'Be careful, there were rumours about a tiger being sighted around here a few days back.'

*

We stared at him as he walked away towards Nainital. Darkness engulfed us again. But this time, it was a blessing for me because I did not want Suraiyya to see the drops of cold sweat forming on my forehead.

Suppressing the spike of primal terror that ran through my chest, I started walking with Suraiyya. I had noted under the light of the tribal's torch that the road ahead was straight up to a point. My plan was to proceed slowly and keep lighting a matchstick at intervals.

'Suraiyya, what would Anil and Lubayna be thinking about us?'

'They would have presumed that we stayed back in Nainital,' she said, glumly. 'They shouldn't have left without us.'

I lit the first matchstick. We had nearly reached the bend. We crossed it with the matchstick alight. We could now take a few steps with confidence.

Suraiyya asked, 'Was it not their duty to give us company?'

'But . . .'

'No one deserts a friend in need like this.'

'But you just said that they must have presumed that we stayed back in Nainital.'

She went quiet.

I lit another matchstick. 'You are forgetting one thing, Suraiyya. There is a vast difference between them and us. We appreciate light classical music like thumri, *dadra* and ghazals. They like pop music and Bollywood songs. We look for beauty in flowers, butterflies and the forests, they look for it in the concrete jungle. We discuss the works of Satyajit Ray and Ravi Shankar, while they spend hours chatting about Raj Kapoor and Nargis's love affair.'

'What are you trying to say?'

'Only this much—we shouldn't expect the same emotional sensitivity from others.'

The matchbox was half-empty by now. The night too was half over. It was almost 1 a.m. and there was a perceptible change in the darkness. Its intensity was cracking. We could

discern the shapes of trees. The craggy outline that delineates
the hills from the sky was also emerging. We were becoming
fearless. In fact, without realizing it, we had begun to enjoy
our midnight jaunt. Arm in arm and cheek to cheek, we
glowed like a pair of Diwali lamps.

I said, 'Jaanu, I feel like singing.'

'You mean croaking?'

'I'm not kidding. I'm getting an uncontrollable urge to
sing at the top of my voice.'

'Go ahead then. You won't be bombarded with rotten
eggs and tomatoes here.'

Suraiyya too was in high spirits.

'Is my voice that awful?'

'Who says that? But let me put it this way—your voice
sounds much sweeter when you are not singing.'

'All right. I shall not sing, but if you don't mind, I will
recite a ghazal.'

'Whose is it?'

'Ahmed Hamdani.'

'I haven't heard the name.'

'He is originally from Meerut, but settled in Karachi after
the Partition. Recently, his collection of ghazals titled *Pyaasi
Zameen* appeared in the market.'

'*Irshaad* (Please go ahead)!'

'If you don't like the opening lines, feel free to stop me
from reciting further.'

She enthusiastically gave me the green light: '*Irshaad!*'

'Main raahein na kya kya badalta raha,
Magar saath sahaara toh chalta raha.'

(I changed so many routes, but misfortune continued to
escort me).

As Suraiyya's knowledge of Urdu was limited, I told her
the meaning of 'sahaara', which means desert.

'That much Urdu I also know, you clown,' she said.

'Sorry,' I said, and continued:

Diye to bahut kuchh jalaye magar
Mere ghar mein ek khauff palta raha.'

(I lit many lamps, but fear continued to breed in my house).

'Wah!'

'Ghata aayi hai to baras jayegi,
Yun hi umar bhar main bahalta raha.'

(Since the clouds have gathered, it is bound to rain, thus I beguiled myself all my life).

This time, Suraiyya was ecstatic. 'Wah! Wah! Khoob!'

'Tere lutf par bhi koi kya jeeye,
Ye suraj to har roz dhalta raha.'

(Who can live on your charm alone, this life is fading away every day).

We didn't need the matchsticks any more. As the night grew brighter, we could see the road ahead clearly. Putting the matchbox in my pocket, I continued with the ghazal:

'Gila kya kisi ka yahan har taraf,
Bas ek aag thi jisme jalta raha.'

(There is no one to be blamed, there was a raging fire all around in which I burnt).

'Aabid, please recite this couplet again.'

I repeated the lines and then delivered the concluding lines:

'Bujha dil toh kuchh zakhm ki lau badhi,
Mein kuchh is tarah bhi sambhalta raha.'

(When the heart cooled down, the flame of the wound leapt up. I managed to survive this way too).

I don't know if Suraiyya appreciated this final couplet as much as the earlier lines, but a tiger definitely roared in response from the forest, chilling us to the bone. We froze. In the dead of the night, the echoes of the roar reverberated in our ears.

From the boom of the sound, we knew that the tiger was nearby. It was a matter of a few seconds—life and death. We needed to think fast and act faster. But we were both shell-shocked.

My situation was worse. I could not even shudder. Terror had made Suraiyya grab me tighter. Until she released her grip, we could not even run for our lives. How many steps we would manage was a different matter altogether.

Just then, I had a brainwave. I remembered that animals keep away from fire. I immediately took out the matchbox from my pocket, lit one matchstick and lit a fire using the dry leaves on the ground.

Suraiyya recovered a little. 'I'm keeping the bonfire alight,' I said, quickly assigning her a task. 'You get some dry twigs.' She got busy. I scrabbled together some more leaves and threw them to the fire. Flames leapt up.

At the same time, across the road, at the rise of the hill, the tiger appeared. Forgetting everything, we looked at this rare sight. The grace with which the magnificent beast stood with its neck held high mesmerized us.

The tiger turned its neck and deigned to look at us. Now the full impact of the precariousness of our situation hit us: we were safe only until the bonfire was on. The moment the blaze died out, we would too.

I made Suraiyya sit near the fire and picked up a few thick twigs. The tiger too appeared to be in no hurry and sat down where it had been standing. Its amber eyes, focused on us, were glowing like burning coals. Our eyes too were fixated on them.

'It seems like we will have to sit here till morning,' I whispered to Suraiyya.

'Can't we shoo it away?'

'It's not your pet.'

'What if we throw burning twigs at it?'

'It might move away from our sight, but we won't be able to move freely. It's also possible that this cunning beast might hide somewhere and pounce on us the moment we move away from the fire.'

Suraiyya kept looking at me steadily.

'It's not safe for us to take even a single step. But, if you wish, you may draw a few quick sketches. No tiger is going to pose for you again,' I quipped.

'My . . . my hands are still shaking.'

The battle lines were drawn on both the sides. The messenger of death was not willing to move from where he was sitting, while we were not able to budge from where we sat.

*

I looked at my wristwatch. It was 2 a.m. By this time, there had been a significant change in the blackness of the night. It was opening up like a moonlit night. We could see the tiger's colour and discern the stripes on its body.

Around 3 a.m., the tiger got up and roared. We trembled nervously. The next moment, I got up too. I pulled out a burning branch. Suraiyya froze. Her eyes, staring at the tiger, were like saucers. She clutched my leg with both her hands. It seemed that the tiger would climb down the hill any moment and devour us.

It stood still for a while, staring us down and growling, and then abruptly turned around and padded away. *Had it lost hope? Had it got tired of waiting and left?*

I did not have to wait long for an answer. In the distance, I heard the rumble of a truck approaching. The tiger must have heard it before us. Perhaps it spotted the headlights from the hilltop and understood that it was not his lucky day. Roaring to express displeasure, it had disappeared into the woods.

We soon saw the headlights around the curve and then the truck. I ran and stood in the middle of the road. Still brandishing the burning branch in one hand, I waved my arms, signalling the truck to stop. The beat-up truck clattered to a halt. I threw away the branch, held Suraiyya's hand and boarded the truck.

On reaching Bhavali at 4 a.m., we found out that Anil and Lubayna had not returned from Nainital. It would not be surprising if, like us, they too had missed the last bus. I couldn't help laughing—the laughter quivered in the sacred predawn air. 'Now, tell me, what would they be thinking about us?'

Some moments of silence followed. Then Suraiyya spoke, 'Cursing us for deserting friends in need.'

24

Iqbal was ready to leave the house. He stuffed the five hundred-rupee notes into his pocket when Gul Banu asked, 'Where are you going?'

'I have a job to finish.' *Why did his mother, who never enquired, question him today?*

'Someone had come to see you last night.'

'Did he give his name?'

'He said people call him Bhadak.'

He had sent a message to Hamid Bhadak two days back. He wanted to meet him once before taking any action. 'Okay, I'll first go to his house,' he told his mother.

After half an hour, he entered Do Tanki locality near J.J. Hospital and walked along Tinkar Lane. This was the same lane where the so-called don of Bombay, Dawood Ibrahim, lived with his four brothers. Dawood at this point had not yet taken a serious step into the world of smuggling. He was barely in his teens. Of course, he was already buying a few contraband watches or an odd gold biscuit to turn a small profit.

*

'Did you know him?' I interrupted Sufi and was taken aback by his reply.

'He used to work under me.'

I was now even more intrigued.

'What work?'

'Sometimes we smuggled fabric from Japan. Dawood used to buy a piece or two from me.'

'Then?'

'He used to sit with a basket on the footpath of Musafir Khana lane to sell it.'

Musafir Khana lane near Crawford Market is notorious in Bombay as a street market for smuggled goods; a launching pad for many an upstart and optimist. Young lads like Dawood used to eke out a living in their early days by selling contraband goods here. Once a year, for the record, the police would conduct bogus raids.

I asked him again, 'What was Dawood like in those days?'

'Like any other tapori.'

'What does that mean?'

'He was just one of the boys working under me.'

'Was there anything special about him?'

'He was a coward. I've seen other boys bashing him up. But, I don't recollect seeing him beating anyone up.'

In those days, in Do Tanki, Ayub Lala led a gang of pickpockets. He did not want another thug to raise his head in his territory.

Dawood had hesitantly entered the field of smuggling. To establish his dominance, Lala never missed an opportunity to humiliate him. Dawood too, on sighting him, would change directions and vanish into bylanes. In case of an accidental encounter, Lala would plant a couple of stinging slaps on Dawood and claim his entire day's earnings. Dawood would not forget these insults.

*

Iqbal climbed up the stairs of a dilapidated building and knocked on a closed door. While waiting in the passage, a question cropped up in his mind. *Is it right to save a murderer from the gallows?*

He would have returned had the door not opened the next moment. Hamid's middle-aged wife, Salma, was standing before him with a downcast face. Iqbal introduced himself and stepped inside.

The building was a chawl, just like Abbasi Manzil, where each family lived in a single room. But Hamid's family had two rooms: one could almost call it a two-room apartment.

The interior of the house was like a museum that had long run out of space. In the first room jostled a cheap sofa set, a couple of chairs, two oversized cupboards and a glass-fronted showcase crammed with forgotten curios. The desperate attempt at creating an impression of wealth was completed by a rectangular aquarium. The walls were a cracked pink that had seen better days.

As Iqbal settled down in a chair, Salma switched on the fan. 'What will you have? Tea or a cold drink?'

Always uncomfortable talking to women, he asked, 'Is there no one at home?'

'The boys have gone to school. The elder one had morning college today. My husband has gone to meet the lawyer. It will take him some time to return.' As an afterthought, she added, 'Didn't he visit you last night?'

'I wasn't at home.'

As Salma turned to leave the room, Iqbal stopped her. 'I've just had breakfast.'

'But you have come to our home for the first time.'

'Can I have a look at Hamid's photographs?'

Salma nodded.

She returned after a while with a glass of Rooh Afza sherbet in one hand and an album in the other. 'This one has our marriage photos,' she said, placing the glass before him.

Taking a sip, Iqbal started looking at the sepia-toned pictures. There were years of difference between Salma the delicate hennaed bride in a salwar-kameez and this tired Salma standing in the shapeless nightgown before him. He struggled to reconcile the image of that coy slip of a girl in the album with this matronly woman in the room.

But, as of now, his mission was to familiarize himself with Hamid, that too the present-day middle-aged Hamid, not the Hamid from thirty years ago.

Taking another sip, he asked Salma, 'Don't you have any recent photographs of Hamid?'

'There are some in an envelope at the end of the album.'

He turned the bulk of the album pages in one swift move and opened the envelope. The fourth photograph, in which Hamid was standing in a garden wearing a T-shirt and pants, was what Iqbal was looking for.

He assessed Hamid's height. He had a taut body with a thin face and high cheekbones. Though he had crossed fifty, his hair had not greyed.

Replacing the photographs in the envelope, he closed the album. Salma was still standing before him. 'Iqbal bhai, will you really save my husband?'

'It's Allah who saves or sinks. Man's duty is to strive.'

'I don't believe this.'

'Why?'

'Singh Sahib said over the phone that if anyone can save me from becoming a widow, it's you. For me, you are the saviour, you can give us a new life . . .'

A child wailed from inside the second room. Iqbal took another sip of the sherbet and stood up. 'My work is done. I'll now take your leave.'

'At least finish the sherbet.'

As Iqbal was about to move towards the door, a one-year-old infant crawled through the curtains separating the two rooms babbling 'Abba! Abba!' Seeing a stranger, the baby started howling bitterly. For a few moments, Iqbal imagined Hamid at the gallows and the child weeping seeing his father hanging by the rope. Unable to bear the thought, Iqbal turned around and walked out of the room.

He arrived at the municipal hospital with the child's wailing still ringing in his ears. At the same time, the age-old question was stuck like a thorn in his side: *should a murderer be hanged for his crime?*

He thought about it more seriously than ever before while heading towards the hospital's morgue. He started debating with himself. Only God has power over life and death. If death was written in Hamid's fate, no messiah would be able to save him. In case Iqbal succeeded in his mission, he had no right to claim to have gifted Hamid a new life.

*

Sufi's argument, though logically sound, did not satisfy me. I had to interrupt again.

'If I agree with your views, then would that mean the government has no right to punish a criminal?'

He countered with another question: 'What are your views on capital punishment?'

'I'm not in favour. Many intellectuals share my view. But there are scholars who favour the death penalty.'

'Why are you against it?'

'The murderer has committed a crime. If the law gives him capital punishment, it commits another murder. Then what is the difference between the two?'

Sufi listened silently.

'Secondly,' I continued, 'sometimes even an innocent person gets implicated in a murder case. There have been a few cases in which an innocent person was hanged.'

'That means that to save an innocent person from the gallows isn't wrong!'

'But Hamid was not innocent.'

'The law doesn't say so.'

'Even after the murder?'

'Murder is a charge. Charges can be framed. But until it's proved, even the law holds the person innocent. That's why the government gives him the right to defend himself.'

'That right is within the law. But you would be going beyond the law.'

'Aabid Bhai, you don't approve of the state executing somebody. If I stop that killing by going around the law, you don't approve of that either. After all, what do you want? Should I also sit silently like you and watch the tamasha of legally executed murders?' He continued evenly, 'Besides, I have total faith in God, as you know. You don't offer namaz, don't fast during Ramzan, don't read the Koran and yet you also must believe in Allah or some divine being?'

'I do.'

'Then tell me, if even a leaf can't move without His will, who was I to save Hamid?'

I was rendered speechless. Sufi's arguments were iron-clad but they failed to convince me.

*

The constable standing guard outside the morgue stopped Iqbal.

'One of my neighbours is missing. We had lodged a complaint with the police a week ago. So far, there has been no news. I thought maybe he met with an accident and was brought here.'

'Have you got a permission letter?'

'From?'

'The superintendent. You see that office across? You will get a stamped slip from there on producing a carbon copy of the police complaint. Fill that slip . . .'

Iqbal took out a Rs 100 note from his pocket and slipped it into the constable's palm.

The constable softened and, as he put the note in his pocket, said, 'The morgue in-charge has gone out for chai. He should be back in a few minutes.'

'I don't need him.'

The constable opened the gate marked 'No Entry'. Iqbal felt as if he had stepped into a vast refrigerator with muzzy tube lights. The freezing air reeked with the rank and pungent smell of disinfectants.

Recovering from the initial revulsion, he started examining the unclaimed bodies. Most of the bodies were racked in long, rectangular drawers that could be pulled out from the wall. A few corpses, perhaps because of the lack of space, were lying on the floor. There was a card on each body for identification. Each card was numbered and had a brief description.

Iqbal was looking for a middle-aged male body that would match Hamid's height. It would be better if the complexion also matched his. But among the corpses there, some were brutally crushed beyond recognition, some were without limbs; one had just the torso and no head. Words couldn't describe the grotesque scene before him.

The faces were mutilated into every shape in which the human countenance can be: bruised, flattened, slashed, puffed and putrified. Some of the faces—jagged, discoloured teeth, sunken cheeks and hideous leers—were so horrific they appeared like B-grade horror film monstrosities. So far, he had not come across a single body that remotely resembled Hamid.

He would not be able to execute his plan if he did not get a body that met his requirements. He began pulling out the drawers one after the other. When he closed the last drawer, he realized that he had not inspected the cadavers on the floor.

Bending over, he lifted the sheet from the first corpse that lay near his feet. He was chilled to the bone. He simply kept staring at it. This was Bali's body. *How did this happen?*

Bali, whom he had detested right from the start, was Inspector Bharucha's informer. *Had someone bumped him off? Had some gang taken revenge? Was DK responsible for his death?*

It was Bali who had recently alerted Inspector Bharucha about the gold being smuggled in from Versova. However, no one knew about this secret. Iqbal too had only guessed that this was what had happened. It was possible that DK too might have figured this out and decided to get him bumped off.

Bali had no particular enemy. He was a *khabri*—an informer. Whichever gang his eyes fixed on, that would become his target. Wherever he saw a chance to make a quick buck, he would inform the police. Had he been only DK's enemy, it would have been easier to say, but Bali spied on many gangs in Bombay. Crooks from every gang were behind bars thanks to his tip-offs to the police.

What surprised Iqbal was the fact that the body had just one mark, besides the post-mortem exam cuts. His skull had been cracked open. Whoever had killed him had made quick work of it.

Bali's corpse wasn't what he was searching for, but an unclaimed body next to Bali fit the bill. It was around five-and-a-half-feet tall, practically the same height as Hamid's. The complexion matched too.

Iqbal came out and told the constable, 'He's here.'

'Who?'

'The neighbour I was looking for.'

'Are you certain?'

'Hundred per cent.'

'You will have to fill up a form to take possession of the body.'

Iqbal took out another Rs 100 note. 'Can I get a blank identification card?'

By this time, the morgue attendant had returned and was smoking a bidi. The constable sent him to the administration department to fetch a blank card.

Iqbal wrote Hamid's full name and address on the card. He replaced the nameless identification tag on the unclaimed body with this new card. The main task was over. The rigmarole that followed was bothersome but not difficult. Now that he had the body, the next job was to bury it. By evening, this was accomplished with help from Altaf and a few other boys.

*

The next day, he took a taxi to the office of the municipal corporation. He filled up a form here to get Hamid's death certificate made. The first copy cost Rs 3. The duplicates cost Re 1 each. He took the original and two copies, went out and called DK from a public telephone booth.

'Iqbal here. Your work has been done.'

'Hmm.'

'Hamid's verdict is to be delivered on Monday, right?'

There were three days to go.

'I need to meet you once before that.'

'What are you doing right now?'

'Nothing.'

'I'll be at the Taj Hotel poolside in an hour.'

*

Iqbal's taxi stopped near Taj Hotel at 2 p.m. While paying the fare, he cast a glance at the sea. It was high tide. Crashing on the Gateway of India fortifications, the crests of the waves were exploding into a fine spray on to the pavement.

Iqbal entered the hotel, crossed the Taj art gallery and walked through the jasmine-scented lobby. There was an imposing glass door between the lobby and the swimming pool. He could see the poolside from within.

As he opened the glass door, his eyes began searching for DK. Stepping into the afternoon sun, the crystal blue swimming pool seemed like an oasis in front of Iqbal, a haven with lawn chairs and tables and tropical plants strewn abundantly around it. It being lunchtime, there were very few people around. One could see only about a dozen foreigners lazing around or swimming. Three white-skinned women in bikinis were sunbathing.

Before Iqbal could spot DK, the latter saw him. Hearing his name, Iqbal turned in bewilderment. DK, who had finished his swim, showered and changed into a clean kurta-pyjama, was standing before him. He was wearing Kolhapuri chappals and a thin gold chain around his neck. However, that was not the reason for Iqbal's astonishment.

Next to DK was Kiran dressed in a pistachio churidar suit. It was evident from her face that she too had just returned after a dip with DK. She looked disconcerted—perhaps, she too didn't expect to see Iqbal here.

'Do you know this girl?'

He had met Kiran several times. Perhaps DK knew this. On the other hand, maybe, he did not know. It did not seem proper to speak about a girl's private life—it may also hurt her feelings.

Kiran understood why he was tight-lipped. She had always had a soft corner for Iqbal. She replied to DK's question. 'He doesn't know me, but I'm familiar with him.'

'How can that be?'

'I've seen him in Singh's room.'

'And he has not seen you?'

'Right.'

'You think I'll buy that?' DK's lips curled into a thin smile.

'You will have to. Iqbal doesn't look directly at women.'

DK burst into a hearty laugh and said, 'My dear Kiran, your beauty won't be appreciated here. Please go to our room. I'll wrap up in half an hour and join you.'

Iqbal appreciated the gracious way DK had asked Kiran to leave. After she left, they sat on the lawn chairs across each other. There was a table between them.

'What will you have?' DK asked, hailing a passing server.

'I had lunch a few minutes ago.'

'Sure? I'm not so good at playing the diligent host.'

'I can imagine how hungry you must be after swimming. Please go ahead and order, I'll have fresh lime juice.'

Perhaps he was planning to eat with Kiran because he only ordered a beer. Once the server left, he turned to Iqbal. 'What did you want to talk about?'

Iqbal placed three papers before him. 'This is Hamid's death certificate. The other two are copies.'

At first, DK didn't seem to follow. Hamid was alive, the court was to deliver the verdict in the murder case on Monday and Iqbal was saying that . . .

He picked up a copy and glanced at it. It bore the date and genuine seal of the municipal corporation. Now, he read the form carefully. The death certificate was authentic. 'What do we do with this?'

'When the court opens on Monday, we need to get Hamid's son to appear with the death certificate.'

DK stared steadily at Iqbal. In a flash, he understood the game plan. All these days, he had been getting news from Singh about Iqbal's magical talents. Today, Iqbal had pulled a rabbit out of the hat in front of his eyes.

It was clear that a dead person cannot be awarded a death sentence. As soon as the death certificate would be produced before the judge, the case would be closed. The case files would be left to gather dust. After going underground for a couple of months, Hamid would be able to start working again.

It was only when the waiter placed a beer mug and a glass of lime juice on the table that DK realized that he had remained silent for quite some time. 'How did you manage to get this death certificate?'

'I went to the morgue. There, I found a corpse resembling Hamid. I placed a card on it with all the necessary details. Now, we only need to make the file disappear.'

'What file?'

'After the case is closed, the government will retain Hamid's file in its godown. So long as the file is there, the sword will hang over Hamid's neck.' Iqbal sipped on the lime juice and continued. 'If that file is destroyed, there would be no chance of reopening Hamid's case in the future because all the evidence would also be destroyed with it.'

'That's not difficult,' DK said, gulping down the beer from the mug. 'For a hundred rupee note, the court's peon will gladly set fire to the entire godown, not just the file.'

The mention of money reminded Iqbal that he had not given an account of the Rs 500 he had taken from DK. He finished the lime juice, took out some currency notes from his pocket and said, 'Rs 200 to the constable at the morgue, Rs 250 for the burial, Rs 4 for the taxi fare from home to the municipal corporation's office and Rs 5 for the original death certificate and two copies for which the receipt is enclosed. Please check the balance.'

This time, DK laughed so loudly that the three foreign tourists turned to glare at him. DK was not bothered.

'Iqbal! You don't have to give accounts for this petty sum. From today, you are my partner.'

'But . . .'

'Forget these scraps of paper. Like me, you were born to play in millions.'

*

At the end of this section of the interview, I asked Sufi a question that was bothering me. 'The face of the corpse you had chosen did not resemble Hamid's. Nobody questioned the difference?'

'There would have been questions raised had there been an inquiry. But who the hell in our bureaucracy has time for such inquiries?'

I wondered what would happen if the government, instead of importing expensive computers, employed live computers like Iqbal to benefit the country.

25

Iqbal had planned to live in the plush apartment gifted by DK only for a couple of days. He was firm in his resolve to return the keys after that. However, a small incident at the home front blew a cannonball-sized hole in his resolution.

He had pulled Razzak out of school and got him a job at his neighbour's shoe shop. This not only put an end to his mischief but also brought about an unexpectedly positive change in him. He would happily get ready every morning and leave with Noor Mohammed. He would return home with him late in the evening after closing the shop.

Iqbal was pleased. Firoze too had obtained 70 per cent marks in the final year of high school and joined a college: a dream had come true. He thanked Allah for this many a time during namaz.

His chest would be close to bursting with gratitude on the first day of the month when Razzak would place his salary in Gul Banu's hand: his hard-earned money. He used to get Rs 600 a month after working diligently like a pack mule. Iqbal had quietly arranged to deposit the entire amount in a bank account in Razzak's name so that whenever he decided to launch his own business, he would have the required capital.

That day too, when Razzak placed his salary in his
mother's hand, Iqbal was sitting on the prayer mat turning
the beads on the tasbih after offering namaz, his face radiant
with love. After completing his prayers, he extended his
hand, held Razzak by the wrist and made him sit beside
him. 'If you continue to put in hard work, one day you
will become a big boss and ten employees will be working
for you.'

'Really, bhaijaan?'

'That's why we aren't taking a single paisa from your
salary for domestic use.'

'If you aren't using my salary, then how are you managing
the kitchen?'

Iqbal was taken aback.

'You are in college,' Razzak added. 'This year, Firoze too
has joined a commerce institute. I'm the only earning member
of the family. And if my entire salary is being deposited in the
bank, how are the household expenses met?'

Iqbal realized that his younger brothers were no more
children and he could not keep them in the dark. But
neither did he want his secret second life to be revealed to
his brothers.

'I do a part-time job.'

'What kind of job?'

'I know how to drive.'

Razzak remembered how Iqbal had brought home a car
one fine morning a few years ago and taken Firoze and him
for a drive. He presumed that the car belonged to his elder
brother's employer. Convinced, he left quietly. However, that
night, Iqbal could not sleep. Like monsoon clouds, several
dark thoughts rolled through his mind, casting shadows upon
his face.

His younger brothers called him 'bhaijaan' affectionately. *What would they think if they found out that the person they worshipped, their gold standard of virtue, was in reality a bad penny? If the secret leaked out, would they not hate him?*

The next morning, he left for the new apartment. He had not seen it yet. He read the address only when he opened the slip of paper as he boarded a taxi. The name of the building was Usha Sadan. It was near the Colaba post office.

One of the reasons why he had decided not to get his family there was that in those days Colaba was notorious: every few days its name would appear in newspaper headlines because the police would raid an apartment in the bylanes and expose a liquor den, or sometimes bust a dance school or massage parlour that was in fact a brothel. It was impossible for an outsider to know which building was inhabited by respectable families and which one by racketeers.

The taxi stopped near the post office. After paying the fare, Iqbal started walking around checking the apartment names, looking for Usha Sadan. He didn't have to walk far, it was practically across the street. He entered the building and went up to apartment number seven on the third floor. He inserted the key in the lock and turned it. The door did not open.

He rechecked the address on the slip of paper and then cross-checked it with the apartment number embossed on the top of the door. Everything was correct. He again leaned over to try to force the key into the keyhole. But before he could turn it, as if by magic, the door opened from inside.

Kiran stood before him in a revealing nightie. Iqbal stared at her face in surprise. There was bewilderment in her eyes too.

'Come,' she said with a smile after the initial fluster, stepping aside. 'Welcome.'

As he stepped inside, it struck him that compared to the swanky Sagar Darshan apartment, this one was modest. However, all the essential things were there in order. There was a golden cage in the balcony. A sad-looking bird with a colourful tail was perched inside. The same melancholy emanated from the faded walls of the apartment too.

'I didn't know that I would get a surprise gift along with the apartment,' Iqbal mused, sitting down on the sofa.

Kiran did not hear a word. She was intoxicated after seeing Iqbal. God had answered her prayers. Iqbal, the man she loved from afar, had come close today.

'Will you have tea? Coffee?' she asked abruptly. Realizing her error, she added, 'Oh, I forgot, you don't really care for tea or coffee. You also don't touch beer. I'll check if there is a lemon in the fridge, I can make you some nimbu sherbet. If not, you'll have to make do with a milkshake.'

Without waiting for Iqbal's response, she dashed out of the room. Kiran's suggestion about lime juice made Iqbal wonder. He had once had a glass of lime juice with DK at Taj Hotel. That time, Kiran was waiting for DK in one of the rooms. He must have mentioned it to her.

When she returned to the drawing room, she wore a white dupatta with green stripes like a shawl over her nightdress. The tray in her hands held a glass of lime juice. She placed it on the centre table and sat on the sofa across him. From time to time, their lowered eyes momentarily found each other.

After a while, he asked, 'Didn't you know?'

'What?'

'That this apartment belongs to me?'

'And who do I belong to?'

'I thought you knew that.'

'Suppose I don't?'

'Then, remember this: everything in this apartment is mine . . .'

Kiran's heart skipped a beat. Iqbal had never expressed himself so directly before. Until today, he had barely even looked directly into her eyes.

'. . . except that bird with the colourful tail,' Iqbal added.

'If everything in the apartment belongs to you, why not the bird?'

'Because it's caged.'

The barb in Iqbal's comment was not lost on Kiran. The bird entertained guests who played with it, caressed it for a while and then left. Her bright eyes lost their gleam. She stared at him, arms folded over her chest, as if he had dealt her a heavy blow. After a few thoughtful moments, she asked, 'Iqbal, are you a real man?'

'Do you doubt it?'

She nodded a yes. 'Every man who came into my life considered himself a real man.'

'And whom do you consider a real man?'

'The one who can open the cage and offer the bird the wide-open sky.'

'What's the guarantee that the bird won't return?'

'Why would she? The sky is big and blue.'

'Because the cage is golden.'

'Golden or silver, a cage is a cage. And if the man who opens the cage has a heart of gold, why would the bird choose a golden cage?' Kiran got up and sat beside Iqbal. 'And you are that man. DK says you are destined to live in a palace, to play in millions, but all that is trivial compared to your love. I want neither a palace nor a lavish lifestyle. If you but ask, I'm prepared to live with you on the pavement. You may not believe it, but Kiran, who the world sees only in five-star hotels, was born under the open skies.'

Iqbal stared at the bird fluttering inside the golden cage.

Suddenly a thought struck him. *If the apartment belonged to DK, then who was Kiran? Had DK also bought her with this house?* Finally, he asked her, 'What is your relationship with DK?'

'What do you want to know?'

'DK knows that I am not interested in women. Does he want to test my integrity?'

'I don't get you.'

'I can understand someone presenting me with an apartment. I can also understand that a furnished house can have a sofa set, bed, fridge and radio. But I can't believe that you too can be a part of the furnishings.'

'I'm not!'

'Then what are you doing here?'

She laughed. 'You are asking a strange question. What am I doing in my own house! I'm entertaining a guest!'

'Is this really your apartment?'

'Should I show you my ration card? My passport? Or do you want to see the rent receipt?'

'Then did DK play a prank on me?'

'DK knows how to laugh at a joke, not to crack one.'

Iqbal took out the slip of paper on which the address was written and glanced at it again. 'The area is Colaba. The building is called Usha Sadan. The house number is seven and it's on the third floor.'

'It can't be! That's my address,' Kiran snatched the slip of paper from Iqbal's hand.

After reading the address, she began giggling. Gradually, her giggle turned into a full-throated laugh. Then she pumped his hand and congratulated him. 'Welcome, Iqbal! From today, you are my neighbour. Come, let me show you your apartment.'

She did not release his hand. She pulled him along behind her to a closed door a few apartments down the passage. 'Where is the key?'

He took out the key from his pocket and looked at the number embossed on top of the door. It was apartment number one. He had mistaken the number scribbled in haste as seven instead of one; apartment seven was Kiran's.

As the door opened, Iqbal looked in amazement. He had entered a super-luxurious air-conditioned apartment that could rival the homes of the Tatas and Birlas. Beside him stood Kiran in her nightie covered with a striped dupatta. Behind them, the door closed.

Kiran came before him and put both her arms around his waist. Fluttering her eyelashes like a movie star she said, 'I've read somewhere that it is God's will that we should love our neighbour.'

'Not somewhere, it's in the Bible—and the words are in a very different context.'

'What can I do? When a person doesn't understand signs, one is compelled to use words. But, why are you silent?'

'Sometimes silence speaks louder than words.'

This admission was enough solace for Kiran. She rested her head on Iqbal's chest. She felt as if she had received a new lease of life. As if Iqbal's pure love had washed away all her sins. Iqbal patted her head and gently nudged her apart. He saw that her face was wet with tears.

'Don't cry, Kiran.'

Wiping off her tears with one end of the white dupatta, she said, 'These are tears of joy, they just overflowed.'

'So much that your face got drenched?'

'So much joy has never flooded my life,' she said. 'And I can prove it.' Iqbal looked puzzled so she clarified, 'Tonight,

I'll cook the best Chinese meal you have ever tasted in your life.'

*

Iqbal stood in Kiran's balcony as she cooked in the kitchen. He gazed at the wide arch of the sky. It was a cloudy day, casting a muted grey pall over the city.

At last, love had entered his life, trampling over his principles, faith and beliefs. Slowly, it had entered his heart and was now flowing through his veins. How did it happen? More surprising was the object of his affections. He knew Kiran was a call girl. Any rich man could buy her for a night by throwing some cash.

He had seen Kiran in Singh's room on many occasions. DK too, he knew, had spent some hours with her at Taj Hotel. Countless men would have entered her life, rising and crashing like uncountable waves. And yet, she had entered deep into the recesses of Iqbal's heart: who has ever understood the mysteries of the heart?

This much he could say with confidence: he had not been attracted to Kiran's body but to her tender heart. Bodies are cheap in this city, but the heart is priceless. No power on earth can buy it. Iqbal had won a precious pearl without asking for it, and he had accepted it too.

Had he erred by accepting it?

*

The path of crime on which Iqbal was marching all through the day had not been his choice. From his childhood till his youth, he had made every effort to hold fast to the path of virtue. In the end, he had quietly accepted the place where he stood today as God's will.

Kiran's life too had moved parallel to his. She was the daughter of a *banjaran*, a gypsy. *Where did her family come from? Who were they?* She did not know. Recalling her childhood, she remembered only one thing clearly: her house was a tinkling, bedecked bullock cart.

One year, this wagon would camp under the chinar trees in Kashmir while the next year it would set base on the banks of the Ganga in Benares. Sometimes, they would put up tents in a city for weeks and, at times, they would halt in a village for months together. Sitting at the foot of the wagon, her mother used to sell sunglasses, while her father found work as a blacksmith.

Her memories of her family ended abruptly at the age of six. Try as she might, what happened after that was lost in the mists of time: *Did someone lure her away? Was she kidnapped?* Nothing was clear. A man had picked her up from one end of the country and brought her to the other end.

The costumes had changed. The people had changed. The call of the birds had changed. The train journey had been long, and she had cried throughout the journey.

However, the end was happy. She found herself on the outskirts of Delhi, in a palatial bungalow overlooking the railway tracks. She had a mountain of toys to play with. There was a doting mother and father to provide for her. She had been sold to the childless Dutt family; she was their newly adopted daughter.

*

Mrs Dutt showered so much love on her that she all but forgot her real parents in a year or two. What remained was a vague cloud of memories, which too dispersed like a fog when she tried to step into it. The fog devoured her real name too.

Mrs Dutt's first problem was to think of a perfect name for her newly adopted daughter. Mr Dutt had little interest in the daughter or in her name. He was a businessman who owned a plastic toy factory. He used to leave for Shahdara at 9 a.m. sharp. When he returned home at 9 p.m., he would invariably be swaying.

So addicted was he to alcohol that he would start drinking in his office before lunch. He would drink for hours. In between he would polish off namkeen snacks. By sunset, two-three pegs would remain. Those he would save for the journey from the factory back home.

He would never have agreed to illegally adopting a child had his lonesome, barren wife not slipped into depression. After five years of craving for marital bliss, she finally lost patience. The bickering started. It's all part of being married, the husband thought initially, not the end of the world. But the clashes grew more fierce; the arguments continued through the night. Finally, to pacify her, he was compelled to place a living, breathing doll in his wife's lap—the cheap plastic toy maker had to pay a thug Rs 5000 to buy the most expensive toy.

In moments of deep affection, Mrs Dutt would whisper to the little girl, 'You have come like a golden ray of sunshine (kiran) into my desolate life.' One day as she said this, the word 'kiran' struck a chord in her heart. The gypsy's daughter was rechristened Kiran.

*

Kiran was sharp when it came to academics. Once she got admission into a regular school, she astonished the students and teachers with the scope of her knowledge. Nature had taught her much during her vagabond life—the earth was her school, college and university. She did not have to make any extra effort to memorize books; her irrepressible curiosity about life was enough.

As their bullock cart house would trundle through a forest, she would sit next to her father, holding the reins of the bullocks and observing new trees, flowers, leaves, animals and birds. On seeing a new animal, she would ask, 'Papa, what's that?'

'That's called a mongoose. The mongoose and snake fight fiercely.'

'Who wins in the end?'

'Whoever is strong. A large snake like the python can devour the mongoose.'

When the cart would pass through a valley of flowers, the kaleidoscope of butterflies floating over the flowers would cast rainbows in the little girl's wide eyes. Water lilies, mirabilis, marigold, narcissus and a variety of other flowers whose names were not known to the children in the city, were etched in her heart.

As bright little Kiran grew up, she started to understand her new parents' personal life better—there was a wide gulf between Mr and Mrs Dutt. By the time she was ten, she figured this out. The husband and wife didn't share a bedroom. Mrs Dutt slept with Kiran in a separate room.

*

The time at which Mr Dutt returned home from work changed. The husband who used to return by 9 p.m. now returned drunk after midnight, and that too not alone: some new woman would accompany him every time. He would spend the night with this woman, under the same roof and on the same bed in which he used to sleep with his wife.

There was a huge quarrel the day he first brought a prostitute into the house. By now Mrs Dutt had learnt to ignore it, but her anguish did not remain hidden from Kiran.

She was suffering silently. Day by day she was shrivelling, becoming weaker. Finally, she was so weak that it became difficult for her to breathe. These were her last days; the beginning of Kiran's college days.

*

Before her death, Mrs Dutt called her husband, placed Kiran's hand in his and made a last request, 'You may not have accepted this girl as your daughter, but she calls you "papa". It's your responsibility to take care of her when I am no more. After she completes her studies, it's your duty to find a young man she approves of and get her married.'

Mr Dutt released Kiran's fingers and reassuringly held his long-suffering wife's hand. 'Even if you hadn't reminded me, I would have done the same.'

When Mrs Dutt closed her eyes for the last time, there was a smile on her face, tears in Kiran's eyes and gloom in the house.

Stillness descended on the eight-room bungalow. The wind started ricocheting on the empty walls, howling around the rooms. The curtains billowed ominously. Kiran could not sleep that night. In fact, she would not sleep peacefully again after that night. She was not used to sleeping alone. At times, she would wake up in the middle of the night with a start and stare fearfully at the empty walls, listening to the wagons being shunted.

*

One night, when she was staring blankly at the ceiling, trying hard to sleep, the door to her room opened with a bang. She sat up. Mr Dutt was silhouetted in the doorway. Today, he had returned at midnight but alone.

Watching Kiran staring fixedly at him, he asked, 'Why are you still awake?'

'I've been feeling uneasy in this room ever since mom died.'

'Then come to my room.'

'Where will you sleep, papa?'

'My bed is big enough for three people to sleep on it.'

Kiran thought for a while before answering. 'I'll sleep here tonight. From tomorrow, I'll make arrangements to sleep in the guest room.'

'Don't you trust me?'

The wagons clashed with a bang.

'What are you saying?' she said, startled by his tone.

'Precisely what is going on in your dirty mind.'

'No, papa. I just don't want to bother you.'

In the dark recesses of Mr Dutt's alcohol-fogged and guilt-ridden mind, Kiran's innocent remark was translated as a snide attack on his habit of bringing prostitutes to his bed.

'Have I ever brought a woman home after your mother died?'

Kiran did not reply. This made him even more incensed.

'Come, get up!'

She stared at him. The devil was in his bloodshot eyes. Without giving Kiran a chance to think further, he bolted the door and drew the curtains. The hunter had trapped his prey. The helpless bird fluttered and screamed and thrashed in vain. Outside, the shunting continued. Clatter, clatter; bang, bang.

This continued for a month. Every morning, the hunter would lock the cage before leaving for the factory, only to open it when he staggered in late at night, drunk. Kiran was rattled and shaken to the core. Every night, she prayed: *This night should have no tomorrow.*

She desperately wanted to escape. But where would she go? The last resort was to hang herself, but she did not believe in suicide; she considered women who committed suicide to be cowards.

Things became complicated when she became pregnant. It became imperative for Mr Dutt to take the bird out of the cage, for an abortion.

The next week, he made arrangements with a doctor and took her to a nursing home. The very next day after the abortion, Kiran slipped away from the nursing home.

She did not have any cash. However, she had a gold chain around her neck and an expensive watch on her wrist. She sold both, bought a ticket for Bombay and boarded the Frontier Mail.

A full-figured, motherly woman was traveling on the same train. Had Kiran known that the woman was deep in the flesh trade, she would not have gone to her house on reaching Bombay. She would not have fallen prey to this racket. She would also not have become the most sought-after call girl in India. But then she would not have met Iqbal: if you look closely enough at coincidences, you can see God's fingerprints.

*

When the food was ready, Kiran came out into the balcony. Iqbal was still standing there, lost in thought.

'Iqbal!'

He turned. Kiran's face was beaming. 'I hope you are insured,' she said.

'Is the food poisoned?'

'I'm a terrible cook and yet you accepted my invitation with a smile. It's mandatory to warn you about the risk involved.'

Heading inside with her, Iqbal said, 'I think I heard you saying something about serving me the best Chinese food I have ever eaten in my life.'

'That you'll know only after tasting it. You still have time to change your mind.'

The banter continued as they discovered common ground. Iqbal realized that, like a chameleon, Kiran had taken on the colour of Bombay. Hers had been almost a rural upbringing where the nights were starkly divorced from day and filled with unending pools of silence. But Bombay never slept; and now she was at home in this sleepless city, amidst the traffic and factories and the long, hooting foghorns in the distance.

Inside, he stopped abruptly. Before him, on a long centre table was a handsome spread of fried rice, sweet corn soup, Russian salad, three types of sauces and two glasses of Coca-Cola. To appease the god of love, Kiran had wisely made a generous offering to the stomach.

From the aromas wafting in the room, Iqbal already knew he would be eating till his clothes split at the seams. He pulled up a chair. Kiran sat on the edge of the bed. The table was between them. 'Wait a second,' she said. 'To properly relish a Chinese dish, you must first savour the sweet aroma.'

By now, Iqbal was desperate to wolf everything down. He quickly said his bismillah and pounced on the food just as the telephone rang. Iqbal's hand froze over the plate of fried rice.

Kiran walked across the room and lifted the receiver.

'Hello!'

'The boss has called you in the evening.'

The voice from the receiver was so clear that Iqbal could hear every word.

'I can't come today.'

'Do you have another booking?'

'No.'

'Then stop these nakhras! Boss is in a good mood today. I won't be surprised if he gifts you a diamond ring.'

'I won't be able to come even if your boss gifts me the Koh-i-noor,' Kiran said with finality. 'I'm on leave for a week.'

Iqbal understood.

As he took his first bite he asked, 'Why did you lie?'

'It is not time yet to tell the truth.'

'When will it come?'

'When you accept me as your wife.'

The sincerity in Kiran's words plunged like a dagger into his soul.

26

' $\mathbf{A}$ abid! Marry me,' Suraiyya said desperately.

We were sitting in an Irani restaurant on top of the Hanging Gardens. One could survey the entire city like a king from here while relishing chocolate ice cream.

Getting married was simple for me. I only needed to find a *qazi* and in the presence of two witnesses accept Suraiyya as my wife. *But what about the responsibilities that would come with it?*

I did not have my own house. I shared a single room in Dongri's Sultan Mansion with my younger brother, mother, uncle and grandmother.

On top of that, my paternal uncle had partitioned the room after his marriage. He and my aunt occupied half of it, while the other members slept in the other half. Fed up of this crammed sleeping situation, I had taken to sleeping under the sky on the building's fifth-floor terrace.

The problem was not just that of a home, but of money too. What I earned from the cartoons was enough only for me. Whatever remained after my expenses was spent on purchasing art material. It would be impossible for me to fulfil familial obligations after marriage.

*

There was a reason behind Suraiyya's desperation for marriage. She could not go to Mombasa during the vacation after our first year. In the second year, we went to Nainital. When she could not go to visit her family in the third year either, her mother, accompanied by her elder brother, Abbas Ali, came to Bombay. They were staying at Oberoi Hotel.

Suraiyya begged me, 'Aabid, we won't get such a golden opportunity to introduce you to my mother.'

'How will you introduce me?'

'As a friend, philosopher and guide.'

'Won't they doubt it?'

'What if they do? In any case, we are going to get married even if they don't like it. But it's my duty to introduce you to my family. This is also necessary so that I can mount pressure for marriage when the right time comes.'

'That's right. But . . .'

'But what?'

'I . . . I don't know why I'm not mentally prepared to meet your mother.' *It's a recipe for disaster, I wanted to add but could not. The words were stuck in my throat.*

*

Eventually, Suraiyya compelled me to come with her. This was her first mistake. Her mother and brother immediately realized from Suraiyya's flushed face that there was more than just friendship between the two of us. On top of that, she was wearing a cherry pink churidar with big silver buttons and a transparent dupatta.

Abbas Ali's comment was pointed. 'Suraiyya, I've never seen such a glow of happiness on your face before.'

'Shouldn't I be happy?'

'I thought your face would be dull. You haven't seen Mother for two years!'

'That's true. I perked up the moment I got the news about her arrival.'

This was just the thin end of the wedge. I sat quietly, trying to read the expressions. Suraiyya's mother had sized me up with a single sweeping glance. I am sure that she must have noticed one of my toes peeping out of my worn-out canvas shoes.

Once the formalities were over, Abbas Ali looked at me. It was evident from his eyes that my presence was not welcome for whatever private discussion they planned to have. Suraiyya too noticed it.

'Bhaijaan, Aabid isn't a stranger. He has stood by me like a rock in this alien city. You need not feel hesitant to say anything in his presence.'

This was Suraiyya's second mistake. It confirmed whatever doubts they had regarding our relationship. Yet, they remained quiet.

Breaking the awkward silence, Suraiyya asked them both, 'Now tell me, what's the matter you want to discuss?'

Her mother opened her purse and fished out a photograph. Abbas Ali gave it to Suraiyya. From where I was sitting, I could tell it was the photograph of a young man—wearing a suit, standing in a hotel lobby.

'Who's he?' Suraiyya asked.

'He is the owner of a hotel in London.'

'So?'

'He has asked for your hand in marriage.'

As if lightning had struck her, her face turned white in a flash. But the next moment, she recovered and took charge of her emotions.

'I don't even know him!' she protested.

'He knows you,' Suraiyya's mother explained. 'We had mailed your photograph along with some basic information about you. He immediately gave his consent. Since then, six months have passed. Every month he writes asking for confirmation. What should we tell him?'

A thick, uncomfortable silence descended on all of us. Again, Suraiyya's mother looked at me. This time, her eyes focused on the hole in my shoes. I too did not try to hide it by curling that foot behind my ankle. That hole and the peeping toe were the truth of my life. That was my true introduction to the millionaire family sitting before me.

'Please understand, Mom!' Suraiyya finally reasoned. 'I don't want to think of marriage till I'm through with my studies.'

'Who's asking you to get married now. We just need your consent. The marriage will happen only when you are ready.'

'It'd be better if you ask him if he is willing to wait for two years.'

'And if he agrees?'

'Then I'll let you know my decision.'

'Remember one thing, if he agrees to wait for you, then you won't have the moral right to refuse him.'

*

Suraiyya's mother returned to Mombasa after staying in Bombay for a week. But in her wake, a pall of gloom descended over our relationship. The slowly-approaching sound of sledgehammer blows from an impending doom started echoing in our ears. The fourth-year examinations had just finished when an unexpected letter came from Mombasa.

The young man from London was prepared to wait for Suraiyya not just for two but three years. He wanted Suraiyya, after getting her diploma from Bombay, to study one more year at London's Royal Academy of Arts.

As long as we were together, we were free from all worries. So long as Suraiyya was in Bombay, no one could separate us. *Despite this assurance, why was it that our hearts throbbed with fear? Why was Suraiyya suddenly desperate to marry? Had her confidence been shaken? Or was it that she had intuitively sensed what was to manifest in the near future?*

*

'Suraiyya!' I said, turning my attention away from the view of the city. 'The question isn't just about marriage, but what after it? For that, I will need at least a few months to prepare.'

'I'm not asking for us to live together after marriage. I'll stay in the hostel and you stay in your house till all arrangements are made.'

'What's the point of such a marriage?'

After thinking for a while, she asked, 'All right, how much time do you need?'

'There are still eight months to go for the final examinations . . .'

'NO!' Her sudden cry made the others around glance at us. 'It will be too late by then.'

'Please, at least let me complete what I am saying first. I'll start looking for some extra work from today. My income will double or triple in a few months. Meanwhile, with the help of some friends I'll arrange for a one-room-kitchen on rent in the suburbs. But remember, after marriage you too will have to slog with me for at least a year.'

'And after that?'

'On securing a first-class diploma, I'll get a secure job that pays a five-figure salary with the art department at a big company like Air India.'

She put both her arms around my neck and kissed me on the mouth, which was still full of chocolate ice cream. That was our final kiss—long, passionate and deep, and in a public place.

*

There was no place for kisses between Iqbal and Kiran. Seen from the point of view of the elders, theirs was a platonic love. At times, an emotional Kiran would rest her head on his shoulders and Iqbal would caress her head reassuringly. Even the idea of embracing her tightly was a sin to him.

The main reason for this was Iqbal's complete faith in Islam. To view women like mothers or sisters was part of his upbringing. His scholarly study of Islam had only strengthened this idea. Defying this religion and upbringing, love had marched into his life. Kiran was the first, and last, woman to enter his heart.

This truth was not hidden from Kiran. She deeply understood Iqbal's chaste nature. He was not sex-obsessed like other men. Else, at the slightest indication from him, Kiran would joyfully have dropped her clothes and offered her body to him.

Now Iqbal had more than one reason to accept DK's gift. He had originally planned to stay here alone for a few days so he had only brought some clothes and things of daily use, as well as all his college books to study in peace.

Kiran lived in another flat on the same floor. A telephone was the link between them. This phone was in Kiran's house and Iqbal received all his calls and messages there. Another link between them was lunch. Kiran would prepare lunch every day and either call him over to her flat or, if he was busy, go to his apartment with the food. There, they would eat lunch together in an air-conditioned room. Their relationship was from sunrise to sunset; every evening, they would go their own solitary ways.

Those days, Iqbal had two obsessions: his college education and his smuggling profession. Like a mother-in-law hands over the keys of the house to her daughter-in-law, DK had handed over the business to Iqbal.

*

Iqbal started studying the gold-smuggling racket closely. Of course, his computer-like brain had already gathered many useful pieces of information. One was that middlemen or brokers played a vital role in smuggling. These intermediaries were important links between the traffickers and the traders (mainly jewellers).

For example, on the sale of a gold biscuit that weighed ten tolas, the broker would take a commission of Rs 50. There are 100 biscuits in a jacket. Therefore, his net profit would come to Rs 5000 per jacket. And the gold market was flooded with innumerable jackets every day.

Some broker would buy five jackets from Sufi, while another would buy twenty-five. It all depended on the broker's financial strength. The one who bought five jackets earned a net profit of Rs 25,000 a day, while the one who bought twenty-five jackets earned as much as Rs 1,25,000. Moreover, these brokers would charge commissions from both the parties. That meant double the profits. At times even more.

The daily fluctuation in the price of gold depends on the bullion markets of London and New York. First, the London market opens at noon to determine the price of gold in pounds sterling. Accordingly, the price of gold is decided in every country on the basis of the foreign exchange rate. This price remains stable till 3 p.m. when the American market opens. Then the price of gold either goes up, down or remains stable. If the price increases, then the profit on sale too increases. Sometimes, because of a shortage of supply of gold, its price shoots up. The resulting profit too is pocketed by the brokers.

*

One day, as Kiran returned after shopping for groceries, she saw an imported car parked below the building. *Whose car could it be?* She came up and got busy in the kitchen, cooking Iqbal's favourite dishes, humming to herself. In her heart, she was already wedded to him and had taken upon herself all his responsibilities; this was joyful for her.

After about fifteen minutes, Iqbal entered her house and stood near the bedroom door, which was next to the kitchen.

'Kiran, with your permission, may I make a phone call?'

'Of course not!' she replied, feigning anger.

'Do you want me to go down to the post office to make the call?'

She turned the knob on the gas stove to low and walked up to him.

'Iqbal, am I a stranger?'

'No.'

'Is this house unfamiliar?'

He shook his head.

'Then why did you ask for permission? Didn't I tell you . . .'

'It's an old habit.'

'It's high time you changed it.'

'Old habits die hard.'

'I'll get cross with you.'

'I know how to make you happy.'

'Really?'

'Let the time come.'

In theatrical fashion, she stomped her feet and plumped herself on the bed. 'I'm cross with you,' she said, pouting. 'Now you can cry, implore or roll at my feet all you want—I don't want to speak to you or have anything to do with you again. Good luck, mister!' With that she defiantly covered her mouth with her hands.

Iqbal could not suppress his laughter. 'Hey hey,' he said with a charming smile, 'I had decided to take you out on a drive after lunch. And here you are . . .'

Kiran remembered the car she had seen downstairs. Instantly removing both hands covering her mouth, she blurted out, 'That Mercedes parked downstairs is yours?'

'Of course. But unfortunately, I can't take you.'

'But why not?'

'Because you don't want to have anything to do with me!'

'You scoundrel!' She was about to put her hands around his neck when the pressure cooker whistled.

She dashed towards the kitchen and Iqbal went for the phone. It was necessary to inform the boss about the 300 jackets that had been dumped in his flat the night before.

*

He had been with DK just two days earlier. They were heading together to the Cricket Club of India (CCI), the high-profile watering hole of Mumbai's neo-rich and aristocrats. Their car stopped outside the club, and as Iqbal stepped out, his eyes stopped upon a Mercedes-Benz 190 parked across the street.

'What are you looking at?' DK asked.

'It's a beautiful car.'

'Hmm . . .'

'It runs on diesel. Must be worth seventy–eighty grand.'

'Possible,' DK shrugged, as if he was not interested.

*

When Iqbal returned home the previous night, Singh was standing downstairs with the car. 'It seems as if you have cast a spell over the boss. You make a wish, the genie fulfils it,' Singh remarked with a tinge of jealousy, handing him the car keys, but Iqbal had barely heard him—he was mesmerized like a child getting an expensive toy. Even in the dark, the vehicle gleamed.

'Have you disposed of the consignment?' DK asked him over the phone.

'I'll do it tomorrow.'

There was silence on the line. Holding the consignment overnight involved a double risk—the threat of a police raid and the possibility of a price crash.

'Do you think the price will go up after the opening of the dollar market?'

'No, but the prices will shoot up after the London exchange opens tomorrow.'

'How come?'

'Inflation is on the rise there. The pound will crash and gold prices will shoot up.'

'All right.' DK hung up.

*

After lunch, Iqbal took Kiran for a joyride in his new car.

'How much did you buy it for?'

'DK gifted it to me.'

'What was the occasion?'

'Because I dropped the middlemen from the gold business.'

With the middlemen gone, Iqbal would earn an additional profit of Rs 5000 per jacket. This meant that for each consignment of 100 jackets, he would earn at least Rs 5 lakh more.

'To whom will you sell the gold now?'

'To the middlemen only.'

Kiran's eyes widened but she didn't comprehend fully. The shiny new car streaked past Marine Drive to the clear seaside stretch along Haji Ali. Her hair flew in the breeze.

In those years, the golden period of gold smuggling, the market was completely under DK's control. He was the only one smuggling jackets in bulk. The middlemen were left with no option but to come on bended knee before Iqbal.

Although the gold being smuggled was in hundreds of tons, it was still much less than the demand of the market. So, the same middlemen were now buying gold from Iqbal without charging him commission.

Kiran was confused. 'But no broker will do business without his commission.'

'You aren't wrong,' Iqbal said, as he drove with an easy grace. 'But you missed a crucial point. His commission from the other party is still there. Instead of a double commission, he has to make do with one. There is another advantage in this for us. Whenever there is a price rise after the London or American markets open, we get the benefit of that increase also.'

'How was it earlier?'

'Earlier, before both the markets opened for the day, the broker used to buy it from us at the prevailing market price. When the price shot up, the broker would enjoy all the upside.'

'And if the prices fall?'

'You can anticipate this using a bit of intelligence.'

'How?'

'*Time* magazine publishes the price of every foreign currency and market rates. Bullion merchants need to study it.'

After winding through Bombay, the car stopped in the parking lot of Sun-n-Sand Hotel. Both of them crossed the lobby and sat by the poolside on cane chairs under a rainbow-coloured umbrella. Iqbal looked at his wristwatch. The sun had set.

'Tell me! What do you want?' he asked.

Kiran smiled, small and mischievous. 'What else does anyone need as long as you are by their side?'

'Mango milkshake!' Iqbal replied playfully and asked the waiter to get two glasses.

Though Iqbal dealt in millions every day, he never got a single paisa in his hand. Of course, if he wished, he could withdraw as much money as he wanted any time. But a person who never smoked, never touched liquor, kept away from women and vices, how much would a man like that need?

*

'Sufi!' I asked for clarification. 'You said you transacted in millions every day and yet never got cash in hand. What's the use of a partnership?'

'Money gets deposited into the joint account of the partners.'

'How many partners were there?'

'Five—DK, Singh, me and two others.'

'You have not mentioned these two partners before.'

'You may call them sleeping partners. They seldom played an active role. But they were useful for the safety of our business.'

'Were they top officials?'

'DK had involved them because they were very influential. For example, one of the two was the son of the chief minister.'

Sufi did not have to say more; I understood. As for the transactions worth millions, he threw some light on the role of the 'bankers', who were the backbone of illicit business.

Normally, businessmen carry out their transactions through banks, but then the money involved is clean. Even a child knows that black money cannot be deposited into a bank. Then where is it hoarded? How is it used for transactions? To clarify: DK used to buy gold worth millions. How did he make the payments? He used to sell gold worth millions in India. How did he receive these huge amounts of money? Did he actually receive millions in cash?

No.

His business was handled by trading firms whom the mafia called 'bankers'. There are many such small and big firms in Bombay, of which five are well-known.

If you visit one of these firms in Kalbadevi, you will be in for a surprise. In a congested locality, in a dilapidated, barely-upright building, there is a single-room *kothri* which houses this firm. Inside, on the mattressed floor, you will find three cylindrical bolsters, a telephone, a trusty ancient safety vault bearing the brand name 'Rahmatullah' and a calendar with pictures of gods and goddesses.

These firms have the government's licence to legally carry on a money lending business. But while the licence is to transact in business worth around Rs 20 lakh, they actually deal in crores.

'Are the officials of the tax department ignorant of the duplicity of these bankers?'

He smiled as if I had cracked a joke. 'Can such massive deals take place without the knowledge of the government?'

'Then why are no raids conducted on these firms?'

'Which official has the guts? Moreover, it's not easy to trap them.'

'That means they too are as powerful as the mafia.'

'Those who play in millions are never weak. Besides, they have the implicit backing of the underworld. Still, the Income Tax (IT) department does carry out occasional raids. In 1990, a banking firm was raided. The firm had to cough up forty-five lakhs to quietly settle the case.'

'What if the official had refused to take the bribe?'

'Obviously, he would have been transferred to some godforsaken place.'

Sufi further explained that though these firms are known as 'bankers', there is no need of a slip book or a cheque book. Here honesty still survives in its pristine form. Just one's word is enough to transfer millions overnight from one account to another.

It must be noted that neither party holds any cash even though they have both placed their funds with the bankers.

Let us take an example. DK sells gold worth Rs 1 crore in the market. A jeweller buys it and informs the banker over the phone. The banker, in turn, telephones DK to inform him that Rs 1 crore has been deposited into his account.

The common man may ask as to where the bankers keep the money? Actually, they too do not keep more than a few million rupees. The rest is kept in circulation as loans on interest to others or as investment in other businesses.

'The bankers must be charging a fee for handling your money?'

'In those days, they used to charge thirty rupees a day for every *peti* (Rs 1 lakh) deposited with them.'

Sometimes, an average trafficker would need a few lakh rupees to buy gold. He too would contact the banker, who would give him the money at an interest rate of Rs 100 a day for every peti. The trafficker would buy the gold in the afternoon, turn a profit of Rs 25,000 and return the capital along with the interest to the banker in the evening.'

'What will the bankers do if someone wants a huge amount in cash?'

'What do you mean by huge?'

'Let's say five crores.'

'In that case, the bankers need at least twenty-four hours so that they can withdraw some part of the investment that is put into different businesses. Sometimes, when this too isn't possible, they contact other bankers. These five main bankers are like the five fingers of a hand. They come to each other's help when needed,' Sufi continued, 'There are occasions when a huge quantity of smuggled gold arrives but the broker does not have the money to buy it. He then offers partnership to the bankers. For example, say the gold is worth ten crores and the broker has only two crores. In such a case, he would make a proposition to the banker. But it may not be possible for the banker to arrange for so much cash immediately. So, the banker contacts other bankers and forms a syndicate that would buy gold from the mafia and sell it.'

I brought up another point. 'This explains the transactions done with Indian currency. What about the transactions done abroad?'

'What transactions?'

'DK was buying gold from Dubai. How did he make payments to the trader in Dubai?'

'Sometimes, the gold is imported against the export of silver of the same value. But this is done only when the price of silver is high in the international market. Otherwise, the Indian bankers know how to exchange Indian currency into foreign currency.'

'How do they do this?'

'They have branches abroad. They only need to inform that branch over the phone about how much money is to be deposited into which account against the purchase of so much gold at so-and-so rate.'

*

'Iqbal! What have you decided?' Kiran asked him finishing her glass of mango milkshake.

'About what?'

'We are both adults now . . .'

'So?'

'If we want, we can get married and start a family.'

'I haven't given it any thought.'

'I'll give you a week to think it fully through,' she said after consideration. 'But don't forget, there are only two options before me—either marriage or . . .'

She did not need to complete her sentence. Iqbal understood: if he did not marry her, she would be forced to continue along the dark road that destiny had chosen for her.

27

Iqbal smiled as he scanned the newspaper headlines before leaving for college the following morning. The pound had started stumbling. The impact of the London Stock Exchange would be felt in markets throughout the world. The price of gold would shoot up. A profit of Rs 3 lakh was now assured on the sale of the 300 jackets that he had held overnight.

Textbooks in hand, he was locking the flat when he heard Kiran approaching. As he turned to look at her, she stopped at a distance. She was wearing a maxi dress.

'Phone for you,' she said and turned away.

'Who is it?'

'Boss.'

He came into the bedroom, put his books down on the bed and lifted the receiver. Kiran watched him from the kitchen as she prepared breakfast.

'Did you like the car?'

Iqbal realized that he hadn't thanked the chief for having gifted him the car.

'Yes . . . It's a nice car.'

'I hope you aren't saying that just for courtesy's sake.'

'It's really fabulous . . . top-class.'

'A Rolls-Royce belonging to a former Maharaja has come up for sale. A Rolls-Royce is considered one of the best cars in the world. If you don't like that Mercedes, we can go in the evening and have a look at it.'

'DK, a Rolls–Royce suits kings, not stewards.'

There was nothing to laugh about and yet, as was his habit, DK laughed out aloud. He then came to the point. 'If the steward permits, I'd like to withdraw some money.'

'All that's there is yours.'

'No. Don't be under that illusion. Whatever is there belongs to us all, to all the partners. And more importantly, you have been appointed the treasurer. No partner can withdraw a single paisa without your permission. This was decided unanimously in the last meeting—and I'm no exception to that rule.'

Even though he was not the boss, Iqbal felt like he was the real power behind the throne; and at the other end of the line, DK was holding out a begging bowl.

'How much do we have in the account?'

'Around Rs 30 crore.'

DK did some calculations and asked, 'This week, has any partner withdrawn any amount?'

'Singh urgently needed Rs 5 lakh.'

'He had struck a property deal in Chandigarh so perhaps he invested it there,' he said and added, 'I need Rs 50 lakh deposited into my Swiss account.'

Iqbal's eyes widened. His Dongri mentality came to the fore. For a person who had sold candies by the roadside and lifted pots of water for tenants in Abbasi Manzil to earn a few rupees, Rs 50 lakh was a staggering amount.

He was about to shoot back, 'So much?' when he bit his lip. He was no more selling chikki but gold biscuits. He was dealing in millions. If Rs 50 lakh was removed from a corpus of Rs 3 crores, the earth would not slip away from beneath their feet. Besides, the boss had to make the payment for contraband goods brought in from other countries. Sometimes, such transactions were done through his Swiss account.

'I'll instruct the bankers,' Iqbal said.

'Thanks, what are your plans for the coming Sunday?'

'I've begun preparations for the final examinations.'

'Work hard all week, but don't forget you are spending Sunday evening with me at the racecourse.'

Even after the call had ended, Iqbal kept staring at the receiver as if he was seeing it for the first time. Emerging from the kitchen, Kiran looked at him with amusement. 'Have flowers begun blossoming from it?' she teased, wiping her hands with a napkin.

'Kiran!' Iqbal smiled, returning the receiver to the cradle. 'This DK is a strange fellow. He can withdraw as much money as he wishes by instructing the bankers over the phone. And yet, he won't touch a paisa without my permission.'

'Is that why you are preening like a peacock?'

'Shouldn't I be?'

'DK isn't as simple as you think.'

'Who told you?'

'My experience. He doesn't have a neck.'

'What do you mean?' Iqbal asked, tickled.

'Have you ever seen his neck?'

Iqbal was surprised by her question. He didn't realize that Kiran observed the men who entered her life so minutely.

'So a man without a neck is a shrewd person?'

'To be blunt, he is a swine.'

'And what about the person who has a long neck?'

'A fool.'

'What does my neck indicate?'

'That's what I fail to grasp,' Kiran shrugged. 'Your neck isn't long, yet you are a prize idiot.'

'How come?'

Because you can't see that you are being manipulated by the top bosses for their personal gains. Instead of saying this, Kiran put both her arms around his waist and asked, 'Tell me honestly, would you have fallen in love with me if you were wise?'

Iqbal nodded and explained, 'Now I understand the reason for my foolishness. I was quite a clever chap till I fell in love with you.'

'Very smart! Now, tell me, are you planning to go to college today without breakfast?'

'I completely forgot!' With this, he pushed Kiran aside and picked up his books from the bed and rushed out.

Reaching the ground floor, his feet stopped near the car. The urge to impress the students by going to college in the Mercedes was tempting. Then, he walked across the street and hailed a taxi. It was a fifteen-minute drive. He spent it pondering over Kiran's proposal.

Kiran wanted to marry him. He too was dreaming of a settled life with her. Yet, why was something pricking deep in his heart? Why was he not getting a clear yes from his brain? Was it the fear of society? Whether a prostitute is from lowly Kamathipura or posh Altamount Road, marrying her would damage Iqbal's reputation. Friends and acquaintances may not dare to say anything to his face, but they would certainly laugh behind his back. And how humiliated would he feel in front of those friends who had spent a night with Kiran? Would he not die of shame if he had happened to bump into DK or Singh with his new wife?

No.

Iqbal didn't care two hoots for society. He had fallen in love knowing her truth. He loved Kiran with all his heart, but his brain was still in his control—examining the matter from every angle.

He was neither a saint nor a social reformer on a mission to reform 'fallen' women. He wanted to make Kiran his wife because among all the girls he had come across, only she understood him deeply; her nature was in tune with his. *Then what was the unknown fear that was stopping him?*

Did he suspect that Kiran, accustomed to sleeping with a variety of men, would start hunting again because a single man would not be able to satisfy her?

No.

He had full faith—in himself and in Kiran. Given the chance, he was confident that Kiran would never look back at her past; she would prove to be as loyal as Sita.

Was he afraid that he would not be able to ensure her happiness after marriage? To some extent, this was true. There was nothing certain in Iqbal's life. He did not know where he would be tomorrow; nobody knew if he would be locked behind bars.

This scenario, however, was unlikely: DK's powerful protection surrounded him. However, DK was not God. Else, Hamid would not have reached the gallows. Had Iqbal not pulled off his trick at the last minute, he would have been hanged.

However, after thinking some more, Iqbal felt that this fear too was unfounded. Kiran knew everything about his life. Like Iqbal, she too was ready to marry him after knowing everything about him.

Another normal fear could arise that Iqbal was a Muslim, while Kiran was a Hindu. The decision between persons of different religions to marry inevitably triggered off a chain of problems: *which matrimonial rites would be followed—Hindu or Muslim? Would Kiran agree to change her religion? Would Iqbal be ready to marry her in an Arya Samaj temple?*

The answer to this question too was quite simple. Both of them were intelligent. If this problem cropped up, neither would Kiran have to convert into a Muslim nor

Iqbal to a Hindu. They could just go to the registrar's office and get married.

Despite examining the issue of marriage under a microscope, he could not identify the needle that was pricking him. He was in no hurry—Kiran had given him a week and today was just the second day. He decided that if he failed to find the answer until the last day, he would go ahead and marry Kiran.

*

Iqbal's complications were different from mine. It had been two months since Suraiyya and I had sealed our decision to get married. During these sixty days, I had doubled my income from Rs 500 to Rs 1000, even though my back was breaking from working long nights.

I had also somehow arranged for a house, a miracle indeed. In a new colony near Santacruz railway station, a friend of mine who needed a studio to paint had booked a small apartment and then got the news that he had been selected for the Rockefeller scholarship. Before he could start working in his new studio, he had to fly to America for a year. I met him with my problem. He was so glad that he thanked me as if I had done him a great favour.

His problem was that if he kept the new house locked for a long time, a thief could break into it. If he gave the house on rent to a stranger, it would create an equally big headache if he refused to vacate the apartment on his return.

I got the keys to our new house within twenty-four hours. I only had to pay the society dues and the electricity bill, which would amount to hardly Rs 200. Everything was going so smoothly that I began doubting my good fortune.

We felt blessed. We both belonged to the same religion. We both shared the same values. We both loved the open sky and each other. Had there not been the unsurmountable wall of wealth between the two of us, we need not have even thought of taking such a desperate step.

I knew that our bold step would upset elders on both sides. There would be an uproar. On my side, there would be a few outbursts; but on her side, there would be nothing less than an explosion.

People in hovels always eye palaces, goes an old saying. Economically, I stood on a lower pedestal. I could not blame Suraiyya's family for thinking that I had lured her for her wealth—it's normal for rich parents to think this way.

Around the same time, a middle-class boy named Bharat Dave, the elder brother of dramatist Shailesh Dave, fell in love with a wealthy Muslim girl, Nannu Sajan, from our college. The violent calamities that befell them after they declared that they had got married secretly were spine-chilling. I too was treading down the same precarious path.

Suddenly, I thought of an idea. In fact, Suraiyya's original suggestion of getting married secretly and not telling anyone till our final examinations fitted well with my plan.

'Suraiyya!' I told her the next day at the art school. 'If luck is on our side, then without hurting our elders' feelings we are going to get married in grand style!'

'How?'

'By using our secret marriage as a weapon. We will get married but won't make it public.'

'Then?'

'After the finals, you just tell your family that you want to marry the person of your choice . . . that's me.'

'We both know that they won't agree.'

'You should ask them the reason.'

It would be difficult for her mother to answer honestly—they would not admit that they were rejecting their daughter's choice only because he was poor.

'And suppose they admit to it?'

'Question them. Ask if you are marrying the boy or his bank balance?'

'They may reply that they have chosen the young man from London considering both the factors.'

'Assert that for you he is a total stranger, while you know me for the last three and a half years.'

This conversation was like digging a ditch with a fork, yet a thorough rehearsal was critical to ensure that everything went off smoothly.

'What if they still don't agree?'

'Then play the trump card of love. Assure them about my character. Encourage them to verify my background.'

'I will assure them that though he is a Muslim, he neither offers namaz nor fasts during Ramadan,' Suraiyya said blithely. 'To verify your character I will give them actor Dharmendra's address. They can confirm with him who initiated you into alcohol. And I can add that long before you got hooked to the bottle, you had picked up a childhood habit of smoking.'

'I'm worried about our future and you are trying to be funny?'

'Did I say anything wrong?'

'After quitting films, I gave up drinking even the single peg that I used to take every night. To be precise, after meeting you.' Trying to underplay the gravity of the situation, I quipped, 'Just because you like the blue-eyed boy from London, you need not pick on me.'

She smiled, looked into my eyes and said, 'Indeed, he looked dashing in the photograph.' When this had no effect on my smugness, she added, 'He is as rich as a lord—he is the owner of a five-star hotel in London. At least I won't have to cook after marriage.'

'You think you will have to cook in my house?'

'Provided you have something at home to cook!'

'Your jest expresses a profound truth, Suraiyya,' I said, turning serious again. 'You're a painter, I'm a painter. It's with much slogging that the fire in an artist's hearth is lit. It's still not too late. If you wish to marry him, live a life of comfort and luxury, hobnob amongst the rich and famous, I've no right to stop you.'

'Won't you be sad?'

That was true. I couldn't contemplate life without her. She had become as necessary to me as painting—being separated was terrifying. Yet I said, 'I've known only sorrow since childhood. One more misfortune will not make any difference. At least, you will be happy.'

'Aabid! I'm sorry to say that though you are so close, you are still miles away from me! How can you imagine that I'll be happy without you?'

'I want what's best for you.'

'And what about me?' she said with a cutting edge in her voice, 'If I wanted a life of comfort and luxury, I would not have been sitting here with you in the public garden! Don't you forget that I've loved you more than my mother. I did not see her face for three years and you are advising me to marry someone else! Aren't you ashamed?'

I immediately accepted my mistake, but it took me more than fifteen minutes to pacify her. I drew the conversation back to the main subject. 'You must make every possible effort to make your family agree to our marriage. Yet, if they stick to their guns, use our secret marriage as a weapon. Show them the nikah certificate. They will surrender.'

After pondering over my suggestion for a while, Suraiyya raised a very pertinent question, 'What if they agree even before I show them the certificate?'

'Then what?'

'They will ask us to go through another nikah.'

This thought had not occurred to me. If they agreed to our marriage, and if they found out that we were already married, it would surely create bitterness. And if we didn't let them know about our secret, we would have to perform the nikah ceremony for a second time, which too would be unethical. 'We will quietly go for a civil marriage,' I suggested. Suraiyya agreed.

For our wedding, I needed a lawyer, not a bearded qazi. The next day, through a friend, I arrived at a lawyer's office. He agreed, for a small fee, to solemnize our marriage at the registrar's office in the Old Customs House. We chose Friday.

For the auspicious day, I bought a new pair of terylene pants and a handloom shirt. A polished pair of leather boots replaced my torn canvas shoes. I stood before the full-size mirror in the cupboard, all ready.

My mother, who was sewing a quilt near the window, commented, 'All dressed up like a bridegroom! Who's getting married?'

'Me!' I quipped facetiously, though it was true.

'You have been quietly shopping for the past few days, as if we are all blind! Tell me the truth, where are you going?'

'I'm just a witness. A friend of mine is getting married secretly. . .' my voice trailed off.

I do not know if my lie convinced her or not, but she stared at me without speaking for a long time. 'Don't *you* ever do such a thing,' she finally said gravely. 'My heart will break into pieces.'

The shine on my face peeled like plaster off a wall. Until then, I had not thought about my mother who had brought me up grinding chillies and accepting every humiliating, menial job she could find. It had never struck me that my secret marriage would shatter her dreams of proudly seeing me seated on horseback as a bridegroom.

I was shaken to the core. On one side was my mother's untiring affection and on the other my true love. My tragedy was that from where I stood, there was no return.

I left the house before 10 a.m. I had to buy a gold ring, pick up Suraiyya from the girls' hostel and go to the registrar's office where our lawyer and two witnesses would be waiting.

I took a taxi and went to a jeweller's shop at Opera House. I had never bought gold before. Noting my bewilderment, the salesperson put me at ease with a broad smile.

I asked to see the latest designs in rings. He placed before me a catalogue. My eye fell on one elegant design. The price was Rs 1700.

The salesman added, 'And it will take at least two days to make it.'

Dismayed, I started looking at ready-made rings.

'Are you looking for a wedding ring?'

I nodded.

'Have you brought a sample ring for the size?'

I was confused again. I finally chose one ring of her approximate size, paid Rs 1400, jumped into the waiting taxi and reached the girls' hostel. A spacious sense of transcendent joy permeated every pore of my body. It was 11 a.m. I had informed Suraiyya last evening that I would be at the main gate at 11 a.m. We had to reach the registrar's office by 11.30 a.m.

*

Suraiyya was not at the gate. I felt a knot in my stomach. This had never happened before. We were so punctual that we strived to arrive before time. It being a working day, the hostel was almost deserted. I waited outside the gate for five minutes and then called the security guard. When he came, I gave him the room number and requested him to call Suraiyya.

'She isn't here.'

'She is expecting me,' I pressed. 'She must be inside somewhere.'

'I told you, she isn't there!'

'Where has she gone?'

'How do I know?'

'But . . .'

'She hasn't returned since last night.'

'Rubbish! I dropped her myself right here last evening.'

Sensing this was escalating into argument, the watchman suggested that I meet the hostel superintendent. I too was fed up of his tactless replies. The name of the superintendent was Ms Bastikar. She was a chromium-plated middle-aged Maharashtrian lady with fine white hair drawn into a bun on the nape of her neck. She had shrewd eyes, but her cold, handsome face was impressive.

As I entered the office on the ground floor of the hostel, she lifted her bespectacled face from a register, and considered me.

'Yes?'

'I've come to see Suraiyya.'

'And may I know who you are?'

'Her boyfriend.'

'Have a seat.'

I had not come here to sit and chat. There was a desk between us with chairs for visitors. I stayed put behind a chair.

'I'm in a hurry,' I told her.

She again asked me to sit.

I was baffled. A heavy silence pulsated ominously in the air. I realized that until I obeyed her, this lady would not open her mouth. I pulled a chair and sat down.

Before replying, she took off her glasses and wiped them with a filigreed handkerchief. Then she said slowly, 'Suraiyya left for Mombasa by the night flight.'

Had I not sat down, I would have collapsed.

28

Suraiyya had not ditched me; her brother, Abbas Ali, had forcibly taken her away. In effect, she was legally kidnapped.

According to her friend Lubayna, when Suraiyya had returned to the hostel the previous evening, Abbas Ali was waiting in the lobby for his sister.

It was natural for Suraiyya to be surprised at seeing her elder brother, that too in her hostel, without any notice.

'How come?' was all she could think of saying.

'I had to come unexpectedly for a day on business. Thought I would meet you. Have you had dinner?'

'No.'

'Come, let's eat together at the Taj and chat awhile.'

'The hostel gate closes at eight,' she said, showing her watch. 'It's already eight.'

'You don't have to worry about that. I've got the late pass from your superintendent.'

Suraiyya thought quickly. If she did not go out with Abbas Ali now, she would have to give him time in the morning, which would be worse. She agreed to go with her brother.

Lubayna said this much. The rest I learnt from the superintendent. Abbas Ali had not taken a late pass. He had told the superintendent that Suraiyya's mother was terminally ill and that the doctors had given up all hope. So, he had especially flown down to Bombay to take Suraiyya back.

When an elder member of the family, armed with a solid reason, personally comes to take charge of his ward, the superintendent has no right to meddle.

From this information, I could guess that after making Suraiyya sit in the taxi, her brother, instead of taking her to Taj Hotel, headed straight for the airport. He must have arranged for everything, including the flight tickets.

I was certain that when Suraiyya discovered the deception, she must have fought tooth and nail to escape, but she had not succeeded.

My wedding night was the most unforgettable night of my life. I lay under the open sky on the terrace. I could neither tell anyone about my anguish nor bear it. I could only toss about helplessly on my mattress.

As the night progressed, my agony increased. I wanted to scream. A high wind picked up, forewarning a coming storm. Windows began slamming against each other. In the distance, the sound of a breaking windowpane pierced the silence of the night.

I was not alone on the terrace. Like worms in a gutter, other tenants of our five-storeyed chawl too were sprawled around me.

One by one, rolling their mats with the pillows and cursing the weather, they went back to the refuge of their rooms. I slept all alone. After midnight it started raining—God's feeble attempt to douse the bonfire of all of my dreams.

*

Where the heart rules, the pain is always intense. The seed of Iqbal and Kiran's love may have sprouted, but it progressed only after a careful consideration of all aspects of life, and its end too was to come after much mental deliberation.

Our love had been blind because our wild hearts ruled over our minds; their love could see all too clearly because their minds examined everything, kept everything in check.

Both couples dived into the ocean of love, but one took the plunge with eyes closed while the other kept them open. And when the eyes are open, the dark hour of separation is not an unbearable agony, the heart does not shatter into a million pieces and the very foundation of life does not get demolished.

*

As the week progressed from Monday rapidly towards Sunday, Iqbal's confusion steadily increased. His heart was getting more and more desperate to marry Kiran, but his mind was holding him back. *What was the reason?* He found the answer in his college textbook, while reading a chapter on genetics.

*

Telling me about his decision, Sufi explained the principle of genetics. 'If one colour is mixed with another, the third colour contains elements of both the colours. For example, when the colour red is mixed with white, it creates pink, a new colour which is half red and half white. The same principle is applicable to a child born between a man and a woman.'

What Sufi concluded from this was that if he married a prostitute, the child thus born would also have some predisposition towards promiscuity or immorality. If the child were a girl, she may even be inclined to follow in her mother's footsteps. Sufi did not want this to happen.

According to this theory of genetics, the rehabilitation of a prostitute is neither wise nor effective. Well-meaning social workers who bestow the status of a wife on a fallen woman are mistaken; at least, they should not compound the error by producing children.

However, zealous proponents of modern genetic theories forget one thing. The principles of genetics have been confirmed by science, but they are not 100 per cent accurate. The character of a child depends on his or her upbringing. The environment determines the child's development. Moreover, a child's predisposition is also influenced by the state of mind of a man and a woman during coitus.

This means that though a woman may not be a saint before and after copulation, if a divine feeling takes over during climax, it will impact her pregnancy. That is why it is not necessary that a mafia don's son will always turn out to be a criminal; the son of a pandit may turn out to be a gangster.

History tells us that Angulimal was a ruthless dacoit. He earned this name because he used to cut off the fingers of his victims, make a garland out of them and wear it around his neck. But when God entered his heart, he quit the path of sin and surrendered to the Buddha. Could genetics explain this?

You might be familiar with the romantic legend of Jesal and Toral, in which the pure love of Toral transforms the dreaded dacoit Jesal. Mary Magdalene too was said to be a prostitute in her time, until Jesus Christ awakened her heart to the path of righteousness. When Christ was being crucified, this so-called 'sinful woman' was given the sacred duty of washing his feet, following which she was no longer a fallen soul but worshipped as a saint. Can genetics explain this?

In that crucial hour of decision, had Sufi investigated the subject of genetics a little more thoroughly, Kiran would have been his wife. We could attribute the eventual outcome to Sufi's incomplete and bookish knowledge—he called it all a part of the play of destiny.

*

Before letting Kiran know about his decision, he invited her to dinner at Palm Grove Hotel. It was Sunday. Her deadline was expiring that night. Though he was dead tired from spending the evening at the racecourse with DK, he had driven from Mahalaxmi to Juhu.

'What will you have?' Iqbal asked her.

They were sitting near the outdoor pool facing the Arabian Sea. Kiran had come dressed in a silk sari—a stunning red one with a contrasting black border and blouse.

'That depends on your answer. If your answer is positive, then whatever money you have in your pocket won't be enough.'

Iqbal pulled out his wallet and rifled through the notes with a small laugh.

'I have at least Rs 3000.'

'My tastes are more expensive than that.'

'What if the answer is negative?'

'Then a bottle of liquor will do.'

'A full bottle?'

'Yes.'

Iqbal ordered Chinese starters for himself and a bottle of Scotch for Kiran. Without saying a word, he had answered her question. Kiran's face betrayed no emotion though she was gutted from within.

'Have you ever had a full bottle before?' Iqbal asked her.

'Never.'

'Why today?'

'I need to get drunk tonight! Otherwise my dreams will haunt me all night.'

'I thought you had strong willpower.'

'I do, but certainly not as rock-hard as yours.'

'Is that what you think of me?'

'You are the one who has made the decision.'

'That's my misfortune. It's true that I've loved you from the bottom of my heart. Though both of us are smiling now, it has been equally painful for me, if not more. But it's also true that we will overcome the jolt in a few days.'

The waiter came and first placed a bottle of Scotch and a glass in front of Kiran who started drinking immediately. After a while, a bowl of sweet corn soup was placed before Iqbal.

Eating a spoonful, he began afresh, 'Kiran, I have a request to make.'

'Yes?'

'Tonight we will be parting as lovers, but in the future, can't we remain friends?'

'We were always only friends and we are ending our friendship tonight.'

'Are you already high?' Iqbal asked, puzzled.

'I'm just on my second peg.'

'Then why do you say that?'

'A love in which there is no place for even a kiss—call it love or friendship—what difference does it make? I don't want you in my life. I don't want you to see me.'

'Don't I even deserve that much?'

'Of course, you deserve it, but I don't want to test your restraint.' With every peg, Kiran's tone was becoming more bitter and more cutting. 'I buried my past just for you. Now I'll have to resurrect the old Kiran. Again, men will start coming into my life and it will be painful for you to see it.'

'If you want, you can chart a new path for yourself,' Iqbal said, trying to placate her. 'Your studies are still incomplete. Finish college. As a friend, I'll be more than happy to take care of all your financial responsibilities.'

'And then?'

'After graduating, you can take up a job of your choice.'

'And then?'

'Marry a young man of your choice.'

'Who will marry a slut?'

'Once you get a degree and a job, all will be forgotten, even your past . . .'

'That's what you think. And I'm not a Mirabai who can devote her entire life to worship. I'm an ordinary woman. I have a heart. What will I do when that heart longs for a man?' Kiran's voice now edged a note higher. 'Should I hire a gigolo then to satisfy my physical needs? No, Iqbal, I'm not the type who secretly enjoys debauchery while pretending to be a devi in public. Whatever I do, I'll do it openly. I have that much courage—to take on society as I am.' The intoxication was showing on her flushed face now. 'And who is this society? The same motherfucker who I respected as a father, who raped me night after night for a month? The same husbands who keep their wives in the dark to strip naked before a whore and are called gentlemen by day? Iqbal, I don't wear a mask. But I don't wear blinders either. Even after six pegs, I can see clearly. I can think clearly.'

After the seventh peg, her dark eyes flashing, she went on. 'A ray of hope had appeared before me. I thought I would step out of the darkness and embrace the light. Perhaps that is not my destiny. I'm a gypsy child. How can I have a house? The open sky above and the earth below is what we call home. And here I was—dreaming of finding refuge within four walls.'

She burst out laughing wildly—as if she had cracked a joke which only she understood.

Then she wagged a finger at Iqbal. 'You must be thinking that I've been hurt by your decision. Don't be under that illusion! Remember, the proposal for marriage was not yours but mine. I had requested you to consider it. That was my right, and, whenever I exercise my rights, I never forget that the other person too has some rights. I gave you the right to accept me or reject me. And . . . and I was prepared for whatever you decided. Had I not been prepared, I'd have been extremely miserable right now. Perhaps like other foolish broken-hearted girls I too would have considered suicide, or ended up in a mental asylum. But I'm not like that, Iqbal. I didn't commit suicide even when that bastard father of mine raped me for the first time.'

Suddenly, she got up and offered him her hand. 'Good luck, Iqbal!'

So far, Iqbal had only tasted the soup. Kiran's heart-breaking anguish beneath her defiant laughter had stopped him from eating a single morsel.

Instead of shaking hands with Kiran, he got up. 'Come, let me drop you home.'

Pulling her hand away she said, 'There's no need.' She turned and walked unsteadily in the general direction of the door. She did not get far—after a few steps, she swooned and dropped to the ground in her bridal-red sari.

*

However tough the heart may be, it is bound to suffer when the thread of love snaps. It took Kiran a week to recover and get back to her old profession. With time, her unrequited love affair with Iqbal was to become a rosy memory of a time when everything seemed possible—even happiness.

*

I could only imagine Suraiyya's plight. To recover from the trauma, like me, it would take her many, many years. Like a fish pulled out of water, she would flail and gasp, wail and bang her head against the wall but to no avail. Finally, she would surrender to her family like a slave condemned. Her body would go through the wedding rituals, her heart would be calling me.

Unlike Suraiyya, I could not cry. It was not in my nature to shed tears. I could not bang my head against walls, so I suffered in silence. A fire raged within me day and night. The liquor bottle was beckoning me—*Devdas found peace here, why don't you try?*

During those hellish days, the one wise choice I made was that I did not seek solace in liquor. On the very first day that I had tasted liquor, I had resolved that I would never touch it in times of sorrow. And I doggedly stuck to my resolve. God know for how many months I suffered silently this way.

I was aware that sharing one's sorrows with friends lightens the load. However, ever since Suraiyya had entered my life, I had no close friend left.

Lubayna and Anil were my friends. Through the back lane that linked St Xavier's college with our arts school, they used to walk with me and comfort me every evening. Sometimes, they used to get tickets for a film screening or a play. But I never felt like joining them; the last thing I needed was pity. As if someone had poisoned the air on campus, I kept away from the college. Yet, I could feel the same breeze on my face. I'd remember the first date at the zoo, our moonless walk in the pitch-dark night in Nainital, our last kiss. Every nook and corner had memories—every path we had walked hand in hand, every bend we had turned, every café where we had whispered promises. What else was left in this godforsaken life?

Every morning, a question cropped up: *where would I spend the day?* The days of Moharram had begun. In memory of the martyrs of Karbala, these are ten days of communal mourning. On the final day, a fire-walking ritual is also organized. Back in those days, this ceremony used to take place at Palghar, a couple of hours' journey from Bombay.

I went there with a friend. It was 11 p.m. In a grave-sized trench, a bed of red-hot coals was burning. Devotees were beating their chests, raring to prove their faith through the trial by fire. This included children as well as the elderly. To whip up the frenzy further, drums were being beaten on one side, while on the other crowds were furiously chanting: 'Ya Hussain, Ya Ali'.

One after the other, the devotees started stepping on to the hot coal. I stared quietly. An old question reared its head: *if these children can jump on to the coal, why am I watching from afar?* Following the queue of devotees, I too went ahead. Walking steadily across the nine foot-long bed of coals, I reached the other side safely.

The next morning, I learnt that almost all the devotees who had jumped into the fire the previous night had burnt their feet. I recalled then, that a few years back, my uncle, to win Allah's favour, had walked on fire and scorched his soles. Till date, I have failed to unravel the mystery of why my feet didn't burn that night.

More questions arose that morning. *Was the decision to jump into the fire sane? Whether consciously or not, was it not a suicide attempt? For how much longer could I continue like this?*

In the end, I realized that my pain would destroy me. If I continued to silently suffocate in my solitary prison, I would surely collapse. It was necessary for me to give expression to my feelings. So, I dropped my brush and picked up a pen.

I was an artist. I had nothing to do with literature. I had not even heard the names of the doyens of Gujarati literature of that period such as Chunilal Madia and Umashankar Joshi. I had learnt to write children's stories by reading Disney comics. Mushtaq Jalili had taught me the art of writing scripts for movies. Besides a handful of short stories, I had also written a couple of one-act plays for inter-college drama competitions.

Perhaps I would not have ventured to write an original play if Jalili had had enough time for me. He used to write a play every year for our college, and I used to have a tough time goading him to write it. Dilly-dallying had become his second nature. Only after making me chase him for days, he would deliver the manuscript. At last, I got fed up. It was not in my nature to fall at anyone's feet.

In the fourth-year inter-college drama competition, for the first time in my life, I wrote a play; my old habit of challenging myself came to the rescue once again. The name of the play was 'Bus Stop'. I played the lead character. This Hindi play met with unexpected success. I won the prize for best acting. The director of the play was Bharat Dave.

Among the spectators were future superstar Rajesh Khanna and actor-writer Kader Khan. Both of them were students at the time. Besides, legendary director K. Asif's chief assistant, Sultan Ahmed, too had come to watch my play. Impressed by my performance, he came backstage.

'Aabid!' he said, introducing himself. 'Asif Sahib has come up with a film project that will have an entirely new cast and there is a comic role of a tailor that you would be perfect for. I would love you to come and meet Asif Sahib.'

I laughed and replied,. '*Miya*, acting is only my hobby! The day I make it my profession, I'll forget my art.'

He was terribly disappointed. He could not believe that someone could have the audacity to refuse to work with the director who had made the all-time classic *Mughal-e-Azam*.

After the death of K. Asif, when Sultan Ahmed became an independent director and was making his first film, he again offered me the role of a comedian.

I was firm in my resolve. I never wanted to become an actor. Neither did I want to become a writer. Yet the grief of my separation from Suraiyya had made me an author. Excavating all the memories I could not share with anyone, I scribbled over 500 pages. I felt as though a very heavy load had been taken off my shoulders.

Those days, in our neighbourhood in Dongri, there lived an affable kabaadi (scrap dealer). Though his name was Mohammed Husein Meghani, everyone affectionately called him 'Rata'—perhaps a teasing wordplay on the fact that he was neither a wealthy tycoon like Tata nor a Bata.

Every morning, before going to Bhat Bazaar to sell old books and magazines, he would peep into my room. He was curious. *What could this painter be writing round the clock?* And yet, he did not have the courage to disturb me.

One day, we bumped into each other on the stairs. 'What do you write the whole day?'

'I don't know,' I replied.

'How many pages have you written?'

'Around 500, I guess.'

'And you don't know what you have written?'

'I know what I've written, but I don't know what to call it.' *An autobiography? A novel? A piece of junk? I could not tell.*

He stared at me for a few moments. 'What will you do with it?'

'You may take it if you want.'

'You know very well that I deal in waste paper.'

'I also know that you are an honest dealer. You won't cheat me while weighing my scrap papers.'

That same day I handed over a heap of handwritten pages to him. At the time I was not aware that our friend Meghani was in touch with the publishers of Gujarati books, and that too with Shivji Ashar, the owner of Swati Prakashan, known for handpicking the new-wave writers.

First, Meghani read my manuscript himself and then submitted it to Swati Prakashan. A fortnight later, early one morning, he walked into my single-room house and stared at me in amazement. I wondered what was up—had horns grown on my head in the night?

'Saala!' he abruptly began saying. 'You wrote such a brilliant novel and you want me to believe you don't know what it is!' Now it was my turn to look at him in amazement. He continued talking nineteen to the dozen but in short, what I understood was that Shivji Ashar had agreed to publish my novel, and that I would be paid a minimum guarantee of Rs 500 as royalty.

Overnight, my name was included in the list of young Turks of Gujarati literature. Upon its publication, the novel *Tutela Farishta* (Fallen Angels) became the talk of the town. But before that, I had failed in my final-year art examinations.

*

Like me, Iqbal too had always been a first-class student. But his tragedy unfolded differently.

After breaking up with Kiran he vacated the Usha Sadan flat and moved to Sagar Darshan building. In those days, conjunctivitis had seized Bombay. Just two days before the

final examinations, he fell victim to this epidemic. He did
not lose hope. To fulfil his father's dream of him becoming
a doctor, he put eye drops and sat for the examination but
failed to answer any of the questions. He could not read a
single question.

29

If a diligent student, who ranks in the top five from the first to the fifth year of college, fails in the final examinations, you can imagine his plight. To rub salt on my wounds, college mates and even acquaintances didn't miss the opportunity to offer condolences.

Someone said, 'Aabid, a great injustice has been done to you. You must fight it out.' Another fellow said that the examiners were orthodox old fogeys who could not understand my abstract visual style. Someone else blamed the examination system, while another saw it as proof of the obvious communal bias.

I was interested neither in their condolences nor in the reasons they offered. My greatest concern was for my mother. She was living on a thin strand of hope. She would sometimes tell the neighbours proudly, 'This year, my son will pass with flying colours, get a job with a four-figure salary—our days of misery will soon be over.'

Even in her dreams, she used to see me wearing a tie and carrying a briefcase, like a bureaucrat going to office.

How would I face her? If I told her the truth, it would destroy her. If I lied, my face would betray me. As it is, my mother had started suspecting me given the changes in my behaviour.

Earlier, I used to return home whistling and chirping like a bird. After Suraiyya's forced deportation, my face looked as if I had just returned from the funeral of a close friend. My mother did comment on the change, but I simply scoffed.

*

The day the results were declared, I thought seriously before going home and, at last, decided to tell the most spectacular lie of my life. My acting skills were about to be tested. Acting on the stage is comparatively easier then acting in real life. On stage, I never cared about whether the audience was impressed. I was not a professional actor nor had I been trained. So my problem was that I had to not only impress but also fully convince this single spectator.

At the corner of our street, I bought a box of sweets. With a showman's smile, I entered the dimly-lit house as if I was stepping on to a brightly-lit stage. With all the conviction I could summon, I said, 'Ma! Your son has become a graduate!'

My mother was scouring the dishes in the kitchen. She immediately turned her head to look at me. For a few long moments, she just stared intently without saying a word. Under her piercing gaze, I felt as if the smile I had held on my lips would fall off and I too would collapse. But finally, the meaning of my words hit home. She hurriedly washed her hands and dried them on her dupatta. 'Why wouldn't you succeed! I've been praying every day for you after namaz.'

Before she could say anything more, I stuffed a peda into her mouth. She placed a peda into my mouth too and then took the box from my hand to gleefully distribute the sweets to the neighbours.

I felt my legs tremble and leant on a chair to steady myself. I couldn't; I slumped into it. I had never experienced such pressure on stage. It was as if this one-minute performance had sucked away a year of my life. Beads of sweat from my forehead trickled down to my neck. My only satisfaction was that I had succeeded in my effort. I had saved my mother from drowning in an inconsolable pool of sorrow.

*

Iqbal, meanwhile, was conquering peak after peak of success. His hope of retracing his steps and becoming a doctor had proven to be another illusion. Now, there was no one to stop him. Even the sky could not contain his ambitions now. His net spread from Kashmir to Kanyakumari.

This did not mean that honest customs officials like Khan and Rustomji had given up or perished—their vigilant eyes were keeping a constant watch on Iqbal. Their helplessness was that they could not arrest him without evidence.

The cat-and-mouse game between the customs officials and smugglers was relentless. On uncovering Iqbal's game plan, Khan and Rustomji would lay a trap only to realize later that the artful dodger had changed his strategy at the last minute.

Howsoever daring the smugglers may be, they have always this fear of the naval ships guarding the coastal frontiers. They also need to steer clear of the coast guard.

Many coast guard officers were on the payroll of the smugglers, but I had neither read nor heard about a gang that had convinced the captain of a naval ship to work as a carrier.

When Sufi broached the subject, I don't know why I had the suspicion for the first time that he might be bragging. I have seen this weakness in quite a few traffickers that I have had the chance to encounter. Since I did not believe him, I showered on him a barrage of questions.

'Where did you meet this captain?'

'At the CCI club.'

'Then?'

'Then what?'

'How did you entrap him?'

'The way I'd lured other customs officials.'

'I want to know the exact method.'

'Method? I've never thought about it.'

'Obviously you don't go to him with a briefcase stuffed with hard cash and ask him to do the job.'

'Oh, no!'

'Then?'

'It's true that the colour of money plays a vital role in this, but how to use it is an art.'

As if recollecting something, he elaborated, 'Generally, a man's face reveals his character. Going a little deeper, a man's eyes reflect the deepest secrets of his psyche. When I first look into a person's eyes, I determine whether the fish will take the bait or not. If I see even a slight hope, I begin casting my line.'

After a long discussion, a rough picture of the methodology emerged before my eyes. We can describe the strategy as 'terror of tomorrow'. For example, on being introduced to a senior official in a five-star hotel or a club, Iqbal would casually bring up the subject of integrity. He would begin saying things to provoke him. If an officer does his job honestly, how does the government reward him? Just a petty pension, which is not enough to run even the kitchen. Secondly, after retirement, he has to surrender the government apartment that he has lived in all his life. If the officer has not made alternate arrangements, his family is out on the street. And how can an honest government servant, who barely makes both ends meet, raise the lakhs of rupees needed to purchase a house in a city like Bombay?

The Bombay Police (now called Mumbai Police) is a case in point. As if their pitiful salary is not humiliating enough, there are many police officers with families who are not even provided accommodation. Some of them live in dilapidated barracks that resemble stables, while others live in tandoor oven-like corrugated shacks in slums.

To buy these police officers there is no need to paint bleak pictures of their future. The stark terror of their present lives is already dancing before their eyes. In short, the underworld is well aware of this weakness of government servants and takes full advantage of it. Of course, money has its own magnetism too.

If an upright officer does not have a TV at home, but his corrupt colleague has not only a TV but a VCR as well, this would pinch him somewhere, and in a moment of weakness he would put aside his principles and accept the values of the day.

Iqbal had not ensnared the captain of the naval ship in just one meeting. After the formal introduction, he had gradually built a rapport with him. The captain was intrigued for Iqbal knew a 101 different ways to make money, both honest and crooked. Who would not be intrigued by such a wizard?

Iqbal had even taught DK some new tricks. One of them was about making the most of the bill of exchange. This was similar to trading in the slump and boom of the capital market but was safer than speculation. At least that's what Sufi said.

Whoever has an account in the Swiss bank can multiply his capital rapidly by just sitting at home, without lifting a finger. To master this skill, it is necessary to know the currency rates of different countries, which are published every week in *Time* magazine, because the prices keep fluctuating.

Iqbal had called for the last six months' issues of *Time* and studied them closely. He had acquired a fairly good insight into the circumstances under which the rate of the currency of a country weakened. For example, if the Japanese yen became stronger, the rate of the American dollar would fall and this would subsequently impact other currencies as well.

Based on his study, Iqbal would tell DK which currency's rate was likely to go up. Immediately, DK would call Switzerland and instruct his bank to convert 50 per cent of his capital from dollars to yen. In a couple of days, when the price of the yen rose, DK's capital in the bank would increase by a few lakh dollars.

When Iqbal informed him that the rate of Germany's deutsche mark would shoot up, DK would make a long-distance call and instruct: convert the currency from yen to the mark.

*

Over time, Iqbal and the naval captain grew close. The captain felt that it was time to test Iqbal because in their last meeting he had claimed that by making simple calculations he could predict which horse would win the next race.

'You will accompany me to the racecourse this Sunday,' the captain instructed him. 'And I'll bet on the same horse on which you will put money.'

'Very sorry, sir,' he said humbly. 'I don't gamble.'

'You can predict with certainty which horse is going to win and yet . . .'

'Sir, my religion considers gambling a sinful act.'

'Fair enough,' the captain conceded. 'I'll play alone, but you must be by my side. Don't forget, if I lose, I'll extract every last penny from you.'

'Take double, sir,' he said with such blithe confidence that the captain was speechless

*

Iqbal did not know much about horse racing. He had accompanied DK a couple of times to the Mahalaxmi racecourse, but that was all. He had seen DK win both the times. He guessed that there must be some ploy.

After a few days, he found out the secret from DK— the winning horse was the one which DK's jockey secretly fed some powder mixed in jaggery. Sufi was not clear as to what that concoction was. He could only conjecture that the mixture must contain some strong drug, like the steroids unscrupulous sportsmen injected before international games.

'Can't it be detected in the sweat of the horse after the race?' I asked.

'Of course. In case of a doubt, there would be a medical test of the horses, but there wasn't much awareness in those days. Moreover, DK didn't make his horse win every race.'

The captain did not have full confidence in Iqbal even on the day of the race. He hesitatingly played Rs 1000 on Iqbal's pick.

'This is chicken feed, sir!' Iqbal blurted out. 'You won't get such a golden opportunity to win again. Play a lakh and become a crorepati.'

He laughed, 'Where would I get such an obscene sum to bet on a horse. I'm an ordinary captain of a ship.'

'I thought you would pawn your house and jewellery and play big.'

'The house belongs to the government and the jewellery to my wife.' Sighing, he let slip the truth. 'Plus, I'm still not sure if trusting you will make me sink or . . .'

*

The results were out in an hour. Like magic, the captain's Rs 1000 had tripled. Now he was completely under Iqbal's spell. He was also addicted to the races. Just like a dog follows its master wagging its tail, the captain became Iqbal's loyal pet.

Every weekend and on holidays, Iqbal and the captain met at the CCI. The captain guzzled beer, while Iqbal sipped his lime juice. They would chat for hours. DK would watch the show from a distance. In fact, he was a CCI member. Iqbal used to sign in as DK's guest and without realizing it, their newest asset, the naval captain, was also his guest.

In the obsession to become a millionaire overnight, a greedy person forgets that without self-interest, even a mother does not nurse her baby.

Before revealing the name of the horse the next time, Iqbal made a shrewd move. 'Sir, can I ask for a small favour?'

'You don't have to ask, just say the word, mate! You want to fix someone a job in the navy, or want somebody promoted?'

'No, no, I believe it's not ethical to interfere in the government's affairs.'

'If more Indians were as wise as you, our country would beat China to pulp.'

'I'll be obliged if you could take delivery of a parcel.'

The captain stared at him unblinkingly. Iqbal did not have to clarify that the parcel meant a large gunny bag of gold-lined jackets. The captain was wise enough to grasp this much. His dilemma was whether to become a millionaire overnight or stick to his principles?

A dilemma signalled a crack—a weak moment. Iqbal had created it. And now he began to exploit the breach: 'Sir, you don't have to pawn your wife's jewellery to bet in tomorrow's race. All the same, if you wish to turn down my request, be blunt. I won't mind at all.'

The captain smiled faintly.

*

The castle had been captured, but the problem was that DK's horse was not participating in the following Sunday's race—only the week before he had got his horse to win.

Next Sunday was this season's last race. It was essential that the captain win that race. The very next day, gold biscuits worth Rs 1.25 crore coming from Dubai were to be unloaded on to the naval ship. If the captain lost the race, the entire game could turn turtle. He might also realize he had been duped and in his frustration it wouldn't be surprising if he decided to take revenge on Iqbal.

That night, he put forth his problem before DK. In front of Iqbal, DK made phone calls to two jockeys and announced the name of a horse: Wonder Prince. 'Tell the captain to play on it. There are 99 per cent chances of it winning tomorrow's race.'

How was this possible? Before Iqbal could ask this question, he got an answer. 'It's Wonder Prince's turn to win the closing race.'

*

When Iqbal delved deeper, he learnt that there was not much difference between how the results of Bombay's infamous matka gambling were manipulated and the outcome of the bets at the racecourse was managed.

In Bombay's matka gambling, people gambled on numbers ranging from zero to nine. Those days, Ratan Khatri was known as the matka king. Every evening, he used to open three cards from a pack of playing cards; the pack did not contain the jack, queen and king.

The numbers on the three open cards were added and the single number finally arrived at was made public. Those who had placed Re 1 on this number would get Rs 9 in return.

The lower classes, and especially daily-wage labourers, were addicted to it. Millions of rupees were played each day.

Now, suppose an overwhelming majority of people betted on the number five, and the same number came up as the winning number, the bookies would go bust. It is natural that in such a situation, this won't ever be declared the winning number.

The same principle applies to horse racing. Racing experts, after going through the breed and track record of every horse, select one as the hot favourite. When the word spreads, hundreds of punters bet on that horse. If that horse really wins, the club and the bookies will go into mourning.

Albeit, those betting on a horse with the highest possibility of winning get lesser returns—at the rate of one and a half to twice the amount. For the horse which is likely to come second and yet comes first, one gets three times the amount placed on it. Similarly, if a horse likely to stand third comes first, those who have put their bets on him would get eight to nine times their money. In other words, those who played a thousand would get almost Rs 9000.

Suppose a horse named Aflatoon is tipped as a sure-shot to win the race. Knowing this, only a fool would gamble on the horse that is likely to come second or third. And yet, those new to this game, or crackpots habituated to do the exact opposite of what society does, could place their bets on such a horse and, by the sheer dint of luck, become millionaires overnight.

The information DK had obtained was that the jockey of the horse on which the highest bets were expected was instructed to keep his horse ahead of the rest until the very end. On the last bend, he was to loosen the rein and give a slight jerk. His horse, which would be running at full speed, would miss a few steps. Taking advantage of this, the horse in second place, Wonder Prince, would overtake it.

That's exactly what happened.

Iqbal had whispered the name of the horse to the captain and generously offered him Rs 50,000. This amount was, in fact, an advance for the service the captain was to render later. The captain did not yet have the courage to risk the entire amount on a horse. Hesitantly, he placed only half. His horse came first, and his Rs 25,000 became one lakh. Overnight, he had become a *lakhpati*.

*

I asked Sufi, 'I can now understand how you enticed the captain. But how you used the naval ship to your advantage is not clear.'

Now Sufi explained to me the most shocking modus operandi of the traffickers: 'The launch from Dubai carrying the gold biscuits entered Indian waters in the dead of the night and returned after unloading the consignment on the naval ship. The captain, with the help of two confidantes, hid the consignment in his own cabin.'

Some of the naval officers have residential quarters on Madh Island, which is at one end of Bombay. This is where their families live. The naval officers go there by motor boats to spend the weekends and holidays.

The captain and his two confidantes became the 'carriers' of the gang. They would stuff the jackets into their bags and take them to their residence on the island. From there, the gang would take the consignment and deliver it to the Sagar Darshan apartment.

*

I have already mentioned that Iqbal had expanded his frontier from Kashmir to Kanyakumari. There was a compelling reason behind this. A strong rumour had been in circulation for the past few weeks that there was going to be a great upheaval in the gold market. The future of smuggling looked dim.

All smugglers, small or big, were playing their last innings. Iqbal was no exception. Customs officers Rustomji and Khan were shadowing his every move.

*

'Iqbal,' DK suggested, 'please see that the captain doesn't land in trouble because of us.'

'He will go down not because of us but for his greed,' Iqbal replied. 'Just today he called up to ask why last month had gone dry.'

'Greed eventually lures everyone, even saints and sufis. But it has failed to seduce you.'

Iqbal was surprised. 'What do you mean?'

'You are not withdrawing anything from the pool?'

'Who said that? I take Rs 5000 every month.'

As was his habit, DK laughed uproariously. Rs 5000, in a game of millions, is like a grain of sand in a desert. After a while, he tried to tempt Iqbal, 'Don't you feel like blowing up some money ever?'

'On what?'

Iqbal's question was also valid. After all, how much does a parsimonious person need? He had no addictions and no expensive hobbies. There had been a slight increase in his expenses when he was in love with Kiran. Sometimes, he would take her out for dinner to a five-star hotel. But now there was no love in his life.

Out of the money that he withdrew every month, he sent half the amount to his mother. He set aside Rs 500 for his younger brother Firoze, who was in college. He kept only

Rs 2000 for himself. From this amount too, some money remained unspent.

'Okay,' said DK. 'Whenever you feel like it, take as much money as you like. You don't have to take anyone's permission. Now tell me, why haven't you given the captain any work in the last one month?'

'I've heard that he is to be transferred soon.'

'That means the government has smelt a rat.'

'Perhaps. And that fool doesn't even realize that a sword is hanging over his head.'

Iqbal placed a catalogue before DK. 'Just glance through it.'

DK picked it up and as he leafed through the glossy pictures he realized that it was a catalogue of a foreign helicopter firm. 'You want to buy one?'

Iqbal nodded. 'If you permit.'

DK was bemused. *What would this kid, who had not even bought a bicycle with the money from the partnership, do with a helicopter?*

30

DK glanced at the catalogue again. 'These are old models of helicopters.'

'You can say these are the leftover scrap from World War II, which is why they are very cheap,' said Iqbal. 'The cheapest one, an eight-seater, is going for a song, for just Rs 7 lakh.'

'The cost is immaterial,' DK said, placing the catalogue on the coffee table. 'The problem is how to buy it.'

'Leave that to me.'

'But this catalogue is from Germany and we can't buy from them without the government's approval.'

'Says who?'

'If you buy it illegally, where will you keep it?'

'Why on earth would we want to keep it!'

'Then what's the point of buying it?'

Iqbal suddenly realized that DK was under the impression that he wanted to buy the helicopter for his personal use. He wanted to laugh out loud like DK but didn't. Instead, he explained his idea.

On one hand, there were omens of an imminent crash in the gold market, while on the other, the customs were tightening the noose on traffickers. These were the days for daredevils to mint money. These were the times for the clever mice to snatch away the cheese at the last second, without falling into the trap.

Customs had set up the last mousetrap on the naval ship. Only after receiving concrete evidence, the officials had laid their net. Now they only needed to wait to round them up red-handed. Just as a deer catches a whiff of danger, Iqbal got wind of the trap. He had spotted mysterious unidentified faces near the residential quarters of the naval officers on Madh Island. This was enough indication for the alert Iqbal. Picking up a haul of crores of rupees, he had snuck away.

The utility of the naval ship too had expired in the last one month. He had dropped the captain unceremoniously. However, before that, he had opened two new avenues. One was to land the smuggled goods by helicopter on the Andaman Islands and the other was to open a new channel in Madras and smuggle in consignments from there.

*

Let us first look at the helicopter concept. The Andaman and Nicobar Islands comprise thirty-five islands, of which only eight are inhabited. The others are a no man's land, completely deserted. Tourists from Madras often visited these. Elephanta, Uran and other small islands near Bombay too are good for a day's picnic, but these islands have the local population as residents. On the deserted islands of Andaman, there are only tall grass, forest, rocks and the rolling ocean all around.

Iqbal, after days of intensive study, had presented this unique blueprint. Then he waited quietly while the boss made up his mind: DK was sceptical, experienced and extremely cautious. At heart, he was still a shrewd baniya.

Playing with his thin gold necklace, DK asked, 'Iqbal, a helicopter will bring the consignment to the island, drop it there and then return. Is that right?'

'Absolutely.'

'Won't the radars detect it?'

His question was not misplaced. Every aircraft, whether big or small, is bound to get detected on entering Indian air space.

'No.'

'How?'

'Radars can't detect aircraft that fly at a low altitude. Our helicopter, after entering India's air space, will dive and fly at four feet above the sea level. For that, I have a German pilot in mind. He was an ace aviator in the last world war.'

'Hmm . . .' DK was pleased. 'The consignment will have to be brought from the island to the city first. What arrangements have you made for that?'

'Every day, steam launches take day-trippers from Madras to these islands. I've appointed the boatman of one of these launches for our job. Only he'll know the 'drop' spot of the consignment on the island. He'll bring the goods back on his return trip. From there it will not be difficult to transport them to Bombay in a truck.'

Iqbal's other stratagem was to smuggle goods in by hoodwinking customs officials in Madras.

The customs department was on alert not only at the Bombay port but also in Madras, Calicut and Calcutta. It had become difficult for cargo ships, which were legally entering the Indian ports, to hide contraband goods. These ships were often raided, inspected and their captains subjected to interrogation.

For instance, if the customs officials detected over a dozen boxes of wristwatches on the ship, the captain would have to provide a satisfactory explanation. He had to furnish an inventory of goods listing the names of the companies to which the cargo belonged. If there was no mention of the wristwatches in the inventory, these would be confiscated. The captain too would land into trouble.

DK's gang smuggled in not just gold, but also whisky, wristwatches, transistor radios, Japanese fabrics and other such goods which were in demand in the Indian market. These contraband goods, like the gold biscuits, used to come in Arab launches or in cargo ships. After customs stepped up vigil, bringing smuggled goods in using cargo ships had become almost impossible.

Iqbal realized that the customs officials inspected only those cargo ships that brought in goods imported by Indian firms. But if a ship anchored at an Indian port for refuelling or other valid reasons, the customs department would not touch it.

DK gave Iqbal's plan the green signal. Iqbal took the plunge with passion as if he, like Faust, had signed a pact with the devil. He, who had so far grossed millions with Bombay as his centre, now spent most of his time outside Maharashtra. Sometimes he was needed in Calcutta and sometimes in Porbandar; sometimes it was Kanyakumari and, at times, Puri. Often, he would drive hundreds of miles on a truck loaded with contraband goods to Bombay.

*

Iqbal's world had expanded, while mine had shrunk. My college life having ended, my mother and other family members started looking at me with hope, like Indian farmers gaze at the sky waiting for rain.

It was now difficult for me to get a secure job within the art department of established government organizations like Air India or the Weavers' Service Centre. Having failed in the finals, I did not have a diploma. In government establishments, they first look at your credentials and then at your talent.

After my estrangement from Suraiyya, my cartoon features in *Ramakadu* and *Parag* were discontinued, but my comic strip 'Dhabbuji' was still going strong in *Dharmayug*. I used to get Rs 15 per strip. My monthly income was Rs 60.

Gradually, all my family members accepted reality. They had given up hope. Not just that, the elders were certain that they would have to bear my load throughout my life, even though I was earning enough to meet my expenses. I would also contribute some money at home when I earned extra. However, nobody was satisfied.

Where was that worthy son who would leave for office every morning with a leather briefcase in his hand and a tie around his neck, and at the end of the month obediently hand over his salary to his mother? Instead, here was a good-for-nothing son who chipped in Rs 100 once in a blue moon.

I stopped contributing even that after I got a place for my studio. I was a painter and was determined to go ahead with it. That was not easy. Maintaining a white elephant would have been easier. I was not in the least compelled to raise my income. Even though I was least interested in cartooning and writing, I reluctantly continued with them.

The place I had set up as my studio was a 10 foot by 10 foot room. This cubicle was on the ground floor of the same Habib Hospital in which I had spent a month recovering from typhoid.

My joy knew no bounds. I neatly laid out all my art material: a three-legged easel, boxes of paints, paper rolls, brushes and inviting blank canvases.

I used to begin work enthusiastically every morning only to find that as the hours passed somehow my spirited ideas were dissipating into despair and frustration. I would try to think about something beautiful, something positive and sinister skeletons would start dancing before me. I started drawing a fantasy heaven and, on completing the painting, I realized the canvas depicted hell.

Why? Why was it happening? Who held the key to my thoughts? What was that hidden power that covered my gorgeous muse Suraiyya's face with repulsive pockmarks?

The title of my second canvas was 'Tears of Blood'. The painting depicted blood oozing out from the eyes of a labourer. It haunted me like a still from a horror film.

*

It was my nature, and still is, to reflect on the day's events before going to bed every night. One evening, I wrestled with these questions seriously and without finding an answer, I fell asleep.

That night, I had a strange dream. I saw that a huge ant the size of an adult was trying to climb a mountain with a hillock on its head, panting all the way up. Suddenly, its legs slipped and it tumbled, the hillock crushing it to death. At the same time, a piece of white cloud floated down from the sky and gently covered the dead ant like a shroud.

I woke up the following morning with the dream of the crushed ant fresh in my mind. With my first cup of tea, I tried to interpret it. The ant represented me and its effort to climb a mountain with a heavy load on its head symbolized my struggle. Perhaps the end of the dream warned that, if I continued my pessimism, the struggle would result in tragedy.

Right or wrong, I found some comfort with this analysis. Yet, when I left for the studio, the corpse of the ant wearing the white cloud as a shroud accompanied me.

After a while, when I entered my room in the hospital, I was stunned—someone covered in a white sheet lay on the floor near the wall. I was certain it was the crushed body of the ant. All the same, I managed to bring my wild imagination under control. The reality set in: *who really was under the sheet? A sleeping man or a dead one?* I slowly pulled the sheet off and felt as if I had pulled the carpet from beneath my feet: there really was a corpse before me.

It dawned on me that the place given to me to use free of charge was the hospital's spare storage room. This room lay vacant most of the time, until a patient passed away. Sometimes, no one would expire for weeks and sometimes more than one patient would drop dead in a single day.

The body would be removed from the ward and shifted to my room. It would remain there until the relatives of the departed claimed it. I suffered from profound claustrophobia, yet, I continued painting. The question of finding another place did not arise. As I said, with empty pockets it takes a lifetime to find a roof in this city.

I gritted my teeth and started hectic preparations in the mortuary for my first exhibition. I was working round the clock, sometimes alone, sometimes in the company of a corpse or two. With each passing day, the atmosphere of the room influenced me a little more.

All the canvases that I painted here carried the stench of dead bodies. The subject and colours of the paintings were pessimistic. The dark colours would have an immediate impact on the onlookers, their expressions would change as if someone had thrown up all over the canvas.

When the show opened, the critics were full of praise for my so-called experiment. Commercially, it was a flop. I had learnt my first lesson.

*

The combination of certain gloomy colours can have a devastating effect. No one would want to buy a painting with repulsive colours and hang it in his house. Of course, the choice of subject also plays an important role. However, the average buyer, who does not understand abstract art, buys a canvas because a certain combination of bright, pleasing colours strikes a chord somewhere.

In this way, each of my flop shows taught me a lesson. But they also plunged me deeper into a financial crisis. Finally, like a losing gambler, I played the final game.

*

While I was neck-deep in debt after my disastrous first show, Iqbal was sitting on a gold mine. Bank notes were raining hard and were being deposited with the bankers. From there, the money was transferred to secret accounts in Switzerland, Dubai and Hong Kong. That was DK's job.

Iqbal did not have the time to keep track of the accounts. His responsibility was to experiment and find new ways of earning money. He was making such quick progress that his four partners were stupefied.

DK, meanwhile, had taken back the responsibility of maintaining the accounts from Iqbal and given him a free rein like an unharnessed racehorse. To quote Kiran, he was strutting like a peacock. But he did not know that his reins were in DK's hand.

But even a prized racehorse, when it becomes lame, is shot dead. DK was not going to shoot him, but he would ensure that he was lame at the right time. Iqbal would realize it only after he tumbled down to the starting point of this game of snakes and ladders.

*

For whom did Iqbal do all this? Why did he do it? His own needs were a reflection of his mentality, which was still that of Dongri—where wealth is built one paisa at a time. If one can walk, one does not take a bus and if one can go by a bus, one does not hire a taxi. The expensive car that DK had gifted him was gathering dust in the compound of Sagar Darshan building.

*

Sufi prefers to go on foot or take a bus even today. If an old friend proposes to him that he start a lucrative smuggling business in partnership, Sufi asks him, 'For whom?' Occasionally, he offers quotes from the Koran or the Gita as replies. One of them was, 'Neither does this body belong to me nor do I belong to this body. It is made of fire, water, air, earth and sky. In the end, it will merge with these elements. But the soul is immortal. Then, what is a human being? Why does he lust for riches?'

But this did not matter to him when he was young. His attention was solely focused on how to do something outstanding, something groundbreaking in the field of smuggling.

First, he removed the risk involved in crossing by introducing the technique of dumping the bag of gold biscuits into the sea. In the process, he had saved hours that were wasted otherwise.

Then he suggested the idea of safely moving the bags from under the sea to another place. His idea which saved Hamid from the gallows was also a master stroke.

Like an energetic young manager who brings about beneficial changes in the workings of a corporation, Iqbal had introduced several measures after joining DK's gang. The most important among these was the elimination of the middleman in gold smuggling. This enabled the gang to earn lakhs of rupees more on every transaction.

During our interview, Sufi used the word 'company' instead of 'gang'. According to him, all the partners were thorough gentlemen. They were out-and-out businessmen and today which businessman does not cheat the government?

*

While Iqbal's idea of employing a helicopter had proved to be successful, the other idea of hoodwinking the customs officials in Madras did not last long.

The last time, a dubious Chinese ship coming from Seychelles and heading for Hong Kong had entered the Madras port on the pretext of a problem in its boiler room. Iqbal was there to take the delivery. He was sitting in the dock's Udipi canteen, sipping tea with Dagdu. Both of them were chatting, having dosas for breakfast. Earlier, they had stuffed themselves with a plate of idlis.

'Boss,' Dagdu asked, opening his mouth to stuff in the dosa, 'why is our business jittery since the past few weeks?'

'You won't understand.'

'Am I that dumb? You explain, I'll understand.'

'How can I explain when I don't know the cause myself?'

However, he thought it necessary to shed some light on the subject. 'The price of gold is going to increase in the world market. That means it will soar higher than the price in our country. It's not yet clear as to what would be the impact; yet, my gut feeling says that it's going to shake the very foundation of our business. I won't be surprised if it breaks the backbone of our jewellers as well as our boss. Our days are numbered.'

Dagdu had just opened his mouth wide to take the last bite of the dosa when his jaws froze. His eyes were fixed on a car that had just entered the dock.

'*Aaichya*!' He put back the dosa on the plate. 'We're screwed, boss!'

The car stopped right in front of the canteen. The taut-shouldered customs officer from Bombay, Khan, alighted. Despite his dark sunglasses, Dagdu had identified him.

Dagdu was about to escape when Iqbal caught him by the wrist. He had almost got up from his seat but sat down again. Iqbal got up.

'Hello, Mr Khan!' Iqbal walked out with a smile to shake hands with him. 'What a pleasant surprise to see you here!'

'I'm pleased too.'

The cat and mouse game started once again. Both knew the real reason behind the other's presence. Khan had come down to Madras following Iqbal. He had not anticipated running into him. He wanted to catch Iqbal red-handed, which would not be possible now.

'Would you like a cup of tea, sir?' Iqbal asked.

Khan looked into the canteen. 'That guy sitting over there shivering like a dry leaf, is he your colleague Dagdu?' he asked.

'Yes, sir.'

'Has he seen a ghost?'

'He saw you and got scared,' Iqbal replied fearlessly. 'I tried to convince him that without proof nobody can touch us. But this nitwit won't believe . . .'

'He knows that I don't need proof to arrest him.' Khan shoved Iqbal aside and headed for Dagdu.

According to the information Khan had received, Iqbal had become active in Madras, but he was unaware of the modus operandi the wizard had adopted. He was really surprised by what he learnt from his phone conversation with the Madras customs officials. According to them, it was true that Iqbal was in Madras, but he was apparently into the transport business.

Fools! Khan thought to himself. *If Iqbal was in any business, it could only be smuggling.*

Iqbal took one long stride and caught up with Khan. By this time Dagdu had relaxed a bit, yet he was shuddering inside. The apprehension was visible on his face.

Khan sat opposite him. Iqbal sat on a third chair. Some flies had started hovering over the half-eaten dosa. Khan's penetrating gaze was fixed on Dagdu.

'Khan Sahib!' Iqbal said. 'The dosa here is to die for.'

'One can imagine, seeing the number of flies,' Khan shot back and asked for a cup of tea instead.

Iqbal beckoned a lungi-clad boy and placed an order for two cups of tea and a glass of lime juice. Looking at Khan, Iqbal asked, 'Sir, may I ask a personal question?'

'Go ahead.'

'How many years of service do you have left?'

'Are you worried?'

'No, no, sir. I asked you in a different context. I just wanted to tell you that a senior officer from the navy recently retired. Can you believe that he will get only Rs 400 as monthly pension?'

'What do you mean?'

'He has four children, a wife and old parents. How will he manage in just Rs 400? Moreover, he has been asked to vacate his house.'

'What's new?'

'Will your honesty too go six feet under after your retirement?'

'No. I will go to my village, Jaawra, after retirement where I have my ancestral home. It's not difficult to live there on Rs 400 a month. Besides, by the time an official retires, his children are grown up and start earning. So, I don't have to look after mine. On the contrary, if needed, they will support me.'

He paused for a while and then exposed Iqbal's game plan. 'If you are trying to buy me like this, you better take note of this. I'm not a gullible person like your navy captain friend who is rotting in prison. Also, once I've had my tea, I'm taking Dagdu with me.'

Dagdu was shaken as if he had been electrocuted by a loose wire dangling from the roof of the canteen. Iqbal's brain too betrayed him. He had not anticipated the tables to turn so unexpectedly.

As the canteen boy brought two cups of tea and a glass of lime juice, the captain of the Hong Kong ship appeared on the deck. As per instructions, this was the time to send a man from the ship to the canteen to establish contact with Iqbal. Iqbal was to disclose at what time and how he would be taking the delivery of the contraband goods, especially the wristwatches from Seychelles.

From the deck, he focused his binoculars and saw Iqbal and Dagdu sitting with a customs official in the canteen. He presumed that the official was on Iqbal's payroll, else why would he be sitting there chatting over a cup of tea? He gave a crew member Iqbal's description and sent him down.

From afar, Iqbal saw him approaching. This time, his knees buckled.

31

Having finished his tea, Khan got up. He glared at Dagdu. This meant that he had to get up too. Dagdu shot a scared look at Iqbal.

'Sahib!' Iqbal said, throwing a final glance at the approaching sailor from the Chinese ship. 'How about taking me instead? I'm ready to come.'

'Not today. Have patience, it will be your turn next.'

Dagdu got up reluctantly.

'But, sir! You won't get the information you are looking for from him.'

'I'll decide about that after the *dandabedi*.'

Dandabedi, Iqbal explained to me, is the technique of extracting information from a criminal in which he is made to lie down on a bench and the soles of his feet are battered with a rod.

According to Sufi, the first few blows hurt the body, but the ones that follow affect the mind as the soles become numb. Each blow feels like a hammer on the head.

Explaining the process in detail, Sufi said that because of the beatings, the swollen feet look like a bad case of elephantiasis. If the accused is presented before the court on the same day and he shows his feet to the magistrate, the customs officials would be in the soup. The magistrate would blast them for abuse. But the officials are no fools. Before taking the accused to court, they force him to jump like a monkey. It is very painful but it reduces the swelling.

Dagdu shivered to the bone on hearing the word dandabedi. As Khan dragged him out of the canteen holding him by the wrist, the Chinese sailor entered.

Through his binoculars, the captain of the ship had observed Iqbal and Khan to be in a good mood, but the sailor had seen a different picture. As if he was a stranger, the sailor entered the canteen and sat on an empty chair. Iqbal silently praised his presence of mind.

Khan gave him a cursory glance and left with Dagdu. Iqbal got up from his seat and went up to the sailor.

'What happened?' the sailor asked him, placing an order for a glass of milk.

'The customs have caught whiff of our plan. Their suspicion will be confirmed once my associate spills the beans.'

'What next?'

'Leave the dock.'

'That's not possible,' he said, sipping the warm milk. 'The ship has just anchored.'

As per protocol, before anchoring, the ship needs to take permission from the port authorities with a valid reason for doing so. The captain had sought permission to anchor on the grounds that he needed to buy some parts from the city to carry out repairs in the boiler. If the ship suddenly started moving, even a porter would become suspicious.

Iqbal thought for a while. 'Has the captain mentioned wristwatches in his manifest?'

'We never needed to do so in the past.'

'Today you will need it. Rush back and get the watches entered in the list.'

'In whose name?'

Iqbal jotted down the name of a Sri Lankan party on a slip of paper. The Chinese emptied the glass of milk in one gulp and rushed back to the ship.

Now, Iqbal thought about Dagdu.

Dagdu was industrious. He was particularly useful for donkey work, having worked as a coolie at VT station. He was also a seasoned fighter, provided Iqbal or some other member of the gang stood by him. Left alone, he turned from a lion into a lamb. He was particularly afraid of the police and the customs officials. Eagle-eyed Khan had spotted this weakness.

*

At the Madras customs office, Khan pushed Dagdu into a room and asked him to lie down on a table. Dagdu knew the horror of dandabedi was about to begin. He had curled his hands up into tight balls. His legs were uneasy. This was not his first time.

As a coolie, he had developed great skill in petty theft. He made the suitcase of a passenger disappear as smoothly as Houdini made an elephant disappear. Yet, he was caught. The reason was obvious: he had used the trick too often. Just as a smart audience member grasps a conjurer's trick by watching it repeatedly, the railway police had quickly solved the mystery and arrested him. That was his first experience of dandabedi.

He was young, daring and considered himself a mighty Maratha warrior—he did not confess to anything. Then the railway police used dandabedi on him. He could not take it. In just seven blows he confessed and was sentenced to six months' imprisonment.

Prison proved to be a boon for him. Previously he knew only one way to steal, there he mastered ten sophisticated techniques. It was as though having completed high school in the outside world, he had come to college in the jail for further studies. After six months, when he came out, he was a graduate: he had earned a degree in crime. But no degree comes in handy when subjected to dandabedi.

*

This time, before Khan could deal the first blow, Dagdu gave in. Khan was speechless. Even in his wildest dreams he could not imagine that a person could employ such an ingenious way for smuggling.

There was no point in keeping Dagdu under custody as Khan did not have any proof against him. He did not believe in wasting the court's time or his own by presenting a case without concrete evidence. He also knew that by this time Iqbal would have arranged for a competent lawyer for Dagdu's release.

Still, there was a ray of hope. If he raided the ship right away, he could seize the large consignment of wristwatches, arrest the captain, detain the entire ship till the court proceedings were on and thus bring the business to a standstill. Instilling such a fear was essential to curb trafficking. In the future, wary ship owners would think a hundred times before employing captains who had links with the underworld.

Khan, accompanied by seven officers of the Madras customs, immediately left in two cars. He thought on the way: just as the doctor who understands the disease must also know its cure, the man who makes the blueprint of crime must also know the trick to slip away—Iqbal was such a man.

Iqbal carefully considered all aspects whenever he made any plan. He would plug all loopholes and also keep an escape route ready. He would implement a plan only after ensuring that it was foolproof. This was why he was able to give sleepless nights to officials of the police and the customs department. And even on this day, in the game of cat and mouse in Madras, he would emerge victorious.

By the time Khan's team arrived on the ship, the contraband wristwatches had been included in the captain's manifest. The captain promptly presented the list to the officials. Khan realized this was the escape route. His shoulders slouched in defeat.

On reaching the headquarters in Bombay, a thought struck him—was the name and address of the Sri Lankan party, to whom the wristwatches apparently belonged, real or fake?

*

The investigation into the matter, which took two days, revealed that there was no such firm by that name in Sri Lanka, and there was no such building as was claimed to be its head office. But by then the ship had left India's territorial waters. And Iqbal?

He had left Madras for Bombay in a truck carrying the contraband goods from Andaman Island, where the helicopter had landed. Dagdu was sitting by his side on the passenger's seat. He had driven the truck for three hours. It was now Iqbal's turn. He knew that guilt must be biting Dagdu, but he did not feel it proper to broach the subject. Finally, it was Dagdu who broke the silence.

'Boss, are you mad at me?'

'Why?'

'Because I confessed.'

'Not at all!'

'Sure?'

Iqbal nodded. It was night. The truck was passing through a forest. Under the headlights, the road, the trees and bushes emerged, illuminated, and were again shrouded in darkness.

'Then, why are you silent?'

'It seems that you have not listened to the radio.'

'What's there to listen to except for the *Binaca Geetmala*? Yes, sometimes I do listen to the *Hawa Mahal* programme.'

After a pause he asked, 'What have you heard?'

'The dollar and pound have crashed. The price of gold has shot up in the foreign market.'

'*Chyaaila!*' Dagdu cursed.

That meant a deadly blow to the enterprise. Smuggling can be profitable only when the prices of gold in the international market are lower compared to the price in India. Who would soil his hands in a business that does not have even a small profit margin? The future looked bleak. The truck rolled in silence for a while.

'Now what?' Dagdu asked.

'That only the chief can tell.'

'What do you feel?'

'We might have to shut the gold business down for a few months. I won't be surprised if we are compelled to take *sannyas* for a year.'

Right now, Iqbal's main concern was disposing of the bag of gold biscuits worth Rs 80 lakh that was hidden amid the coconut-laden truck. He had to jettison the entire consignment at whatever profit he could make on reaching Bombay tomorrow. He was even prepared to sell on a no-profit, no-loss basis.

*

My main worry at the time was to get out of the debt trap I had landed in after my first flop painting exhibition, and to prepare for a new one. All put together, I had borrowed about Rs 5000. This year, I would need at least Rs 6000 to hold my next show.

Following the ban on the import of art materials, the prices of colours and canvases had increased, and the Indian companies manufacturing art materials were not yet up to the international standard. The Indian colours were like dust and the canvas was worse than jute sacks. Yet, I felt that my kismet was changing for the better.

Nisa Bandookwalla, who had studied in art school with me, had a spacious apartment in which she had set aside a room for painting. One day, when I met her at Jehangir Art Gallery, I told her about my predicament. 'I have a pretty big studio,' she said. 'Aabid, if you paint by my side, I'll be inspired to work more.'

I thanked her.

The next day, I fetched all my belongings from the hospital morgue and placed them in her Colaba apartment.

But as soon as one major problem was solved, a new one cropped up at home. The elders in my family—my mother, uncle, aunt and grandmother—had conspired to get me married as soon as possible.

The decision greatly pleased my mother, who no longer considered me a worthy fellow. The field of arts (including theatre, dance and music) is looked upon suspiciously by Indian families even today. My old mother was no exception. She believed that if a boy is pinned down with responsibilities, his life will get back on track.

This is another wrongly-held belief and there is no solution to it. I was helpless. I shuddered at the thought of marriage. There was more than one reason for it.

The foremost was the responsibility it entailed. If I were to get married, I would be liable to take care of my wife. And even worse, if by mistake she were to bear a child, I would have no option but to quit my dream and take up a steady job, even if the salary was only Rs 500. After all, I would have to run the house. Many talented artists have squandered their entire lives in making both ends meet.

Secondly, artists are moody because they are deeply involved in their art. No wife, even if she is highly educated, can tolerate it. After becoming a wife, the average woman feels that she has acquired real estate, not a husband, and feels obliged to enforce her rights, which is the beginning of marital conflict.

Settling down with Suraiyya was a different proposition. There was near total absence of conflict. There was also no possibility of becoming a burden on each other because both of us were from the same profession and had similar natures; we deeply understood each other's feelings. Only a fortunate man gets such a woman; I was not that man.

*

I was determined not to get enmeshed in marriage. Whatever the temptation, by finding some or the other fault, I would try to reject it. That is exactly what I did when the first proposal came.

The girl was a beautician. Her passport-sized photograph was placed before me. The elders eagerly looked at me. I sat quietly.

My mother could not stand my silence. 'What's there to think about? We have seen the girl and she will be a perfect match. Besides, she draws a salary of Rs 300 a month. If you like, we can invite her home.'

'She looks alright, but . . .'

'But what?'

I had seen the girl a couple of times as she crossed our lane. I asked knowingly, 'One cannot make out her features and complexion from this photograph. How does she look?'

'She's slightly dark, but definitely not ugly.'

At the end of this discussion, I was given seven days to decide, to which I readily agreed. I knew how to extend a week's time to a fortnight and a fortnight to a month.

*

Iqbal did not know what lay in store for him. Two days after getting the gold biscuits from Madras, he met DK at his residence. 'Have you sold the entire consignment?' was the first question.

Iqbal nodded.

'At what price?'

'We were able to recover our investment.'

DK had not expected that.

Heaving a sigh of relief, he said, 'We would have been in deep trouble had the Rs 80 lakh drowned.'

'How?'

'Our party from Dubai came by the night flight. This time, he has demanded part payment in cash.'

*

The Dubai party was the sheikh who sent the gold. He used to come to Bombay once or twice a year to settle the accounts and would book three suites at the Taj Hotel. He occupied the one in the middle while the two adjoining ones remained vacant so that no one could move into them during his stay. 'An alert man is always happy' was the Sheikh's favourite proverb; the second one was 'Even walls have ears'.

Iqbal failed to understand why a few lakh rupees had become a matter of concern. He did not feel it proper to ask DK. After all, he was the boss.

'Do you have any appointment now?'

Iqbal shook his head in the negative.

'Then let's go and meet the sheikh.'

Both of them came out of the Marine Drive flat, drove to the hotel and went up to the second floor. The corpulent sheikh was lounging half-sunk into a plush sofa, listening to Egypt's popular singer Umme Laila's song on a record player and eating chicken lollipops from a silver tray. To Iqbal, the sheikh looked a picture-perfect symbol of western gluttony.

Seeing DK accompanied by Iqbal, he turned off the music. DK closed the door behind him and both of them quietly sat on the sofa across the sheikh.

Let me clarify something here—there is no ban on the import or export of gold in Dubai. The sheikh was a bullion merchant. He did not cheat his government because he never violated his country's laws.

*

The last four months' accounts were to be settled. During this period, gold worth Rs 7 crore had been smuggled into India, that too on word of mouth.

Neither was there a written contract between the two parties nor any document. Long-distance calls played a major role in whatever was agreed to by both the parties. The phone calls lasted only a few seconds. In the conversation, the word 'peti' meant a lakh of rupees and 'khokha' meant a crore.

For instance, if DK wanted to import gold worth Rs 1 crore, he would only say, 'Please send one khokha.' These code words are used even today.

After the formalities were over, DK took out two slips of paper from the pocket of his kurta. The sheikh took out his pocket diary. They tallied the dates and checked when and how many khokhas of gold had been imported.

The question of either side committing a mistake did not arise. There was no question of betrayal either. In this respect, both of them were impeccable businessmen, else four months' accounts would not have been settled in just four minutes. DK tore up the account slips, threw them into the waste basket, and asked, 'Now, tell me Sheikh Sahib, what would you like to see this time?'

'I've heard that striptease has been introduced here just like in Paris.'

'Right.'

'How is it?'

'I've never been there.'

That was true. DK was never interested in girls who undressed in public. Of course, he had no scruples if a beautiful woman bared herself in private.

'I've heard that the striptease in the newly opened The Blue Nile Hotel in Colaba is worth watching.'

'I'll have dinner there,' said the sheikh. 'It seems that the future of our trade won't be as bright as before.'

'It will be bleak for at least four to six months. I think this compulsory retirement is necessary.'

'What will you do?'

'Rest for a few months and then plan something new.'

'You have partners . . .'

'That partnership has been dissolved now.'

Iqbal was growing increasingly disturbed. Firstly, DK had not thought it necessary to introduce him as a partner to the sheikh—this had pinched him. Then, DK had casually made this explosive announcement about the partnership. Yet, Iqbal remained quiet. The final jolt was yet to come.

Their conversation over, DK got up, saying, 'My car will be in the parking lot. You can go out for dinner at your convenience.' Iqbal too got up with him. As they turned to walk away, the sheikh said, 'I hope the car won't be empty!'

'Oh!' DK stopped. 'I'd totally forgotten. Whom should I send?'

'Who had accompanied me to the Elephanta caves last time?'

DK had over a dozen call girls on his list. It was difficult for him to remember such small details. He pretended to rack his memory when the sheikh reminded him, 'She had a colourful bird in a golden cage in her balcony.'

'Kiran?'

'That's the one!'

Iqbal was shaken even though he had parted ways with Kiran and had no reason to feel anguished.

32

Going down in the lift, DK said to Iqbal, 'The bastard chose the most expensive girl. The rate of the dollar has crashed, but her charges have shot up. Now she demands Rs 5000 a night.'

Once they were in the car, DK asked Iqbal, 'Have you thought about the future?'

Iqbal shook his head.

'In fact, you need not.'

He listened quietly.

'You haven't tasted blood yet. Sometimes I wonder how you manage to live in this dirty pond and stay untouched like a lotus?'

'I'll have to find something to do.'

'Maybe not. You will get more than enough from the partnership. I mean you can spend your whole life doing nothing.'

'True, but an industrious person can't sit idle.' That was when Iqbal realized that instead of heading towards Marine Drive, the car was going in the opposite direction.

'You are absolutely right. I'd read somewhere that an empty mind is the devil's workshop. Tell me, do you want to open a shop? Set up a factory? Tell me, yaar, I'm with you. It's not a bad idea to start a new business either.'

Before answering DK's question, Iqbal put forth his own doubt. 'My share . . . how many crores will I get?'

As was his habit, DK burst out laughing uproariously. The car continued to move silently through the streets. 'How many crores!' he repeated and continued laughing. 'Iqbal, my friend, I must admit I'm losing my edge. But I'm not the only idiot. Many veteran officers too have been fooled by your innocent face.'

Iqbal was confused. As he could not understand what DK was trying to say, he asked, 'Fooled?'

'The lotus is soiled. You have tasted blood. You are dreaming of crores.'

Now Iqbal understood the truth.

'I'm just asking for the share I deserve . . .'

'Where were you sleeping all these days? I asked you time and again to withdraw a few million and blow it up. Didn't I? But you were firm in your resolve, never taking more than Rs 5000 a month and now when the treasury has been cleaned out . . .'

Iqbal was stunned. DK had indeed told him to withdraw a few million rupees and blow it up. However, he had never said that like all the other partners, he too should withdraw sizeable amounts every month to invest in other enterprises.

Initially, when the reins were in Iqbal's hand, the partners used to borrow lakhs of rupees on one pretext or another, as loans—at least that is what he thought. He was under the illusion that partnership meant sharing the profit equally and that his share was being kept aside.

'You are disappointed,' DK said, noticing Iqbal's crestfallen face.

Iqbal looked at DK. The greatest swindler in history looked like a saint compared to him.

'A dead elephant is worth more than a living one,' DK continued. 'We have deposited enough money in your account to help you form your own smuggling network, if you so desire.'

At this moment, Iqbal was interested neither in criminal businesses nor in regular ones. *He had shown more loyalty than a dog. He had given a big chunk of the best period of his life, his youth, his blood and his sweat. What did he get in return?*

Trickery.

Treachery.

And a stab in the back.

Without using a knife, DK had slaughtered him as a goat is sacrificed on Bakri Eid. And to top it all, he was being chided like a foolish child who was to blame for this mistake. His cheeks were burning as he battled an enormous urge to scream.

'How much is there?' he asked, trying to gather himself.

'Ten lakhs in cash and *Al Kabir*. On top of that, the car worth eighty thousand and the apartment in Sagar Darshan are yours to keep.'

This demolished another of Iqbal's illusions. He had never been gifted the car and the apartment: both belonged to the partnership and were handed to him for official use. He had thought that the boss had generously gifted these to him as goodwill gestures. This time, he was enraged at his own stupidity. It was too late to regret though.

He came back to his senses as the car stopped near Usha Sadan. Kiran still lived there on the third floor.

'Iqbal,' DK said, still sitting in the car, 'if I go up, she will rob me. If you ask, she will be reasonable. Try to strike a deal for Rs 3000.'

Iqbal looked straight into his eyes and shot back, 'In this short life, I've committed many crimes knowingly or unknowingly, but I've never been a pimp.'

DK once again threw his head back and exploded in laughter. It was a liberating laugh, like steam that escapes after being confined for too long.

*

'Sufi!' I interrupted. 'I can understand that you were entitled to your share and that you should have got at least Rs 10 crore, but when your requirement was limited to Rs 5000 a month, what difference did it make?'

'A lot.'

'How?'

'I wanted to switch over to a regular business. I had already thought through my plans. I wanted to buy a factory that manufactured drums, which had gone out of business. It required an investment of Rs 40 lakh. And . . .'

I chided, 'How can a person neck-deep in trafficking think of renouncing it all for a boring regular life?'

'Anyone living under constant pressure gets such an idea some time or the other. Why did the Chambal dacoits surrender before Jayaprakash Narayan the moment they got an opportunity in 1972? Were they not minting money by robbing innocent people?'

Satisfied that I found his reply convincing, he continued, 'Aabid Bhai, our community is economically backward. That's why most of our youth have remained uneducated. Where there is no education, there is hunger. My deepest desire was to eradicate this unemployment and hunger. If I could have started a couple of small-scale industries, I could have offered jobs to young Muslim men and prevented them from following the destructive path of easy money.'

To my ears, these were not Sufi's words, this was his wretched childhood speaking. It was the ache of hunger that he had suffered as a helpless child growing up in Dongri which was calling out.

*

Sufi is a Muslim but not an orthodox fanatic. When he offers namaz, he understands every word of it—most Muslims do not know the meaning of the Arabic verses from the Koran that they recite while praying. Sufi often astounded friends with his knowledge of Islam.

He believes that Allah would be happier if people helped orphans rather than spending money on rituals and congregations. Because of his views, the mullahs often lambast him. Islam, which is close to socialism, imposes zakat on Muslims. In simple terms, it is a tax at 2.5 per cent of one's income. Muslims are required to compulsorily set aside this amount for the welfare of the poor.

The other Islamic tax is called *khums*. Khums, which literally means 'one-fifth', mandates that one-fifth of certain items which a person acquires as profit in business must be paid as tax. However, there is a difference of opinion in the Islamic community about this tax. According to Sufi, it was introduced only because of the jihads at the dawn of Islam. During the time of Prophet Mohammed and the caliphs that followed, there used to be holy wars and the soldiers of the victorious army would rob the enemy. This practice of looting was prevalent even before the advent of Islam, but no religion had imposed tax on it because no religion needed it. Islam was desperate for funds. Why?

Sufi explained, 'The newly-converted Muslims and the soldiers of Islam were impoverished. Many of them did not even have swords. 'This new tax of 20 per cent on the *maal-e-ganimat* (the spoils of war) benefited the poor foot soldiers.'

According to him, it was necessary to note that on the battlefield, the victorious army would get weapons and animals like camels and horses instead of currency because no soldier carried hard cash while going to war.

Whatever was plundered was presented before the chief of the army. The value of the seized goods was assessed and 80 per cent of its value was distributed among the soldiers while the chief retained the remaining 20 per cent. This 20 per cent, which comprised weapons and beasts, was used to arm the new recruits of the Islamic army.

Some present-day religious leaders have not only imposed khums on all Muslims, but they also insist that a part of it goes into their own pockets.

Sufi remembers one particular incident when a mullah committed the blunder of demanding khums from him. He simply asked the mullah, 'Maulana, what's the meaning of khums?'

'The holy Koran has prescribed zakat as well as khums. The latter is on maal-e-ganimat.'

'What's maal-e-ganimat?'

'The spoils of war collected by the soldiers of the holy war.'

'I've neither participated in a war nor have I robbed a soldier. How can khums apply to me?'

The mullah was perplexed. Perhaps no one had argued with him before. 'Brother, khums is levied on every Muslim.'

'Why?'

'That's Allah's order.'

'On which page of the Holy Koran?'

The question tied the mullah in knots. Sufi enjoyed this immensely. Whenever someone tried to make a fool of him, he preferred that, instead of telling him directly that he was an idiot, to make the other person realize this by quoting his own words. This was his way of having fun.

Before the mullah could reply, Sufi asked, 'Who's entitled to receive khums?'

'The poor, the orphans, the aalim . . .'

The Arabic word 'aalim' means the learned one. So it ostensibly applied to the mullah, who is supposed to be knowledgeable in matters of religion.

'Maulana!' Sufi asked again, 'Is it also written in the Holy Koran that the aalim is entitled to receive khums?'

'Listen, brother, if you want to offer khums, it is all right. Else, it's your wish. You will be held guilty in the court of the Almighty.'

'When did I say that I don't want to offer it? I just want to understand before giving it . . .'

'What do you want to know?'

'How much do you expect to receive by way of khums?'

The question raised the mullah's hopes. He softened and replied, 'My entire year's household expenses.'

'How much does it come to?'

'More than Rs 8000 a month. A person who has five children and a wife would need at least that much.'

'I too have an equal number of members in my family. Yet, my household expenses are much less than yours.'

'That depends on one's lifestyle.'

'What do you mean?'

'We are not miserly as far as our food habits are concerned. The children need a double-egg omelette each for breakfast. Besides, they also need jam, butter and juice. It is necessary to give them wholesome food for their physical development. Moreover, we never cook our food in vegetable or refined oil. We use only pure ghee.'

Sufi listened patiently and then asked, 'Can Prophet Mohammed—peace be upon him—be called an aalim?'

The mullah was provoked again. 'You should have the common sense to know that he was the father of all aalims.'

'What was his diet?'

As the mullah glared at him, Sufi reminded him of an incident from the Prophet's life. One day, when the Prophet sat down for supper, his daughter placed before him three dishes. One contained salt, the other milk and the third one had bread.

Surprised, the Prophet said, 'You have placed three dishes before me. What is the occasion? Don't you know that there shouldn't be more than two?' Before the daughter could reply, he picked up the bowl containing milk, gave it to her and ate the bread with salt.

Sufi did not have to spell out to the mullah sitting across him that he was not worthy of being called an aalim.

*

When Sufi begins to talk, he talks for hours. He picks up a point to begin with. To prove that point, he goes on adding new topics. In the process, I get so engrossed that I forget the main issue. Take for instance today's discussion. The dialogue had begun with his share in the partnership that he deserved. Then it veered towards zakaat, khums and the poor mullah.

'I'm not a social worker,' he came back on track. 'I've never dreamt of becoming a leader. I consider it my duty to help if I can.'

'Can you give me an example?'

'Of what?'

'An example of someone whom you helped, who prospered in life.'

'Don't ask me. Ask in the neighbourhood.'

'But why not you?'

'Islam says that when you do charity, your left hand shouldn't know what your right hand does.'

He was right. In fact, he had never bragged about his charity, which was in lakhs. He had never uttered a word.

From what I could gather from other sources, Sufi had over Rs 10 lakh—at a time when a lakh meant something—set aside in lieu of zakaat, financial assistance to the poor of the Khoja community, for the education of underprivileged students and institutions providing employment to widows.

He had also donated Rs 2 lakh to the Jain Vidyalaya at Prarthana Samaj. He also did not forget leprosy patients on Eid. He sent a money order of Rs 25 to each of the patients on his list. Earlier, he would send Rs 75. In all, Rs 3000 was thus distributed.

The list of Sufi's secret donations is quite long. However, he never reveals his name and insists that it should not be displayed on plaques.

One can imagine that if he had received Rs 10 crore from DK, he would have invested the money in businesses that would have given employment to the poor and the needy.

And yet, he was not disappointed. It was a wake-up call. He had received a golden opportunity to start afresh. He grabbed it with both hands. He rented out the steam launch, *Al Kabir*, to the Koli fishermen. Now it was used to catch fish and brought him Rs 4000 a month.

From the cash that he had received from DK, he set aside Rs 2 lakh to start a new business and bought a flat in suburban Khar for his family.

He got an additional Rs 1.5 lakh by selling his room in Dongri's Abbasi Manzil. He deposited that money in his brothers' bank accounts.

He still had the apartment in Sagar Darshan building and the car. He was in no hurry to sell off the apartment because the property rates on Warden Road were shooting up. The car had not yet been disposed of. He was expecting to get about Rs 60,000 for it.

There was no longer a need for him to live away from his family. Smuggling had become a thing of the past. With him were his mother and youngest brother, Razzak, who still worked in the footwear shop. He was no more a kid. He was a seventeen-year-old young man.

Firoze had joined a commerce college, but he left it for a job at a chemist's shop. He desired to open his own shop one day.

*

A new sun had risen in his life. The days of adventure and tension had been replaced by days of leisure. After many years of continuous work, he had been gifted an enforced vacation. He was bursting with ideas. Initially, he was unable to pinpoint which direction to adopt. What profession should he take up? Where should he begin?

Weeks rolled by with Iqbal making plans and then scrapping them. In the third month, a new business opportunity popped up, courtesy Dagdu.

Following the dissolution of the partnership, all members of the gang had scattered. The members of the lowest rung, in particular, had become unemployed. Some of them had started a gang of pickpockets, while others had joined matka gambling dens. Someone became a carrier, while another got into bootlegging. Dagdu was planning to go back to being a coolie at VT railway station with some new tricks up his sleeve.

'I wouldn't advise you to do that,' Iqbal told him.

'But why not?'

'You are already notorious. As soon as any passenger reports theft, the police will come knocking on your door, even if someone else has done the job. I have a feeling that you won't be happy there.'

'Then what should I do?'

'Seek employment.'

'Who will give me a job?'

'You can also start a small business.'

'That would require capital.'

'Haven't you saved anything?'

'You think a man with two wives and nine children can have savings? I must have saved about Rs 8000–9000. But one cannot even buy a tempo with that money.'

'Suppose you can buy a tempo for Rs 8000. What will you do?'

'Boss!' His face lit up. 'I live near Sassoon Docks where tempos are in great demand.'

'How come there is so much work there while the tempo owners are sitting idle here?'

'I don't know that but I'm certain that no tempo leaves empty from there.'

'All right. Meet me after two days.'

Little did he know then that he was stepping into the new world of the prawn mafia.

33

In those two days, Iqbal himself went to Sassoon Docks and asked around. He found that there was indeed a great demand for tempos. However, most tempo owners preferred not to ply there. *Why?*

There was a wholesale fish market at the Colaba port area. Kolis from distant areas would come in boats to dump their catch here. Tons of fish used to arrive every morning. Seasonally, the rates of the fish were determined according to the size and quality, and wholesale and retail brokers would throng to buy fish by the ton here.

Fish rots if kept outside water for long. Hence, it has to be disposed of as soon as possible. The easiest way to do so was to sell them to companies like Castle Rock, Bombay Fisheries and Britannia which export fish in the Wagle Industrial Estate of Thane at the other end of Bombay.

The transporters did not like to carry the fish in their tempos. There were two main reasons for their reluctance. One, Hindus who were vegetarians were naturally averse to hauling fish across the city. Secondly, tempos carrying fish suffered more wear and tear. Because of the salt water, the inside of the tempo was adversely affected and its paint wore off very fast. The exposed parts rusted quickly. This reduced the life of the tempo. However, despite these drawbacks, the business was profitable.

Sufi meditated over all this information for two days. On the third day, he finalized everything and decided to back Dagdu. In those days, a tempo was priced at Rs 32,000. Dagdu put in Rs 8000 and Iqbal offered an equal amount. He took the remainder as a loan from a bank and bought Dagdu a tempo. Dagdu's life was back on track.

Every day, he would stuff the tempo with fish from Sassoon Docks and unload it at the factories in Thane. From the income, he would make a living, keep aside a part for the bank loan and buy a bottle of country liquor in the evening. He was a happy man.

He continued for about a month, when suddenly he was struck by a bolt of lightning: watching the daily auction of fish at Sassoon Docks, he remembered his former boss.

*

Iqbal had not decided on his line of business yet. If someone like Dagdu came to him for advice, he would get engaged in the problem for a few days. He did not believe in helping blindly—he would investigate the matter and sponsor the person only if he found the case to be genuine.

'Boss!' Dagdu told Iqbal one evening. 'I have an excellent business proposal.'

Iqbal resisted the urge to smile. 'Go ahead.'

'From tomorrow, come to Sassoon Docks to buy fish in wholesale.'

'Seriously?'

'Yes, seriously.'

'Then?'

'Then what? Load the fish into my tempo and sell the stock to factories in Thane,' Dagdu said and then added, 'You don't understand such a simple thing?'

'How much capital would be needed?'

'Ah . . .?'

'How many thousands do we have to put out for purchasing the stock every day?'

Dagdu scratched his head.

'At least you would know the profit margin?'

'I don't know all that,' he accepted, hanging his head.

'Then what made you so confident about putting my neck on the line?'

'I thought that since the brokers buy tons of fish every day, there must be a terrific profit. Otherwise, why should anyone come early in the morning to breathe in the stench?'

Dagdu had a point. Iqbal thought that the margin of profit in the business must really be very high. He had plenty of time on hand and set about investigating the matter with his usual thoroughness.

*

Every morning after an early breakfast, Iqbal would go to Sassoon Docks. Dagdu would meet him there. Like a local tourist guide, Dagdu would amble around leisurely with Iqbal, educating him with pride on the seafood business.

'Here, the highest demand is for prawns. The brokers always pounce on it first. Hundreds of kilos of prawns are sold in the time it takes to bat an eyelid. See those two huge baskets? Arrey, the same ones on which the crows are sitting. There must be around ten kilos of prawns in each.'

'But you said tons of goods arrive here,' Iqbal asked after surveying the market on the very first day. 'Here there is nothing but a few baskets.'

'These are just the samples.'

'Meaning?'

'Fishermen anchor their boats laden with fish at the dock and bring a basket or two to the jetty. Similarly, all the boat owners present two baskets each as samples. Now, there will be an auction.'

*

Gradually, Iqbal began to comprehend. One could guess the quality of fish from the two baskets. The best-quality prawns were the famed giant tiger prawns.

Each tiger prawn weighs about one quarter of a kilogram. Thus, a kilo only has four or five prawns. These best-quality prawns are bought by five-star hotels. They also fetch high prices in the export market. The next best prawns are called white or medium prawns because of their colour and size. Last come the tiny shrimps—these are dried, mixed with salt and chillies, and fried to serve as snacks with alcoholic drinks. In terms of flavour and looks, there is not much difference between dry fried prawns and chivda.

*

In that day's auction in the wholesale market, the opening bid for prawns was set at Rs 8 per kilo. Here, Iqbal noted that the broker who had bid after examining the sample had to buy the entire stock of prawns after the deal was finalized.

'Dagdu!' Iqbal called, seeing him slink away. 'Where are you going?'

'My master has finalized his deal. I'll have to leave with the catch.'

'Wait for me.'

'You will join me?' Dagdu asked, surprised.

'Shouldn't I?'

'You will have to use an oxygen mask or the stench will blast your head off,' he grinned, dashing after the Kolis carrying basketloads of fish on their heads. Crows hovered over them, pecking from the baskets.

Iqbal gave the market one last look. All the brokers were Marathas and illiterate. They had all started out doing small petty jobs like Dagdu and worked their way up to become brokers. Though they earned substantial profits, there had been no change in their attitude, attire or behaviour.

Two of them were wearing dirty dhotis and equally dirty kurtas. One wore a knee-long, loose half-pant and a bush shirt. Yet, they all looked like birds of the same feather in their peaked Gandhi caps. Iqbal, dressed smartly in a sparkling white safari suit, stood out.

Iqbal arrived before Dagdu started the tempo. Dagdu's employer, Duttaram, who also dressed exactly like Dagdu, was standing at the back of the tempo with a fisherwoman.

The stench of the prawns attacked Iqbal as he tried to sit beside Dagdu. For a moment, he felt like bolting. However, he was relieved after the tempo started—the wind was blowing on their faces and carrying the stench away behind them.

As the tempo sped towards Thane, Iqbal thought about Duttaram who was standing in the midst of tons of prawns smoking a bidi and wooing the fisherwomen. *Was he not offended by the stomach-churning stench?*

Initially, that great Maratha too must have felt wretched like him. Then, gradually he must have become accustomed to it. After all, Dagdu too had become habituated to the smell. *My dear Iqbal*, a voice echoed within, *you too will get accustomed to it one day*.

On reaching Thane, the tempo stopped opposite the Bombay Fisheries factory. Immediately, they began the process of unloading the prawns into a water tank. After washing, the prawns were weighed on giant scales and sent into the factory. There, the heads and shells were removed while the remaining peeled meat was packed into airtight cans for export.

Iqbal made some mental notes. The original rate of the prawns was Rs 8 per kilo. The purchase officer of the factory bought each for Rs 9. Thus, there was a profit of Re 1 per kilo. Given that the entire stock was of two tons, the profit worked out to Rs 2000. After deducting the rent of the tempo and the wages, a single broker earned a net profit of Rs 1950 per day.

He felt that if he bought ten tons of prawns from the market, he could earn Rs 9000 a day. To begin with, Iqbal cautiously purchased just one ton. When he loaded the prawns into the tempo and came to the factory, Iqbal himself was washed clean along with the prawns.

This was just the beginning. In this so-called legal trade, unlike the criminal world of smuggling, a person's word did not carry any weight. This was a cut-throat business. Those whom he had dismissed as uneducated, unsophisticated Marathas were in fact the prawn mafia.

Iqbal realized that he had stepped into the territory of an entirely new breed of gangsters. There was no question of backing out now. Having once stepped on to the battlefield, he did not believe in fleeing. He decided to fight the crooked mafia, but this battle wasn't going to be fought with guns and grenades; it was going to be a battle of wits. Without touching the enemy, he had to make them lick the dust.

*

But before that, let's see what happened on the first day. Seeing Iqbal throw his hat into the ring, the prawn sharks welcomed him as if he were one of them. They allowed him to buy two baskets of the best-quality prawns. These were samples from a one-ton consignment. Then, he loaded the consignment into Dagdu's tempo and went straight to the factory in Thane. When the purchase officer put the consignment on to the measuring scale, the one-ton consignment became three-quarters. He was surprised and got suspicious about the authenticity of the scales.

'I hope the scale is correct.'

Purchase Officer Rangacharya looked at him and asked, 'What makes you suspicious?'

'I had purchased one ton.'

The purchase office wanted to laugh at this amateur. He blithely asked, 'Have you thought about why we put the consignment into the water tank before putting it on the scale?'

'To clean it.'

'That we can do even after weighing it.'

'Then?'

The purchase officer explained, 'Try to understand. The fishermen bring the prawns frozen in ice crystals, which the naked eye can't see. The ice melts after we put the prawns into the water tank, and with that the weight too drops. But you have been completely duped. Between the top and bottom layer of prawns only a thick slab of ice was packed.'

The consignment worth Rs 8000 was reduced to Rs 6000. Besides, there was also a difference in the quality of prawns between the samples and the actual stock. In the first transaction, Iqbal could not even recover his investment, let alone earn a profit.

Yet, he stepped into the ring the next day again. The brokers had not expected it. They had presumed that after being cleaned like a prawn he wouldn't make the mistake of showing up again. They were mistaken. With the readiness to gamble at least Rs 1 lakh, Iqbal now fully plunged into the new business. Moreover, he was spoiling for a fight: he had decided to take an eye for an eye, a tooth for a tooth.

Had the prawn mafia not played this dirty trick on him, he would have perhaps got bored and left the business on his own. Since childhood, the flame of his life had sparked highest in moments of death-defying challenges. In this business, there was actually neither stress nor challenge; he would have been bored soon enough of such a lifeless life.

He needed thrill even in mundane business. And now he found that here. His computer-like brain started working again. Sadly, before it could compute a plan, the whole game changed.

*

The brokers, meanwhile, secretly formed a syndicate and announced a rate that was 50 paise lower than the market price. The trick was that either all the fishermen should sell their catch to the syndicate or no one would buy from them. It was nothing but blackmail—in a cut-throat business you can't cry for fair play. The syndicate had killed two birds with a sharp stone: they had cut Iqbal to size and slashed the rate too.

Iqbal, already once-bitten, knew that it would be foolhardy to accept the challenge and buy out the entire stock. Nor was there any time to think. The fishermen, considering their own good, had already sold their entire stock to the syndicate. Iqbal returned home, tired and defeated.

He vanished from the scene for a whole week. In those seven days, his brain worked through fresh computations and one fine morning, he turned up once again. The syndicate members realized that this adversary could not be scared away so easily. They decided the day's rate and announced it before the fishermen: Rs 7.5. The fishermen did not have enough funds to challenge the monopoly. If they protested and the syndicate members left without purchasing, their entire stock would rot.

As the syndicate members went forward to lift the stock, Iqbal sprung a surprise. 'I'll pay Rs 8.' All the fishermen, along with the five members of the syndicate, were taken aback.

'Rs 8.5,' announced Duttaram, the leader of the syndicate, after some hurried consultation with the other members.

'Rs 9.'

On one side were the five bosses of the prawn mafia, on the other side was Iqbal. Both the parties knew that Rs 9 was the selling price. Buying the catch at this rate would not only be unprofitable, but the rent of the tempo and the labour charges would also have to be shelled out from one's own pocket.

Increasing the rate beyond that would lead to losses. The syndicate could not commit such a blunder. At the same time, they did not want to lose the battle.

They discussed amongst themselves and finally Duttaram gave the fishermen a veiled threat. 'It's your choice. Sell your stock at Rs 8.5 per kilo to the syndicate or at Rs 9 per kilo to Iqbal Seth. But don't you forget! We are here to stay but Iqbal Seth may not be here tomorrow.'

The threat had the weight of truth behind it. Before Iqbal, several other traders had tried to penetrate the fish market, but the shark-like brokers had trapped them so badly that none had returned.

Iqbal watched silently. The rivals had made a good move. They had not bid further, yet they had made a move. Not only that, their words had the desired effect. The fishermen were looking at each other in stunned silence.

If Iqbal really did withdraw after a couple of days, the syndicate members were bound to take revenge on them. These days, they were fixing the daily rate of the prawns at Rs 7 per kilo instead of Rs 8. In the future, they may quote still lower!

The fishermen clashed. Like the murder of crows that scrabbled over the fish baskets, squawking raucously while fighting over scraps of dead fish, the fishermen too started squabbling.

There were two Muslims among these Kolis. Whenever a God-fearing Muslim gets embroiled in such a situation, he never thinks of the future. What does one get by worrying about tomorrow? The beneficent and merciful Allah will take care.

'We won't ever get such a high price!' declared one of them. The other fishermen hesitated. Before they could pick sides, Iqbal played the trump card, 'Rs 9.5.' Dagdu was thrilled to see his boss in full form again.

The syndicate members were dumbfounded. The dispute among the fishermen was immediately resolved. Everyone unanimously handed over the stock to Iqbal. This time, the syndicate members had to limp away defeated.

The stock was one and a quarter ton, or 1250 kilos. Iqbal had suffered a loss of 50 paise per kilo. However, for a person who had spent a week carefully planning the strategy to make Rs 50 lakh from this business, this loss was a pittance. By incurring a petty loss, he had also taken control over the whole business. The monopoly had finally slipped away from the brokers. Iqbal was the new don of the prawn mafia.

This routine continued for a few days. Every morning, both the parties would come to Sassoon Docks. Both the rivals would make their bids. Iqbal would sit tight after bidding for Rs 9 per kilo. He knew that the syndicate would not go beyond that.

*

Let us now look at Iqbal's strategy in detail. On the first day, he had suffered an insignificant loss, about Rs 700. From the second day, he had to bear the expense of just the rent for the tempo and labour charges for a week. However, from the third week, he started making a profit.

Surprisingly, during the auction, he never bid low. Of course, he was also not in a position to lower the rates. Then how was he miraculously turning a profit?

Of the eight brokers who supplied prawns to the seafood factories located in Wagle Industrial Estate, five were the main agents. Once the tussle between Iqbal and these five members of the syndicate began, the smaller suppliers withdrew from the business and started trading in pomfret and other varieties of fish in the local market. Thereafter, Iqbal cut out the syndicate and became the sole supplier of prawns.

There were four factories and the demand had doubled. Knowing this, he deliberately sold the entire haul to only one factory. It was but natural that the other three factory owners would begin squirming. If Iqbal went on supplying all the prawns to just one client, the other three would have to close down.

The purchase officers of the factories were perplexed. The way the prawn mafia had cornered the fishermen by forming a syndicate, Iqbal too had trapped the big companies. Within two days, the purchase officers of the other three factories were standing before Iqbal with folded hands. 'There, I get a rate of Rs 9 per kilo,' Iqbal told them. 'If you can afford to pay Rs 9.5, I'll supply to you as well.'

They did not have any other option. If they wanted to keep the company running and not lose export orders, they would have to accept the rate Iqbal demanded.

From the third day, Iqbal started supplying prawns to all the four companies at the same price. The situation of the brokers too had become pitiable. If they returned empty-handed day after day, they would soon have to wash dishes in a restaurant. An entire month had passed without work. After another fortnight, they realized that there was no option but to surrender to Iqbal Seth.

While the purchase officers had accepted the sudden increase in rates, they had also started contacting brokers at other ports. However, it takes time to put things in order after a sudden and unexpected brake is applied to a system that has been operating smoothly for years.

The purchase officers were about to strike a deal with the new brokers to buy prawns at Rs 9 per kilo when Iqbal promised to lower the rate by 50 paise. This was a clever move. He had come to know that the syndicate was going to surrender soon. In that case, he need not take 50 paise extra from the factories.

The day he made the promise to the purchase officers, the leader of the syndicate, Duttaram, proposed, 'Iqbal Seth! Let's do business together.'

'Together?'

'We are five partners. You are the sixth one.'

'No,' Iqbal said after consideration. 'I don't want to be your partner. But I don't mind doing business with you.'

'How?'

'You do the bidding, fix the market price, but don't sell to anyone besides me.'

They debated the proposal for a few minutes. Though, in reality, there was nothing to discuss: the syndicate was on its knees. The deal was clear. Iqbal wanted to control the prawn market. Against this condition, Iqbal was also giving them what they needed most—the opportunity to earn their bread and butter. From masters they had become pets, yet they accepted the proposal.

*

Iqbal now enjoyed absolute monopoly over the seafood-exporting companies. He was now able to lower or increase the prices from time to time. The real income, 'malai' in Dagdu's words, was right here. He wanted to earn millions and establishing a monopoly was only the first step in that direction. The second step was to enter into a deal with India's global seafood company, Britannia. Here, he committed a Himalayan blunder—one that not only threw him out of the ring, but also out of the entire seafood business.

34

Iqbal fixed an appointment with the general manager (GM) of Britannia at the company's Nariman Point office. GM Karkare welcomed him. Instead of the usual illiterate Marathas who were the suppliers in the seafood business, here was a well-dressed young man standing before him with a briefcase in hand. Not only was Iqbal well-scrubbed and scrupulously clean, he carried a fresh, pressed white shirt in his briefcase when going for a special appointment. Before the meeting, he would change into a new shirt so that he did not smell of fish.

'Yes, Mr Rupani!' Karkare said after offering him a seat, 'What can I do for you?'

'I want to supply your entire quota.'

'Do you know how much our company buys from different suppliers?'

'About eight tons, and your requirement is ten.'

'Absolutely right. What rate will you offer?'

'Rs 9.5 per kilo.'

Karkare did some quick calculations. If he got ten tons daily instead of the usual eight, there would be more profit. Even after deducting the negligible loss on account of the higher rate, the company could turn a profit. Besides, instead of haggling with a bunch of baboons it was better to deal with one educated, well-spoken agent.

'The rate is no problem. But you will have to agree to one critical deal term from our side too.'

'What is that?'

'Without fail, you must supply ten tons daily.'

'Agreed.'

Both parties signed a contract.

*

To expand the business, Iqbal rented an office at Carnac Bunder. He made Dagdu a 25 per cent partner in the business. His job was just to attend the office. His tempo would now ply for Iqbal's company: King's Seafood Company. A receptionist and a driver for the tempo were also appointed.

Every morning, after namaz, Iqbal would go out to make the daily purchase. He had arranged to receive consignments from outside Bombay at Bhaucha Dhakka dock.

*

Here, Sufi provided some interesting information. Kolis, the fishermens' community, are the backbone of the fishery business. They can be both Gujaratis and Marathas. Gujarati Kolis were uprooted from Sassoon Docks following stiff competition between the two communities. Now, they offloaded their catch only at Bhaucha Dhakka.

Iqbal would take the delivery from all the ports and load the fish into the tempo to send it to Britannia. Dagdu supervised operations there. The purchase officer would wash the prawns in the water tank, weigh them, note down the weight and forward them to the different sections of the factory where these were packed in airtight cans.

Everything was going on smoothly. King's Seafood Company was making a net profit of Rs 3,00,000 per month. Dagdu was getting Rs 75,000 as per his 25 per cent share, while the remainder went to Iqbal.

A monthly income of Rs 2–3 lakh in a venture was peanuts for Iqbal. His ambition was to roll in millions. He was aware that the seafood business had untapped potential. India had just begun to explore it. Given a vision and the required capital, an entrepreneur could earn not just millions but billions. Iqbal had the vision. The computer-like brain had served criminals so far, now it was active in a constructive field.

*

Iqbal thought, just as the Alphonso is considered the king of mangoes the pomfret is the queen of fish. If only foreigners developed a liking for the Indian pomfret, the country could have a turnover of crores within a year. Moreover, with so much of foreign exchange coming in, the government too would be happy.

He presented this proposal before GM Karkare who was a younger generation Maratha with a double-graduate degree and foresight to boot. He accepted the proposal and asked for samples.

The next day, Iqbal gave him two pomfrets of outstanding quality. Each of them weighed 1.5 kg. Karkare sent these samples to the London office.

Sufi claims that these two samples of pomfret would have revolutionized the seafood trade. He was the first visionary to have taken an initiative in this direction. Had he survived in the business, he would have been rolling in millions. Within a

few decades, by the '90s, the export of pomfrets was fetching
Rs 50 crore.

*

Before the import order from London arrived, Iqbal's downfall
had begun. As I could see, only he was responsible for his
catastrophe. He had stepped into quicksand by signing the
contract with Britannia. He had started the prawn business
in August–September. He did not know at the time that like
flowers and fruits, prawns too are seasonal. This season starts
before September when a couple of tons of prawn are caught
from each shore.

When he signed the contract with Britannia in November,
it was peak season. He had thought getting the required quota
every month would be easy.

The supply started dwindling by February. The shore from
which he used to get a ton of prawns now started supplying only
three-quarters. But he did not lose heart. He established contacts
at other ports. He replenished the shortage by getting prawns
from Goa. He was swimming upstream against the current.

By March–April, warning bells started ringing. The supply
came down from three-fourths of a ton to one-fourth, or
just 250 kilos. It was the same situation in Bombay and its
surrounding coastal areas.

In order to fulfil his commitment, he had to target
Ratnagiri, Malwan and Vengurla ports. He bought an
Ambassador car that became his house on wheels. He would
roam for miles every day. He would buy from whichever port
he could get the stock, put it in ice, load it on to a truck and
rush it to Bombay. He was exhausting himself day in and day
out. For what? Just to keep his word? Maybe there was some
light at the end of the tunnel.

At this end, the entire responsibility fell on Dagdu. This rustic Maratha was basically honest but unfit to handle administrative jobs. So long as Iqbal was in Bombay, he guided Dagdu. Now, he was all alone.

Frequent delays started occurring in supplies. One day, when the purchase officer of Britannia lost his temper, Dagdu slapped him.

Iqbal came to know of the incident only when he reached Bombay a week later. He realized that it was futile to wander from coast to coast. Moreover, it was too late to appoint an experienced manager now. His energy was drained. There was a shortage of about 50 kilos. It was impossible to avoid defaulting on the contract terms because things were beyond his control. Finally, he wound up his enterprise, King's Seafood Company.

*

Two notable incidents occurred that month: the two samples of pomfret sent to London had the desired result. A massive order for 50 tons was received. This was an excellent opportunity to become a millionaire, but Iqbal, the man who had paved the way, had left the arena. The second incident would take him back to smuggling.

*

Iqbal had failed in just one venture, I had failed in four. My condition had become worse than that of a beggar after four of my painting exhibitions flopped one after the other. The only difference between a beggar and me was that while he could beg, I could not even borrow. I was crushed under heavy debt. My friends slipped into bylanes on seeing me coming down the road. If a friend accidentally bumped into me, he would get rid of me by throwing a Rs 2 note at me. With the money, I would eat some dal-chawal or roti-sabzi and survive for a couple of days more.

My relationship with my family had become confined to me going to the chawl to sleep on the terrace. I was a prodigal son, good for nothing. Sometimes, I used to tiptoe through the house like a thief to change my clothes. I would leave without having tea. I had no right to eat in the house where I did not contribute a dime. Besides, keeping away from home was the best safeguard against the marriage proposals.

*

Iqbal too was worried about marriage. The pressure had been mounting on him after he quit smuggling. Like every mother, his mother too dreamt of her son standing tall in a groom's attire with a fetching bride by his side. Like me, he too was rejecting marriage proposals in his own way. But I lacked his strength to face this oppressive atmosphere.

The increasing stress took a toll on my health. I would feel dizzy while hunting for work and fall down unconscious on roads, footpaths and railway platforms.

The most tragic part about these recurring fits was that when I opened my eyes, the first thing I would see was a bunch of stinking shoes. I would be struggling for fresh air while a few gentlemen would be trying hard to make me smell their shoes. A crowd would gather to watch the tamasha.

They thought I was suffering from hysteria. God alone knows who had educated them with the misinformation that if a convulsive patient falls unconscious, they should make him sniff leather. Of course, I was not suffering from hysteria but from depression. One good thing about getting up after lying

like a log for a few minutes was that I felt as if I had woken up
after a sound sleep. My body would feel fresh and the world
would appear more beautiful. This euphoria, however, did
not last long. After a few hours, the grey clouds of uneasiness
would gather around me again. After a few days, I would again
feel the world swinging around me and collapse on the spot.

*

In those days, vipassana camps had just started in Bombay.
Those were the days when the late J. Krishnamurti used to
conduct public talks for a week once a year on the J.J. School
of Arts campus. Bhagwan Shree Rajneesh (Osho) had also
set up a tent at Azad Maidan. His mesmerizing voice drew
passers-by for his spiritual discourses like ants to honey.

One day, while I was walking past Cama Hospital, the
same voice echoed in my ears. I was going to VT station but
sat down to listen instead. His lecture was very impressive,
but I did not get even a glimpse of the peace of mind I was
hoping for.

The following week I bumped into Girish Vaidya, the
director of films like *Anant* and *Aakrant*. Before I could
exhibit my empty wallet, he said, 'Aabid, I've made special
arrangements for you to have free food for at least ten days.'

'How?'

He wrote an address on a slip of paper and handed it over
to me. The address was that of the vipassana camp. Initially,
these camps would be held in a dharamshala near Gol Deval,
a circular temple.

Lifting my eyes from the slip of paper, I asked, 'Who
organizes these camps?'

'A Marwari.'

I was amused.

Bollywood has created a stereotypical image in our minds about people from different castes and communities. For example, if there is a Parsee character in a film, he would invariably be shown as being eccentric, while in reality the Parsees are an enterprising, successful business community. Similarly, when a Marwari character appears on screen, he is mostly depicted as a Shylock, a bloodsucker. Therefore, it was not surprising that I took some time to digest the idea of a Marwari in a spiritual role.

I decided that there was no harm marching into a camp that offered free food for ten days. Besides, I had been interested in theology since my childhood. Readers already know that my father had lost his mind trying to control the realm of the spirits.

I went to the camp carrying one set of clothes. I met the guru, Shri Satyanarayan Goenka, for the first time in my life. His simplicity, his smile and his truth touched me. I realized during the final day of meditation that a cascade of hidden truth was pouring upon me. I was swimming in a spiritual ocean.

*

When I emerged from the camp after ten days, I was a changed person. The endless chatter had stilled in the quiet of the silent mind. Layers of filth had been washed clean from my mind. Envy and anger had melted away. Compassion, hitherto lying dormant, had surfaced. Everything was clear before my eyes. I had a new vision to solve my predicaments.

The very same problems that had created tension and knocked me off my path were no more a burden. For example, before the ten-day camp, Suraiyya's memory was so vivid and haunting that it had become an anathema. Now, I willingly returned to it sometimes to refresh myself.

The friends who turned their faces away and slipped into bylanes slowly started coming back to me. The reason was the change in my attitude after ten days of diligent meditation.

Earlier, I used to curse the friends who would refuse loans. I was no more the object of their repulsion. My aggression had given way to a smile of compassion. Where there is a smile, there is love. At peace, I started preparing for my fifth painting exhibition.

*

Let us now consider Iqbal's debit and credit accounts. As a trader, he had supplied prawns worth crores of rupees to Britannia in seven months and made a neat profit of Rs 21 lakh. However, after the prawn season was over, the daily catch of prawns dwindled and their rates skyrocketed. As per his contract with the company, he could not raise the price. And to fulfil his obligation of supplying 10 tons of prawns, he had to buy them at twice or thrice the market rate.

A written contract did not mean much for Iqbal. Had he wanted, he could have torn the stamped paper to pieces and walked out. *But what about his word of honour?* This was the first lesson he had learnt from the underworld. Till date, he has never gone back on his word. To honour his word, Iqbal finally had to sell his office, the car he had received from DK, the new Ambassador car and Dagdu's tempo.

The prawns had nibbled away all that Iqbal and Dagdu had earned from the sea. Both of them were jobless again. Iqbal still had a source of income, Rs 4000 as monthly rent for *Al Kabir*. As for Dagdu, his world fell apart.

'Boss!' Dagdu said, 'Your partnership has ruined me.'

'Sometimes it happens in business.'

It was a Friday, one of those late June afternoons when all the trees come into leaf, the air smells of monsoon and the birds sing of rain.

Despite having left Dongri and taken up a new residence in Khar, Iqbal used to visit Dongri every Friday without fail to offer namaz at Khoja Masjid. That day, he was sitting with Dagdu in Café Naaz after offering prayers.

'I wouldn't have even pissed on that business had I known before,' Dagdu said, lighting up a bidi. 'How happy I was driving the tempo. By evening, I would have a Rs 100 note in my pocket. After taking care of other expenses, I would get a full bottle to drink!'

'Whatever God does is for our own good. Tell me the truth, haven't you come down to a quarter from a full bottle?'

'What if I don't get even a peg tomorrow? On top of that, I've to listen to the obscenities of my second wife.' Dagdu called his mistress his second wife. 'The first one is loyal, but this bitch does not allow me to sleep in peace. Do something, boss, else . . .'

'What can I do?'

'What we are born to do . . .'

'That's not possible.'

'The gold market is picking up again. I've seen taporis moving about Zaveri Bazaar with pockets bulging with gold biscuits.'

'Who has stopped you? Go, join them!'

'Boss, to be honest, I don't feel like working with anyone but you.'

'Give me a week's time. I'll find a way out.'

'Legal or . . .?'

'Dagdu, please forget about the forbidden fruit.'

*

As they came out of Café Naaz, customs officer Khan's car stopped before them.

'Get in, son!' Khan smiled, opening the front door.

Iqbal had not committed any crime. He figured that perhaps Khan wanted information regarding some crime. He fearlessly sat down in the front seat beside the officer.

Dagdu crushed the bidi under his shoe and watched wide-eyed. The car headed towards Colaba. 'Don't you want to know where I am taking you?' Khan asked.

'Sir, I've just had lunch. It's obvious that you are not taking me to a hotel.'

'Of course not. But you can say that I'm taking you in and every morsel you've eaten for lunch out.'

'You have to be joking.'

Driving with one hand, Khan opened a briefcase with the other and took out two sheets of paper. 'Read it.'

Iqbal glanced over both the pages and protested. 'This . . . is a white lie.'

'Is Altaf not your colleague?'

When Iqbal was into gold smuggling, there had been a mixed bunch of more than a dozen fellows, including Dagdu and Michael, working under him. Of these, a few felt intimidated by his strong personality and were uncomfortable working under him. Altaf, with the drooping moustache, was one of those who loathed his guts. After the gold smuggling phase ended, the entire gang had dispersed.

Altaf, with the local Lalas' backing, had started smuggling independently using air freight. He had taken two officials into confidence. No one suspected anything for six months. In the seventh month, the government sniffed a rat. He was trapped in the customs' net.

Iqbal had nothing to do with him or his racket. Yet, in his confessional statement before the customs, Altaf had named him. According to his admission, Iqbal was the leader of the air parcel racket—watches worth lakhs of rupees had been smuggled into the country under his supervision.

'It's true that this weirdo worked with me a year ago. But I've nothing to do with this air parcel racket.'

'What are you doing these days?'

'Nothing.'

'How is it that all your colleagues got busy but you are still looking for work?'

'Sir, I've just retired from the prawn business . . .' he was trying to explain when the car stopped across the DRI headquarters.

'We'll discuss the matter upstairs.'

*

Khan walked ahead, holding Iqbal's wrist. Across them was Hotel Waldorf. The entire floor above it was occupied by the DRI. Khan took him to the same room in which he had been interrogated earlier. That time Singh was with him and the duo had successfully hoodwinked Khan and Rustomji.

It was different today. Today, he was innocent and had been brought here for no fault of his. Today, Khan was not going to exonerate him. He was going to extract revenge for every point Iqbal had scored and every game Iqbal had won in the past.

Iqbal noticed that there was the same bench-like table and chair in the room. Khan made him sit on the table and opened with a threat. 'Iqbal, none of your gimmicks are going to work today. It is in your best interest that you confess.'

'But, sir . . .'

'I won't repeat myself.'

'Should I confess despite being innocent? You know well, there is never a loophole in whatever I do. Else, I'd have been caught years ago.'

'All right! Bring in Altaf,' he yelled at someone behind the door.

Iqbal couldn't think of the reason why Altaf would involve him. Maybe Khan was playing a cat-and-mouse game to trap him. However, this was a remote possibility.

As soon as Altaf entered along with Rustomji, Khan asked him, 'Do you know him?'

Altaf looked at Iqbal. Their eyes met. He immediately looked down and said, 'He is Iqbal.'

'Since when do you know him?'

'We were together in gold smuggling.'

'After that?'

'We switched over to other rackets after the slump in the gold market.'

'What exactly did you do?'

'Smuggling through air parcels.'

'Under whom?'

'Iqbal, sir.'

Iqbal stiffened with shock. Now he was sure that this was not a ruse by Khan. Altaf had confirmed his statement in front of Iqbal. *But why? What was the purpose of humiliating him?*

*

And then he remembered. Several years ago, during a midnight crossing, their steam launch had been illuminated twice under the searchlight of a naval ship. Iqbal's colleagues had panicked. They were preparing to abandon the cargo and swim to safety. Altaf had been at the forefront of that plan.

Had he jumped, it would have emboldened the others. Iqbal had pulled him down from the brim of the launch and punched him hard. It had broken his nose. His drooping moustache had been dripping with blood. At the time, Altaf had swallowed the insult but vowed to avenge himself one day. Today was that day.

Khan sniggered. Rustomji brought three peons from outside. All four of them made Iqbal lie down on the table with his face down. He was tied with a rope. Khan began hammering his soles with a rod.

'Tell me,' Khan would repeat with each excruciating blow, 'are you ready to confess?' Iqbal too would declare his innocence after each blow. In half an hour, his soles puffed up like balloons, but he did not budge.

'Khan!' Rustomji finally pleaded, 'He has been screaming himself hoarse that he was into the seafood business. He is also giving the phone number of Britannia's GM. What is the harm in confirming it?'

Khan thought it proper to give it a try. Throwing away the rod, he went out with Rustomji. The three peons stood guard. Iqbal lay on the table like a mute animal writhing in pain. He made a resolution. He had been implicated in the smuggling of wristwatches. He would now actually start smuggling them to teach Khan a lesson.

After fifteen minutes, Rustomji, and not Khan, approached him with a cup of tea and a sandwich. Iqbal slowly sat upright.

'You are really fortunate! Khan had a talk with Mr Karkare. Had he not supported your statement, you would have certainly been rotting behind bars. Come, have tea . . .'

With a stroke of his hand, Iqbal swatted away the teacup, saucer and sandwiches.

35

Iqbal had shared a vital truth with customs officer Khan: whenever he took on a criminal enterprise, he never left a loophole. His blueprint was always watertight. Even in ventures other than smuggling, his fertile brain had been extremely productive—his ingenious idea had rescued DK's man Hamid from the gallows when the brightest lawyers in the country had failed.

If an accused is sentenced to a certain number of years of imprisonment and he does not want to go to jail, Sufi has a solution. If someone wants to avoid paying income tax, he can suggest ways to do that legally within minutes.

Those days, the government had imposed a 240 per cent customs duty on the import of stainless steel. Understandably, a rise in customs duty led to an increase in price. And when the price increases, it boosts smuggling. This nexus between the government and the criminals has been as old as civilization.

One day, a trader friend came to Sufi. 'If you agree to smuggle stainless steel sheets, I'm prepared to buy them all.' Since Iqbal had studied the new budget in the morning paper in minute detail, he smiled and said, 'You don't have to break the law for that.'

'I'll be ruined if I pay 240 per cent duty.'

'There is no need to pay the customs duty either.'

'The customs officials are not my in-laws that they would allow me to import for nothing.'

'That's true. But if you use a bit of common sense, you can import it by paying just 40 per cent duty.'

'How?'

Iqbal showed him the loophole in the budget. The 240 per cent duty was on stainless steel sheets and not on stainless steel angles. The only requirement in the budget was that the angle should be of 45 degrees. This meant that if you bent a flat sheet at 45 degrees, the customs duty would be reduced from 240 per cent to just 40 per cent. Of course, after importing, you could flatten them again.

'Would you not save 200 per cent on customs duty this way?' Iqbal asked.

His trader friend looked at him wonderstruck. He made millions by following Iqbal's suggestion. What did Iqbal get in return? Nothing. He never charged his friends for advice.

*

'Got it,' I told Sufi. 'But how can you keep a convict out of jail once he is sentenced?'

'It's very simple. Send a substitute . . .'

'Why would anyone agree to undergo imprisonment for someone else?'

'There is so much poverty in our country that a man can even go to the gallows for some money.'

'What'll he do with money if he is to die?'

'Won't his wife and children benefit?'

'Suppose someone agrees to undergo imprisonment as a substitute, how much will he get?'

'About Rs 1000 a month. Of this, his family gets Rs 700 and the man gets Rs 300 inside the prison.'

Sufi then went on to explain the procedure. The accused, fearing conviction, has to arrange for a substitute on the day the court is expected to deliver the judgment. If the case is of trafficking, the trial will take place in the court of the chief metropolitan magistrate (Azad Maidan).

There is a provision of a lock-up room in the cellar of the court building. After the court passes the judgment and sentences the convict, the head constable of the concerned police station puts the convict in this same lock-up. Now, the charge of the convict is with the head constable of the court. It is not difficult for crooks to bribe the head constable. The convict escapes from here and a proxy replaces him.

'What if the head constable is honest?'

He smiled, as if I had asked him a silly question, but coolly suggested another way out. 'A police van arrives in the evening to pick up the convicts from the court's lock-up and take them to the prison.'

Generally, an inspector, one driver and two constables are in the van. The godfathers keep the inspectors on their payrolls too. The van stops at a predetermined place between Azad Maidan and Arthur Road jail. The real convict jumps out of the van and a substitute takes his place. The exchange happens in a fraction of a second.

'Don't the jail officials realize that the prisoner has been changed?'

'How would they know? They haven't seen the convict. The jail officials receive only the names of the convicts.'

According to Sufi, no official in the government administration bothers to verify the names. If the prisoner has already been replaced in the lock-up and the police van arrives in the evening to pick up the convicts, the inspector, who only counts the number of heads, will never notice.

If, on a certain day, five persons are sentenced to prison, the inspector counts five heads and is satisfied; a similar head count is carried out in prison. It is not surprising that the underworld takes advantage of such laxity.

Sufi revealed another fact. Not all substitute prisoners are victims of human predicaments. Some of them set up shops inside the prison. They can easily arrange for hashish, liquor or even 'boys'. Besides the Rs 300 they get as substitutes, each of them earns an extra Rs 2000–3000 a month.

For Iqbal, petty tasks like arranging for a prison substitute were child's play. But he needed to be extra careful when it came to smuggling contraband goods worth millions of rupees. He could undertake the venture only after ensuring that the plan was foolproof.

*

After a week's serious planning, he came up with a unique idea that would give Khan sleepless nights. It was to carry out smuggling using transit post parcels.

Just as any business start-up during the incubation phase needs research, in smuggling too many experiments are needed to fine-tune any new idea.

Another month passed. During this month, Iqbal recalled three of his old colleagues—Dagdu, Michael and Sadru.

Wristwatches were to be smuggled. A tsunami of branded watches from Dubai was to hit Indian markets. Iqbal spent three days in Dubai and finalized the deal with a sheikh. In exchange for wristwatches, he was to send silver because the price of silver was rising in the international market.

*

By the following month, the wristwatches started coming into Bombay. Thousands of wristwatches of famous brands like Citizen, Seiko and Favre-Leuba were being sold openly in every corner of the city. Inspector Khan's head reeled. He was stunned by the staggering tide of foreign wristwatches. Yet he was helpless. When a dam bursts, how can a single man stop the flooding?

He was certain that no single thug could dare to carry out smuggling on such a vast scale without the collaboration of top officials. Moreover, Khan would not gain much by arresting taporis who were selling these wristwatches in the retail market. They were merely the leaves of the banyan tree—if he plucked a leaf, another would grow in its place. *How many leaves could he pluck?* The need of the day was to uproot the tree so that neither the trunk, nor the branches, nor the leaves remained. *But where were its roots?*

*

These were the last months of the 1960s. Despite a big dent in profits, Mastan had managed to continue smuggling in gold. Yusuf Patel had become his partner. Mastan used to smuggle in gold and Patel would supply silver to send to Dubai.

The Narang brothers were neck-deep into the smuggling of idols. There was an uproar in India after a rare Natraj statue, which had vanished mysteriously, appeared in the private collection of American billionaire Norton Simon.

The Lalas ruled over Dongri, but Dawood was gradually rearing his head. The Lalas were from Peshawar, while Dawood was a Konkani. The Konkani gang was eager to confront the Lalas.

One Mr Bakhia had engaged an entire island near Daman for his smuggling operations. He had opened an office under the banner of Meena Trading Agency in Dubai with branches in Hong Kong and Kowloon. One of his brothers-in-law was a Congress (I) MLA, while the other managed his Dubai office.

At such a time, when traffickers were exploding like mushrooms, Khan was bound to feel suffocated. He had failed to trace the gang that had flooded the Indian market with wristwatches. He had failed to comprehend even the route through which these had been brought in: air, sea or from across the border.

*

While Khan was trying to sort out the chaos in his head, a tapori hesitatingly entered the office of customs collector Sonawale and sat down facing him.

'Yeah . . .' Sonawale closed the file on his table and yawned. 'What information have you brought?'

'About the wristwatches, sir . . .'

'Go ahead!'

'About the smuggled watches . . .'

'I understand that. What else?'

The tapori was a little muddled. Had he been asked a specific question, he had some shocking dope to offer. But he had never before faced such a senior officer. For a while, he could not think of what to say further.

'The entire city knows that there has been a sudden spurt in contraband wristwatches,' Sonawale said, noticing the young man shrink. 'If you have any concrete information . . .'

'Of course, sahib!' the boy said, gathering courage, 'An entire gang from Dongri is involved.'

Perhaps Customs Collector Sonawale had woken up on the wrong side of the bed that day. Or perhaps he had missed his morning dose of caffeine. He yawned like a bored zoo lion.

Looking blearily at the tapori, he asked again, 'Is that all?'

'The transit post parcel department is being used for smuggling.'

'How?'

'I don't know that but my information is correct.'

'We can't take action on the basis of such vague information.'

Frustration was writ large on the tapori's face. There were two reasons why he had come here. One of them was the reward he would get on the seized contraband goods.

He was about to get up when Sonawale took out a cigar from a small tin box on his table and lit it. 'The wristwatches come by post parcel?'

'Yes.'

'From where?'

The boy kept quiet so Sonawale took a pull at the cigar and prompted, 'From Hong Kong, Japan, Dubai?'

He did not know.

'By which ship do they come?'

He did not know.

'The consignment belongs to the mafia. Obviously, it must not be addressed to a real name.'

'True.'

'Then to whose name does it come?'

The tapori started squirming uncomfortably.

'What is your name?'

'Ali.'

He was a dropout from Habib High School and was determined to snitch on Iqbal.

'Listen, Ali, the transit department receives hundreds of parcels. We can certainly take action if you have some definite information about the parcels carrying the smuggled goods.'

'But . . .'

'To investigate on the basis of such flimsy information, we need manpower. I neither have enough men nor time,' he said, dismissing him with a vaguely reassuring, 'Yet, I'll think about it.'

Ali got up, crestfallen. *Bastards! All of them get paid for doing nothing. No one wants to work.*

*

Returning home by bus, he spotted the CBI headquarters. Until he retired, Inspector Bharucha used to sit here. Ali's face lit up with hope again. He jumped off the bus and entered the building.

Inspector Kanetkar gave him a patient hearing. The information he had received was too specific to be ignored. He immediately phoned the DRI. The DRI was the topmost investigating agency of the customs department—Khan and Rustomji were its crack officers.

Inspector Kanetkar spoke briefly to DRI chief Wadhwa, put down the receiver and wrote something on a piece of paper. He put the paper into an envelope and gave it to Ali. 'Here is the DRI's address. Show it to any peon there, he will guide you to the right officer.'

Ali boarded a bus for Colaba. As the bus moved, he slid into the past.

This was the same Ali who had studied with Iqbal in school. He was the one who had initiated Iqbal into the illicit business. It was through him that Iqbal had met Moghul and started supplying bottles of ethyl alcohol to liquor dens. Thereafter, Ali had joined Mastan's gang and left school but was unable to make much progress, unlike his understudy Iqbal. He had remained a tapori. Frustrated, he decided to earn some extra money and became an informer.

The work of an informer is dangerous. Bali was one and the readers know by now how tragic his end was. Hence, for his own safety, Ali started keeping a tab on minor players and informed the local cops as and when he got some information.

Iqbal was not a small-time operator any more. He had become the kingpin. He had his own gang, a retinue of government officials on his payroll and his own system of working—he had built an entire network for himself. He had also taken care to remain an invisible man of the underworld. DK too was another such man because his name was hardly mentioned in newspapers. Yet, Ali had made Iqbal his target. His second reason was jealousy.

*

When Ali reached the DRI headquarters and entered the cabin of its chief, the latter was anxiously waiting for him. For the first time in his life, he was welcomed with a big smile. Ali's mouth started watering with the promise of a reward. However, his eyes, brimming with malice, were considering a more important outcome: this chief would definitely take action and put Iqbal behind bars for at least five years.

'What's your name?' the chief asked.

Ali gave his full name.

'What do you do?'

'I'm unemployed. I thought that by giving you information about criminals I'll get a reward and serve my country too.'

The chief smiled behind his bushy moustache.

Once the peon brought in two cups of tea, Ali's confidence increased and whatever little doubt he still harboured disappeared. Thinking afresh, he thought that Iqbal would disappear for at least ten years.

Sipping tea from a feather-light china cup, he repeated with gusto all the information he had given to the customs collector and the CBI officer. On top of that, he also disclosed the name: Iqbal.

The chief put his cup down, made notes on a rough pad and looked at him. 'Good. Now tell me, who is this Iqbal?'

'Patli.'

'Patli?'

'Since he is slim, he is known by that name in Dongri.'

He lifted his cup of tea, thought for a while and asked, 'Ali, how many boys work for him?'

'Many, sir. An entire gang.'

'How big is it? Two, five, twenty-five, fifty . . . how many?'

He drank his tea and replaced the cup on the saucer. 'Iqbal heads the gang. There are three directly under him and under those three are twenty-three others, but I don't know how many taporis work under those twenty-three crooks.' He paused and then said, 'I'm sure you have got the full picture!'

'You must know the names of at least a couple of them.'

'Ganpat Chalke.'

'And who is this Chalke?'

'He is an official of the postal department.'

'Where does he sit?'

'At the General Post Office.'

'Are you sure?'

'Of course, sir. I have seen him having tea with Iqbal at a roadside stall.'

The information was enough for the chief. He now knew where to start investigating from. This link would lead him to the others and ultimately trap Iqbal. Once the bishops and knights were eliminated, the king would be forced to abdicate his throne.

After Ali left, chief Wadhwa looked at his pad. He once again went through his notes. To put the matter succinctly, a 'computer' called Iqbal, or Patli, was using the transit department of the GPO to his advantage with the help of a postal official called Ganpat Chalke. *But how?*

It was clear that the watches were being brought surreptitiously through the transit post parcels. It meant that the parcels were coming from abroad in a ship to Bombay and yet they were not for Bombay. That's why they were called transit parcels.

*

Let us understand how the transit division of the postal department works. If a party from Dubai wants to send a parcel to Africa, since there is no direct ship, all the parcels for Africa are loaded on to Bombay-bound ships. Since the ships terminate here, all parcels for Africa are offloaded at Bombay and kept under lock and key in the GPO's transit division. When, in a week or so, an Africa-bound ship anchors at the Bombay port, those transit parcels are loaded on to it.

The question that was bothering the chief was how there could be bungling in the sealed transit parcels when even customs did not have the right to open them.

Suppose some of these parcels contained contraband goods and were stolen from the transit department, then there would be a shortfall in the number of parcels that were offloaded from the Dubai ship. This would also have been noticed at the time of loading the parcels on to the Africa-bound ship.

Yet no one had reported any missing parcels to the DRI until today.

Just to be sure, he made a telephone call to the customs collector. 'Mr Sonawale! Has it ever come to your notice that any of the transit parcels has been stolen?'

'No.'

'Does that mean that the information I've received is incorrect?'

Sonawale realized that the young man who had visited him had gone to the DRI office.

'Even if the information is correct, we don't have any clues to begin investigating.'

'We do have one,' he said, revealing Ganpat Chalke's name. 'Now, I've a request to make.'

'Sure . . .'

'Don't you dare meddle with this case.'

*

Sonawale put the receiver down. After a moment or two of stupefaction, he felt drops of sweat on his forehead. He had failed to extract information from Ali, whereas the DRI chief had been successful in identifying an important link. Moreover, he had been insulted to his face. *How would he salvage the situation unless he meddled in the case?*

The DRI chief pressed the bell button. The peon standing outside popped in. 'Send Mr Khan to my cabin.' Khan was having tea with Rustomji. The peon gave him the chief's message. He was startled. He gulped down the remaining tea and stood up.

'Khan!' the chief said, motioning him to sit. 'You know a young man called Iqbal, right?'

'Sure. But if you are planning to catch him, just forget it.'

'Why?'

'He is a cunning fox. You won't even realize when he sneaks into a field and by the time you realize it, he's already vanished without leaving a single clue.'

'I'm giving you a clue,' the chief smiled, glancing at his note pad. 'Perhaps, this time his vanishing trick won't work.'

After listening to the full story, Khan's heart began to sing with joy. For him to begin an investigation, one clue was more than enough. Through Ganpat Chalke he could easily reach Iqbal. He was determined to catch them both red-handed this time.

36

My fifth exhibition, titled Rhythm and Colours, was neither a success nor a failure. I did recover the expenses from the sale of a few paintings, but I faced the same question again and again: *does it make sense?*

A painter toils for months. *What about the time he invests in his work?* He works hard to prepare for an exhibition. *What about his effort?* Barring this show, I had lost Rs 25,000. The three years of labour I had put in were of no account.

Had I invested the same time, effort and capital on some other enterprise, I would have been in a sound position financially. I would have a modicum of respect in society too; society treats destitute artists like untouchables. The moot question was: *what did I expect from life? Worldly riches or creative satisfaction?*

Those days, a *bhaiyya* from north India sat with his basket on the pavement under our building to sell peanuts and kurmura (puffed rice flakes). By the time I had completed five painting exhibitions, he had bought a shop. He had also booked a flat in a newly constructed building nearby, while I remained where I was, with a joint family in a single room and sleeping on the terrace.

It was very clear that money didn't offer me much contentment. However, I needed money even to survive as an artist. *Where would I find that?*

Generally, there is either an industrialist or a political party backing a painter. There was no one behind me. It was not in my nature to be obsequious and I knew that soliciting a promoter meant compromising with one's principles.

Take the example of artist M.F. Hussain. He had accepted the patronage of the Congress party. During the draconian Emergency period, the party's high command directed him to paint in support of the Emergency. Following the command of the government, he painted a giant-sized canvas in three pieces. Its title was 'Durga-Amba-Kali', the three divine incarnations of the then prime minister, Indira Gandhi.

My predicament was whether to convert my art into a commodity or not. If I turned into a trader, I would not be able to express what I felt. My conscience would be pleading with me to paint what my heart desired, while the customer's demand would be something entirely different.

I knew well that paintings on certain subjects with pleasing colour combinations would sell like hot cakes. Take horses for example. If I started painting horses in vivid colours, I would not need to market them; I would sell as many as I could paint. Hussain did exactly that in the beginning—he flooded the market with horses.

Another gimmick is still life, especially with flower vases. The late K.H. Ara was an expert in this. Whenever in need of money, he would hold an exhibition of paintings of flowerpots or colourful nudes. Who wouldn't want to display a rainbow of pleasing flowers in their living room?

I neither wanted to be a florist nor a horse trader. Had I wanted to do that, I would have preferred to sell peanuts and kurmura like the bhaiyya from north India. *What could I do if I did not want to make compromises? How on earth was I to survive?* That was my quandary. Surely, I didn't want to starve in an attic waiting for my talent to be recognized. Some radical change was needed.

My lifestyle would have been different today if only I had come across the diary of the Italian painter Salvador Dali in my youth. He had written that before becoming an artist, he had decided to become a millionaire. He did not reveal the secret to becoming a millionaire, but he did list the grounds for his choice, the main being the following:

1. Don't have to go to friends with a begging bowl to buy canvases and colours.
2. Don't have to compromise with one's principles.
3. Throw a grand cocktail party for art critics before throwing open one's exhibition.
4. Keep editors, art critics in one's pocket to buy media coverage. This includes newspapers, periodicals, radio and TV channels.

At the young age of twenty, that fellow had understood the secret of success. He knew well that one could buy most of the art critics. By throwing money, one could get oneself interviewed and critiqued as a visionary artist.

What Dali had said about European media held true in India too. Which critic would condemn his host after consuming gallons of liquor at the preview? Besides, it is customary to stuff envelopes containing cash into the pockets of journalists present at the press conference. Don't call it a bribe—the dignified term is 'taxi fare'.

In my case, the reviews of my exhibitions depended entirely on the quality of my work. The art critics used to tear me apart if they found it below their standards. Sometimes, I felt that like the traffic police randomly give blameless drivers speeding tickets to complete their quota, art critics too randomly give struggling artists poor reviews to balance out their gushing paid reviews. But despite the morass in the field of art, honest critics like Sri Nadkarni and the late Jag Mohan stood by me like pillars without asking for a single rupee.

In 1960, sketch pens were introduced into the market. Because I liked the sheen of their colours, I bought a set before embarking on a journey to Mathura and Brindavan (now called Vrindavan). When I returned, I held an exhibition in Bombay of the felt-pen sketches I had drawn of the *kunj gallis*.

When a famous art critic of the *Times of India* could not find any fault with my drawings, he wrote a full column censuring me for using a medium that was not suitable for art.

Vipassana had made me shockproof and so I derived satisfaction in the fact that an English newspaper like the *Times of India* had devoted a full column to my work, even though it was only to shower abuses. At least, it had taken note of my work.

The following month, when Hussain held an exhibition of sketches using the same felt-tip pens, the very same critic praised him to the skies—his headline read 'Innovation in Art'.

That day, I laughed heartily. Crying would have been futile. I had chosen my own battlefield. My misfortune was that I could afford neither bow and arrow nor a sword to fight, and a life-long battle lay ahead. Blaming fate or circumstances was pointless; I was charting out my own destiny.

After attending the Vipassana camp, my relationship with my family too had improved. For the past several months, I had been going home just to spend the nights sleeping on the terrace. I had started spending quite some time solving the day-to-day problems at home. I was contributing as much as possible to my family but it seemed that all they wanted was my head on the chopping block of marriage.

Again, a photograph of a girl was placed before me. This must have been the thirteenth girl! It was evident that everyone in my family was fed up with me. It was also evident that escaping the unlucky number thirteen was not going to be easy.

As usual, I looked at the photograph. 'Not bad. But where will I keep her after marriage?'

The question was not irrelevant.

Seven of us were living in a single room. On top of that, my uncle and aunt alone occupied half of it. I had to go up to the terrace to sleep.

Instead of throwing a fit, my mother confronted me with my own words. 'Did you like the girl?'

'I admit that she seems to be from a good family.'

'Then why deny yourself the richness and satisfaction of family life?'

'But . . .'

'Leave the rest to Allah.'

'Agreed!' I said laughing. 'But, Ma, I won't marry till I have an independent house.'

I knew that our bank balance was zero. In fact, we did not have a bank account. My uncle's salary helped our domestic cart trundle along month after month. Under the circumstances, it was impossible to find a room in Bombay. In the 1960s, the going rate for one room was Rs 50,000.

*

Pleased with myself for executing yet another narrow escape, I set off for Colaba. My studio was near Radio Club. The DRI headquarters were also located there above Waldorf Hotel.

Khan emerged from there, got into his jeep and went straight to the GPO. Half an hour later, he was seated opposite a clerk on the third floor. His finger moved down the list of names in the payroll register.

Khan was not interested in anyone's salary. He was just looking for a name. So far, he had scanned four pages. 'Sahib!' the clerk said, 'Can I be of any help?'

'Ganpat Chalke.'

'What about him?'

'Does he work here?'

'Yes, why?'

Slamming the register shut, Khan looked at him, 'What do you know about him?'

'He has been working here since twelve years.'

'What else?'

'What else do you want to know?'

'Has he ever been accused in the past, any charge sheet?'

The clerk shook his head.

'What is his designation?'

'He was appointed as an officer in our export section last year.'

'There are ten other officers there. What does he do?'

'He handles the Africa-bound parcels.'

'Where would he be now?'

The clerk pointed a finger.

Khan turned his head. There were piles of parcels as well as twenty sets of tables and chairs in the large hall ahead. The employees of the export-booking department were busy. Ganpat Chalke was jotting something down in a file, smoking a bidi.

'Yes?' Ganpat did not even bother to lift his head to look at the unusual guest who had dropped in.

Khan placed his identity card between Ganpat's eyes and the file. Under the table, Ganpat's legs started shaking. A dark cloud passed over his face as he jerked his head up. Khan's sharp eyes noticed that too as he studied him: forty-five years old, medium height, thick black handlebar moustache and dark skin. He was wearing a bush shirt and trousers.

'Are you Ganpat Chalke?'

'Yes.'

'Is it true that you were appointed to the transit division last year, around five months back?'

He nodded.

'Congratulations,' Khan flashed a smile and offered him his hand. Ganpat looked at him wide-eyed. Then, a hesitant smile started creeping back on his face.

Khan withdrew his hand without shaking and announced a fictitious reason for his visit. 'The government is pleased with your work. I've been asked to make some investigations before recommending a promotion. By the way, this is just a formality.'

As if coming to his senses all of a sudden, Chalke jumped up from his seat and stuttered, 'Sssir . . . tttea . . . cccoffee . . .' Khan smiled, glanced at his pockmarked face and stood up, starting for the door.

*

There was radiance on the DRI chief's face when a neatly typed dossier was placed on his table with the lowdown on Chalke. There remained no doubt whatsoever about the veracity of the information Ali had given.

The transit parcels from Dubai, which contained the smuggled wristwatches, were being manipulated in connivance with Chalke. But the same old question raised its head again:

how? To discover the answer, it was necessary to keep an eye on Chalke.

Four days were left for the next ship from Dubai to arrive. They would need strong leads from Chalke in these four days to be able to trap Iqbal. Utmost care had to be exercised. The slightest hint of danger and both birds would fly away.

*

Khan became Chalke's shadow from that day. There was also a need to keep Iqbal under watch—the chief wanted it, but Khan did not feel it was critical at this stage. There was another important reason for this. Iqbal was as sharp as a hawk: he would certainly sense if someone tailed him day and night. If that happened, the DRI's game plan would fail.

Though Customs Collector Sonawale had been explicitly warned not to meddle with the case, he did exactly that. He unleashed a special officer from his team like a hunting dog to track Iqbal's every move.

Khan had also correctly surmised that Chalke was a novice to smuggling and therefore careless. It would be possible to know Iqbal's movements from Chalke's activities. Therefore, he focused his full attention on Chalke.

Dressed in plainclothes, Khan would stalk him from the moment he left home to catch the suburban train. Chalke lived in Kurla, a suburb on the Central line. On his way to the station, he would stop at a paan shop. Khan too would stop at an appropriate distance. Chalke would proceed further after taking a pinch of lime and a packet of tobacco. Khan too would follow.

Khan looked striking in his black sunglasses but to shadow a suspect he could transform his appearance completely. Even though it was not difficult to shadow Chalke, he would disguise himself to avoid attracting unnecessary attention.

Chalke's train would terminate at VT. Khan too would mingle with the crowd after alighting from the bogie behind Chalke's. The GPO's imposing heritage building was close to VT station.

Chalke would walk up to the building and climb the stairs. Khan would take position under a tree or the verandah of a shop. He would remain there until lunch. The moment Chalke would come out for a walk or to meet someone, he would become alert.

Like a shadow separates itself from a man after dark, Khan too would leave him and go home at the end of the day. But before going to bed, he would unfailingly prepare the day's report for the chief.

He followed Chalke for two full days but got no clue. *How could that be!* If Chalke was involved in bootlegging, one would have got at least a couple of clues from him by now. There was every possibility that one of the members of the gang would establish contact with him, but so far no one had tried to do so.

*

Only forty-eight hours were left for the ship from Dubai to arrive. It had now become necessary for Iqbal to approach Chalke. At 11 a.m., he made a telephone call from Khar railway station to the GPO. He was using a public telephone booth. Waiting for Chalke to come on the line, his eyes rested on a man standing in the queue for a railway ticket. The man turned twice and looked in his direction. Iqbal did not attach much importance to him.

'What's the news?' he asked Chalke.

'Cool.'

'Anything new?'

'No,' he replied, then suddenly remembering, added, 'I'm to be promoted. There will be a raise in my salary and designation too.' His words emerged with a force that belied his frail body.

'Really!'

'A man from the DRI had come to give me the good news.'

Iqbal froze.

'What has the DRI got to do with your promotion?'

'Why? The post parcels arrive here via the customs. And the DRI is above the customs. What is surprising if the DRI recommends . . .'

The only surprising part is that that you are not worth the promotion, Iqbal wanted to say. An uneasy silence hung at both the ends of the line.

'Iqbal?'

'Yes.'

'I thought the line got cut. By the way, do you suspect . . .'

'I'll tell you when we meet during the lunch break. But remember, don't try to approach me if I turn away.'

Chalke was puzzled. *Was the good news given by the DRI a ploy? Was it a net to get him? Had someone come to know of the shenanigans in the transit department?*

At 1 p.m., he had his lunch and then went to meet Iqbal. He came up to the staircase making his way through the tables and chairs. Here the clerk from the accounts section accosted him.

'Where to, Chalke?'

'The tea stall.'

'What's wrong with our canteen?'

'They serve coloured water instead of tea.'

'I too have stopped visiting our canteen. For the past one month, I've been going across the road. But today, you will have to offer me a cup.'

'Anything special?'

'I'll disclose it if you promise to treat me.'

'I'll treat you to cream biscuits with the tea. But what's the occasion?'

'An inquiry has been ordered against you.'

*

The two men stepped out of the GPO building and stopped on the pavement. Chalke was looking at the clerk's face.

'Who told you?'

'A fellow from the DRI had come. Hope you haven't done any hanky-panky?'

'I'm getting a promotion.'

'Really! In that case, only cream biscuits won't do.'

'Let me get the increment, I'll treat you to a cake as well.'

Both of them kept walking. A flicker of suspicion crossed Chalke's mind. He knew it was time to be cautious.

While crossing the road, he looked back once. It was not possible to tell if anyone was following him amongst the crowds of people milling about. Crossing over to the opposite footpath with the clerk, he noticed Iqbal behind a partly-covered pigeon's enclosure in the middle of the road.

Their eyes met for a fraction of a second before Iqbal turned away. Chalke understood that someone was monitoring his movements. He quietly proceeded with the clerk and sat down at the roadside stall.

Iqbal's eyes were fixed on Khan while Khan was watching Chalke. Earlier, Iqbal had spotted Sonawale's official at Khar railway station, but he had not cared about it much. In those days, there were no direct trains for VT—one had to change at Bandra.

The official had shown up again when Iqbal got down at Bandra station. Once again, he had ignored the shadow stalking him. He crossed the overbridge and came to the central platform. The official stood at some distance, partly covered by a pillar. Now, Iqbal smelt a rat. Moreover, that official had committed the folly of looking at him audaciously. Iqbal was alert now. He immediately thought of a plan to shake him off.

When the train for VT arrived, Iqbal made a show of boarding it. The official discreetly boarded the next compartment. As soon as the train gathered speed, Iqbal jumped off. It was not safe to travel by train any more: he took a bus from outside Bandra station to get to VT.

*

Chalke and the clerk returned after having tea. Khan followed them. Iqbal was sitting in a nearby hotel, Sher-e-Punjab, with a glass of lassi.

The ship from Dubai was to arrive the next day. Nine post parcels containing smuggled wristwatches were also expected. The information had leaked out and yet he had to recover the wristwatches. To succeed he would have to outwit Khan even though this time Khan knew the plan in advance. *Would he turn out to be the victor or the vanquished?*

37

Sitting in the rented godown at Dongri, Iqbal was lost in thought. He could see that the customs and DRI officials were closing around him. Between the two, the DRI was more dangerous.

He had received a beating from Khan a few months ago, but that had become a provocation rather than a cause for fear. Had Khan not beaten him up mercilessly, he might have started a legal business after retiring from the prawn marketing.

'It's all a matter of destiny,' Iqbal says even today.

There was nothing in the godown other than a table and three chairs, and a telephone. Ghostly cobwebs dangled from the high ceilings. Cartons with the contraband wristwatches were stored here for a short period of time; DK would use an apartment for this purpose. All the goods had to be disposed of at the earliest, which meant within twenty-four hours. This was done very systematically. For example, take the post office. As soon as a pile of letters arrived, it was immediately sorted out and different postmen lifted the mail for their respective postal zones and set out for delivery. Iqbal had made somewhat similar arrangements for the disposal of the wristwatches. He had learnt the tricks of the trade from gold smuggling.

Two elders from the community entered the godown, interrupting his chain of thought. He could not make out who these bearded gentlemen were. He had never seen them before.

'Please be seated,' he said. A thought flashed through his mind. The pressure to get married had been mounting on him for the past several months and, so far, he had managed to evade it. However, never before had the menfolk from the prospective bride's family landed up at his den.

Just as the elders of my family were fed up with my dilly-dallying, Iqbal's family too seemed to have given up. Their constant complaint was that no one would give their daughters to the younger brothers until Iqbal agreed to settle down. Besides, there would be a social stigma attached to the family if the eldest boy remained single. Society would not believe Iqbal's true reason for refusal: he did not want to wreck a girl's life. Instead, society would find fault with him. 'Surely, there must be some fault in the boy. Why else would he refuse to marry?'

The same question was thrown at me too as I also had a younger brother.

Once a stigma got stamped on to the family, the younger brothers too would have to remain single all their lives. If by sheer chance a proposal did come, it wouldn't be from a 'good' family.

Iqbal's mother had discussed the problem with the family, chosen a girl and told him, 'She is a teacher and from a good family. To get such a girl for a wife, one has to be blessed. Be wise, be polite, grab the opportunity.'

Iqbal chuckled, recalling Gul Banu's words: he was determined to bulldoze the proposal. Watching him chuckle to himself, the two men looked at each other questioningly. *Hope the boy is not soft in the head!* Among the two, one was the girl's father, the other was her uncle.

When both the elders looked at him again, Iqbal grinned as if he had just come to his senses. 'What'll you have? Something hot or cold?'

'Nothing, thank you,' the girl's father replied.

'You have come for the first time, have tea at least.'

'We just had it.'

'Then have something cold.' Iqbal directed a tapori standing outside the godown to get two glasses of falooda.

Both the men were pleased with Iqbal's magnanimity. In fact, they had not hoped for anything other than cutting chai. In five minutes, two glasses of ice-cold falooda were placed before them. Both the elders had a sip and the interview commenced.

'What do you sell?' the girl's father asked, scanning the empty godown.

Iqbal had been waiting for the inquisition to begin. Expressing surprise, he shot back, 'The whole of Dongri knows. Didn't anyone tell you?'

The men looked at each other once again. Perhaps they needed more time to understand the truth behind Iqbal's question.

'What does the whole of Dongri know?'

'My business.'

'What is it?'

Just then, one of Iqbal's toughies, Michael, stormed in. 'Boss, we found the rat.'

'Yeah?'

'I've traced the stool pigeon who informed the DRI about us.'

'Who is it?'

'Your childhood buddy.'

'But who?'

'Ali.'

Iqbal opened the drawer. There was a Rampuri knife inside it—a step-lock kind that made seven clicking sounds while unsheathing. Iqbal casually opened the knife in front of the elders and handed it over to Michael. 'Cut that asshole to little pieces so that he doesn't rat on his friends again.'

Together with the elders, Michael's eyes too opened wide. Iqbal had never taken such an extreme step. Besides, Michael had come here hoping for a reward. Instead, he had been told to bump off Ali. It was his duty to obey the master. He closed the knife, slid it into his pocket and left.

Iqbal did not need to explain what business he was into any more. He boldly looked at the two men. They lowered their eyes.

The glasses of falooda were half-full when the telephone rang. Iqbal picked up the receiver. 'Hello!'

It was Dagdu. 'Boss, the cops have seized one of our trucks at Mahim. Please see that the truck and driver are released before an FIR is lodged.'

'Who is the duty officer?'

'Bhonsle.'

'Go there after ten minutes.'

Next, he called up the police station. The deputy officer told him that the truck had run over a pedestrian.

'He won't come back to life. But we need to live together in this fragile world, isn't it?' Iqbal said. The duty officer was wise, he got the message.

Refusing to finish the falooda, both the men were preparing to leave when Iqbal's third colleague, Sadru, dramatically entered the scene like a villain from a Bollywood movie.

'That fucking Sindhi isn't coughing up money. Boss, I don't know what to do with him.'

'Cut his balls and feed the dogs.'

Iqbal thought that this would have been enough for the two wise men. Yet, both the men could not make up their minds about the prospective groom. They had been confidently told that Iqbal was a hardworking and devout person.

'At least finish the falooda,' Iqbal said as they got up to leave.

The two men stopped at the entrance of the godown trying to frame an appropriately civil response. After a few moments, they gave up and rushed out. Iqbal burst out laughing. Little did he know that he would eventually get married to this girl.

Patting his own back, he once again focused his attention on the problem at hand. Smuggling wristwatches through the transit post parcel had been very simple so far. While Iqbal had engaged Chalke, the latter had involved two of his colleagues in the racket. There were three people from the GPO working for him now.

*

The ship from Dubai would anchor at the Bombay dock. The post parcels would be offloaded here first. From here, the parcels would be taken in a postal van to the import section of the foreign post office.

After separating the local parcels, all the transit parcels would be shifted to the export section on the third floor of the GPO. The export booking section was located there and had a staff of about twenty. Here, the transit parcels for different countries would be sorted out and kept in different piles. Chalke was in charge of the transit parcels for Africa's Seychelles port. The smuggled goods came in the parcels bound for this port only.

The parcels themselves carried the label 'Surgical Instruments'. They would be stored here until a ship headed for Seychelles anchored at the Bombay port. Sometimes, this would take up to a week.

During this period, Chalke and his two colleagues would come to office on Sundays on the pretext of working overtime, that too with permission from the superintendent. The superintendent did not have any objection. On the contrary, he was pleased with Chalke and his colleagues. Sometimes, he would commend them in front of the other employees to set an example: Here are my dedicated, committed comrades!

On Sunday, Chalke and his colleagues would swing into action. Undisturbed and in total peace, they could work swiftly. First, they would carefully remove the packing ribbons from each parcel. This took the maximum time because there was a lead seal on these ribbons. It was an art to remove the ribbons while keeping the seal intact. If the seal broke, their fate would be sealed, the conspiracy would be exposed.

Once this delicate task was accomplished, they would tear apart the cloth of the parcel, open the box and extract the watches. Thereafter, stones of the same weight would be filled into these boxes and the parcels would be tied with the ribbons along with the seal. When the ship arrived, these parcels would be sent to Seychelles.

Chalke and his two colleagues would deliver these contraband watches in postbags to Iqbal's godown. *After all, who would suspect a postman coming out of the GPO with a postbag?*

Let us now see what happened to the parcels of stones that were sent to Seychelles. These parcels had bogus addresses on them, and so, the postal department of Seychelles would return them to the first party in Dubai after marking them as 'incomplete address' or some such thing. These parcels would again come to Bombay.

This time, the stones would be removed and pieces of silver of the same weight (nine kilos in each) would be placed into them under Iqbal's supervision and sent back to Dubai where the sheikh and Iqbal's partner received them after paying a fine of 50 dirhams.

*

Before Iqbal could think further, his eyes rested on Michael and Sadru, who were smoking bidis at a tea stall across the road. They couldn't decide whether they should do what Iqbal had asked them to. They threw away their bidis and went to him.

'You fools! What would be the difference between other goons and us if we too acted like them? No one is to be stabbed, no one's balls are to be cut.'

Then why? Michael wanted to ask.

Iqbal smiled. 'To entertain the guests. As for Ali, I'll handle him. You will see, he will curse the day he was born. And just a friendly warning is enough for the Sindhi.'

A relieved Michael and Sadru went out and once again sat at the tea stall. Iqbal picked up his thoughts from where he had left off. His problem was that he was being watched by both the customs and the DRI. The ship for Seychelles carrying nine parcels had arrived and would anchor at the docks tomorrow. He had to remove the wristwatches from the parcels without being caught.

Suddenly, an idea struck him. He picked up the phone and dialled Chalke's number. When he came on the line, Iqbal simply said, 'Go straight home after work. I'll contact you.'

He put down the receiver and went to the GPO. It was time for the shops to pull down their shutters. Some offices had already closed for the day. Chalke would come out exactly at 5.30 p.m. There were still five minutes to go.

*

Khan was standing under a tree, a little distance away from the GPO. Iqbal was watching him from behind a pole on the footpath across the road. Chalke emerged from the GPO building at the usual time. Khan followed him. Iqbal shadowed Khan.

On reaching VT station, Ganpat caught the 5.40 p.m. suburban local. He had boarded the bogie from one entrance while Khan entered from the other. Iqbal boarded the next compartment. The train reached Kurla in less than half an hour.

Chalke got down. Unaware of the danger stalking him, he soon reached home.

Khan waited for two hours a little away from his house. Reassured that Chalke was not going to leave his house now, Khan hailed a taxi. He did not know that Iqbal was trailing him.

To open the parcels containing the contraband wristwatches the next day, it was important to know where Khan would go from here. He hailed another taxi.

'Where to?' the driver asked. Iqbal gave him a Rs 100 note and pointed to the taxi ahead. The driver took a few seconds but finally understood. He followed Khan's taxi and soon reached Ghatkopar. It was 9 p.m.

Khan's taxi stopped near a building in a colony. He paid the fare, got down and slowly entered the gate. After a few minutes, the lights came on in the first-floor apartment.

From a safe distance, Iqbal saw the windows opening up. Khan opened the third window, looked at the dark sky for no apparent reason and walked away into the apartment.

*

The next morning, Iqbal called Chalke at the office. 'Listen! The ship has arrived. Today too, go straight home but don't go to sleep. Besides, this time, your colleagues are not required. Did you understand?'

Chalke just said 'yes' and replaced the receiver. *What was Iqbal's game plan?* He was trying to solve the riddle. *The DRI is suspicious. That means someone close to him had leaked the information. If this guess were true, then the DRI must have put more than one hound after him. One was Khan. Where were the other shadows hiding? Was it necessary to stick his neck out?* This was a crucial question for Chalke. *The temptation of earning a few thousand rupees may even cost him his job and perhaps land him in prison.*

He took the decision in no time. *He would have to ignore Iqbal. It was for his own good.* However, the decision was made by a fly hopelessly stuck in a spider's web.

*

The transit parcels arrived in Chalke's section in the afternoon. The parcels for Seychelles were dumped near him. Both his colleagues, members of the clique, looked at him conspiratorially. He ignored them. Once again suspicion surfaced. *Were they moles? Why had Iqbal asked him to drop them?*

As usual, Chalke went out after lunch to the restaurant across the road, had tea and then returned to his department. He had lost interest in the work. Strain erupted as sweat on his forehead. Whoever crossed his path that day appeared to be a DRI spy.

Suddenly, the telephone on the table started ringing. He was shaken to the core. As if he was lifting a snake and not the receiver, he picked it up nervously. He heard the voice he dreaded the most.

'Chalke!'

'Yes.'

'Meet me in the men's urinal on the second floor in five minutes.'

Now Chalke was breathless with anxiety. Before he could utter a word the line was cut. The real dilemma was now whether to go or not to go. Thoughts started raging in his mind. He was unable to sit quietly and kept fidgeting in his chair. In the same confused state of mind, he got up like a zombie, went down to the second floor and pumping all his willpower into his veins, resolved to say 'no' to Iqbal. Yes, an absolute flat 'no'.

When he entered the toilet, there was no sign of Iqbal. His entire body felt light, as if a mountain had been lifted off his shoulders. To release the last drops of the lingering tension, he unzipped his fly, maintaining some distance from a urinating postman.

As soon as the postman left, the latrine door slowly opened. Chalke turned his head, still pissing, and saw Iqbal standing behind him. He found himself in an embarrassing position.

Before he could zip up and turn to look at him, Iqbal said, 'It's 4 p.m. I'll return exactly at 5.40 p.m. You don't have to do anything. Just remember to leave after all the staff members have left.'

He turned towards Iqbal. 'Please tell me again.'

'This time, I'll be the one taking the risk.'

'You mean . . .'

'When you come out last, I'll stay inside and finish off the work alone at night.'

'But how will you come out?' By this time, Chalke's dilemma had been resolved for some unknown reason. He had merely wanted to be reassured before becoming an accomplice to Iqbal again.

'When you leave, tell the peon that you will be coming early tomorrow. He will offer you the key.'

'What if he doesn't give it?'

'Call him at 8 a.m., get the door opened and send him for a cup of tea. Any more questions?'

Chalke shook his head.

*

Iqbal entered Chalke's department at exactly 5.40 p.m. His men had dumped nine parcels there. All these parcels contained stones. Each parcel, along with the packing, weighed ten kilos.

Since the foreign-bound parcels were received here, there was no reason for anyone to suspect Iqbal. He had come with the parcels posing as a tradesman. Moreover, it being closing time, all the employees were preparing to leave.

Chalke was deceiving himself. *What was the risk?* Nothing. *Where do I figure in the picture?* Nowhere. *What proof do the DRI have?* Fuck the DRI.

As if Iqbal were a genuine customer, Chalke opened his register. By that time, Iqbal's eyes had spotted a safe place to hide. The pile of Hong Kong-bound parcels was the tallest. No one would be able to tell even if an elephant was crouching behind that pile.

Gradually, like the sun hiding behind clouds, he moved towards the pile and slipped behind it. After a while, the employees of the export division left for the day.

The peon was in a hurry to go home but was helpless. He came to Chalke's table. '*Kai Saiba*? Are you determined to work overtime today?'

'Oh, no. But tomorrow I'll have to.'

By the time he came up to the door with the peon, he realized that the superintendent was still working—and from the heap of files on his desk, it appeared that he would have to do a night shift today. Chalke felt his knees go weak. He was in a catch-22 situation. He could neither go out nor come in now. *How could he leave, deserting Iqbal?*

What if the superintendent got up to inspect the parcels? And, what would the peon think if he went back in after having cleaned his desk? He pulled out a handkerchief from his pocket and blew his nose.

Reading his predicament on his pockmarked face, the peon asked, 'Sahib, you aren't feeling well?'

'I'm fine.'

'Then why don't you leave?'

'I'm in a dilemma . . . the chief is still working. I might as well finish some more work. Else, I'll have to come early tomorrow.'

Juggling these thoughts, he returned to his chair. The superintendent looked up from his desk. As their eyes met, Chalke gave a sheepish smile. *A pain in the ass*, he muttered to himself.

Sitting on his chair, he opened the register again. He started entering the details of the parcels that had arrived by the morning ship. That was his work, his responsibility.

Iqbal, who was hiding behind the parcels, felt that luck was not on his side today.

The sun set. The table lamp on the superintendent's desk glowed. Chalke got up and put on the switch. The tube light over his head came on. With the light came fear. He started shivering. He had seen a head appear at the door for a few seconds. *Was it Khan, the one who had interviewed him?*

He was right. Khan was patiently keeping watch like a predator lying in wait.

38

Chalke usually left office every day at 5.30 p.m. He would come out of the GPO building and catch the local train for Kurla. However, the routine was altered today. Naturally, Khan, who had been shadowing him, got suspicious.

He came up to the third floor. Peeping through the door, he saw Chalke busy making entries in a register. At some distance, his boss was engrossed in files. Both of them were working overtime. The sight disappointed Khan. He had hoped to at least find Chalke tampering with the parcels. If that were the case, Khan could have claimed he had hit the jackpot.

New doubts crept up in Khan's mind. *Was Chalke not directly involved in smuggling wristwatches? Was he innocent?* The answers to these questions were not simple. He came down and stood in a dark corner, trying to add up all the questions and filtering the replies. Still, there was some hope at the end of the tunnel.

Exactly at 9.40 p.m., the table lamp on the superintendent's desk was switched off. The circle of light faded. Before going out, the superintendent stopped near Chalke's desk.

'Heavy workload today?'

Chalke got up respectfully and nodded.

'Come early tomorrow.'

For the first time that day, Chalke chuckled. 'Sorry to say but, sir, you really spoil me.'

473

'How come?'

'Who was it that taught us about not keeping today's work for tomorrow?'

'Of course, I had said it. But that was not meant for you. You are an exception, Chalke.' He patted his back and added, 'Come, it's already late.'

'On one condition. If you allow me to come early tomorrow.'

The superintendent smiled from ear to ear.

Chalke closed the register and left with him. As they neared the door, the superintendent himself gave instructions to the peon. 'Mr Chalke will come at 8 a.m. tomorrow.'

'Chalke,' he remembered, 'you live somewhere near Vikhroli, right?'

'Kurla, sir.'

'Your house is on my way. I can drop you.'

Both of them went down the stairs, chatting. In the meantime, the peon closed the windows and the door, and while coming down to the second floor he passed Chalke standing alone. The superintendent had gone to the toilet.

'Where do you live?' Chalke asked the peon.

'Virar.'

'That's quite far. Will you be able to come on time tomorrow?'

'Of course, but with some difficulty. If you don't mind . . .'

'Yes?'

'Keep the key with you.'

Chalke slipped the key into his pocket.

Khan watched the peon emerge from the main entrance of the GPO building and head towards Churchgate station to catch the Virar local. He was merrily singing the song, 'Mera joota hai Japani' from a Raj Kapoor movie.

After a few minutes, Chalke appeared, accompanied by the superintendent. The chief affectionately made him sit in the front, taking the driver's seat himself. The car started and moved away.

Khan sizzled, hissed, sputtered and felt like banging his head against the wall. It was not daylight, else his face would have been the poster of his agony. It was pitch-dark. There was no moon, no stars. If there was anything in it for him, it was only utter frustration.

*

The ship from Dubai had arrived, the parcels had arrived, yet none of the thugs had contacted Chalke, nor had Chalke's behaviour been suspect. Whatever misgiving was left had faded away today. There was no point shadowing the dark. Suddenly, he felt his life draining away and called it a day.

As he took the first step towards VT station, he saw some movement on the opposite footpath. Someone had slipped behind a tree.

Cautiously, he crossed the road, came near the tree and looked in amazement. Customs officer D'Souza stood before him. Dismay was writ large on his face for having been exposed.

'What are you doing here, D'Souza?' Khan frowned.

'To be honest,' he confessed, 'I was asked to keep an eye on Iqbal.'

'But the collector was warned not to meddle in this case.'

'True, but I've to follow the chief's orders.'

The last fortnight had been crazy. Until now, Khan had been blaming his own intelligence and fate for his failure. Now, he realized that the collector's foolish face-saving action had tipped Iqbal off. *Now what?*

'When did you see Iqbal last?' Khan asked, trying to control his rage.

'He was here just before five in the evening.'

'Where exactly?'

'Near that pigeons' enclosure.'

'Then?'

'He vanished suddenly.'

'Then what are you doing here?'

'I suspect that he must be somewhere around here.'

'It's 10.45 p.m. Why should he be here?'

'The parcels from Seychelles have arrived.'

'True.'

'He must have a key to the export section, a duplicate.'

Khan was alarmed. It hadn't struck him so far. There was every possibility of Iqbal entering the GPO after the staff left.

'All right,' said Khan. 'You keep watch here; I'll take a look on the third floor.'

*

Khan climbed the stairs up to the third floor and looked at the door. A strong lock was dangling on it. Inside, Iqbal was sitting comfortably behind the mountain of parcels bound for Hong Kong. He was in no hurry to finish the job. He had the whole night at his disposal.

After Chalke and the superintendent left, as a precautionary measure, he remained seated quietly for two hours. It was possible that someone would have forgotten something and come back for it. The superintendent himself might return. If he had an extra key, Iqbal would be nabbed like an ordinary thief.

*

He waited for half an hour more and came out at the stroke of midnight. He had a small torch that lit up a limited area. Moving nimbly, he came near the parcels for Seychelles. At that time, Khan was yawning, waiting in a dark corner of the passage outside the closed door, hoping for Iqbal to show up. His gut feeling told him that the mouse would not fall into the trap because it had smelt it. His guess was right, and yet he was wrong.

Iqbal disengaged the tin ribbons, with the seals intact, from each of the parcels, removed the wristwatches and replaced them with stones. He placed all the wristwatches into the boxes in which he had brought the stones and closed all of them. He placed the Seychelles parcels, seals intact, where they belonged.

Khan had looked at his wristwatch several times. He looked at it one last time. It was 5 a.m. He gave up hope and quietly went down.

For Iqbal, this was the time to offer morning prayers. However, before that, he needed water to wash his limbs and face.

Carrying the small torch, he went around the large hall in search of water. Soon, he found an earthen pot in a corner. He cleansed his body with the water, and finding a clean spot, settled down to offer namaz.

Gradually, the windowpanes started gleaming. The sun was rising. When the door opened at 8 a.m., he was sitting safely behind the fortress of parcels for Hong Kong. He saw from a small slit between two parcels Chalke marching up to him.

'Iqbal, how will you take out the parcels?'

'My men must have arrived at the gate.'

'Call them. Now.'

Iqbal dashed towards the door. His men were waiting for him in a taxi. Seeing Iqbal coming out of the entrance, they got out. Iqbal sat beside the driver. The three men—Dagdu, Michael and Sadru—rushed upstairs. They were dressed in postmen's uniforms with postbags hanging from their shoulders and a sack each in their hands.

Each of them dumped three parcels into each sack, returned in less than fifteen minutes and sat in the taxi. One sack was placed on the overhead carrier, while the other two were kept in the trunk. The taxi sped towards the godown at Dongri.

*

The DRI chief was baffled. Khan kept watch over Chalke for another week. After the ship for Seychelles docked at the Bombay port, all the tampered parcels were loaded on to it with the seals intact. This time, they were stuffed with stones.

No parcel was missing. All the seals were intact. Impossible! The chief was seething in anger. He had no doubt that the traffickers must have employed some unimaginably ingenious technique.

Every month, two ships arrived from Dubai. The interval was a fortnight, but this time the DRI chief decided that he himself would go to the front. He was to leave his air-conditioned cabin and storm the exports division of the post office because he was confident that Ali had given him correct information. He put forward the same argument on observing Khan's hopes sinking. Yet, Khan did not look convinced.

He argued, 'Sir, even if what you say is true, at least Chalke should have committed some mistake. I shadowed him for twelve days. He met no one, no thug contacted him, nor did he visit any suspicious place.'

'He might have come to know that he is under watch. He must have become cautious.'

Sufi   479

'Suppose you are right, but then what about the parcels? Why were none of the seals broken?'

'Because this time I'm going to break the seals,' he said, slamming his palm on the table.

Khan stared at him.

*

At social gatherings, people gawk whenever I reply to their question about my marriage. They typically ask, 'Aabid Bhai, was yours a love marriage or an arranged marriage?' My answer is, 'A surprise marriage.'

In fact, something like that did happen. When I was returning home one evening from my studio, I came to know from my neighbour at the Dongri newspaper stall that I had got engaged to be married.

I did not believe him because it was impossible for my family to fulfil my condition of marriage. I had told them that I wouldn't marry until I had a room of my own.

When I approached my building, another friend congratulated me. Now I was alarmed. *Had someone in the family won the lottery?* Only then would it be possible for them to buy me a room.

Yes, it was something like that. My uncle worked at the dock. He had served with unstinting honesty for ten years in Ghadiyal Godi (Bhaucha Dhakka), which was known for its corruption. His employer, pleased with his honesty, had made him a 25 per cent partner in the business. No one knew this secret.

The same month, when the year's account was cleared, my uncle got his share—Rs 60,000. With this money, he bought me a room.

The elders of the family had fulfilled my far-fetched condition. Now, there was no way for me to wriggle out of the marriage trap. As I climbed up the stairs, the photograph of the girl shown to me last floated before my eyes. I stopped for a few moments and made a firm decision—I would fulfil all my responsibilities with full commitment.

*

Exactly a week later, the ship from Dubai, *M.V. Damra*, which belonged to the British India Company, docked in Bombay. All the post parcels were dropped at the export section of the GPO on the third floor after passing through the foreign post office. Before that, the DRI chief and Khan had arrived and were chatting with the superintendent.

The sorting of the parcels began. Parcels for different countries were collected in different piles. On one side was the heap of parcels bound for Singapore, while on the other side was the stockpile of parcels for Japan. On the third side was one for Hong Kong while on the fourth side was the stack of parcels for Seychelles.

Chalke, in charge of the parcels for Seychelles, was examining the labels on the parcels. His legs were trembling. The presence of the DRI chief had left him shaken.

After the collating was over, the chief and Khan got up and walked over to Chalke. Feigning naïveté, Khan asked, 'These parcels are for which country?'

'They have come from Dubai and are bound for Seychelles.'

'What's the content?'

'Surgical instruments.'

'Who's the party?'

'Sheikh Abdul Malik,' Chalke read out the name on the label.

'Now tell me, Mr Chalke, if the same sheikh had sent something last month.'

Feigning ignorance, Chalke opened the register on his table and ran his finger through the entries. He lifted his head after some time and stated, 'Last month, he had sent two consignments of nine parcels.'

'What did they contain?'

He again pretended to check the register and said, 'The same thing, sir, surgical instruments.'

By now, the superintendent too had finished his work and stood between the DRI chief and Khan. All the past entries were being examined. The chief's curiosity increased by the minute. The sheikh from Dubai had been exporting surgical instruments to a party in Seychelles for over one and a half years now.

'It seems that the surgeons in Seychelles are in the habit of discarding surgical instruments after single use!' the chief commented sarcastically, looking at Chalke. 'Otherwise, they wouldn't be importing by the dozens every month!'

Chalke remained quiet, but the superintendent gave a new twist to the climax: 'Sir, the puzzle seems more complicated than the Rubik's cube.'

The chief looked at him. 'What do you mean?'

'The party from Seychelles, in whose name these parcels come, is bogus.'

'You mean nobody accepts these parcels there?'

'True. These parcels return to Bombay every month from Seychelles and are then sent back to the original party in Dubai.'

'Amazing! Open them up.'

Chalke and the superintendent were taken aback.

'What did you say?' the superintendent asked.

'I'm curious to see what's inside.'

'Surely you know that we are not authorized to open transit parcels.'

'Of course you aren't. Open the Seychelles' parcels. I take full responsibility.'

With his hands shivering, Chalke broke the seal of a parcel, removed the ribbon and opened it. Everyone, except Chalke, was amazed to see the expensive watches inside the parcel. The chief, however, did notice Chalke's flat expression.

It was just the beginning. All the nine parcels were opened one after the other. There were over 200 watches in each parcel, but no straps. There were two other parcels that contained 100 watches and 100 straps.

*

Sufi says the date was 1 August. The DRI chief confiscated the goods and prepared a list appended by the signatures of three postal department officials as witnesses for the panchnama.

On 3 August, around 3.30 p.m., Chalke was taken into custody under section 108 of the Customs Act (1968). The section provides for the arrest of any person based on suspicion. The next was Iqbal. The DRI raided his godown at 4.30 p.m. At the time, there was only one tapori sitting inside to receive messages on the phone.

The DRI did not find anything incriminating there. Khan, however, received a jolt upon learning that Iqbal had left for his honeymoon.

*

How did this happen despite Iqbal's Oscar-worthy performance to thwart his marriage? Surely, no father would offer his daughter to such a dangerous underworld don.

Sufi informs me that the elders were certainly disappointed with him after the interview but had not lost hope. The reason was their acknowledgment of the other side of the coin. If Iqbal had a dark side, his other side must be equally bright.

Swinging between these two poles like a pendulum, the elders decided to make further inquiries. Iqbal seemed to have read their mind and made a call to his friend in Dongri. 'Safdar! Just listen carefully. Two oldies will visit you in about ten minutes.'

'So?'

'They will ask you some personal questions about me. In fact, whatever they ask, you have to tell them that the boy is a graduate from the school for scoundrels.'

'Yaar, you know very well that I don't lie. I promise to give truthful answers to whatever they ask.'

'You can freely add masala to whatever you say about me.'

'But why?'

'I don't want to spoil anyone's life by marrying her.'

'Are you going to remain single all your life?'

'Maybe.'

'But Islam doesn't favour celibacy.'

'Try to understand, I'm not in a position to marry right now. Can I expect you to deliver a thundering sermon to the visitors about your immoral friend?'

Safdar laughed and put the receiver down. The same moment, the two elders appeared at his door. 'Safdar Bhai?'

He nodded, welcoming them respectfully and offering them chairs. As soon as the formalities were over, they began the interview. The girl's father asked Safdar, 'Is it true that your friend Iqbal offers namaz five times a day?'

'Yes.'

'Every Friday, does he go to the mosque to pray?'

'Of course.'

'Does he keep fast during the holy month of Ramadan?'

'Yes.'

'Does he observe ten days of mourning during Moharram?'

'Yes, he does.'

'Can he be called a scholar in theology?'

'In a way, yes.'

'Now, tell us, if he is addicted to paan, bidi, cigarette, liquor or gambling?'

'Not at all.'

Both the elders looked at each other. Satisfied, they were about to leave when Safdar interjected, 'Wouldn't you like to ask anything more?' They thanked him and left.

*

Iqbal was married into the same close-knit clan as I was.

Iqbal's wife's name is Masooma.

My wife too is called Masooma.

Both of us grew up in the same ghetto and studied in the same school. Our circumstances were the same. Both of us struggled against hunger. Yet, we parted ways and made tracks in diametrically opposite directions.

Iqbal says that it is destiny.

I have already stated earlier that I chose my own path, my own battlefield, my own destiny.

What do you say?

AFTERWORD

THE TALE OF TWO TITANS

Mahanagar, a local Hindi newspaper from Bombay, had serialized this book in 1992. Upon its completion, the author and Iqbal Rupani gave the only interview ever to a publication in an attempt to clarify some of the doubts that may linger in the minds of the readers. This is a translated transcript.

AABID SURTI

Q. To begin with, what triggered the idea of writing this novel?

A. Firstly, let me make it clear once again that this is not a work of fiction. It is a biography. Of course, the form chosen is that of a novel. Normally biographies are so boring to read that readers just put them aside. So, I've tried to make it readable by presenting it in an innovative manner. Beyond that, it's based on fact, not fiction. Except for the names of Suraiyya, Bharucha and Khanvilkar, the other names, incidents, dates and times are true to the best of my knowledge.

Q. But why the underworld?

A. You see, I grew up in Dongri. I lived there from 1940 to 1976 and saw young Muslim boys entering the underworld to survive hunger and unemployment. Other factors like superstition and illiteracy played a major role in the downfall of that society as a whole. I wanted to encompass all that, and a real-life character from the underworld fit the bill.

Q. Don't you feel that knowingly or unknowingly you have glorified the underworld by eulogizing the character of Sufi?

A. Sufi's life has two sides and I've tried to present both in proper perspective. On the one hand he was neck-deep in criminal activities, while on the other he is a devout Muslim who respects all religions. Perhaps, because I have not ignored his positive side, it sounds like he is being extolled . . .

Q. *Sufi: The Invisible Man of the Underworld* is a biography as well as reportage. Have you done journalism too?

A. Of course, but not like you people.

Q. You said that you wanted to paint a true picture of the Muslim community. Please tell us what exactly is the true picture?

A. I divide people into two categories—those who follow knowingly and those who follow blindly. Most Muslims are blind followers of Islam. On top of that, the lack of education compounds their problems. Naturally, they believe whatever the mullahs preach or what the so-called Muslim leadership exhorts.

Since they are uneducated and uninformed, they are unable to identify the real issues. The day this community comes out of the darkness, the so-called leadership will have to pack up their bags and leave. One more tragedy with this community is that the leadership does not emerge from within. If some outsider genuinely tries to help them, he is soon branded a BJP agent, an enemy of Islam. What is urgently needed is a trustworthy leader from within.

Q. Aabid Bhai, you have said that there is nothing fictitious about this book. Then why not disclose DK's identity?

A. Like Suraiyya's name, I had to conceal the identity for some reasons. All the same, I can give one more clue about that mysterious character. His initials are not DK but KD. In the 1960s and 1970s, he was identified by the media but his father always shielded him.

Q. If this is your biography, it's incomplete. Can we expect a second part?

A. Sure, but not in the near future. In this volume, I've covered the period from birth (1935) to marriage (1965). In the second volume I intend to cover the phase from marriage to the present time.

Q. Can we expect to meet the same characters—Suraiyya, Kiran, Iqbal—in that?

A. Iqbal will certainly be there because it's a jugalbandi, which means two together. Regarding the other characters, I'm not sure. Once again, I remind you, in life you can't expect growth like fiction. I mean love–separation–happy ending. In life, we rarely come across the people who have left us. Who knows where Suraiyya is today or where Kiran vanished? Inspector Bharucha is no more, but where did Mr Khan get transferred? You can expect a caravan of new characters and a few of the old.

IQBAL RUPANI (SUFI)

Q. Let's begin from the other end of the book. Ganpat Chalke was arrested in the end. What about you?

A. I was arrested but not sentenced.

Q. Why?

A. The DRI didn't have any proof to convict me, nor did I confess to anything. By the way, does any big fish in our country ever get convicted? I'd say that in the present situation it's nearly impossible. In the name of the culprit, usually some of his associates, like drivers and relatives, are sentenced, most of whom are innocent. Of course, some taporis too are arrested, but never the big fish.

Q. What is the reason for such a situation?

A. In the first place, the officers are not interested in arresting them. In case the crime is glaring and they do decide to arrest them, they are helpless because they are beyond their reach. In the end, if they somehow succeed in arresting them, they fail to convict them. They can't prove anything. Also, in the absence of witnesses the case is shut for good.

Q. But why don't the witnesses come forward?

A. Who would want to visit a court again and again, leaving his job and curse himself for getting into the mess? Nobody knows for how many years a court case will continue. Secondly, the question of safety is vital. When the witness starts getting threats, he goes to the police station. The police tell him, 'Come to us when something serious happens. Even we get threats every day. So what?' Leave aside the witnesses, there is no guarantee of safety for the informers also. We come to know from the customs collector's office itself if someone rats on us. If the collector doesn't want to be the one to disclose the name, he writes the name on a slip of paper and passes it on to the peon. We then know the name and also know how to deal with him.

I know a man who had told the customs about gold worth Rs 14 crore to be smuggled into India. He was assured beyond doubt that his name would remain a secret. On that information, the customs department saw a big catch. The informer got Rs 70,00,000 as a gift cheque. But the cheque was given to him through the peon. The peon swiftly got the cheque xeroxed before delivering it and passed the copy on to the gang. A few days later, the man who had got the cheque was found dead. Now, in such a situation, how can you expect anyone to come forward and be a witness?

Q. Does that mean that it's impossible to stop smuggling?

A. Looking at the laws and the present style of functioning, it seems impossible. One of my cousins was once caught carrying drugs. I met the officer concerned and told him, 'Look, my boy is still scared of prison. If you lock him up once, that fear will go away.

By putting him behind bars, the narcotic trade isn't going to stop. It will be better if you try to rout this racket.'

He asked me how that would be done. I told him to use my cousin as a decoy. Release him with the drugs, I said. Then he will deliver them at the pre-decided place, which is on the border of Holland. He will get his commission. No one will suspect him. After that you just have to get them arrested. The party will lose the fare up to Holland and the stuff too will be seized before it reaches the market. If it's done a few times, the party will go bankrupt. The taporis and the carriers will be automatically thrown out. But the officer didn't agree. He argued about how it would be done, how the superiors wouldn't co-operate to release an arrested runner. I told him the bitter truth and that was that he may get the Presidents' awards by the dozen, but he wouldn't be able to stop trafficking in a hundred years.

Q. Can you give us some inside information about drug trafficking?

A. There are many ways to do it. Also, new ones are invented if required.

Q. Tell us something about the new ones.

A. Nowadays narcotics are often smuggled in the form of an idol.

Q. Please elaborate.

A. This is possible if one has a knowledge of certain chemicals. The drug is converted into pulp using these, and like plaster of Paris, it's moulded into a fancy statue or an idol. It looks so real that you can't figure out even by touching it. Later, using the same chemicals, the idol is converted back into powder form.

Q. What do you think of our government's endeavours to stop drug trafficking?

A. The same as their efforts to stop contraband goods. In fact, in the matter of narcotic drugs it's the worst. For example, if a person is arrested for drug trafficking, he is sentenced to ten years' imprisonment. Now see the fun. Neither the quantity is considered by the law nor the quality. One gets ten years for possessing drugs like heroin and ten years for the soft ones also. Ten years for having ten grams and ten years for having a 100 tonnes. Isn't it foolish?

According to the Prevention of Illicit Trafficking in Narcotic Drugs and Psychotropic Substances Act, hearings of these cases can be held only at the special courts. Now, the government has created only four courts so far. For these, no special judge is appointed. Those same old judges sit on cushioned chairs with 'special' added to their designation. What I mean is that in Bombay alone, there are nearly 5000 cases pending and the judges are just four.

Q. Really?

A. In a month, the maximum number of cases the court can hear is two. Imagine, after how many years will the 5000th case come to a hearing? Fifty? What would you call this? A travesty of justice? The punishment for this offence is ten years by law, but an accused rots in jail for fifty years. Who is guilty? The accused or the system?

One more thing, of the runners arrested in drug trafficking in Bombay alone, thousands are foreigners. They all are rotting in jail because the offence is non-bailable. These are mostly carriers who have taken up this assignment due to poverty or helplessness. By arresting these guys, you can't stop trafficking.

On the contrary, the government will be spending crores of rupees on them in the coming fifty years.

I have a suggestion. They should all be released on Rs 50,000 bail each so that our government gets Rs 5,00,00,000. Also, no visa for these foreigners in the future so that they can't carry out drug trade on our soil. But who in the bureaucracy cares to use intelligence to implement such practical ideas?

Q. Indeed a good suggestion. But in our country the narcotic business is spreading . . .

A. May I tell you an interesting fact? You may not believe it, but it's true that in the name of abolition of narcotics trafficking, so much hue and cry is being created that a common man starts believing that this bogeyman exists. In fact, the reality is totally different.

Q. If it's merely a bogeyman, then where do the people seen taking hash in the dark corners of bylanes and on railway tracks get their quota from?

A. What they get as hash or narcotic substance is some powder with a pinch of the drug. Often, even that is missing.

Q. But they do get a kick.

A. You may call it the placebo effect. Narcotics are so expensive that it's almost beyond the reach of a common man to buy them. You tell me, the addicts you just mentioned, can they afford to buy at Rs 100 a gram? What they get as the drug is an adulterated powder.

Q. Now a few personal questions: what do your brothers do these days?

A. Busy with their own occupations.

Q. The one that God forbids or the one that He approves?

A. (Smiles) The one that He approves.

Q. What are you busy with?

A. I'm into the stock market.

Q. Like Harshad Mehta?

A. Harshad Mehta was an idiot. He aggravated the situation for nothing. If I'd been in his place, I'd have confessed to my offence. The situation wouldn't have worsened. Of course, I'd have been sentenced and you know how our prisons function?

Q. How?

A. They have become free guest houses. Whatever comforts are available in the outside world are also available there, if you have the money.

Q. Is this your own experience or . . .

A. Of course, I'm talking from personal experience. Once I was convicted in a smuggling case. For security reasons, I was transferred to a jail outside Bombay.

There, in the jail, I earned more than I had earned outside. Outside, I had to shell out a rupee to make a call. Inside, the Indian government paid for my calls. I used to sit comfortably in the jail superintendent's office and make calls.

Q. I'd like to ask one more question: why do you make all this public?

A. I believe that if the truth comes out in the open, some change may take place in the system and benefit the common man. If you think that by publishing my interview your readers will be benefited, I'm prepared to sit with you for a month. But I doubt that these imbecile bureaucrats will come to their senses. All these ideas that I've been repeatedly suggesting to different officials all these years have been without any result. All the same, I've not lost hope. This is one more attempt. Maybe this interview appearing in print will create a miracle.

Q. You could have disclosed all this anonymously. Now you might get into trouble.

A. You see, I'm not afraid to face the toughest situation in life because I truly believe even today that without His wish not even a leaf moves. Secondly, these officials couldn't touch me when I was into trafficking, what will they do now?

Q. I'm surprised that you have still stuck to your belief!

A. There is a reason. It's true that I got everything one could desire, but I didn't get what I wanted. If I could have had my way, I'd have become a doctor. Despite Herculean efforts, I couldn't succeed. That confirmed my belief in the supreme power of God's Will.